BRITISH ELECTORAL FACTS 1832-2006

British Electoral Facts
1832-2006

Compiled and edited by
COLIN RALLINGS and MICHAEL THRASHER
(in association with Dawn Cole)

ASHGATE

Published by
Ashgate Publishing Limited
Gower House
Croft Road
Aldershot
Hampshire GU11 3HR
England

Ashgate Publishing Company
Suite 420
101 Cherry Street
Burlington, VT 05401-4405
USA

Ashgate website: http://www.ashgate.com

British Library Cataloguing in Publication Data
British electoral facts, 1832-2006
   1. Great Britain. Parliament - Elections - Statistics
   2. Elections - Great Britain - History
   I Rallings, Colin II. Thrasher, Michael
   324.9'41'08

Library of Congress Control Number: 2007922170

ISBN 978-0-7546-2712-8

Printed and bound in Great Britain by MPG Books Ltd, Bodmin, Cornwall.

B100 000001 9859 48

Contents

(Alphabetical Index available at page 295)

1. General Election Results, 1832-2005 (contd.)

2. General Election Summary Data, 1832-2005

3. Political Parties

3. Political Parties (contd.)

4. Electorate

5. Electoral Administration

6. Boundary Reviews

7. Members and Candidates

13. Electrorate and Electoral Administration, European Parliament Elections 1979-2004

14. European Parliament By-Election Results

ELECTIONS WITHIN THE UNITED KINGDOM

15. General Election Results by Region and Nation, 1955-2005

16. Elections in Major Urban Areas

17. Devolution Elections

LOCAL GOVERNMENT ELECTIONS (GB)

18. Local Government Election Turnout

19. Councillors and Council Control

20. Elected Mayors

21. Local Government Elections - Miscellaneous Information

REFERENDUMS

22. Referendums in the United Kingdom 1973-2004

ELECTORAL IRREGULARITIES
23.Parliamentary Electoral Irregularities 1832-2006

PUBLIC OPINION POLLS
24.Public Opinion Polls at General Elections 1945-2005

25.Public Opinion Polls - monthly data 1945-2006

APPENDIX
Election Records and Trivia

INDEX

Preface

(to 7th edition)

Although this new edition follows the practice of its predecessors in bringing up to date a myriad of information and facts, it also reflects continuing change in the electoral landscape of the United Kingdom. Since 1999 there have been two general elections and one European Parliament election; a second round of elections for the Scottish Parliament and Welsh and Northern Ireland Assemblies; inaugural and subsequent elections for the Mayor and Assembly of the Greater London Authority; referendums and elections relating to new elected mayors in a number of local authorities; and the first, and perhaps only, referendum on the establishment of an elected regional assembly in a part of England. To aid readers in finding their way about this increasingly complex maze, there is now an Index at the end of the book as well as the detailed Table of Contents at the beginning.

We are again grateful to a number of friends and colleagues for helping us to keep track of these developments. To those named in the preface to the sixth edition should be added Brian Cheal, our long-serving Research Assistant; Richard Cracknell and Oonagh Gay of the House of Commons Library; Katy Bere of the Electoral Commission; and Ben Marshall, formerly of the Electoral Commission and now of MORI.

We are also very pleased to elevate our invaluable Projects Administrator, Dawn Cole, to a deserved place on the title page. Dawn has done much of the research for this edition, quite apart from typesetting the entire book.

Once again we encourage readers to contact us with details of any errors detected, together with suggestions for new tables.

Colin Rallings & Michael Thrasher

Local Government Chronicle Elections Centre
Plymouth
September 2006

Preface

(to 6th edition)

The late Fred Craig wrote that of all his reference works he was especially proud of *British Electoral Facts*. He was right to be so proud and we have been aware of the need to preserve his legacy whilst at the same time making a number of changes in content and form.

For this new edition we have not simply up-dated Craig's tables, but have taken the opportunity entirely to re-order the material in the book. We hope that this makes it easier to follow and use. We have added some tables (and removed others) and included significant new information, not least on regional voting patterns in England since 1955, on every parliamentary by-election since 1945, and on elections to the new devolved legislatures. We have also considerably expanded the selection of opinion poll data.

The task of re-setting the book to modern, computer readable standards has been considerable. Mark Besley was initially responsible for scanning pages from the previous edition of *British Electoral Facts* and Dawn Cole has performed valiantly in turning those files into a publishable form.

We are especially grateful to those individuals who have been ready to supply us with data or kind enough to offer suggestions about what they would like to see in a new edition of *Facts*. They include Richard Allen, Simon Atkinson, Bill Bush, David Butler, Rob Clements, David Cowling, Ivor Crewe, David Denver, Danny Dorling, Tony Fox, Anthony King, Chris Long, Iain McLean, James Mitchell, Pippa Norris, Richard Rose, Shamit Saggar, Peter Snow and Lawrence Ware.

The format of the book will allow future editions to be produced relatively quickly and straightforwardly. With that in mind we would welcome readers sending us details of any errors that they may detect, together with suggestions for new tables.

Colin Rallings & Michael Thrasher

Local Government Chronicle Elections Centre
Plymouth
July 2000

Introductory Notes

COALITION CANDIDATES 1918-1922 In the majority of tables, official Coalition candidates are not distinguished from other candidates of the same party. The only exception is in respect of the five Coalition Labour candidates at the General Election of 1918 who could not be classed with other Labour candidates as they were not endorsed by the Labour Party. The Coalition prefix has only been used for official candidates of the Coalition, i. e. those who received the 'coupon', a letter signed by Lloyd George and Bonar Law which was sent to approved nominees.

CO-OPERATIVE PARTY From the General Election of 1922, all Co-operative Party candidates have been endorsed by the Labour Party and sought election as 'Labour and Co-operative'. No distinction is made in the tables between these joint candidates and other Labour candidates.

ELECTORATE As a result of the Representation of the People Act, 1969, those becoming 18 years of age during the period covered by the annual Electoral Register now have the date on which they attain their 18th birthday inserted in the Register and they can vote from that date. This change in the registration procedure meant that it was no longer possible to know the exact electorate in a constituency on a particular date without asking Electoral Registration Officers to go through each register and deduct the number of post-election "dated names" from the total electorate. Before the widespread use of computers this was a laborious task which caused delays in the obtaining of electorate figures and frequently resulted in Electoral Registration Officers providing estimated rather than exact figures.

In 1974, Parliamentary Research Services initiated discussions with the Office of Population Censuses and Surveys, the Home Office, the Press Association, the British Broadcasting Corporation, Independent Television News and a number of interested academics in an attempt to find an acceptable formula for calculating electorates on a particular date. As a result the following formula was used by the media in calculating the electorate from the General Election of October 1974:

Total number of "dated names" on the Register multiplied by the fraction

$$\frac{\text{Number of days from February 17 to Polling Day (both dates inclusive)}}{364 \text{ (or 365 in a Leap Year)}}$$

The following is an example of the calculation:-

Electorate at 16 February	64,162
Number of "dated names"	757
Total	64,919

Using the Electorate Calculator on page 103 and assuming polling day was October 1 the formula would be:

$$757 \times 227/364 \ (0.623626) = 472.084882 \ (\text{truncate})$$

The estimated electorate at October 1 would be:

$$64,162 + 472 = 64,634$$

The figures for electorate given in this book for General Elections and subsequent by-elections from 1974 to 2000 have been calculated using the above formula. For the general elections of 1992 and 1997 an increasing number of Electoral Registration Officers were able to provide exact figures of the electorate 'on the day'.

These have been used where available.

The number of electors is, of course, affected not merely by 'coming of age', but by death, moving house, submitting late claims for inclusion etc. An earlier edition of this book attempted to take account of these factors in calculating an 'adjusted' turnout figure. The formula is outlined in detail in F.W.S. Craig, *British Parliamentary Election Statistics 1918-1970* (Chichester, 1971) and in the chapter on Britain in R. Rose (ed), *Comparative Electoral Behaviour* (New York: Free Press, 1972). An indication of its impact on general election turnout for the period 1950-1997 can be found in Table 4.02.

The Representation of the People Act 2000 introduced a 'rolling register' which allowed electors to be added to or removed from the register throughout the year. With amended registers now published monthly, we have decided to stop using the Electoral Calculator and publishing an 'adjusted' turnout figure.

GAINS AND LOSSES Until 1992 a gain or loss of a seat has been recorded on the basis of the incumbent's party allegiance at the time of the Dissolution or by-election. This means that where an MP changed from one party to another or became an Independent during a Parliament and did not resign immediately, his seat was from then on considered to be held by his new party. From 1992 gains and losses are calculated by reference to the previous general election result. A detailed list of changes of party allegiance since 1900 will be found in David Butler and Gareth Butler, *Twentieth Century British Political Facts,* 8th edition (London: Macmillan 2000) pp. 244-249.

INDEPENDENT LABOUR PARTY From 1900 until August 1932, the Independent Labour Party (ILP) was affiliated to the Labour Party and as their candidates normally received endorsement they are treated as official Labour candidates in the tables. There were however four by-elections where ILP candidates went forward without Labour Party endorsement and they have therefore been classed as ILP and not Labour candidates.

INDEPENDENTS AND MINOR PARTIES The columns headed 'Others' include all Independents and candidates of minor parties and organisations.

LIBERALS AND NATIONAL LIBERALS 1922-1923 In the majority of tables, no distinction is made between (Asquith) Liberal and (Lloyd George) National Liberal candidates. The two groups merged in November 1923 to fight the forthcoming General Election as a united party.

LIBERAL/SOCIAL DEMOCRATIC PARTY ALLIANCE These two parties concluded an electoral alliance for the general elections of 1983 and 1987. Summary information covering the performance of both parties at those elections, and at other types of election from 1982-87 inclusive, is usually aggregated under the 'Liberal' heading.

MULTI-MEMBER SEATS Percentage figures of votes cast and turnout have been adjusted to allow for the multi-member seats which existed prior to 1950. In calculating the percentage of votes, the total votes in multi-member constituencies have been divided by the number of votes which each elector was allowed. In two-member seats each elector had two votes; in three member constituencies prior to 1868 each elector had three votes but from 1868 this was reduced to two votes; in the four-member constituency of the City of London, prior to 1868 each elector had four votes but this was reduced to three votes from 1868.

In calculating turnout prior to 1885, votes in multi-member seats have been counted as one quarter, one third or one half votes which makes no allowance for electors using fewer than the votes allowed to them. The turnout percentages produced are therefore a slight underestimate of the number of electors voting as distinct from the number of votes cast. From 1885 onwards figures of the actual number of electors voting in multi-member seats were, with a few exceptions, generally available and have been used in calculating the turnout.

NATIONAL LIBERAL AND CONSERVATIVE CANDIDATES In the majority of tables, no distinction is made between joint National Liberal and Conservative candidates and other Conservative candidates. In May 1947, recommendations were issued by Lord Woolton, on behalf of the Conservative Party, and Lord Teviot, on behalf of the National Liberal Organisation, which advocated that the two parties should come together in constituencies and form combined associations under a mutually agreed title. Immediately following the 1950 election, a Liberal-Unionist Group was formed in the House of Commons by those MPs elected under the auspices of joint local associations. Owing to local circumstances and preferences, the actual 'labels' used by candidates varied from one constituency to another but for the sake of uniformity the designation National Liberal and Conservative (NL & C) has been used throughout this book. In May 1968 the National Liberal Council was disbanded.

NORTHERN IRELAND Until the General Election of February 1974, no distinction has been made between Unionist, Labour (provided they were endorsed by the Labour Party in London) and Liberal candidates in Northern Ireland and Conservative/Unionist, Labour and Liberal candidates in Great Britain.

From the General Election of February 1974, candidates of the Ulster Unionist Council, Northern Ireland Labour Party and the Ulster Liberal Party have been classed as 'Others' in all the tables. This reflected the changed political situation in Northern Ireland which made it unrealistic to continue the former method of classification.

NOTIONAL RESULTS Occasionally reference is made to the 'notional results' of the 1992 general election. This means that the data are taken from an exercise conducted on behalf of the BBC, ITN, PA News and Sky News to estimate the likely result in each constituency in 1992 if the new, 1997 boundaries had then been in place. This allows a comparison to be made between the 1992 and 1997 results at constituency level. Full details can be found in C. Rallings and M. Thrasher (eds.), *Media Guide to the New Parliamentary Constituencies* (Plymouth: Local Government Chronicle Elections Centre, 1995).

PERCENTAGES F.W.S. Craig tried to ensure that the percentages in his tables summed to 100. In the tables we have compiled percentages do not always sum exactly to 100 because we have adopted the more conventional approach of rounding figures originally calculated to 2 or more decimal places.

SOURCES Unless otherwise stated, all statistics have been compiled from *British Parliamentary Election Results, 1832-1983* (5 volumes) compiled and edited by F.W.S. Craig, from *British Parliamentary Election Results 1983-97* and *Britain Votes 6* compiled and edited by Colin Rallings and Michael Thrasher, and from the 'official results' for 2001 and 2005 compiled and edited by Colin Rallings and Michael Thrasher for the Electoral Commission. Statistics relating to elections in Ireland from 1832-1922 for which detailed constituency results are not included in *British Parliamentary Election Results* have been based on Dr Brian Walker's book *Parliamentary Election Results in Ireland 1801-1922*.

SPEAKER OF THE HOUSE OF COMMONS The Speaker of the House of Commons takes no active part in an election campaign and since 1950 (when the Speaker requested that he be given no party 'label') has sought re-election as 'The Speaker' and not as a party candidate. Until 1997 the Speaker has been regarded as a candidate of the party he represented before his appointment. For the 1997 general election and subsequently the votes cast for the Speaker are included among 'Others'.

STATE OF PARTIES AFTER GENERAL ELECTIONS Throughout this book the state of parties in the House of Commons following a General Election reflects the position after the double and treble elections had been decided but prior to changes caused by election petitions.

SWING 'Swing' is a way of summarising the change in share of the vote between two parties at two points in time. In Table 2.08 two measures of swing are used. Two-party ('Steed') swing is a measure of the change in the percentage share of the vote for the Conservative and Labour parties in terms of the votes cast for those two parties only. Total vote ('Butler') swing measures the change in terms of each party's percentage share of the total votes cast at each election. A fuller explanation may be found in D. Denver, *Elections and Voting Behaviour in Britain* (London: Prentice Hall, 1994) pp.19-20.

UNIVERSITY SEATS From 1918 in the university constituencies returning more than one member, General Elections were conducted by Proportional Representation (single transferable vote). In compiling the tables, figures of first preference votes have been used.

Abbreviations

Parties

AP	Anti-Partitionist (candidate of the Anti-Partition of Ireland League of Great Britain)
APNI	Alliance Party of Northern Ireland
BEP	British Empire Party
BLP	Belfast Labour Party (subsequently Northern Ireland Labour Party)
BM	British Movement
BNP	British National Party
BSP	British Socialist Party
C/Con	Conservative and Unionist Party
CFMPB	Campaign for a More Prosperous Britain
Ch	Chartist
CNP	Cornish Nationalist Party
Co	Coalition
Com	Communist Party of Great Britain
Const	Constitutionalist
Co-op	Co-operative Party
CP	Christian Pacifist
CPE	Communist Party of England (Marxist-Leninist)
Crf	Crofter
CW	Common Wealth Movement
CW Land P	Commonwealth Land Party
CWLP	Commonwealth Labour Party
Dem Lab	Democratic Labour
Dem P	Democratic Party (1942-45)
DP	Democratic Party (1969-71)
EFP	European Federal Party
ENP	English National Party
EP	Ecology Party (formerly People Movement, subsequently Green Party)
EP/WFLOE	Ecology Party/Women for Life on Earth joint candidate
FP	Fellowship Party
FTAPMP	Free Trade Anti-Common Market Party
GP/Green	Green Party (formerly Ecology Party)
H&IA	Highlands and Islands Association
HLL	Highland Land League
HP	Humanist Party
HR	Irish Home Ruler
ICRA	Irish Civil Rights Association
IDA	Independent Democratic Alliance
IIP	Irish Independence Party
ILP	Independent Labour Party
IMG	International Marxist Group
Ind	Independent (indicates an unofficial candidate when placed before a party name)
INDEC	Independent Nuclear Disarmament Election Committee
Irish LP	Labour Party (Dublin)
L	Liberal Party
Lab	Labour Party
Lab/Co-op	Labour Party/Co-operative Party joint candidate

LC	Liberal Conservative
LD	Liberal Democrat (formed from merger of Liberals and SDP in March 1988)
L/Lab	Liberal/Labour
Lib	Liberal (refers, after March 1988, to group which did not join Liberal Democrats)
Loyalist	Independent Loyalist (candidate of the League of Empire Loyalists)
LP'87	Labour Party '87
LPP	Liverpool Protestant Party
LRG	Labour for Representative Government
LU	Liberal Unionist Party
MGC	Mudiad Gweriniaethol Cymru (Welsh Republican Movement)
MK	Mebyon Kernow (Sons of Cornwall) -Cornish Nationalist Movement
MRLP	Monster Raving Loony Party
N	Irish Nationalist/Anti-Partitionist
Nat	National
Nat DP	National Democratic Party
Nat P	National Party (1917-21)
Nat Pty	Nationalist Party (formerly National Front Constitutional Movement)
NBP	New Britain Party
N Dem P	National Democratic Party
NDP	National Democratic and Labour Party
NF	National Front
NFDSS	National Federation of Discharged and Demobilized Sailors and Soldiers
NIEP	Northern Ireland Ecology Party
NI Ind Lab	Northern Ireland Independent Labour Party
NI Lab	Northern Ireland Labour Party
NIP	National Independence Party
NIWC	Northern Ireland Women's Coalition
NL	National Liberal (candidate of Lloyd George's National Liberal Council,1922-23 or of the National Liberal Organization (Liberal National Organization, 1931-48), 1931-68)
N Lab	National Labour Organization
N Lab P	National Labour Party (1981-)
NL & C	National Liberal and Conservative (joint candidate of the Conservative Party and the National Liberal Organization)
NLP	National Labour Party (1958-60)
NLP	Natural Law Party (1992-)
NP	New Party
NSP	National Socialist Party
OSM	Orkney and Shetland Movement
PAL	Party of Associates with Licensees
Pat P	Patriotic Party
PC	Plaid Cymru (Welsh Nationalist Party)
People	People Movement (subsequently Ecology Party)
PL	Pro-Life Party
Prog	Progressive
Prog U	Progressive Unionist Party
Prot U	Protestant Unionist Party (subsequently Ulster Democratic Unionist Party)
R	Irish Repealer
RA	Radical Alliance
Ref	Referendum Party
Rep	Irish Republican
Rep C	Republican Clubs (subsequently Republican Clubs - The Workers Party)
Rep C/TWP	Republican Clubs - The Workers Party (formerly Republican Clubs)
Rep LP	Republican Labour Party

Rev CP	Revolutionary Communist Party
RF	Red Front (candidate of the Revolutionary Communist Party)
SCLP	Scottish Labour Party
SCPGB	Social Credit Party of Great Britain
SD	Social Democrat (candidate of the Campaign for Social Democracy)
S Dem P	Social Democratic Party (formerly Social Democratic Federation) (1907-1911)
SDF	Social Democratic Federation (subsequently Social Democratic Party)
SDLP	Social Democratic and Labour Party
SDP	Social Democratic Party (1981 - 1990)
SF	Sinn Fein - Irish Republican Organisation
SLP	Socialist Labour Party
SLRL	Scottish Land Restoration League
SNP	Scottish National Party
Soc	Socialist
Soc.Env.All.	Socialist Environmental Alliance
SPGB	Socialist Party of Great Britain
SPLP	Scottish (Parliamentary) Labour Party
SPP	Scottish Prohibition Party
SSF	Scottish Socialist Federation
SSP	Scottish Socialist Party
SU	Socialist Unity
SUP	Scottish Unionist Party
SUTCLP	Scottish United Trades Councils Labour Party
SWRC	Scottish Workers Representation Committee
TWP	The Workers Party (formerly Republican Clubs - The Workers Party)
UACM	United Anti-Common Marketeers
UCP	United Country Party
UDP	United Democratic Party
UDUP	Ulster Democratic Unionist Party (formerly Protestant Unionist Party)
UIM	Ulster Independence Movement
UKInd	UK Independence Party
UKUP	United Kingdom Unionist Party
U M	Union Movement
Unity	Opposition Unity (candidate in Northern Ireland opposed to the Government and sponsored by various organisations)
Union	Unionist
United	United Unionist
UnSoc	United Socialist
UPNI	Unionist Party of Northern Ireland
UPUP	Ulster Popular Unionist Party
UU/UUP	Ulster Unionist (candidate of the Ulster Unionist Council)
UUUC	United Ulster Unionist Council
UUUP	United Ulster Unionist Party
VNP	Vectis (Isle of Wight) Nationalist Party
VUPP	Vanguard Unionist Progressive Party
WFLOE	Women for Life on Earth
Wk P	Workers Party
WP	Women's Party
WR	Wessex Regionalist
WRP	Workers Revolutionary Party

General Elections

1. General Election Results, 1832-2005*

*From 1832-1945 inclusive the % share figures have been adjusted to take account of multi-member constituencies. See Introductory Notes.

1.01-1.44 General Election 1832 to General Election 2005

2. General Election Summary Data, 1832-2005

3. Political Parties

Table 1.01: General Election 1832

	Total Votes	%	Candidates	Unopposed	Elected
ENGLAND					
C	193,442	29.2	228	32	117
L	474,542	70.8	488	81	347
Total	**667,984**		**716**	**113**	**464**
WALES					
C	7,466	53.4	19	10	14
L	6,348	46.6	21	12	18
Total	**13,814**		**40**	**22**	**32**
SCOTLAND					
C	9,752	21.0	28	4	10
L	44,003	79.0	70	12	43
Total	**53,755**		**98**	**16**	**53**
IRELAND					
C	28,030	32.1	69	16	28
L	29,013	33.3	55	4	33
R	31,773	34.6	51	14	42
Total	**88,816**		**175**	**34**	**103**
UNIVERSITIES					
C	2,594	76.2	6	4	6
L	813	23.8	2	0	0
Total	**3,407**		**8**	**4**	**6**
GREAT BRITAIN					
C	213,254	28.9	281	50	147
L	525,706	71.1	581	105	408
Total	**738,960**		**862**	**155**	**555**
UNITED KINGDOM					
C	241,284	29.4	350	66	175
L	554,719	66.7	636	109	441
R	31,773	3.9	51	14	42
Total	**827,776**		**1,037**	**189**	**658**

Table 1.02: General Election 1835

	Total Votes	%	Candidates	Unopposed	Elected
ENGLAND					
C	209,964	42.6	278	77	200
L	281,576	57.4	380	100	264
Total	**491,540**		**658**	**177**	**464**
WALES					
C	10,210	63.9	21	11	17
L	5,119	36.1	19	11	15
Total	**15,329**		**40**	**22**	**32**
SCOTLAND					
C	15,733	37.2	33	8	15
L	28,307	62.8	52	15	38
Total	**44,040**		**85**	**23**	**53**

General Election 1835 (contd.)

	Total Votes	%	Candidates	Unopposed	Elected
IRELAND					
C	25,362	42.4	69	19	35
L	34,866	57.6	87	28	68
Total	**60,228**		**156**	**47**	**103**
UNIVERSITIES					
C	-	-	6	6	6
Total	**-**	**-**	**6**	**6**	**6**
GREAT BRITAIN					
C	235,907	42.8	338	102	238
L	315,002	57.2	451	126	317
Total	**550,909**		**789**	**228**	**555**
UNITED KINGDOM					
C	261,269	42.6	407	121	273
L	349,868	57.4	538	154	385
Total	**611,137**		**945**	**275**	**658**

Table 1.03: General Election 1837

	Total Votes	%	Candidates	Unopposed	Elected
ENGLAND					
C	321,124	48.9	348	80	239
L	347,549	51.1	352	60	225
Total	**668,673**		**700**	**140**	**464**
WALES					
C	11,616	52.8	25	11	19
L	10,144	47.2	20	6	13
Total	**21,760**		**45**	**17**	**32**
SCOTLAND					
C	18,569	46.0	35	7	20
L	22,082	54.0	49	15	33
Total	**40,651**		**84**	**22**	**53**
IRELAND					
C	26,694	41.5	70	19	30
L	38,370	58.5	88	34	73
Total	**65,064**		**158**	**53**	**103**
UNIVERSITIES					
C	1,691	90.1	6	4	6
L	186	9.9	1	0	0
Total	**1,877**		**7**	**4**	**6**
GREAT BRITAIN					
C	353,000	48.2	414	102	284
L	379,961	51.8	422	81	271
Total	**732,961**		**836**	**183**	**555**
UNITED KINGDOM					
C	379,694	48.3	484	121	314
L	418,331	51.7	510	115	344
Total	**798,025**		**994**	**236**	**658**

Table 1.04: General Election 1841

	Total Votes	%	Candidates	Unopposed	Elected
ENGLAND					
C	272,755	53.1	374	147	277
L	236,813	46.8	277	62	187
Ch	307	0.1	4	0	0
Total	**509,875**		**655**	**209**	**464**
WALES					
C	4,102	53.2	24	16	21
L	3,605	46.8	16	8	11
Ch	0	0.0	1	0	0
Total	**7,707**		**41**	**24**	**32**
SCOTLAND					
C	9,793	38.3	35	16	22
L	16,356	60.8	40	13	31
Ch	385	0.9	3	0	0
Total	**26,534**		**78**	**29**	**53**
IRELAND					
C	19,664	40.1	59	27	41
L	17,128	35.1	55	30	42
R	12,537	24.8	22	12	20
Total	**49,329**		**136**	**69**	**103**
UNIVERSITIES					
C	-	-	6	6	6
Total	**-**	**-**	**6**	**6**	**6**
GREAT BRITAIN					
C	286,650	52.7	439	185	326
L	256,774	47.2	333	83	229
Ch	692	0.1	8	0	0
Total	**544,116**		**780**	**268**	**555**
UNITED KINGDOM					
C	306,314	50.9	498	212	367
L	273,902	46.9	388	113	271
Ch	692	0.1	8	0	0
R	12,537	2.1	22	12	20
Total	**593,445**		**916**	**337**	**658**

Table 1.05: General Election 1847

	Total Votes	%	Candidates	Unopposed	Elected
ENGLAND					
C & LC	170,407	42.1	319	149	239
L	230,656	57.2	297	92	222
Ch	2,848	0.7	9	0	1
Total	**403,911**		**625**	**241**	**462**
WALES					
C & LC	11,114	89.5	22	15	20
L	1,394	10.5	13	12	12
Total	**12,508**		**35**	**27**	**32**

General Election 1847 (contd.)

	Total Votes	*%*	*Candidates*	*Unopposed*	*Elected*
SCOTLAND					
C & LC	3,509	18.3	23	16	20
L	20,092	81.7	48	21	33
Total	**23,601**		**71**	**37**	**53**
IRELAND					
C & LC	11,258	34.0	49	33	40
L	5,935	20.2	33	11	25
R	14,128	43.6	51	18	36
Others	661	2.2	4	0	2
Total	**31,982**		**137**	**62**	**103**
UNIVERSITIES					
C & LC	9,193	88.2	9	0	6
L	1,234	11.8	2	0	0
Total	**10,427**		**11**	**0**	**6**
GREAT BRITAIN					
C & LC	194,223	43.1	373	180	285
L	253,376	56.2	360	125	267
Ch	2,848	0.6	9	0	1
Total	**450,447**		**742**	**305**	**553**
UNITED KINGDOM					
C & LC	205,481	42.2	422	213	325
L	259,311	53.9	393	136	292
Ch	2,848	0.6	9	0	1
R	14,128	3.1	51	18	36
Others	661	0.2	4	0	2
Total	**482,429**		**879**	**367**	**656**

Table 1.06: General Election 1852

	Total Votes	*%*	*Candidates*	*Unopposed*	*Elected*
ENGLAND					
C & LC	232,407	40.5	332	109	244
L	334,121	59.2	334	56	216
Ch	1,541	0.3	4	0	0
Total	**568,069**		**670**	**165**	**460**
WALES					
C & LC	7,212	54.7	25	14	20
L	5,251	45.3	17	7	12
Total	**12,463**		**42**	**21**	**32**
SCOTLAND					
C & LC	6,955	27.4	31	18	20
L	21,015	72.6	43	15	33
Total	**27,970**		**74**	**33**	**53**
IRELAND					
C & LC	61,672	46.3	66	15	40
L	70,495	53.7	94	17	63
Total	**132,167**		**160**	**32**	**103**

General Election 1852 (contd.)

	Total Votes	%	Candidates	Unopposed	Elected
UNIVERSITIES					
C & LC	3,235	100.0	7	4	6
Total	**3,235**		**7**	**4**	**6**
GREAT BRITAIN					
C & LC	249,809	40.8	395	145	290
L	360,387	58.9	394	78	261
Ch	1,541	0.3	4	0	0
Total	**611,737**		**793**	**223**	**551**
UNITED KINGDOM					
C & LC	311,481	41.4	461	160	330
L	430,882	58.4	488	95	324
Ch	1,541	0.2	4	0	0
Total	**743,904**		**953**	**255**	**654**

Table 1.07: General Election 1857

	Total Votes	%	Candidates	Unopposed	Elected
ENGLAND					
C & LC	168,705	31.7	255	102	185
L	355,913	68.2	362	112	275
Ch	614	0.1	1	0	0
Total	**525,232**		**618**	**214**	**460**
WALES					
C & LC	3,586	34.6	19	15	17
L	7,892	65.4	17	12	15
Total	**11,478**		**36**	**27**	**32**
SCOTLAND					
C & LC	4,060	15.2	19	13	14
L	31,999	84.8	49	25	39
Total	**36,059**		**68**	**38**	**53**
IRELAND					
C & LC	61,741	43.6	52	14	42
L	67,935	47.8	77	27	48
Others	12,099	8.6	19	4	13
Total	**141,775**		**148**	**45**	**103**
UNIVERSITIES					
C & LC	1,620	80.7	6	4	6
L	388	19.3	2	0	0
Total	**2,008**		**8**	**4**	**6**
GREAT BRITAIN					
C & LC	177,971	31.0	299	134	222
L	396,192	68.9	430	149	329
Ch	614	0.1	1	0	0
Total	**574,777**		**730**	**283**	**551**

General Election 1857 (contd.)

	Total Votes	*%*	*Candidates*	*Unopposed*	*Elected*
UNITED KINGDOM					
C & LC	239,712	33.1	351	148	264
L	464,127	65.1	507	176	377
Ch	614	0.1	1	0	0
Others	12,099	1.7	19	4	13
Total	**716,552**		**878**	**328**	**654**

Table 1.08: General Election 1859

	Total Votes	*%*	*Candidates*	*Unopposed*	*Elected*
ENGLAND					
C & LC	152,591	32.9	286	129	209
L	307,949	67.1	330	109	251
Ch	151	0.0	1	0	0
Total	**460,691**		**617**	**238**	**460**
WALES					
C & LC	2,767	63.6	18	14	17
L	1,585	36.4	18	14	15
Total	**4,352**		**36**	**28**	**32**
SCOTLAND					
C & LC	2,616	33.6	17	11	13
L	5,174	66.4	44	34	40
Total	**7,790**		**61**	**45**	**53**
IRELAND					
C & LC	35,258	38.9	67	36	53
L	57,409	61.1	73	26	50
Total	**92,667**		**140**	**62**	**103**
UNIVERSITIES					
C & LC	-	-	6	6	6
Total	**-**	**-**	**6**	**6**	**6**
GREAT BRITAIN					
C & LC	157,974	33.4	327	160	245
L	314,708	66.6	392	157	306
Ch	151	0.0	1	0	0
Total	**472,833**		**720**	**317**	**551**
UNITED KINGDOM					
C & LC	193,232	34.3	394	196	298
L	372,117	65.7	465	183	356
Ch	151	0.0	1	0	0
Total	**565,500**		**860**	**379**	**654**

Table 1.09: General Election 1865

	Total Votes	*%*	*Candidates*	*Unopposed*	*Elected*
ENGLAND					
C	291,238	41.0	308	94	213
L	406,978	59.0	359	88	251
Total	**698,216**		**667**	**182**	**464**

General Election 1865 (contd.)

	Total Votes	%	Candidates	Unopposed	Elected
WALES					
C	1,600	26.0	16	12	14
L	4,565	74.0	21	15	18
Total	**6,165**		**37**	**27**	**32**
SCOTLAND					
C	4,305	14.6	17	7	11
L	43,480	85.4	51	30	42
Total	**47,785**		**68**	**37**	**53**
IRELAND					
C	41,497	44.4	59	27	45
L	51,532	55.6	83	28	58
Total	**93,029**		**142**	**55**	**103**
UNIVERSITIES					
C	7,395	76.5	6	2	6
L	2,266	23.5	2	0	0
Total	**9,661**		**8**	**2**	**6**
GREAT BRITAIN					
C	304,538	40.0	347	115	244
L	457,289	60.0	433	133	311
Total	**761,827**		**780**	**248**	**555**
UNITED KINGDOM					
C	346,035	39.8	406	142	289
L	508,821	60.2	516	161	369
Total	**854,856**		**922**	**303**	**658**

Table 1.10: General Election 1868

	Total Votes	%	Candidates	Unopposed	Elected
ENGLAND					
C	803,637	40.2	334	54	211
L	1,192,098	59.7	412	46	244
Others	969	0.1	1	0	0
Total	**1,996,704**		**747**	**100**	**455**
WALES					
C	29,866	37.9	20	4	10
L	52,256	62.1	29	10	23
Total	**82,122**		**49**	**14**	**33**
SCOTLAND					
C	23,985	17.5	20	3	7
L	125,356	82.5	70	23	51
Total	**149,341**		**90**	**26**	**58**
IRELAND					
C	38,767	41.9	53	26	37
L	54,461	57.9	85	41	66
Others	188	0.2	2	0	0
Total	**93,416**		**140**	**67**	**103**

General Election 1868 (contd.)

	Total Votes	*%*	*Candidates*	*Unopposed*	*Elected*
UNIVERSITIES					
C	7,063	55.4	9	4	6
L	4,605	44.6	4	1	3
Total	**11,668**		**13**	**5**	**9**
GREAT BRITAIN					
C	864,551	38.6	383	65	234
L	1,374,315	61.4	515	80	321
Others	969	0.0	1	0	0
Total	**2,239,835**		**899**	**145**	**555**
UNITED KINGDOM					
C	903,318	38.4	436	91	271
L	1,428,776	61.5	600	121	387
Others	1,157	0.1	3	0	0
Total	**2,333,251**		**1,039**	**212**	**658**

Table 1.11: General Election 1874

	Total Votes	*%*	*Candidates*	*Unopposed*	*Elected*
ENGLAND					
C	905,239	46.2	387	100	280
L	1,035,268	53.8	355	26	171
Others	2	0.0	1	0	0
Total	**1,940,509**		**743**	**126**	**451**
WALES					
C	31,574	39.1	23	5	14
L	57,768	60.9	32	7	19
Total	**89,342**		**55**	**12**	**33**
SCOTLAND					
C	63,193	31.6	36	6	18
L	148,345	68.4	61	16	40
Total	**211,538**		**97**	**22**	**58**
IRELAND					
C	91,702	40.8	54	7	31
L	39,778	18.4	39	1	10
HR	90,234	39.6	80	10	60
Others	2,934	1.2	3	0	0
Total	**224,648**		**176**	**18**	**101**
UNIVERSITIES					
C	-	-	7	7	7
L	-	-	2	2	2
Total	**-**	**-**	**9**	**9**	**9**
GREAT BRITAIN					
C	1,000,006	44.6	453	118	319
L	1,241,381	55.4	450	51	232
Others	2	0.0	1	0	0
Total	**2,241,389**		**904**	**169**	**551**

General Election 1874 (contd.)

	Total Votes	%	Candidates	Unopposed	Elected
UNITED KINGDOM					
C	1,091,708	43.9	507	125	350
L	1,281,159	52.7	489	52	242
HR	90,234	3.3	80	10	60
Others	2,936	0.1	4	0	0
Total	**2,466,037**		**1,080**	**187**	**652**

Table 1.12: General Election 1880

	Total Votes	%	Candidates	Unopposed	Elected
ENGLAND					
C	1,205,990	43.7	390	47	197
L	1,519,576	56.2	372	19	254
Others	1,107	0.1	2	0	0
Total	**2,726,673**		**764**	**66**	**451**
WALES					
C	41,106	41.2	22	1	4
L	59,403	58.8	32	9	29
Total	**100,509**		**54**	**10**	**33**
SCOTLAND					
C	74,145	29.9	43	0	6
L	195,517	70.1	60	12	52
Total	**269,662**		**103**	**12**	**58**
IRELAND					
C	99,607	39.8	57	4	23
L	56,252	22.7	32	1	15
HR	95,535	37.5	81	10	63
Total	**251,394**		**170**	**15**	**101**
UNIVERSITIES					
C	5,503	49.2	9	6	7
L	5,675	50.8	3	0	2
Total	**11,178**		**12**	**6**	**9**
GREAT BRITAIN					
C	1,326,744	42.7	464	54	214
L	1,780,171	57.3	467	40	337
Others	1,107	0.0	2	0	0
Total	**3,108,022**		**933**	**94**	**551**
UNITED KINGDOM					
C	1,426,351	42.0	521	58	237
L	1,836,423	55.4	499	41	352
HR	95,535	2.6	81	10	63
Others	1,107	0.0	2	0	0
Total	**3,359,416**		**1,103**	**109**	**652**

Table 1.13: General Election 1885

	Total Votes	%	Candidates	Unopposed	Elected
ENGLAND					
C	1,675,757	47.5	440	1	213
L	1,809,665	51.4	452	4	238
N	3,489	0.1	2	0	1
Others	40,990	1.0	26	0	4
Total	**3,529,901**		**920**	**5**	**456**
WALES					
C	79,690	38.9	29	0	4
L	119,231	58.3	34	4	29
Others	5,766	2.8	2	0	1
Total	**204,687**		**65**	**4**	**34**
SCOTLAND					
C	151,137	34.3	55	0	8
L	238,627	53.3	70	5	51
Others	57,124	12.4	32	0	11
Total	**446,888**		**157**	**5**	**70**
IRELAND					
C	111,503	24.8	70	2	16
L	30,022	6.8	14	0	0
N	307,119	67.8	92	19	85
Others	2,822	0.6	10	0	0
Total	**451,466**		**186**	**21**	**101**
UNIVERSITIES					
C	2,840	53.7	8	7	8
L	2,453	46.3	2	1	1
Total	**5,293**		**10**	**8**	**9**
GREAT BRITAIN					
C	1,909,424	45.6	532	8	233
L	2,169,976	51.8	558	14	319
N	3,489	0.1	2	0	1
Others	103,880	2.5	60	0	16
Total	**4,186,769**		**1,152**	**22**	**569**
UNITED KINGDOM					
C	2,020,927	43.5	602	10	249
L	2,199,998	47.4	572	14	319
N	310,608	6.9	94	19	86
Others	106,702	2.2	70[1]	0	16[2]
Total	**4,638,235**		**1,338**	**43**	**670**

1. Including 5 SLRL, 3 SDF.
2. Namely:W. Abraham (Glamorganshire, Rhondda—Ind L/Lab);Sir R.Anstruther,Bt.(St.Andrews Burghs—Ind L); J.M. Cameron (Wick Burghs—Ind L); Sir G. Campbell (Kirkcaldy Burghs—Ind L); Dr. G.B. Clark (Caithness—Ind L/Crf); C.A.V. Conybeare (Cornwall, Camborne—Ind L); J. Cowen (Newcastle upon Tyne—Ind L); Hon. W.J.W. Fitzwilliam (Peterborough—Ind L); G. Fraser-Mackintosh (Inverness-shire—Ind L/Crf); G.J. Goschen (Edinburgh, East—Ind L); Sir G. Harrison (Edinburgh, South—Ind L); Dr. R. Macdonald (Ross and Cromarty—Ind L/Crf); D.H. Macfarlane (Argyll—Ind L/Crf); C.S. Parker (Perth—Ind L); Sir E.W. Watkin, Bt. (Hythe—Ind L); J. Wilson (Edinburgh, Central—Ind L).

Table 1.14: General Election 1886

	Total Votes	%	Candidates	Unopposed	Elected
ENGLAND					
C & LU	1,193,289	52.6	432	105	332
L	1,087,065	47.2	347	23	123
N	2,911	0.1	1	0	1
Others	1,791	0.1	3	0	0
Total	**2,285,056**		**783**	**128**	**456**
WALES					
C & LU	60,048	46.1	24	2	8
L	70,289	53.9	32	10	26
Total	**130,337**		**56**	**12**	**34**
SCOTLAND					
C & LU	164,314	46.4	63	2	27
L	193,801	53.6	68	7	43
Total	**358,115**		**131**	**9**	**70**
IRELAND					
C & LU	98,201	50.4	35	3	17
L	1,910	1.0	1	0	0
N	94,883	48.6	97	66	84
Total	**194,994**		**133**	**69**	**101**
UNIVERSITIES					
C & LU	5,034	84.7	9	6	9
L	516	13.8	1	0	0
N	111	1.5	2	0	0
Total	**5,661**		**12**	**6**	**9**
GREAT BRITAIN					
C & LU	1,422,685	51.2	528	115	376
L	1,351,671	48.6	448	40	192
N	3,022	0.1	3	0	1
Others	1,791	0.1	3	0	0
Total	**2,779,169**		**982**	**155**	**569**
UNITED KINGDOM					
C & LU	1,520,886	51.4	563	118	393 [1]
L	1,353,581	45.0	449	40	192
N	97,905	3.5	100	66	85
Others	1,791	0.1	3	0	0
Total	**2,974,163**		**1,115**	**224**	**670**

1. Including approximately 77 Liberal Unionists.

Table 1.15: General Election 1892

	Total Votes	%	Candidates	Unopposed	Elected
ENGLAND					
C & LU	1,788,108	51.1	441	22	261
L	1,685,283	48.0	426	9	190
N	2,537	0.1	1	0	1
Others	29,891	0.8	18	1	4
Total	**3,505,819**		**886**	**32**	**456**

General Election 1892 (contd.)

	Total Votes	%	Candidates	Unopposed	Elected
WALES					
C & LU	78,038	37.2	29	0	3
L	141,465	62.8	34	4	31
Total	**219,503**		**63**	**4**	**34**
SCOTLAND					
C & LU	209,944	44.4	68	0	19
L	256,944	53.9	70	0	51
Others	8,242	1.7	11	0	0
Total	**475,130**		**149**	**0**	**70**
IRELAND					
C & LU	79,263	20.6	59	11	21
L	4,327	1.1	2	0	0
N	308,972	78.1	133	9	80
Others	611	0.2	1	0	0
Total	**393,173**		**195**	**20**	**101**
UNIVERSITIES					
C & LU	3,797	80.9	9	7	9
Others	897	19.1	1	0	0
Total	**4,694**		**10**	**7**	**9**
GREAT BRITAIN					
C & LU	2,079,887	49.5	547	29	292
L	2,083,692	49.6	530	13	272
N	2,537	0.1	1	0	1
Others	39,030	0.9	30	1	4
Total	**4,205,146**		**1,108**	**43**	**569**
UNITED KINGDOM					
C & LU	2,159,150	47.0	606	40	313[1]
L	2,088,019	45.1	532	13	272
N	311,509	7.0	134	9	81[2]
Others	39,641	0.9	31[3]	1	4[4]
Total	**4,598,319**		**1,303**	**63**	**670**

1. Including approximately 45 Liberal Unionists.
2. Including 9 'Parnellites'.
3. Including 3 SPLP, 3 SUTCLP, 2 SDF, 1 joint SSF and SUTCLP.
4. Namely: J.W. Burns (Battersea and Clapham, Battersea —Ind Lab); J.K. Hardie (West Ham, South— Ind Lab); Sir E.W. Watkin, Bt.(Hythe—Ind L); J.H. Wilson (Middlesbrough—Ind Lab).

Table 1.16: General Election 1895

	Total Votes	%	Candidates	Unopposed	Elected
ENGLAND					
C & LU	1,521,938	51.9	442	106	343
L	1,369,598	46.7	342	8	112
ILP	40,056	1.1	21	0	0
N	2,089	0.1	1	0	1
Others	5,675	0.2	9	0	0
Total	**2,939,356**		**815**	**114**	**456**

General Election 1895 (contd.)

	Total Votes	%	Candidates	Unopposed	Elected
WALES					
C & LU	103,802	42.2	31	0	9
L	144,216	56.8	34	2	25
Others	2,677	1.0	2	0	0
Total	**250,695**		**67**	**2**	**34**
SCOTLAND					
C & LU	214,403	47.4	68	4	31
L	236,446	51.7	66	1	39
ILP	4,269	0.8	7	0	0
Others	608	0.1	1	0	0
Total	**455,726**		**142**	**5**	**70**
IRELAND					
C & LU	54,629	26.0	38	13	19
L	15,006	7.1	5	0	1
N	150,870	66.9	104	46	81
Total	**220,505**		**147**	**59**	**101**
UNIVERSITIES					
C & LU	-	-	9	9	9
Total	**-**	**-**	**9**	**9**	**9**
GREAT BRITAIN					
C & LU	1,840,143	50.5	550	119	392
L	1,750,260	48.0	442	11	176
ILP	44,325	1.2	28	0	0
N	2,089	0.1	1	0	1
Others	8,960	0.2	12	0	0
Total	**3,645,777**		**1,033**	**130**	**569**
UNITED KINGDOM					
C & LU	1,894,772	49.1	588	132	411[1]
L	1,765,266	45.7	447	11	177
ILP	44,325	1.0	28	0	0
N	152,959	4.0	105	46	82[2]
Others	8,960	0.2	12[3]	0	0
Total	**3,866,282**		**1,180**	**189**	**670**

1. Including approximately 71 Liberal Unionists.

2. Including 12 'Parnellites'.

3. Including 4 SDF.

Table 1.17: General Election 1900

	Total Votes	%	Candidates	Unopposed	Elected
ENGLAND					
C & LU	1,421,195	52.4	441	139	332
L	1,218,525	45.6	302	12	121
Lab	53,100	1.4	13	0	1
N	2,044	0.1	1	0	1
Others	13,628	0.5	6	0	1
Total	**2,708,492**		**763**	**151**	**456**

General Election 1900 (contd.)

	Total Votes	%	Candidates	Unopposed	Elected
WALES					
C & LU	63,932	37.6	21	1	6
L	105,837	58.5	33	10	27
Lab	9,598	3.9	2	0	1
Total	**179,367**		**56**	**11**	**34**
SCOTLAND					
C & LU	237,217	49.0	70	3	36
L	245,092	50.2	66	0	34
Others	3,921	0.8	3	0	0
Total	**486,230**		**139**	**3**	**70**
IRELAND					
C & LU	45,614	32.2	28	11	19
L	2,869	2.0	1	0	1
N	89,011	57.4	100	58	81
Others	11,899	8.4	6	0	0
Total	**149,393**		**135**	**69**	**101**
UNIVERSITIES					
C & LU	-	-	9	9	9
Total	**-**	**-**	**9**	**9**	**9**
GREAT BRITAIN					
C & LU	1,722,344	51.0	541	152	383
L	1,569,454	46.5	401	22	182
Lab	62,698	1.9	15	0	2
N	2,044	0.1	1	0	1
Others	17,549	0.5	9	0	1
Total	**3,374,089**		**967**	**174**	**569**
UNITED KINGDOM					
C & LU	1,767,958	50.3	569	163	402 [1]
L	1,572,323	45.0	402	22	183
Lab	62,698	1.3	15	0	2
N	91,055	2.6	101	58	82 [2]
Others	29,448	0.8	15 [3]	0	1 [4]
Total	**3,523,482**		**1,102**	**243**	**670**

1. Including approximately 68 Liberal Unionists.
2. Including 5 Independents.
3. Including 1 SWRC.
4. Namely: Sir J. Austin, Bt. (Yorkshire, Osgoldcross—Ind L).

Table 1.18: General Election 1906

	Total Votes	%	Candidates	Unopposed	Elected
ENGLAND					
C & LU	2,050,800	44.3	435	3	122
L	2,255,358	49.0	421	14	306
Lab	288,285	5.3	43	0	26
N	2,808	0.1	1	0	1
Others	60,358	1.3	28	0	1
Total	**4,657,609**		**928**	**17**	**456**

General Election 1906 (contd.)

	Total Votes	%	Candidates	Unopposed	Elected
WALES					
C & LU	65,949	33.8	20	0	0
L	128,461	60.2	34	12	32
Lab	11,865	3.5	2	0	1
Others	4,841	2.5	1	0	1
Total	**211,116**		**57**	**12**	**34**
SCOTLAND					
C & LU	225,802	38.2	69	0	10
L	336,400	56.4	70	1	58
Lab	16,897	2.3	4	0	2
Others	17,815	3.1	8	0	0
Total	**596,914**		**151**	**1**	**70**
IRELAND					
C & LU	63,218	47.0	23	6	15
L	26,572	19.7	9	0	3
Lab	4,616	3.4	1	0	0
N	32,223	23.9	85	73	81
Others	8,052	6.0	5	1	2
Total	**134,681**		**123**	**80**	**101**
UNIVERSITIES					
C & LU	16,302	60.6	9	4	9
L	4,266	19.4	2	0	0
Others	5,203	20.0	3	0	0
Total	**25,771**		**14**	**4**	**9**
GREAT BRITAIN					
C & LU	2,358,853	43.0	533	7	141
L	2,724,485	49.6	527	27	396
Lab	317,047	5.8	49	0	29
N	2,808	0.1	1	0	1
Others	88,217	1.6	40	0	2
Total	**5,491,410**		**1,150**	**34**	**569**
UNITED KINGDOM					
C & LU	2,422,071	43.4	556	13	156[1]
L	2,751,057	49.4	536	27	399[2]
Lab	321,663	4.8	50	0	29
N	35,031	0.7	86	73	82
Others	96,269	1.7	45[3]	1	4[4]
Total	**5,626,091**		**1,273**	**114**	**670**

1. Including approximately 25 Liberal Unionists.
2. Including 'Russellite' candidates in Ireland.
3. Including 8 SDF, 5 SWRC.
4. Namely: W. O'Brien (Cork City—Ind N);T.H.Sloan (Belfast, South—Ind C);J.W. Taylor (Durham, Chester-le-Street—Ind Lab); J.Williams (Glamorganshire, Gower—Ind L/Lab). Taylor's candidature had for technical reasons not been endorsed by the Labour Representation Committee but he joined the Parliamentary Labour Party upon election.

Table 1.19: General Election 1910 (January)

	Total Votes	%	Candidates	Unopposed	Elected
ENGLAND					
C & LU	2,645,914	49.3	453	5	233
L	2,291,062	43.0	405	1	188
Lab	403,358	6.9	62	0	33
N	2,943	0.1	1	0	1
Others	44,768	0.7	19	0	1
Total	**5,388,045**		**940**	**6**	**456**
WALES					
C & LU	116,769	31.9	33	0	2
L	195,288	52.3	29	0	27
Lab	60,496	14.9	5	0	5
Others	5,090	0.9	2	0	0
Total	**377,643**		**69**	**0**	**34**
SCOTLAND					
C & LU	260,033	39.6	70	0	9
L	354,847	54.2	68	0	58
Lab	37,852	5.1	10	0	2
Others	7,710	1.1	4	0	1
Total	**660,442**		**152**	**0**	**70**
IRELAND					
C & LU	68,982	32.7	29	8	19
L	20,339	9.6	7	0	1
Lab	3,951	1.9	1	0	0
N	123,704	54.1	104	55	81
Others	3,553	1.7	1	0	0
Total	**220,529**		**142**	**63**	**101**
UNIVERSITIES					
C & LU	12,709	61.3	9	6	9
L	4,621	22.3	2	0	0
Others	3,411	16.4	1	0	0
Total	**20,741**		**12**	**6**	**9**
GREAT BRITAIN					
C & LU	3,035,425	47.1	565	11	253
L	2,845,818	44.1	504	1	273
Lab	501,706	7.8	77	0	40
N	2,943	0.0	1	0	1
Others	60,979	0.9	26	0	2
Total	**6,446,871**		**1,173**	**12**	**569**
UNITED KINGDOM					
C & LU	3,104,407	46.8	594	19	272[1]
L	2,866,157	43.5	511	1	274
Lab	505,657	7.0	78	0	40
N	126,647	1.9	105	55	82[2]
Others	64,532	0.8	27[3]	0	2[4]
Total	**6,667,400**		**1,315**	**75**	**670**

1. Including approximately 32 Liberal Unionists.
2. Including 11 Independents.
3. Including 9 S Dem P, 1 SPP.
4. Namely: A.C.Corbett (Glasgow, Tradeston—Ind L); S. Storey (Sunderland—Ind C).

Table 1.20: General Election 1910 (December)

	Total Votes	%	Candidates	Unopposed	Elected
ENGLAND					
C & LU	2,035,297	48.8	436	54	233
L	1,849,098	44.4	362	14	187
Lab	300,142	6.4	44	2	34
N	2,458	0.1	1	0	1
Others	11,630	0.3	8	0	1
Total	**4,198,625**		**851**	**70**	**456**
WALES					
C & LU	81,100	33.8	20	0	3
L	117,533	47.9	30	10	26
Lab	47,027	17.8	7	1	5
Others	1,176	0.5	1	0	0
Total	**246,836**		**58**	**11**	**34**
SCOTLAND					
C & LU	244,785	42.6	57	1	9
L	306,378	53.6	67	11	58
Lab	24,633	3.6	5	0	3
Others	1,947	0.2	3	0	0
Total	**577,743**		**132**	**12**	**70**
IRELAND					
C & LU	56,408	28.6	26	9	17
L	19,003	9.6	7	0	1
N	129,262	60.3	105	53	83
Others	2,925	1.5	2	0	0
Total	**207,598**		**140**	**62**	**101**
UNIVERSITIES					
C & LU	2,579	58.1	9	8	9
L	1,857	41.9	1	0	0
Total	**4,436**		**10**	**8**	**9**
GREAT BRITAIN					
C & LU	2,363,761	47.0	522	63	254
L	2,274,866	45.2	460	35	271
Lab	371,802	7.4	56	3	42
N	2,458	0.0	1	0	1
Others	14,753	0.3	12	0	1
Total	**5,027,640**		**1,051**	**101**	**569**
UNITED KINGDOM					
C & LU	2,420,169	46.6	548	72	271 [1]
L	2,293,869	44.2	467	35	272
Lab	371,802	6.4	56	3	42
N	131,720	2.5	106	53	84 [2]
Others	17,678	0.3	14 [3]	0	1 [4]
Total	**5,235,238**		**1,191**	**163**	**670**

1. Including approximately 36 Liberal Unionists.
2. Including 10 Independents.
3. Including 2 S Dem P, 1 SPP.
4. Namely: F.Bennett-Goldney (Canterbury—Ind C).

Table 1.21: General Election 1918 (14 December*)

	Total Votes	%	Candidates	Unopposed	Elected
ENGLAND					
Co C	3,097,350	38.9	318	40	295
Co L	962,871	11.6	95	12	82
Co Lab	39,715	0.3	4	1	3
Co NDP	121,673	1.6	15	0	8
Co Ind	9,274	0.1	1	0	1
(Total Co)	*(4,230,883)*	*(52.5)*	*(433)*	*(53)*	*(389)*
C	317,281	3.7	34	0	20
L	1,172,700	14.7	232	2	25
Lab	1,811,739	22.6	291	6	42
Co-op	37,944	0.5	7	0	1
N	8,225	0.1	2	1	1
Nat P	94,389	1.2	26	0	2
NDP	20,200	0.2	7	0	0
NFDSS	12,329	0.1	5	0	0
Others	345,188	4.4	114	1	5
Total	**8,050,878**		**1,151**	**63**	**485**
WALES					
Co C	20,328	3.9	2	0	1
Co L	207,377	39.2	19	4	17
Co NDP	22,824	4.3	1	0	1
(Total Co)	*(250,529)*	*(47.4)*	*(22)*	*(4)*	*(19)*
C	39,264	7.4	6	0	3
L	51,382	9.7	10	2	3
Lab	163,055	30.8	25	5	9
Others	24,804	4.7	8	0	
Total	**529,034**		**71**	**11**	**35**
SCOTLAND					
Co C	336,530	30.8	34	1	28
Co L	221,145	19.1	28	7	25
Co Lab	14,247	1.3	1	0	1
Co NDP	12,337	1.1	2	0	0
(Total Co)	*(584,259)*	*(52.3)*	*(65)*	*(8)*	*(54)*
C	21,939	2.0	3	0	2
L	163,960	15.0	33	0	8
Lab	265,744	22.9	39	0	6
Co-op	19,841	1.8	3	0	0
NDP	4,297	0.4	1	0	0
Others	66,671	5.6	21	0	1
Total	**1,126,711**		**165**	**8**	**71**
IRELAND					
C	289,213	28.4	36	0	23
N	228,902	22.0	56	0	6
SF	495,345	47.0	100	25	72
Others	25,765	2.6	12	0	0
Total	**1,039,225**		**204**	**25**	**101**

General Election 1918 (contd.)

	Total Votes	%	Candidates	Unopposed	Elected
UNIVERSITIES					
Co C	18,530	45.2	8	0	8
Co L	5,197	12.7	3	0	3
(Total Co)	*(23,727)*	*(57.9)*	*(11)*	*(0)*	*(11)*
C	3,757	9.2	4	0	2
L	742	1.8	1	0	0
Lab	5,239	12.8	6	0	0
N	1,070	2.6	2	0	0
SF	1,762	4.3	2	0	1
Others	4,673	11.4	6	0	1
Total	**40,970**		**32**	**0**	**15**
GREAT BRITAIN					
Co C	3,472,738	35.6	362	41	332
Co L	1,396,590	14.3	145	23	127
Co Lab	53,962	0.6	5	1	4
Co Ind	9,274	0.1	1	0	1
Co NDP	156,834	1.6	18	0	9
(Total Co)	*(5,089,398)*	*(52.2)*	*(531)*	*(65)*	*(473)*
C	382,241	3.9	47	0	27
L	1,388,784	14.2	276	4	36
Lab	2,245,777	23.0	361	11	57
Co-op	57,785	0.6	10	0	1
N	9,295	0.1	4	1	1
Nat P	94,389	1.0	26	0	2
NDP	24,497	0.3	8	0	0
NFDSS	12,329	0.1	5	0	0
SF	1,762	0.0	2	0	1
Others	441,336	4.5	149	1	8
Total	**9,747,593**		**1,419**	**82**	**606**
UNITED KINGDOM					
Co C	3,472,738	32.5	362	41	332
Co L	1,396,590	12.6	145[1]	23	127
Co Lab	53,962	0.4	5[2]	1	4
Co Ind	9,274	0.1	1	0	1
Co NDP	156,834	1.5	18	0	9
(Total Co)	*(5,089,398)*	*(47.1)*	*(531)*	*(65)*	*(473)*
C	671,454	6.2	83[3]	0	50[4]
L	1,388,784	13.0	276	4	36[5]
Lab	2,245,777	20.8	361	11	57
Co-op	57,785	0.6	10	0	1[6]
N	238,197	2.2	60	1	7
Nat P	94,389	0.9	26	0	2
NDP	24,497	0.2	8	0	0
NFDSS	12,329	0.1	5	0	0
SF	497,107	4.6	102	25	73[7]
Others	467,101	4.3	161[8]	1	8[9]
Total	**10,786,818**		**1,623**[10]	**107**	**707**

* Before 1918 polling took place over several weeks -see Table 5.02.

1. Excluding 14 candidates who received the 'coupon' (the endorsement given to officially approved candidates) but repudiated it.

2. Of the five Coalition Labour candidates, only two were official and received the 'coupon'. They were J.R. Bell (Kingston-upon-Hull, South-West) and J. Parker (Staffordshire, Cannock). They were however incorrectly designated in the official list of Coalition candidates as National Democratic Party and Liberal respectively.

General Election 1918 (contd.)

3. The majority of Conservative candidates supported the Coalition although not all received the 'coupon'. There were also numerous other candidates, among them members of the National Party and National Democratic Party and at least half the Independents, who were certainly not opposed to the Coalition and the figures of votes polled by the official Coalition candidates must underestimate very considerably the number of electors who supported the Coalition.

4. Including three members of the Ulster Unionist Labour Association who were elected for Belfast constituencies and ran under the title 'Labour-Unionist'.

5. This is in fact an overestimate of the number of non-Coalition Liberals as nine who had not received the 'coupon' accepted the Coalition Whip upon election. They were: Sir F.D. Blake, Bt. (Northumberland, Berwick-upon-Tweed); G.P. Collins (Greenock); Hon. W.H. Cozens-Hardy (Norfolk, Southern); J. Gardiner (Perthshire and Kinross-shire, Kinross and Western); S.G. Howard (Suffolk, Sudbury); G. Lambert (Devon, South Molton); J.T.T. Rees (Devon, Barnstaple); Sir W.H. Seager (Cardiff, East); E.H. Young (Norwich). A few other Liberals were, with reservations, general supporters of the Coalition and the number of anti-Coalition Liberals (commonly called 'Free' or 'Asquithian' Liberals) who were prepared to follow Asquith's leadership was estimated by *The Times* in January 1919, to be about fourteen members who could be relied upon to consistently oppose the Coalition Government. The other non-Coalition Liberals at first adopted an independent attitude but as opposition to the Coalition grew, they tended to drift into the Asquith group.

6. Joined the Parliamentary Labour Party upon election.

7. The actual number was 69 as four Sinn Fein candidates were returned for two constituencies. They were: E. de Valera (Clare, East and Mayo, East); A. Griffith (Cavan, East and Tyrone, North-West); J.E. MacNeill (Londonderry, and National University); W.L.J. Mellows (Galway, East and Meath, North). The Sinn Fein members did not take their seats in the House of Commons.

8. Including 4 HLL, 3 BSP, 3 NSP, 3 SLP, 1 SPP, 1 WP.

9. Namely: R.H. Barker (Yorkshire, Sowerby); N.P. Billing (Hertfordshire, Hertford); H.W. Bottomley, (Hackney, South); J.J. Jones (West Ham, Silvertown—NSP); F.H. Rose (Aberdeen, North—Ind Lab); Sir O. Thomas (Anglesey—Ind Lab); J.C. Wedgwood (Newcastle-under-Lyme—Ind L); Sir R.H. Woods (Dublin University—Ind C). Jones, Rose and Sir O. Thomas joined the Labour Party immediately after being elected. Wedgwood joined the Labour Party in August 1919. Sir O. Thomas resigned from the Labour Party in July 1919. Sir R.H. Woods accepted the Conservative Whip upon election.

10. The number of persons seeking election was 1,611 owing to the fact that in Ireland nine candidates contested two constituencies each and one contested four constituencies.

Table 1.22: General Election 1922 (15 November)

	Total Votes	%	Candidates	Unopposed	Elected
ENGLAND					
C	4,809,797	41.5	406	29	307
L	2,260,423	19.6	271	3	44
NL	950,515	7.6	97	2	31
Lab	3,370,430	28.8	340	2	95
Com	9,693	0.1	2	0	0
N	12,614	0.1	2	1	1
Others	282,958	2.3	38	0	7
Total	**11,696,430**		**1,156**	**37**	**485**
WALES					
C	190,919	21.4	19	1	6
L	74,996	8.4	11	1	2
NL	230,961	25.8	19	1	8
Lab	363,568	40.8	28	1	18
Others	32,256	3.6	3	0	1
Total	**892,700**		**80**	**4**	**35**
SCOTLAND					
C	379,396	25.1	36	0	13
L	328,649	21.5	48	1	15
NL	288,529	17.7	33	1	12
Lab	501,254	32.2	43	1	29
Com	23,944	1.4	3	0	1
Others	47,589	2.1	5	0	1
Total	**1,569,361**		**168**	**3**	**71**
NORTHERN IRELAND					
C	107,972	55.8	12	9	10
N	90,053	36.3	2	0	2
Others	9,861	7.9	1	0	0
Total	**207,886**		**15**	**9**	**12**
UNIVERSITIES					
C	14,214	54.8	9	3	8
L	4,075	15.7	4	1	1
NL	1,312	5.0	2	0	2
Lab	2,097	8.1	3	0	0
Others	4,255	16.4	4	0	1
Total	**25,953**		**22**	**4**	**12**
GREAT BRITAIN					
C	5,394,326	38.0	470	33	334
L	2,668,143	18.8	334	6	62
NL	1,471,317	10.4	151	4	53
Lab	4,237,349	29.9	414	4	142
Com	33,637	0.2	5	0	1
N	12,614	0.1	2	1	1
Others	367,058	2.6	50	0	10
Total	**14,184,444**		**1,426**	**48**	**603**

General Election 1922 (contd.)

	Total Votes	%	Candidates	Unopposed	Elected
UNITED KINGDOM					
C	5,502,298	38.5	482	42	344
L	2,668,143	18.9	334	6	62 [1]
NL	1,471,317	9.9	151	4	53 [1]
Lab	4,237,349	29.7	414	4	142
Com	33,637	0.2	5 [2]	0	1
N	102,667	0.4	4	1	3
Others	376,919	2.4	51 [3]	0	10 [4]
Total	**14,392,330**		**1,441**	**57**	**615**

1. Two National Liberals, T.M. Guthrie (Moray and Nairnshire) and J. Hinds (Carmarthenshire, Carmarthen) accepted the Liberal Whip upon election bringing the party's strength up to 64 members.
2. For details of Communists who secured endorsement as official Labour candidates see Table 7.07 in the fifth edition of this book.
3. Including 1 SPP.
4. Namely: H.T.A. Becker (Richmond—Ind C); J.R.M. Butler (Cambridge University—Ind L); J.M.M.Erskine (Westminster, St. George's—Ind C); G.R. Hall Caine (Dorset, Eastern—Ind C); A. Hopkinson (Lancashire, Mossley); G.W.S. Jarrett (Kent, Dartford—Const); O.E. Mosley (Middlesex, Harrow); G.H. Roberts (Norwich); E. Scrymgeour (Dundee—SPP); Sir O. Thomas (Anglesey—Ind Lab). Becker, Erskine, Hall Caine and Roberts were subsequently granted the Conservative Whip.

Table 1.23: General Election 1923 (6 December)

	Total Votes	%	Candidates	Unopposed	Elected
ENGLAND					
C	4,732,176	39.8	444	24	221
L	3,572,335	29.9	362	3	123
Lab	3,549,888	29.7	350	1	138
N	10,322	0.1	2	1	1
Others	62,364	0.5	8	0	2
Total	**11,927,085**		**1,166**	**29**	**485**
WALES					
C	178,113	21.1	19	0	4
L	299,314	35.4	31	3	11
Lab	355,172	42.0	27	2	19
Others	12,469	1.5	1	0	1
Total	**845,068**		**78**	**5**	**35**
SCOTLAND					
C	468,526	31.6	52	0	14
L	422,995	28.4	59	4	22
Lab	532,450	35.9	48	0	34
Com	39,448	2.4	4	0	0
Others	37,908	1.7	4	0	1
Total	**1,501,327**		**167**	**4**	**71**
NORTHERN IRELAND					
C	117,161	49.4	12	8	10
N	87,671	27.3	2	0	2
Others	37,426	23.3	2	0	0
Total	**242,258**		**16**	**8**	**12**

General Election 1923 (contd.)

	Total Votes	%	Candidates	Unopposed	Elected
UNIVERSITIES					
C	18,565	58.1	9	3	9
L	6,837	21.4	5	1	2
Lab	2,270	7.1	2	0	0
Others	4,285	13.4	3	0	1
Total	**31,957**		**19**	**4**	**12**
GREAT BRITAIN					
C	5,397,380	37.7	524	27	248
L	4,301,481	30.1	457	11	158
Lab	4,439,780	31.0	427	3	191
Com	39,448	0.3	4	0	0
N	10,322	0.1	2	1	1
Others	117,026	0.8	16	0	5
Total	**14,305,437**		**1,430**	**42**	**603**
UNITED KINGDOM					
C	5,514,541	38.0	536	35	258
L	4,301,481	29.7	457	11	158
Lab	4,439,780	30.7	427	3	191
Com	39,448	0.2	4[1]	0	0
N	97,993	0.4	4	1	3
Others	154,452	1.0	18[2]	0	5[3]
Total	**14,547,695**		**1,446**	**50**	**615**

1. For details of Communists who secured endorsement as official Labour candidates see Table 7.07 in the fifth edition of this book.
2. Including 1 BLP, 1 SPP.
3. Namely: G.M.L. Davies (University of Wales—CP); A. Hopkinson (Lancashire, Mossley); R.H. Morris (Cardiganshire—Ind L); O.E. Mosley (Middlesex, Harrow); E. Scrymgeour (Dundee—SPP). Davies and Mosley joined the Labour Party shortly after the election and Morris was granted the Liberal Whip.

Table 1.24: General Election 1924 (29 October)

	Total Votes	%	Candidates	Unopposed	Elected
ENGLAND					
C	6,460,266	47.7	440	13	347
L	2,388,429	17.6	280	2	19
Lab	4,467,236	32.8	414	2	109
Com	39,416	0.3	6	0	1
Const	185,075	1.4	12	0	7
N	-	-	1	1	1
Others	21,136	0.2	6	0	1
Total	**13,561,558**		**1,159**	**18**	**485**
WALES					
C	224,014	28.4	17	0	9
L	244,828	31.0	21	1	10
Lab	320,397	40.6	33	7	16
Total	**789,239**		**71**	**8**	**35**

General Election 1924 (contd.)

	Total Votes	%	Candidates	Unopposed	Elected
SCOTLAND					
C	688,299	40.7	56	0	36
L	286,540	16.6	34	3	8
Lab	697,146	41.1	63	0	26
Com	15,930	0.7	2	0	0
Others	29,193	0.9	1	0	1
Total	**1,717,108**		**156**	**3**	**71**
NORTHERN IRELAND					
C	451,278	83.8	12	2	12
SF	46,457	9.9	8	0	0
Others	21,639	6.3	2	0	0
Total	**519,374**		**22**	**2**	**12**
UNIVERSITIES					
C	30,666	57.9	9	1	8
L	8,940	16.9	4	0	3
Lab	4,308	8.1	4	0	0
Others	9,086	17.1	3	0	1
Total	**53,000**		**20**	**1**	**12**
GREAT BRITAIN					
C	7,403,245	45.9	522	14	400
L	2,928,737	18.2	339	6	40
Lab	5,489,087	34.0	514	9	151
Com	55,346	0.3	8	0	1
Const	185,075	1.1	12	0	7
N	-	-	1	1	1
SF	0	0.0	0	0	0
Others	59,415	0.4	10	0	3
Total	**16,120,905**		**1,406**	**30**	**603**
UNITED KINGDOM					
C	7,854,523	46.8	534	16	412
L	2,928,737	17.8	339	6	40 [1]
Lab	5,489,087	33.3	514	9	151
Com	55,346	0.3	8	0	1
Const	185,075	1.2	12 [2]	0	7
N	-	-	1	1	1
SF	46,457	0.2	8	0	0
Others	81,054	0.4	12 [3]	0	3 [4]
Total	**16,640,279**		**1,428**	**32**	**615**

1. Including F.E.Guest (Bristol, North) whose name was originally given in the list of constitutionalist candidates. In the final list his name was omitted and although supported officially by the local Conservative Association he ran as a Liberal.

2. Of the twelve who ran as Constitutionalists, six [W.L.S. Churchill (Essex, Epping); J.E. Davis (Durham,Consett);Sir H.Greenwood,Bt.(Walthamstow, East); C.E.Loseby (Nottingham,West); A.H.Moreing (Cornwall,Camborne); J.L.Sturrock (Tottenham,North)] were ex-Liberals, most of whom subsequently joined the Conservative Party. The other six candidates [W.Allen (Stoke-on-Trent,Burslem); J.H.Edwards (Accrington);A.England (Lancashire,Heywood and Radcliffe); H.C.Hogbin (Battersea,North); Sir T.Robinson (Lancashire,Stretford); J.Ward (Stoke on-Trent, Stoke)] were Liberals and their names appear to have been included in the official list of Liberal candidates. Those elected were: (Conservatives)—Churchill, Sir H. Greenwood, Bt. and Moreing. (Liberals)—Edwards, England, Sir T. Robinson and Ward.

3. Including 1 NI Lab, 1 SPP.

4. Namely: Dr.E.G.G.Graham-Little (London University); A.Hopkinson (Lancashire, Mossley),E.Scrymgeour (Dundee—SPP).

Table 1.25: General Election 1929 (30 May)

	Total Votes	%	Candidates	Unopposed	Elected
ENGLAND					
C	7,177,551	38.8	469	2	221
L	4,340,703	23.6	422	0	35
Lab	6,850,738	36.9	467	0	226
Com	15,377	0.1	12	0	0
N	-	-	1	1	1
Others	117,876	0.6	17	0	2
Total	**18,502,245**		**1,388**	**3**	**485**
WALES					
C	289,695	22.0	35	0	1
L	440,911	33.5	34	0	9
Lab	577,554	43.9	33	0	25
Com	8,143	0.6	3	0	0
PC	609	0.0	1	0	0
Total	**1,316,912**		**106**	**0**	**35**
SCOTLAND					
C	792,063	35.9	65	0	20
L	407,081	18.1	45	0	13
Lab	937,300	42.3	66	0	36
Com	27,114	1.1	10	0	0
SNP	3,313	0.2	2	0	0
Others	76,070	2.4	4	0	2
Total	**2,242,941**		**192**	**0**	**71**
NORTHERN IRELAND					
C	354,657	68.0	10	1	10
L	100,103	16.8	6	0	0
N	24,177	6.6	3	2	2
Others	31,116	8.6	3	0	0
Total	**510,053**		**22**	**3**	**12**
UNIVERSITIES					
C	42,259	55.4	11	1	8
L	19,940	26.2	6	0	2
Lab	4,825	6.3	3	0	0
Others	9,200	12.1	2	0	2
Total	**76,224**		**22**	**1**	**12**
GREAT BRITAIN					
C	8,301,568	37.5	580	3	250
L	5,208,635	23.5	507	0	59
Lab	8,370,417	37.8	569	0	287
Com	50,634	0.2	25	0	0
N	-	-	1	1	1
PC	609	0.0	1	0	0
SNP	3,313	0.0	2	0	0
Others	203,146	0.9	23	0	6
Total	**22,138,322**		**1,708**	**4**	**603**

General Election 1929 (contd.)

	Total Votes	%	Candidates	Unopposed	Elected
UNITED KINGDOM					
C	8,656,225	38.1	590	4	260
L	5,308,738	23.5	513	0	59 [1]
Lab	8,370,417	37.1	569	0	287
Com	50,634	0.2	25	0	0
N	24,177	0.1	4	3	3
PC	609	0.0	1	0	0
SNP	3,313	0.0	2	0	0
Others	234,262	1.0	26 [2]	0	6 [3]
Total	**22,648,375**		**1,730**	**7**	**615**

1. Including Sir W.A. Jowitt (Preston) who joined the Labour Party one week after the election.
2. Including 1 SPP.
3. Namely: Dr. E.G.G. Graham-Little (London University); N. Maclean (Glasgow, Govan—Ind Lab); Sir R.H.S.D.L. Newman, Bt. (Exeter); Miss E.F. Rathbone (Combined English Universities); Sir T. Robinson (Lancashire, Stretford); E. Scrymgeour (Dundee—SPP). Maclean was re-admitted into the Parliamentary Labour Party in February 1930.

Table 1.26: General Election 1931 (27 October)

	Total Votes	%	Candidates	Unopposed	Elected
ENGLAND					
C	10,453,349	57.8	427	31	398
L	1,007,510	5.8	85	1	19
Nat	100,193	0.6	4	0	4
NL	632,155	3.4	28	3	23
N Lab	292,688	1.5	17	0	11
(Total Nat)	*(12,485,895)*	*(69.1)*	*(561)*	*(35)*	*(455)*
Ind L	31,989	0.2	2	0	0
Lab	5,464,425	30.2	428	2	29
Com	21,452	0.1	15	0	0
NP	20,721	0.1	16	0	0
Others	58,552	0.3	10	0	1
Total	**18,083,034**		**1,032**	**37**	**485**
WALES					
C	240,861	22.1	14	0	6
L	157,472	14.5	10	0	4
NL	75,717	7.0	5	2	4
N Lab	24,120	2.2	1	0	1
(Total Nat)	*(498,170)*	*(45.8)*	*(30)*	*(2)*	*(15)*
Ind L	71,539	6.6	4	0	4
Lab	479,547	44.1	30	4	16
Com	17,754	1.6	3	0	0
NP	11,300	1.0	2	0	0
PC	1,136	0.1	1	0	0
Others	9,100	0.8	2	0	0
Total	**1,088,546**		**72**	**6**	**35**

General Election 1931 (contd.)

	Total Votes	%	Candidates	Unopposed	Elected
SCOTLAND					
C	1,056,768	49.5	56	3	48
L	205,384	8.6	14	3	7
NL	101,430	4.9	8	2	8
N Lab	21,803	1.0	1	0	1
(Total Nat)	*(1,385,385)*	*(64.0)*	*(79)*	*(8)*	*(64)*
Lab	696,248	32.6	57	0	7
Com	35,618	1.4	8	0	0
NP	3,895	0.2	5	0	0
SNP	20,954	1.0	5	0	0
Others	32,229	0.8	1	0	0
Total	**2,174,329**		**155**	**8**	**71**
NORTHERN IRELAND					
C	149,566	56.1	12	8	10
(Total Nat)	*(149,566)*	*(56.1)*	*(12)*	*(8)*	*(10)*
Lab	9,410	5.0	1	0	0
N	123,053	38.9	3	0	2
Total	**282,029**		**16**	**8**	**12**
UNIVERSITIES					
C	5,381	18.9	9	7	8
L	2,229	7.9	2	1	2
N Lab	2,759	9.7	1	0	0
(Total Nat)	*(10,369)*	*(36.5)*	*(12)*	*(8)*	*(10)*
NP	461	1.6	1	0	0
PC	914	3.2	1	0	0
Others	16,691	58.7	3	0	2
Total	**28,435**		**17**	**8**	**12**
GREAT BRITAIN					
C	11,756,359	55.0	506	41	460
L	1,372,595	6.4	111	5	32
Nat	100,193	0.5	4	0	4
NL	809,302	3.8	41	7	35
N Lab	341,370	1.6	20	0	13
(Total Nat)	*(14,379,819)*	*(67.3)*	*(682)*	*(53)*	*(544)*
Ind L	103,528	0.5	6	0	4
Lab	6,640,220	31.1	515	6	52
Com	74,824	0.4	26	0	0
NP	36,377	0.2	24	0	0
PC	2,050	0.0	2	0	0
SNP	20,954	0.1	5	0	0
Others	116,572	0.5	16	0	3
Total	**21,374,344**		**1,276**	**59**	**603**

General Election 1931 (contd.)

	Total Votes	*%*	*Candidates*	*Unopposed*	*Elected*
UNITED KINGDOM					
C	11,905,925	55.0	518	49	470
L	1,372,595	6.5	111	5	32
Nat	100,193	0.5	4	0	4
NL	809,302	3.7	41 [1]	7	35
N Lab	341,370	1.5	20	0	13
(Total Nat)	*(14,529,385)*	*(67.2)*	*(694)*	*(61)*	*(554)*
Ind L	103,528	0.5	6 [2]	0	4
Lab	6,649,630	30.9	516 [3]	6 [4]	52 [5]
Com	74,824	0.3	26	0	0
N	123,053	0.3	3	0	2
NP	36,377	0.2	24	0	0
PC	2,050	0.0	2	0	0
SNP	20,954	0.1	5	0	0
Others	116,572	0.5	16 [6]	0	3 [7]
Total	**21,656,373**		**1,292**	**67**	**615**

1. Although standing as National Liberals and using a separate election organisation, the National Liberal candidates had their names included in the official list of Liberal Party candidates and those elected were claimed by the Liberal Party as their members. It appears that it was not until after the Liberal Party withdrew its support from the National Government in September 1932, that the party finally accepted that National Liberals could no longer be classed with Liberals who had stood without the National prefix.

2. Of the Liberal candidates opposed to the National Government, the four who secured election (the Lloyd George family group) took their seats on the Opposition Benches in the House of Commons and were subsequently joined by the other Liberal M.P.s who decided to cross the floor and go into opposition when the new Parliamentary Session opened on November 21, 1933. D. Lloyd George never again sat on the Liberal Benches from the time of the 1931 election until his elevation to the Peerage in 1945. He always occupied the corner seat on the Opposition (Labour) Front Bench.

3. Including 25 candidates who did not receive official endorsement. Of this number, 24 were members of the ILP (including 19 official ILP nominees, the remaining 5 although members of the ILP were the nominees of trade unions and Constituency Labour Parties) and refused to sign a form accepting the Standing Orders of the Parliamentary Labour Party, a condition of endorsement which was introduced just prior to the election. The remaining case of a candidate not receiving endorsement was at Glasgow, Hillhead where the candidate, although adopted by the Constituency Labour Party, was refused endorsement on the grounds that neither local finance or organisation warranted the adoption of a candidate. The total votes polled by the 25 non-endorsed candidates were 324,893.

4. Including 1 unendorsed.

5. Including six unendorsed members: G. Buchanan (Glasgow, Gorbals); D. Kirkwood (Dumbarton Burghs); J. McGovern (Glasgow, Shettleston); J. Maxton (Glasgow, Bridgeton); R.C. Wallhead (Merthyr Tydfil, Merthyr); J.C. Wedgwood (Newcastle-under-Lyme). McGovern, Maxton and Wallhead formed an ILP Parliamentary Group and were joined by Buchanan and Kirkwood. Wedgwood remained an Independent. Subsequently Kirkwood, Wallhead and Wedgwood re-entered the Parliamentary Labour Party.

6. Including 2 CW Land P, 1 LPP, 1 SPP.

7. Namely: Sir E.G.G. Graham-Little (London University—Nat Ind); A. Hopkinson (Lancashire, Mossley—Nat Ind); Miss E.F. Rathbone (Combined English Universities).

Table 1.27: General Election 1935 (14 November)

	Total Votes	%	Candidates	Unopposed	Elected
ENGLAND					
C	8,997,348	49.4	423	14	329
Nat	13,250	0.1	1	0	0
NL	673,597	3.4	31	2	22
N Lab	303,742	1.6	18	0	6
(Total Nat)	*(9,987,937)*	*(54.5)*	*(473)*	*(16)*	*(357)*
L	1,108,971	6.3	132	0	11
Lab	7,054,050	38.5	452	3	116
ILP	18,681	0.1	5	0	0
Others	103,396	0.6	16	0	1
Total	**18,273,035**		**1,078**	**19**	**485**
WALES					
C	204,099	23.4	14	0	6
Nat	35,318	4.1	2	0	1
NL	36,156	4.2	3	1	3
N Lab	16,954	1.9	1	0	1
(Total Nat)	*(292,527)*	*(33.6)*	*(20)*	*(1)*	*(11)*
L	157,091	18.0	12	0	6
Lab	395,830	45.4	33	10	18
Com	13,655	1.6	1	0	0
ILP	9,640	1.1	1	0	0
PC	2,534	0.3	1	0	0
Total	**871,277**		**68**	**11**	**35**
SCOTLAND					
C	962,595	42.0	58	1	35
Nat	4,621	0.2	1	0	0
NL	149,072	6.7	9	0	7
N Lab	19,115	0.9	1	0	1
(Total Nat)	*(1,135,403)*	*(49.8)*	*(69)*	*(1)*	*(43)*
L	174,235	6.7	16	0	3
Lab	863,789	36.8	63	0	20
Com	13,462	0.6	1	0	1
ILP	111,256	5.0	11	0	4
SNP	25,652	1.1	7	0	0
Total	**2,323,797**		**167**	**1**	**71**
NORTHERN IRELAND					
C	292,840	64.9	12	6	10
(Total Nat)	*(292,840)*	*(64.9)*	*(12)*	*(6)*	*(10)*
N	101,494	18.3	2	0	2
Rep	56,833	16.8	3	0	0
Total	**451,167**		**17**	**6**	**12**
UNIVERSITIES					
C	39,418	50.7	8	2	7
NL	7,529	9.6	1	0	1
(Total Nat)	*(46,947)*	*(60.3)*	*(9)*	*(2)*	*(8)*
L	2,796	3.6	1	0	1
Lab	11,822	15.2	4	0	0
SNP	3,865	5.0	1	0	0
Others	12,348	15.9	3	1	3
Total	**77,778**		**18**	**3**	**12**

General Election 1935 (contd.)

	Total Votes	%	Candidates	Unopposed	Elected
GREAT BRITAIN					
C	10,203,460	47.4	503	17	377
Nat	53,189	0.2	4	0	1
NL	866,354	4.0	44	3	33
N Lab	339,811	1.6	20	0	8
(Total Nat)	*(11,462,814)*	*(53.2)*	*(571)*	*(20)*	*(419)*
L	1,443,093	6.7	161	0	21
Lab	8,325,491	38.6	552	13	154
Com	27,117	0.1	2	0	1
ILP	139,577	0.6	17	0	4
PC	2,534	0.0	1	0	0
SNP	29,517	0.1	8	0	0
Others	115,744	0.5	19	1	4
Total	**21,545,887**		**1,331**	**34**	**603**
UNITED KINGDOM					
C	10,496,300	47.8	515	23	387
Nat	53,189	0.3	4	0	1
NL	866,354	3.7	44	3	33
N Lab	339,811	1.5	20	0	8
(Total Nat)	*(11,755,654)*	*(53.3)*	*(583)*	*(26)*	*(429)*
L	1,443,093	6.7	161	0	21 [1]
Lab	8,325,491	38.0	552	13	154
Com	27,117	0.1	2	0	1
ILP	139,577	0.7	17	0	4
N	101,494	0.3	2	0	2
PC	2,534	0.0	1	0	0
Rep	56,833	0.2	3	0	0
SNP	29,517	0.1	8	0	0
Others	115,744	0.6	19 [2]	1	4 [3]
Total	**21,997,054**		**1,348**	**40**	**615**

1. Including R.H. Bernays (Bristol, North) and the Hon. J.P. Maclay (Paisley) who although elected as Liberals without prefix, supported the National Government. Bernays accepted the National Liberal Whip in October 1936.
2. Including 1 LPP, 1 SCPGB.
3. Namely: Sir E.G.G. Graham-Little (London University—Nat Ind);A.P. Herbert(Oxford University);A.Hopkinson (Lancashire, Mossley—Nat Ind); Miss E.F. Rathbone (Combined English Universities).

Table 1.28: General Election 1945 (5 July)

	Total Votes	%	Candidates	Unopposed	Elected
ENGLAND					
C	7,575,577	37.0	461	0	159
Nat	105,862	0.5	8	0	1
NL	587,752	2.7	38	0	7
(Total Nat)	*(8,269,191)*	*(40.2)*	*(507)*	*(0)*	*(167)*
L	1,913,917	9.4	265	0	5
Lab	9,972,519	48.5	494	1	331
Com	53,754	0.3	15	0	1
CW	106,403	0.5	21	0	1
ILP	6,044	0.0	2	0	0
Others	217,192	1.1	59	0	5
Total	**20,539,020**		**1,363**	**1**	**510**

General Election 1945 (contd.)

	Total Votes	%	Candidates	Unopposed	Elected
WALES					
C	241,380	18.1	21	0	3
Nat	11,306	0.9	1	0	0
NL	64,043	4.8	5	0	1
(Total Nat)	*(316,729)*	*(23.8)*	*(27)*	*(0)*	*(4)*
L	198,553	14.9	17	0	6
Lab	779,184	58.5	34	1	25
Com	15,761	1.2	1	0	0
PC	14,321	1.1	6	0	0
Others	6,123	0.5	2	0	0
Total	**1,330,671**		**87**	**1**	**35**
SCOTLAND					
C	878,206	36.7	62	0	24
NL	85,937	3.6	6	0	3
(Total Nat)	*(964,143)*	*(40.3)*	*(68)*	*(0)*	*(27)*
L	132,849	5.6	22	0	0
Lab	1,144,310	47.9	68	0	37
Com	33,265	1.4	5	0	1
CW	4,231	0.2	2	0	0
ILP	40,725	1.7	3	0	3
SNP	30,595	1.3	8	0	0
Others	39,774	1.7	8	0	3
Total	**2,389,892**		**184**	**0**	**71**
NORTHERN IRELAND					
C	392,450	53.7	12	1	8
(Total Nat)	*(392,450)*	*(53.7)*	*(12)*	*(1)*	*(8)*
Lab	65,459	11.4	5	0	0
CWLP	14,096	2.9	1	0	0
N	148,078	18.8	3	0	2
Others	99,682	13.2	3	0	2
Total	**719,765**		**24**	**1**	**12**
UNIVERSITIES					
C	13,486	11.7	3	0	3
Nat	16,011	13.8	1	0	1
(Total Nat)	*(29,497)*	*(25.5)*	*(4)*	*(0)*	*(4)*
L	7,111	6.1	2	0	1
Lab	6,274	5.4	2	0	0
PC	1,696	1.5	1	0	0
Others	71,269	61.5	16	0	7
Total	**115,847**		**25**	**0**	**12**

General Election 1945 (contd.)

	Total Votes	%	Candidates	Unopposed	Elected
GREAT BRITAIN					
C	8,708,649	35.7	547	0	189
Nat	133,179	0.5	10	0	2
NL	737,732	3.0	49	0	11
(Total Nat)	*(9,579,560)*	*(39.3)*	*(606)*	*(0)*	*(202)*
L	2,252,430	9.2	306	0	12[1]
Lab	11,902,287	48.8	598	2	393
Com	102,780	0.4	21	0	2
CW	110,634	0.5	23	0	1
ILP	46,769	0.2	5	0	3
PC	16,017	0.1	7	0	0
SNP	30,595	0.1	8	0	0
Others	334,358	1.4	85	0	15
Total	**24,375,430**		**1,659**	**2**	**628**
UNITED KINGDOM					
C	9,101,099	36.2	559	1	197
Nat	133,179	0.5	10	0	2
NL	737,732	2.9	49	0	11
(Total Nat)	*(9,972,010)*	*(39.6)*	*(618)*	*(1)*	*(210)*
L	2,252,430	9.0	306	0	12[1]
Lab	11,967,746	48.0	603	2	393
Com	102,780	0.4	21	0	2
CW	110,634	0.5	23	0	1
CWLP	14,096	0.1	1	0	0
ILP	46,769	0.2	5	0	3
N	148,078	0.4	3	0	2
PC	16,017	0.1	7	0	0
SNP	30,595	0.1	8	0	0
Others	434,040	1.6	88[2]	0	17[3]
Total	**25,095,195**		**1,683**	**3**	**640**

1. Including G. Lloyd George (Pembrokeshire) who had accepted office in the National (Caretaker) Government and supported Churchill.
2. Including 5 Dem P, 1 LPP, 1 SPGB.
3. Namely: C.V.O. Bartlett (Somerset, Bridgwater—Ind Prog); J. Beattie (Belfast, West—Ind Lab); Sir J. Boyd Orr (Combined Scottish Universities); W.J. Brown (Warwickshire, Rugby); Sir E.G.G.Graham-Little (London University—Nat Ind); H.W. Harris (Cambridge University); A.P. Herbert (Oxford University); W.D. Kendall (Lincolnshire, Grantham); K.M. Lindsay (Combined English Universities); D.L. Lipson (Cheltenham—Nat Ind); Rev. Dr. J. Little (Down—Ind C); Sir M. Macdonald (Inverness-shire and Ross and Cromarty, Inverness—Ind L); J.H. Mackie (Galloway—Ind C); J. MacLeod (Inverness-shire and Ross and Cromarty, Ross and Cromarty—Ind L); D.N. Pritt (Hammersmith, North—Ind Lab); Miss E.F. Rathbone (Combined English Universities); Sir J.A. Salter (Oxford University). Mackie was granted the Conservative Whip in March 1948 and Beattie joined the Irish Labour Party in 1949. Sir M. Macdonald and MacLeod aligned themselves with the National Liberal Party in the House of Commons.

Table 1.29: General Election 1950 (23 February)

	Total Votes	%	Candidates	Unopposed	Elected
ENGLAND					
C	9,820,068	41.0	466	0	243
NL & C	679,324	2.8	38	0	10
(Total C)	(10,499,392)	(43.8)	(504)	(0)	(253)
L	2,248,127	9.4	413	0	2
Lab	11,050,966	46.1	505	0	251
Com	55,158	0.2	80	0	0
Others	100,805	0.4	26	0	0
Total	**23,954,448**		**1,528**	**0**	**506**
WALES					
C	320,750	21.0	29	0	3
NL & C	97,918	6.4	6	0	1
(Total C)	(418,668)	(27.4)	(35)	(0)	(4)
L	193,090	12.6	21	0	5
Lab	887,984	58.1	36	0	27
Com	9,048	0.6	4	0	0
PC	17,580	1.2	7	0	0
Others	2,184	0.1	2	0	0
Total	**1,528,554**		**105**	**0**	**36**
SCOTLAND					
C	1,013,909	37.2	57	0	26
NL & C	208,101	7.6	11	0	5
(Total C)	(1,222,010)	(44.8)	(68)	(0)	(31)
L	180,270	6.6	41	0	2
Lab	1,259,410	46.2	71	0	37
Com	27,559	1.0	16	0	0
SNP	9,708	0.4	3	0	0
Others	27,727	1.0	13	0	1
Total	**2,726,684**		**212**	**0**	**71**
NORTHERN IRELAND					
C	352,334	62.8	12	2	10
Lab	67,816	12.1	5	0	0
Irish LP	52,715	9.4	2	0	0
N	65,211	11.6	2	0	2
SF	23,362	4.2	2	0	0
Total	**561,438**		**23**	**2**	**12**
GREAT BRITAIN					
C	11,154,727	39.5	552	0	272
NL & C	985,343	3.5	55	0	16
(Total C)	(12,140,070)	(43.0)	(607)	(0)	(288)
L	2,621,487	9.3	475	0	9
Lab	13,198,360	46.8	612	0	315
Com	91,765	0.3	100	0	0
PC	17,580	0.1	7	0	0
SNP	9,708	0.0	3	0	0
Others	130,716	0.5	41	0	1
Total	**28,209,686**		**1,845**	**0**	**613**

General Election 1950 (contd.)

	Total Votes	*%*	*Candidates*	*Unopposed*	*Elected*
UNITED KINGDOM					
C	11,507,061	40.0	564	2	282
NL & C	985,343	3.4	55	0	16
(Total C)	*(12,492,404)*	*(43.4)*	*(619)*	*(2)*	*(298)*
L	2,621,487	9.1	475	0	9
Lab	13,266,176	46.1	617	0	315
Com	91,765	0.3	100	0	0
Irish LP	52,715	0.2	2	0	0
N	65,211	0.2	2	0	2
PC	17,580	0.1	7	0	0
SF	23,362	0.1	2	0	0
SNP	9,708	0.0	3	0	0
Others	130,716	0.5	41 [1]	0	1 [2]
Total	**28,771,124**		**1,868**	**2**	**625**

1. Including 4 AP, 4 ILP, 2 SPGB, 1 MGC, 1 SCPGB.
2. Namely: J. MacLeod (Inverness-shire and Ross and Cromarty, Ross and Cromarty—Ind L). He joined the Liberal-Unionist Group in May 1951.

Table 1.30: General Election 1951 (25 October)

	Total Votes	*%*	*Candidates*	*Unopposed*	*Elected*
ENGLAND					
C	10,855,287	45.6	463	0	259
NL & C	767,417	3.2	39	0	12
(Total C)	*(11,622,704)*	*(48.8)*	*(502)*	*(0)*	*(271)*
L	537,434	2.3	91	0	2
Lab	11,630,467	48.8	506	0	233
Com	7,745	0.0	5	0	0
Others	27,745	0.1	8	0	0
Total	**23,826,095**		**1,112**	**0**	**506**
WALES					
C	421,525	27.6	30	0	5
NL & C	49,744	3.3	3	0	1
(Total C)	*(471,269)*	*(30.8)*	*(33)*	*(0)*	*(6)*
L	116,821	7.6	9	0	3
Lab	925,848	60.5	36	0	27
Com	2,948	0.2	1	0	0
PC	10,920	0.7	4	0	0
Others	1,643	0.1	1	0	0
Total	**1,529,449**		**84**	**0**	**36**
SCOTLAND					
C	1,108,321	39.9	57	0	29
NL & C	240,977	8.7	13	0	6
(Total C)	*(1,349,298)*	*(48.6)*	*(70)*	*(0)*	*(35)*
L	76,291	2.7	9	0	1
Lab	1,330,244	47.9	71	0	35
Com	10,947	0.4	4	0	0
SNP	7,299	0.3	2	0	0
Others	3,758	0.1	4	0	0
Total	**2,777,837**		**160**	**0**	**71**

General Election 1951 (contd.)

	Total Votes	%	Candidates	Unopposed	Elected
NORTHERN IRELAND					
C	274,928	59.4	12	4	9
Lab	62,324	13.5	4	0	0
Irish LP	33,174	7.2	1	0	1
N	92,787	20.0	3	0	2
Total	**463,213**		**20**	**4**	**12**
GREAT BRITAIN					
C	12,385,133	44.0	550	0	293
NL & C	1,058,138	3.8	55	0	19
(Total C)	*(13,443,271)*	*(47.8)*	*(605)*	*(0)*	*(312)*
L	730,546	2.6	109	0	6
Lab	13,886,559	49.4	613	0	295
Com	21,640	0.1	10	0	0
PC	10,920	0.0	4	0	0
SNP	7,299	0.0	2	0	0
Others	33,146	0.1	131	0	0
Total	**28,133,381**		**1,356**	**0**	**613**
UNITED KINGDOM					
C	12,660,061	44.3	562	4	302
NL & C	1,058,138	3.7	55	0	19
(Total C)	*(13,718,199)*	*(48.0)*	*(617)*	*(4)*	*(321)*
L	730,546	2.6	109	0	6
Lab	13,948,883	48.8	617	0	295
Com	21,640	0.1	10	0	0
Irish LP	33,174	0.1	1	0	1
N	92,787	0.3	3	0	2
PC	10,920	0.0	4	0	0
SNP	7,299	0.0	2	0	0
Others	33,146	0.1	13 [1]	0	0
Total	**28,596,594**		**1,376**	**4**	**625**

1. Including 1 AP, 3 ILP, 1 BEP.

Table 1.31: General Election 1955 (26 May)

	Total Votes	%	Candidates	Elected
ENGLAND				
C	10,586,790	47.8	480	279
NL & C	578,646	2.6	29	14
(Total C)	*(11,165,436)*	*(50.4)*	*(509)*	*(293)*
L	571,034	2.6	95	2
Lab	10,355,892	46.8	510	216
Com	15,405	0.1	11	0
Others	28,363	0.1	9	0
Total	**22,136,130**		**1,134**	**511**

General Election 1955 (contd.)

	Total Votes	%	Candidates	Elected
WALES				
C	383,132	26.7	28	5
NL & C	45,734	3.2	4	1
(Total C)	*(428,866)*	*(29.9)*	*(32)*	*(6)*
L	104,095	7.3	10	3
Lab	825,690	57.6	36	27
Com	4,544	0.3	1	0
PC	45,119	3.1	11	0
Others	25,410	1.8	1	0
Total	**1,433,724**		**91**	**36**
SCOTLAND				
C	1,056,209	41.5	59	30
NL & C	217,733	8.6	12	6
(Total C)	*(1,273,942)*	*(50.1)*	*(71)*	*(36)*
L	47,273	1.9	5	1
Lab	1,188,058	46.7	71	34
Com	13,195	0.5	5	0
SNP	12,112	0.5	2	0
Others	8,674	0.3	2	0
Total	**2,543,254**		**156**	**71**
NORTHERN IRELAND				
C	442,647	68.5	12	10
Lab	35,614	5.5	3	0
Irish LP	16,050	2.5	1	0
SF	152,310	23.6	12	2
Total	**646,621**		**28**	**12**
GREAT BRITAIN				
C	12,026,131	46.1	567	314
NL & C	842,113	3.2	45	21
(Total C)	*(12,868,244)*	*(49.3)*	*(612)*	*(335)*
L	722,402	2.8	110	6
Lab	12,369,640	47.4	617	277
Com	33,144	0.1	17	0
PC	45,119	0.2	11	0
SNP	12,112	0.0	2	0
Others	62,447	0.2	12	0
Total	**26,113,108**		**1,381**	**618**
UNITED KINGDOM				
C	12,468,778	46.6	579	324
NL & C	842,113	3.1	45	21
(Total C)	*(13,310,891)*	*(49.7)*	*(624)*	*(345)*
L	722,402	2.7	110	6
Lab	12,405,254	46.4	620	277
Com	33,144	0.1	17	0
Irish LP	16,050	0.1	1	0
PC	45,119	0.2	11	0
SF	152,310	0.6	12	2
SNP	12,112	0.0	2	0
Others	62,447	0.2	12 [1]	0
Total	**26,759,729**		**1,409**	**630**

1. Including 2 ILP.

Table 1.32: General Election 1959 (8 October)

	Total Votes	%	Candidates	Elected
ENGLAND				
C	11,037,998	47.7	484	302
NL & C	521,242	2.3	25	13
(Total C)	(11,559,240)	(50.0)	(509)	(315)
L	1,449,593	6.3	191	3
Lab	10,085,097	43.6	511	193
Com	12,204	0.1	10	0
Others	21,635	0.1	13	0
Total	**23,127,769**		**1,234**	**511**
WALES				
C	441,461	29.6	31	6
NL & C	44,874	3.0	3	1
(Total C)	(486,335)	(32.6)	(34)	(7)
L	78,951	5.3	8	2
Lab	841,450	56.4	36	27
Com	6,542	0.4	2	0
PC	77,571	5.2	20	0
Others	408	0.0	1	0
Total	**1,491,257**		**101**	**36**
SCOTLAND				
C	1,060,609	39.8	59	25
NL & C	199,678	7.5	11	6
(Total C)	(1,260,287)	(47.2)	(70)	(31)
L	108,963	4.1	16	1
Lab	1,245,255	46.7	71	38
Com	12,150	0.5	6	0
SNP	21,738	0.8	5	0
Others	19,120	0.7	4	1
Total	**2,667,513**		**172**	**71**
NORTHERN IRELAND				
C	445,013	77.2	12	12
L	3,253	0.6	1	0
Lab	44,370	7.7	3	0
SF	63,415	11.0	12	0
Others	20,062	3.5	1	0
Total	**576,113**		**29**	**12**
GREAT BRITAIN				
C	12,540,068	46.0	574	333
NL & C	765,794	2.8	39	20
(Total C)	(13,305,862)	(48.8)	(613)	(353)
L	1,637,507	6.0	215	6
Lab	12,171,802	44.6	618	258
Com	30,896	0.1	18	0
PC	77,571	0.3	20	0
SNP	21,738	0.1	5	0
Others	41,163	0.2	18	1
Total	**27,286,539**		**1,507**	**618**

General Election 1959 (contd.)

	Total Votes	%	Candidates	Elected
UNITED KINGDOM				
C	12,985,081	46.6	586	345
NL & C	765,794	2.7	39	20
(Total C)	*(13,750,875)*	*(49.4)*	*(625)*	*(365)*
L	1,640,760	5.9	216	6
Lab	12,216,172	43.8	621	258
Com	30,896	0.1	18	0
PC	77,571	0.3	20	0
SF	63,415	0.2	12	0
SNP	21,738	0.1	5	0
Others	61,225	0.2	19 [1]	1 [2]
Total	**27,862,652**		**1,536**	**630**

1. Including 2 ILP, 1 FP, 1 NI Ind Lab, 1 NLP, 1 SPGB, 1 UM.
2. Namely; Sir D.Robertson (Caithness and Sutherland—Ind C).

Table 1.33: General Election 1964 (15 October)

	Total Votes	%	Candidates	Elected
ENGLAND				
C	9,894,014	43.1	500	256
NL & C	212,014	0.9	11	6
(Total C)	*(10,106,028)*	*(44.1)*	*(511)*	*(262)*
L	2,775,752	12.1	323	3
Lab	9,982,360	43.5	511	246
Com	24,824	0.1	22	0
Others	48,287	0.2	42	0
Total	**22,937,251**		**1,409**	**511**
WALES				
C	398,960	27.6	34	6
NL & C	26,062	1.8	2	0
(Total C)	*(425,022)*	*(29.4)*	*(36)*	*(6)*
L	106,114	7.3	12	2
Lab	837,022	57.8	36	28
Com	9,377	0.6	5	0
PC	69,507	4.8	23	0
Total	**1,447,042**		**112**	**36**
SCOTLAND				
C	981,641	37.3	65	24
NL & C	88,054	3.3	6	0
(Total C)	*(1,069,695)*	*(40.6)*	*(71)*	*(24)*
L	200,063	7.6	26	4
Lab	1,283,667	48.7	71	43
Com	12,241	0.5	9	0
SNP	64,044	2.4	15	0
Others	4,829	0.2	5	0
Total	**2,634,539**		**197**	**71**

General Election 1964 (contd.)

	Total Votes	%	Candidates	Elected
NORTHERN IRELAND				
C	401,897	63.0	12	12
L	17,354	2.7	4	0
Lab	102,759	16.1	10	0
Rep	101,628	15.9	12	0
Rep LP	14,678	2.3	1	0
Total	**638,316**		**39**	**12**
GREAT BRITAIN				
C	11,274,615	41.7	599	286
NL & C	326,130	1.2	19	6
(Total C)	*(11,600,745)*	*(42.9)*	*(618)*	*(292)*
L	3,081,929	11.4	361	9
Lab	12,103,049	44.8	618	317
Com	46,442	0.2	36	0
PC	69,507	0.3	23	0
SNP	64,044	0.2	15	0
Others	53,116	0.2	47	0
Total	**27,018,832**		**1,718**	**618**
UNITED KINGDOM				
C	11,676,512	42.2	611	298
NL & C	326,130	1.2	19	6
(Total C)	*(12,002,642)*	*(43.4)*	*(630)*	*(304)*
L	3,099,283	11.2	365	9
Lab	12,205,808	44.1	628	317
Com	46,442	0.2	36	0
PC	69,507	0.3	23	0
Rep	101,628	0.4	12	0
Rep LP	14,678	0.1	1	0
SNP	64,044	0.2	15	0
Others	53,116	0.2	47[1]	0
Total	**27,657,148**		**1,757**	**630**

1. Including 3 Loyalists, 2 INDEC, 2 Pat P, 2 SPGB, 1 BNP, 1 FP, 1 N Dem P.

Table 1.34: General Election 1966 (31 March)

	Total Votes	%	Candidates	Elected
ENGLAND				
C	9,542,577	42.1	501	216
NL & C	149,779	0.7	9	3
(Total C)	*(9,692,356)*	*(42.7)*	*(510)*	*(219)*
L	2,036,793	9.0	273	6
Lab	10,886,408	48.0	511	286
Com	33,093	0.1	34	0
Others	44,045	0.2	35	0
Total	**22,692,695**		**1,363**	**511**

General Election 1966 (contd.)

	Total Votes	*%*	*Candidates*	*Elected*
WALES				
C	396,795	27.9	36	3
L	89,108	6.3	11	1
Lab	863,692	60.7	36	32
Com	12,769	0.9	8	0
PC	61,071	4.3	20	0
Total	**1,423,435**		**111**	**36**
SCOTLAND				
C	960,675	37.6	71	20
L	172,447	6.8	24	5
Lab	1,273,916	49.9	71	46
Com	16,230	0.6	15	0
SNP	128,474	5.0	23	0
Others	638	0.0	2	0
Total	**2,552,380**		**206**	**71**
NORTHERN IRELAND				
C	368,629	61.8	12	11
L	29,109	4.9	3	0
Lab	72,613	12.2	4	0
N	22,167	3.7	1	0
Rep	62,782	10.5	5	0
Rep LP	26,292	4.4	1	1
Others	14,645	2.5	1	0
Total	**596,237**		**27**	**12**
GREAT BRITAIN				
C	10,900,047	40.9	608	239
NL & C	149,779	0.6	9	3
(Total C)	*(11,049,826)*	*(41.4)*	*(617)*	*(242)*
L	2,298,348	8.6	308	12
Lab	13,024,016	48.8	618	364
Com	62,092	0.2	57	0
PC	61,071	0.2	20	0
SNP	128,474	0.5	23	0
Others	44,683	0.2	37	0
Total	**26,668,510**		**1,680**	**618**
UNITED KINGDOM				
C	11,268,676	41.3	620	250
NL & C	149,779	0.5	9	3
(Total C)	*(11,418,455)*	*(41.9)*	*(629)*	*(253)*
L	2,327,457	8.5	311	12
Lab	13,096,629	48.0	622	364
Com	62,092	0.2	57	0
N	22,167	0.1	1	0
PC	61,071	0.2	20	0
Rep	62,782	0.2	5	0
Rep LP	26,292	0.1	1	1
SNP	128,474	0.5	23	0
Others	59,328	0.2	38 [1]	0
Total	**27,264,747**		**1,707**	**630**

1. Including 4 UM, 3 BNP, 2 SPGB, 1 FP, 1 ILP, 1 N Dem P, 1 Pat P, 1 RA.

Table 1.35: General Election 1970 (18 June)

	Total Votes	%	Candidates	Elected
ENGLAND				
C	11,282,524	48.3	510	292
L	1,853,616	7.9	282	2
Lab	10,131,555	43.4	511	217
Com	20,103	0.1	35	0
NF	10,467	0.0	9	0
Others	62,631	0.3	56	0
Total	**23,360,896**		**1,403**	**511**
WALES				
C	419,884	27.7	36	7
L	103,747	6.8	19	1
Lab	781,941	51.6	36	27
Com	6,459	0.4	8	0
NF	982	0.1	1	0
PC	175,016	11.5	36	0
Others	28,525	1.9	2	1
Total	**1,516,554**		**138**	**36**
SCOTLAND				
C	1,020,674	38.0	70	23
L	147,667	5.5	27	3
Lab	1,197,068	44.5	71	44
Com	11,408	0.4	15	0
SNP	306,802	11.4	65	1
Others	4,616	0.2	8	0
Total	**2,688,235**		**256**	**71**
NORTHERN IRELAND				
C	422,041	54.2	12	8
L	12,005	1.5	4	0
Lab	98,194	12.6	7	0
Nat DP	10,349	1.3	2	0
Prot U	35,303	4.5	2	1
Rep LP	30,649	3.9	1	1
Unity	140,930	18.1	5	2
Others	29,642	3.8	7	0
Total	**779,113**		**40**	**12**
GREAT BRITAIN				
C	12,723,082	46.2	616	322
L	2,105,030	7.6	328	6
Lab	12,110,564	43.9	618	288
Com	37,970	0.1	58	0
NF	11,449	0.0	10	0
PC	175,016	0.6	36	0
SNP	306,802	1.1	65	1
Others	95,772	0.3	66	1
Total	**27,565,685**		**1,797**	**618**

General Election 1970 (contd.)

	Total Votes	%	Candidates	Elected
UNITED KINGDOM				
C	13,145,123	46.4	628	330
L	2,117,035	7.5	332	6
Lab	12,208,758	43.1	625	288
Com	37,970	0.1	58	0
Nat DP	10,349	0.0	2	0
NF	11,449	0.0	10	0
PC	175,016	0.6	36	0
Prot U	35,303	0.1	2	1
Rep LP	30,649	0.1	1	1
SNP	306,802	1.1	65	1
Unity	140,930	0.5	5	2
Others	125,414	0.4	73 [1]	1 [2]
Total	**28,344,798**		**1,837**	**630**

1. Including 5 DP, 4 N Dem P, 2 SPGB, 1 BM, 1 ILP, 1 MK, 1 VNP.
2. Namely: S.O.Davies (Merthyr Tydfil—Ind Lab).

Table 1.36: General Election 1974 (28 February)

	Total Votes	%	Candidates	Elected
ENGLAND				
C	10,508,977	40.2	516	268
L	5,574,934	21.3	452	9
Lab	9,842,468	37.7	516	237
Com	13,379	0.1	23	0
NF	76,865	0.3	54	0
Others	124,995	0.5	113	2
Total	**26,141,618**		**1,674**	**516**
WALES				
C	412,535	25.9	36	8
L	255,423	16.0	31	2
Lab	745,547	46.8	36	24
Com	4,293	0.3	6	0
PC	171,374	10.8	36	2
Othen	4,671	0.3	3	0
Total	**1,593,843**		**148**	**36**
SCOTLAND				
C	950,668	32.9	71	21
L	229,162	7.9	34	3
Lab	1,057,601	36.6	71	40
Com	15,071	0.5	15	0
SNP	633,180	21.9	70	7
Others	1,393	0.0	4	0
Total	**2,887,075**		**265**	**71**

General Election 1974[F] (contd.)

	Total Votes	%	Candidates	Elected
NORTHERN IRELAND				
UDUP	58,656	8.2	2	1
UU (Anti-Assembly)	232,103	32.3	7	7
VUPP	75,944	10.6	3	3
(Total UUUC)	*(366,703)*	*(51.1)*	*(12)*	*(11)*
APNI	22,660	3.2	3	0
NI Lab	17,284	2.4	5	0
Rep C	15,152	2.1	4	0
SDLP	160,437	22.4	12	1
Unity	17,593	2.5	2	0
UU (Pro-Assembly)	94,301	13.1	7	0
Others	23,496	3.3	3	0
Total	**717,626**		**48**	**12**
GREAT BRITAIN				
C	11,872,180	38.8	623	297
L	6,059,519	19.8	517	14
Lab	11,645,616	38.0	623	301
Com	32,743	0.1	44	0
NF	76,865	0.3	54	0
PC	171,374	0.6	36	2
SNP	633,180	2.1	70	7
Others	131,059	0.4	120	2
Total	**30,622,536**		**2,087**	**623**
UNITED KINGDOM				
C	11,872,180	37.9	623	297
L	6,059,519	19.3	517	14
Lab	11,645,616	37.2	623	301
Com	32,743	0.1	44	0
NF	76,865	0.2	54	0
PC	171,374	0.5	36	2
SNP	633,180	2.0	70	7
Others	848,685	2.7	168 [1]	14 [2]
Total	**31,340,162**		**2,135** [3]	**635**

1. Including all candidates in Northern Ireland and 9 WRP, 6 CPE, 6 IDA, 6 People, 4 SD, 3 IMG, 1 BM, 1 CFMPB, 1 MK, 1 N Dem P, 1 NIP, 1 WR.

2. The twelve members for Northern Ireland constituencies (7 UU, 3 VUPP, 1 SDLP, 1 UDUP) and E.J. Milne (Blyth—Ind Lab); D. Taverne (Lincoln—Dem Lab).

3. The number of persons seeking election was 2,133 as one candidate contested three constituencies.

Table 1.37: General Election 1974 (10 October)

	Total Votes	%	Candidates	Elected
ENGLAND				
C	9,414,008	38.9	515	253
L	4,878,792	20.2	515	8
Lab	9,695,051	40.1	516	255
Com	7,032	0.0	17	0
NF	113,757	0.5	89	0
Others	82,429	0.3	114	0
Total	**24,191,069**		**1,766**	**516**
WALES				
C	367,230	23.9	36	8
L	239,057	15.5	36	2
Lab	761,447	49.5	36	23
Com	2,941	0.2	3	0
PC	166,321	10.8	36	3
Others	844	0.1	3	0
Total	**1,537,840**		**150**	**36**
SCOTLAND				
C	681,327	24.7	71	16
L	228,855	8.3	68	3
Lab	1,000,581	36.3	71	41
Com	7,453	0.3	9	0
NF	86	0.0	1	0
SNP	839,617	30.4	71	11
Others	182	0.0	2	0
Total	**2,758,101**		**293**	**71**
NORTHERN IRELAND				
UDUP	59,451	8.5	2	1
UU	256,065	36.5	7	6
VUPP	92,262	13.1	3	3
(Total UUUC)	*(407,778)*	*(58.1)*	*(12)*	*(10)*
APNI	44,644	6.4	5	0
NI Lab	11,539	1.6	3	0
Rep C	21,633	3.1	5	0
SDLP	154,193	22.0	9	1
UPNI	20,454	2.9	2	0
Others	41,853	6.0	7	1
Total	**702,094**		**43**	**12**
GREAT BRITAIN				
C	10,462,565	36.7	622	277
L	5,346,704	18.8	619	13
Lab	11,457,079	40.2	623	319
Com	17,426	0.1	29	0
NF	113,843	0.4	90	0
PC	166,321	0.6	36	3
SNP	839,617	2.9	71	11
Others	83,455	0.3	119	0
Total	**28,487,010**		**2,209**	**623**

General Election 1974 [O] (contd.)

	Total Votes	%	Candidates	Elected
UNITED KINGDOM				
C	10,462,565	35.8	622	277
L	5,346,704	18.3	619	13
Lab	11,457,079	39.3	623	319
Com	17,426	0.1	29	0
NF	113,843	0.4	90	0
PC	166,321	0.6	36	3
SNP	839,617	2.9	71	11
Others	785,549	2.7	162 [1]	12 [2]
Total	**29,189,104**		**2,252** [3]	**635**

1. Including all candidates in Northern Ireland and 25 CFMPB, 13 UDP, 10 WRP, 8 CPE, 7 ICRA, 5 People, 1 MK, 1 SPGB.
2. The twelve members for Northern Ireland constituencies (6 UU, 3 VUPP, 1 UDUP, 1 Ind Rep, 1 SDLP).
3. The number of persons seeking election was 2,231 as one candidate contested twelve constituencies and another contested eleven constituencies.

Table 1.38: General Election 1979 (3 May)

	Total Votes	%	Candidates	Elected
ENGLAND				
C	12,255,514	47.2	516	306
L	3,878,055	14.9	506	7
Lab	9,525,280	36.7	516	203
Com	6,622	0.0	18	0
EP	38,116	0.1	50	0
NF	189,150	0.7	297	0
WRP	11,708	0.0	53	0
Others	67,805	0.3	118	0
Total	**25,972,250**		**2,074**	**516**
WALES				
C	526,254	32.2	35	11
L	173,525	10.6	28	1
Lab	795,493	48.6	36	22
Com	4,310	0.3	8	0
EP	1,250	0.1	2	0
NF	2,465	0.2	5	0
PC	132,544	8.1	36	2
WRP	114	0.0	1	0
Others	633	0.0	3	0
Total	**1,636,588**		**154**	**36**
SCOTLAND				
C	916,155	31.4	71	22
L	262,224	9.0	43	3
Lab	1,211,445	41.5	71	44
Com	5,926	0.2	12	0
EP	552	0.0	1	0
NF	104	0.0	1	0
SNP	504,259	17.3	71	2
WRP	809	0.0	6	0
Others	15,163	0.5	8	0
Total	**2,916,637**		**284**	**71**

General Election 1979 (contd.)

	Total Votes	%	Candidates	Elected
NORTHERN IRELAND				
UDUP	70,975	10.2	5	3
UPNI	8,021	1.2	3	0
UU	254,578	36.6	11	5
UUUP	39,856	5.7	2	1
Others	36,989	5.3	1	1
(Total 'Loyalist')	*(410,419)*	*(59.0)*	*(22)*	*(10)*
APNI	82,892	11.9	12	0
IIP	23,086	3.3	4	0
Nl Lab	4,411	0.6	3	0
Rep C/TWP	12,098	1.7	7	0
SDLP	126,325	18.2	9	1
Others	36,656	5.3	7	1
Total	**695,887**		**64**	**12**
GREAT BRITAIN				
C	13,697,923	44.9	622	339
L	4,313,804	14.1	577	11
Lab	11,532,218	37.8	623	269
Com	16,858	0.1	38	0
EP	39,918	0.1	53	0
NF	191,719	0.6	303	0
PC	132,544	0.4	36	2
SNP	504,259	1.7	71	2
WRP	12,631	0.0	60	0
Others	83,601	0.3	129	0
Total	**30,525,475**		**2,512**	**623**
UNITED KINGDOM				
C	13,697,923	43.9	622	339
L	4,313,804	13.8	577	11
Lab	11,532,218	36.9	623	269
Com	16,858	0.1	38	0
EP	39,918	0.1	53	0
NF	191,719	0.6	303	0
PC	132,544	0.4	36	2
SNP	504,259	1.6	71	2
WRP	12,631	0.0	60	0
Others	779,488	2.5	193 [1]	12 [2]
Total	**31,221,362**		**2,576** [3]	**635**

1. Including all candidates in Northern Ireland and 10 SU, 7 WR, 6 CFMPB, 3 MK, 3 SCLP, 2 FP, 2 NBP, 2 UCP, 2 Wk P, 1 CNP 1 ENP, 1 SPGB.

2. The twelve members for Northern Ireland constituencies (5 UU, 3 UDUP, 1 Ind Rep, 1 Ind UU, 1 SDLP, 1 UUUP).

3. The number of persons seeking election was 2,569 as one candidate contested six constituencies and another contested three constituencies.

Table 1.39: General Election 1983 (9 June)

	Total Votes	*%*	*Candidates*	*Elected*
ENGLAND				
C	11,711,519	46.0	523	362
L	3,658,903	14.4	267	10
SDP	3,056,054	12.0	256	3
(Total L/SDP)	*(6,714,957)*	*(26.4)*	*(523)*	*(13)*
Lab	6,862,422	26.9	523	148
BNP	14,364	0.1	52	0
Com	6,368	0.0	22	0
EP	46,484	0.2	90	0
NF	27,065	0.1	60	0
WRP	3,280	0.0	18	0
Others	86,187	0.3	189	0
Total	**25,472,646**		**2,000**	**523**
WALES				
C	499,310	31.0	38	14
L	194,988	12.1	19	2
SDP	178,370	11.1	19	0
(Total L/SDP)	*(373,358)*	*(23.2)*	*(38)*	*(2)*
Lab	603,858	37.5	38	20
BNP	154	0.0	1	0
Com	2,015	0.1	3	0
EP	3,510	0.2	· 7	0
PC	125,309	7.8	38	2
WRP	256	0.0	1	0
Others	1,216	0.1	5	0
Total	**1,608,986**		**169**	**38**
SCOTLAND				
C	801,487	28.4	72	21
L	356,224	12.6	36	5
SDP	336,410	11.9	36	3
(Total L/SDP)	*(692,634)*	*(24.5)*	*(72)*	*(8)*
Lab	990,654	35.1	72	41
BNP	103	0.0	1	0
Com	3,223	0.1	10	0
EP	3,854	0.1	11	0
SNP	331,975	11.8	72	2
WRP	262	0.0	2	0
Others	388	0.0	2	0
Total	**2,824,580**		**314**	**72**

General Election 1983 (contd.)

	Total Votes	*%*	*Candidates*	*Elected*
NORTHERN IRELAND				
UDUP	152,749	20.0	14	3
UPUP	22,861	3.0	1	1
UU	259,952	34.0	16	11
Others	1,134	0.1	1	0
(Total 'Loyalist')	*(436,696)*	*(57.1)*	*(32)*	*(15)*
APNI	61,275	8.0	12	0
EP	451	0.1	1	0
SDLP	137,012	17.9	17	1
SF	102,701	13.4	14	1
TWP	14,650	1.9	14	0
Others	12,140	1.6	5	0
Total	**764,925**		**95**	**17**
GREAT BRITAIN				
C	13,012,316	43.5	633	397
L	4,210,115	14.1	322	17
SDP	3,570,834	11.9	311	6
(Total L/SDP)	*(7,780,949)*	*(26.0)*	*(633)*	*(23)*
Lab	8,456,934	28.3	633	209
BNP	14,621	0.0	54	0
Com	11,606	0.0	35	0
EP	53,848	0.2	108	0
NF	27,065	0.1	60	0
PC	125,309	0.4	38	2
SNP	331,975	1.1	72	2
WRP	3,798	0.0	21	0
Others	87,791	0.3	196	0
Total	**29,906,212**		**2,483**	**633**
UNITED KINGDOM				
C	13,012,316	42.4	633	397
L	4,210,115	13.7	322	17
SDP	3,570,834	11.6	311	6
(Total L/SDP)	*(7,780,949)*	*(25.4)*	*(633)*	*(23)*
Lab	8,456,934	27.6	633	209
BNP	14,621	0.0	54	0
Com	11,606	0.0	35	0
EP	53,848	0.2	108 [1]	0
NF	27,065	0.1	60	0
PC	125,309	0.4	38	2
SNP	331,975	1.1	72	2
WRP	3,798	0.0	21	0
Others	852,716	2.8	291 [2]	17 [3]
Total	**30,671,137**		**2,578** [4]	**650**

1. Including three joint EP/WFLOE candidates who polled 1,341 votes, but excluding one candidate in Northern Ireland who polled 451 votes.

2. Including all candidates in Northern Ireland and 11 MRLP, 10 WR, 5 Nat Pty, 4 PAL, 4 Rev CP, 2 FTACMP, 2 MK, 2 NBP, 2 Wk P, 1 CNP, 1 FP, 1 N Lab P, 1 SPGB, 1 WFLOE.

3. The seventeen members for Northern Ireland constituencies (11 UU, 3 UDUP, 1 SDLP, 1 SF, 1UPUP).

4. The number of persons seeking election was 2,574 as one candidate contested five constituencies.

Table 1.40: General Election 1987 (11 June)

	Total Votes	%	Candidates	Elected
ENGLAND				
C	12,546,186	46.2	523	358
L	3,684,813	13.6	271	7
SDP	2,782,537	10.3	252	3
(Total L/SDP)	*(6,467,350)*	*(23.8)*	*(523)*	*(10)*
Lab	8,006,466	29.5	523	155
Com	4,022	0.0	13	0
GP	82,787	0.3	117	0
Others	26,711	0.1	83	0
Total	**27,133,522**		**1,782**	**523**
WALES				
C	501,316	29.5	38	8
L	181,427	10.7	20	3
SDP	122,803	7.2	18	0
(Total L/SDP)	*(304,230)*	*(17.9)*	*(38)*	*(3)*
Lab	765,209	45.1	38	24
Com	869	0.1	1	0
GP	2,221	0.1	4	0
PC	123,599	7.3	38	3
Others	652	0.0	1	0
Total	**1,698,096**		**158**	**38**
SCOTLAND				
C	713,081	24.0	72	10
L	307,210	10.4	36	7
SDP	262,843	8.9	36	2
(Total L/SDP)	*(570,053)*	*(19.2)*	*(72)*	*(9)*
Lab	1,258,132	42.4	72	50
Com	1,187	0.0	5	0
GP	4,745	0.2	12	0
SNP	416,473	14.0	71	3
Others	4,137	0.1	4	0
Total	**2,967,808**		**308**	**72**
NORTHERN IRELAND				
UDUP	85,642	11.7	4	3
UPUP	18,420	2.5	1	1
UU	276,230	37.8	12	9
Others	20,138	2.8	2	0
(Total 'Loyalist')	*(400,430)*	*(54.8)*	*(19)*	*(13)*
APNI	72,671	10.0	16	0
NIEP	281	0.0	1	0
SDLP	154,087	21.1	13	3
SF	83,389	11.4	14	1
TWP	19,294	2.6	14	0
Total	**730,152**		**77**	**17**

General Election 1987 (contd.)

	Total Votes	*%*	*Candidates*	*Elected*
GREAT BRITAIN				
C	13,760,583	43.3	633	376
L	4,173,450	13.1	327	17
SDP	3,168,183	10.0	306	5
(Total L/SDP)	*(7,341,633)*	*(23.1)*	*(633)*	*(22)*
Lab	10,029,807	31.5	633	229
Com	6,078	0.0	19	0
GP	89,753	0.3	133	0
PC	123,599	0.4	38	3
SNP	416,473	1.3	71	3
Others	31,500	0.1	88	0
Total	**31,799,426**		**2,248**	**633**
UNITED KINGDOM				
C	13,760,583	42.3	633	376
L	4,173,450	12.8	327	17
SDP	3,168,183	9.7	306	5
(Total L/SDP)	*(7,341,633)*	*(22.6)*	*(633)*	*(22)*
Lab	10,029,807	30.8	633	229
Com	6,078	0.0	19	0
GP	89,753	0.3	133	0
PC	123,599	0.4	38	3
SNP	416,473	1.3	71	3
Others	761,652	2.3	165 [1]	17 [2]
Total	**32,529,578**		**2,325**	**650**

1. Including all candidates in Northern Ireland and 14 RF, 10 WRP, 5 MRLP, 4 HP, 2 BNP, 1 FP, 1 OSM, 1 SPGB.
2. The seventeen members for Northern Ireland constituencies (9 UU, 3 UDUP, 1UPUP, 3 SDLP, 1 SF).

Table 1.41: General Election 1992 (9 April)

	Total Votes	*%*	*Candidates*	*Elected*
ENGLAND				
C	12,796,772	45.5	524	319
Lab	9,551,910	33.9	524	195
LD	5,398,293	19.2	522	10
Green	156,463	0.6	223	0
NLP	57,415	0.2	272	0
Others	187,653	0.7	263	0
Total	**28,148,506**		**2,328**	**524**
WALES				
C	499,677	28.6	38	6
Lab	865,663	49.5	38	27
LD	217,457	12.4	38	1
PC	154,947	8.9	35	4
Green	7,073	0.4	14	0
NLP	1,231	0.1	9	0
Others	2,729	0.2	8	0
Total	**1,748,777**		**180**	**38**

General Election 1992 (contd.)

	Total Votes	*%*	*Candidates*	*Elected*
SCOTLAND				
C	751,950	25.6	72	11
Lab	1,142,911	39.0	72	49
LD	383,856	13.1	72	9
SNP	629,564	21.5	72	3
Green	8,391	0.3	19	0
NLP	2,095	0.1	19	0
Others	12,931	0.4	15	0
Total	**2,931,698**		**341**	**72**
NORTHERN IRELAND				
C	44,608	5.7	11	0
UU	271,049	34.5	13	9
UDUP	103,039	13.1	7	3
UPUP	19,305	2.5	1	1
SDLP	184,445	23.5	13	4
APNI	68,665	8.7	16	0
SF	78,291	10.0	14	0
NLP	2,147	0.3	9	0
Others	13,544	1.7	16	0
Total	**785,093**		**100**	**17**
GREAT BRITAIN				
C	14,048,399	42.8	634	336
Lab	11,560,484	35.2	634	271
LD	5,999,606	18.3	632	20
PC	154,947	0.5	35	4
SNP	629,564	1.9	72	3
Green	171,927	0.5	256	0
NLP	60,741	0.2	300	0
Others	203,313	0.6	286	0
Total	**32,828,981**		**2,849**	**634**
UNITED KINGDOM				
C	14,093,007	41.9	645	336
Lab	11,560,484	34.4	634	271
LD	5,999,606	17.8	632	20
PC	154,947	0.5	35	4
SNP	629,564	1.9	72	3
Green	171,927	0.5	256	0
NLP	62,888	0.2	309	0
Others	941,651	2.8	366 [1]	17 [2]
Total	**33,614,074**		**2,949** [3]	**651**

1. Including all candidates in Northern Ireland except the 11 Conservative and 9 NLP candidates.

2. The seventeen members for Northern Ireland constituencies (9 UU, 3 DUP, 1UPUP, 4 SDLP).

3. The number of persons seeking election was 2,946 as one candidate contested three constituencies and another two constituencies.

Table 1.42   General Election 1997 (1 May)

	Total Votes	*%*	*Candidates*	*Elected*
ENGLAND				
C	8,780,881	33.7	528	165
Lab	11,347,882	43.5	527	328
LD	4,677,565	18.0	527	34
Green	60,013	0.2	85	0
NLP	25,958	0.1	160	0
Referendum	746,624	2.9	445	0
UK Ind	103,521	0.4	182	0
Others	316,268	1.2	491	2
Total Vote	**26,058,712**		**2,945**	**529**
WALES				
C	317,145	19.6	40	0
Lab	886,935	54.7	40	34
LD	200,020	12.3	40	2
PC	161,030	9.9	40	4
Green	1,718	0.1	4	0
NLP	516	0.0	5	0
Referendum	38,245	2.4	35	0
UK Ind	616	0.0	2	0
Others	13,837	0.9	17	0
Total Vote	**1,620,062**		**223**	**40**
SCOTLAND				
C	493,059	17.5	72	0
Lab	1,283,350	45.6	72	56
LD	365,362	13.0	72	10
SNP	621,550	22.1	72	6
Green	1,721	0.1	5	0
NLP	1,922	0.1	14	0
Referendum	26,980	1.0	67	0
UK Ind	1,585	0.1	9	0
Others	21,219	0.8	48	0
Total Vote	**2,816,748**		**431**	**72**
NORTHERN IRELAND				
C	9,858	1.2	8	0
UU	258,349	32.7	16	10
UDUP	107,348	13.6	9	2
UKUP	12,817	1.6	1	1
Prog U	10,928	1.4	3	0
APNI	62,972	8.0	17	0
SDLP	190,814	24.1	18	3
SF	126,921	16.1	17	2
NLP	2,208	0.3	18	0
Others	8,547	1.1	18 [1]	0
Total Vote	**790,762**		**125**	**18**

General Election 1997 (contd.)

	Total Votes	*%*	*Candidates*	*Elected*
GREAT BRITAIN				
C	9,591,085	31.5	640	165
Lab	13,518,167	44.3	639	418
LD	5,242,947	17.2	639	46
PC	161,030	0.5	40	4
SNP	621,550	2.0	72	6
Green	63,452	0.2	94	0
NLP	28,396	0.1	179	0
Referendum	811,849	2.7	547	0
UK Ind	105,722	0.3	193	0
Others	351,324	1.2	556	2
Total	**30,495,522**		**3,599**	**641**
UNITED KINGDOM				
C	9,600,943	30.7	648	165
Lab	13,518,167	43.2	639	418
LD	5,242,947	16.8	639	46
PC	161,030	0.5	40	4
SNP	621,550	2.0	72	6
Green	63,991	0.2	95	0
NLP	30,604	0.1	197	0
Referendum	811,849	2.6	547	0
UK Ind	105,722	0.3	193	0
Others	1,129,481	3.6	654[2]	20[3]
Total Vote	**31,286,284**		**3,724**[4]	**659**

1. Including one Green candidate who polled 539 votes in Belfast North.

2. Including all candidates in Northern Ireland except the 8 Conservative,18 NLP and 1 Green candidates.

3. The eighteen members for Northern Ireland constituencies (10 UU, 2 DUP, 1UKU, 3 SDLP and 2 SF), together with Ms. B. Boothroyd (Speaker —West Bromwich West) and M. Bell (Independent—Tatton).

4. The number of persons seeking election was 3,718 as one candidate contested four constitutencies, one three constituencies and another two constitutencies.

Table 1.43: General Election 2001 (7 June)

	Total Votes	%	Candidates	Elected
ENGLAND				
C	7,705,870	35.2	529	165
Lab	9,056,824	41.4	529	323
LD	4,246,853	19.4	528	40
UK Ind	374,775	1.7	392	0
Green	158,173	0.7	135	0
Others	328,267	1.5	475	1
Total Vote	**21,870,762**		**2,588**	**529**
SCOTLAND				
C	360,658	15.6	71	1
Lab	1,001,173	43.3	71	55
LD	378,034	16.3	71	10
SNP	464,314	20.1	72	5
UK Ind	3,236	0.1	11	0
Green	4,551	0.2	4	0
SSP	72,516	3.1	72	0
Others	29,219	1.3	35	1
Total Vote	**2,313,701**		**407**	**72**
WALES				
C	288,665	21.0	40	0
Lab	666,956	48.6	40	34
LD	189,434	13.8	40	2
PC	195,893	14.3	40	4
UK Ind	12,552	0.9	25	0
Green	3,753	0.3	6	0
Others	15,293	1.1	33	0
Total Vote	**1,372,546**		**224**	**40**
NORTHERN IRELAND				
C	2,422	0.3	3	0
UU	216,839	26.8	17	6
UDUP	181,999	22.5	14	5
UKUP	13,509	1.7	1	0
APNI	28,999	3.6	10	0
SDLP	169,865	21.0	18	3
SF	175,933	21.7	18	4
Others	20,808	2.6	19	0
Total Vote	**810,374**		**100**	**18**
GREAT BRITAIN				
C	8,355,193	32.7	640	166
Lab	10,724,953	42.0	640	412
LD	4,814,321	18.8	639	52
SNP	464,314	1.8	72	5
UKIind				
390,563	1.5	428	0	
PC	195,893	0.8	40	4
Green	166,477	0.7	145	0
Others	445,295	1.7	615	2
Total Vote	**25,557,009**		**3,219**	**641**

General Election 2001 (contd.)

	Total Votes	%	Candidates	Elected
UNITED KINGDOM				
C	8,357,615	31.7	643	166
Lab	10,724,953	40.7	640	412
LD	4,814,321	18.3	639	52
SNP	464,314	1.8	72	5
PC	195,893	0.7	40	4
UK Ind	390,563	1.5	428	0
Green	166,477	0.6	145	0
Others	1,253,247	4.8	712 [1]	20 [2]
Total Vote	**26,367,383**		**3,319** [3]	**659**

1. Including all candidates in Northern Ireland except the 3 Conservative candidates.
2. The eighteen members for Northern Ireland constituencies together with M.J. Martin (Speaker—Glasgow Springburn) and R.T. Taylor (Independent Kidderminster Hospital and Health Concern—Wyre Forest).
3. The number of persons seeking election was 3,313 as one candidate contested four constituencies, one three constituencies, and another two constituencies.

Table 1.44: General Election 2005 (5 May)

	Total Votes	%	Candidates	Elected
ENGLAND[1]				
C	8,114,979	35.7	529	194
Lab	8,050,366	35.5	529	286
LD	5,201,129	22.9	528	47
UK Ind	576,817	2.5	443	0
Green	250,510	1.1	173	0
Others	510,501	2.2	615	2
Total	**22,704,302**		**2,817**	**529**
SCOTLAND				
C	369,388	15.8	58	1
Lab	907,249	38.9	58	40
LD	528,076	22.6	58	11
SNP	412,267	17.7	59	6
UK Ind	8,859	0.4	22	0
Green	25,760	1.1	19	0
SSP	43,514	1.9	58	0
Others	38,774	1.7	50	1
Total	**2,333,887**		382	**59**
WALES				
C	297,830	21.4	40	3
Lab	594,821	42.7	40	29
LD	256,249	18.4	40	4
PC	174,838	12.6	40	3
UK Ind	20,297	1.5	31	0
Green	7,144	0.5	11	0
Others	41,540	3.0	48	1
Total	**1,392,719**		**250**	**40**

General Election 2005 (contd.)

	Total Votes	%	Candidates	Elected
N. IRELAND				
C	2,718	0.4	3	0
UU	127,414	17.8	18	1
UDUP	241,856	33.7	18	9
APNI	28,291	3.9	12	0
SDLP	125,626	17.5	18	3
SF	174,530	24.3	18	5
Others	17,167	2.4	18	0
Total	**717,602**		**105**	**18**
GREAT BRITAIN[1]				
C	8,782,197	33.2	627	198
Lab	9,552,436	36.1	627	355
LD	5,985,454	22.6	626	62
SNP	412,267	1.6	59	6
PC	174,838	0.7	40	3
UK Ind	605,973	2.3	496	0
Green	283,414	1.1	203	0
SSP	43,514	0.2	58	0
Others	590,815	2.2	713	4
Total	**26,430,908**		**3,449**	**628**
UNITED KINGDOM[1]				
C	8,784,915	32.4	630	198
Lab	9,552,436	35.2	627	355
LD	5,985,454	22.0	626	62
SNP	412,267	1.5	59	6
PC	174,838	0.6	40	3
UK Ind	605,973	2.2	496	0
Green	283,414	1.0	203	0
Others	1,349,213	5.0	873 [2]	22 [3]
Total	**27,148,510**		**3,554** [4]	**646**

1. The election in Staffordshire South was postponed following the death of a candidate—See Table 5.11. The results of the postponed election are included with these totals.

2. Including all candidates in Northern Ireland except the 3 Conservative candidates.

3. The eighteen members for Northern Ireland constituencies together with M.J. Martin (Speaker—Glasgow Springburn); R.T. Taylor (Independent Kidderminster Hospital and Health Concern—Wyre Forest); P.J. Law (no label—Blaenau Gwent) and G. Galloway (Respect—Bethnal Green and Bow).

4. The number of persons seeking election was 3,522 as one candidate contested thirteen constituencies, one eight constituencies, two four constituencies each, one three constituencies, and five two constituencies each.

Table 2.01: Summary Results of General Elections 1832-2005 (UK)

Election	Con %	Con MPs[1]	Lab %	Lab MPs	Lib %	Lib MPs[2]	Other %	Other MPs	Govt.	Majority[3]
1832	29.4	175 *	-	-	66.7	441	3.9	42	Lib	225
1835	42.6	273 *	-	-	57.4	385	-	-	Lib	113
1837	48.3	314	-	-	51.7	344 *	-	-	Lib	29
1841	50.9	367	-	-	46.9	271 *	2.2	20	Con	77
1847	42.2	325	-	-	53.9	292 *	3.9	39	Lib	None
1852	41.4	330	-	-	58.4	324 *	0.2	-	Con	7
1857	33.1	264	-	-	65.1	377	1.8	13	Lib	100
1859	34.3	298	-	-	65.7	356 *	0.0	-	Lib	59
1865	39.8	289	-	-	60.2	369 *	-	-	Lib	81
1868	38.4	271	-	-	61.5	387 *	0.1	-	Lib	115
1874	43.9	350	-	-	52.7	242 *	3.4	60	Con	49
1880	42.0	237	-	-	55.4	352 *	2.6	63	Lib	51
1885	43.5	249	-	-	47.4	319 *	9.1	102	Con	None
1886	51.4	393 *	-	-	45.0	192	3.6	85	Con	116
1892	47.0	313	-	-	45.1	272	7.9	85	Lib	None
1895	49.1	411	-	-	45.7	177 *	5.2	82	Con	153
1900	50.3	402	1.3	2	45.0	183 *	3.4	83	Con	135
1906	43.4	156 *	4.8	29	49.4	399	2.4	86	Lib	129
1910(J)	46.8	272 *	7.0	40	43.5	274	2.7	84	Lib	None
1910(D)	46.6	271 *	6.4	42	44.2	272	2.8	85	Lib	None
1918	38.7	382 *	20.8	57	25.6	163	14.9	105	Coal	283[4]
1922	38.5	344	29.7	142	28.8	115 *	3.0	14	Con	74
1923	38.0	258	30.7	191	29.7	158 *	1.6	8	Lab	None
1924	46.8	412	33.3	151	17.8	40 *	2.1	12	Con	210
1929	38.1	260 *	37.1	287	23.5	59	1.3	9	Lab	None
1931	60.7	522 *	30.9	52[5]	7.0	36[6]	1.4	5	Nat	492
1935	53.3	429 *	38.0	154	6.7	21	2.0	11	Nat	242
1945	39.6	210 *	48.0	393	9.0	12	3.4	25	Lab	147
1950	43.4	298 *	46.1	315	9.1	9	1.4	3	Lab	6
1951	48.0	321	48.8	295	2.6	6	0.6	3	Con	16
1955	49.7	345 *	46.4	277	2.7	6	1.2	2	Con	59
1959	49.4	365	43.8	258	5.9	6	0.9	1	Con	99
1964	43.4	304 *	44.1	317	11.2	9	1.3	-	Lab	5
1966	41.9	253	48.0	364 *	8.5	12	1.5	1	Lab	97
1970	46.4	330	43.1	288 *	7.5	6	3.0	6	Con	31
1974(F)	37.9	297 *	37.2	301	19.3	14	5.6	23	Lab	None
1974(O)	35.8	277 *	39.3	319	18.3	13	6.7	26	Lab	4
1979	43.9	339	36.9	269 *	13.8	11	5.4	16	Con	44
1983	42.4	397	27.6	209	25.4	23	4.6	21	Con	144
1987	42.3	376 *	30.8	229	22.6	22	4.4	23	Con	101
1992	41.9	336	34.4	271	17.8	20	5.8	24	Con	21
1997	30.7	165	43.2	418	16.8	46	9.3	30 *	Lab	178
2001	31.7	166	40.7	412	18.3	52	9.4	29 *	Lab	166
2005	32.4	198	35.2	355	22.0	62	10.4	31 *	Lab	65

*Including the Speaker. See Introductory Notes.

1. Including Liberal Conservatives, 1847-59; Liberal Unionists, 1886-1910(D); National, National Liberal and National Labour, 1931-45.

Summary Results of General Elections 1832-2005 (UK) (contd.)

2. Including both Liberal and National Liberal, 1922; Independent Liberal, 1931; SDP/Liberal Alliance, 1983-87; Liberal Democrat 1992 onwards.

3. This figure represents the majority of the Government over all other parties combined. The Speaker has been excluded when calculating the majority.

4. Theoretical majority. 73 Sinn Fein members did not take their seats.

5. Including 6 unendorsed.

6. Of this total, 4 Liberals opposed the National Government and are counted with the Opposition in calculating the overall majority.

Table 2.02: Summary Results of General Elections 1832-2005 (GB)

Election	Con %	Con MPs[1]	Lab %	Lab MPs	Lib %	Lib MPs[2]	Other %	Other MPs
1832	28.9	147	-	-	71.1	408	-	-
1835	42.8	238	-	-	57.2	317	-	-
1837	48.2	284	-	-	51.8	271	-	-
1841	52.7	326	-	-	47.2	229	0.1	-
1847	43.1	285	-	-	56.2	267	0.6	1
1852	40.8	290	-	-	58.9	261	0.3	-
1857	31.0	222	-	-	68.9	329	0.1	-
1859	33.4	245	-	-	66.6	306	0.0	-
1865	40.0	244	-	-	60.0	311	-	-
1868	38.6	234	-	-	61.4	321	0.0	-
1874	44.6	319	-	-	55.4	232	0.0	-
1880	42.7	214	-	-	57.3	337	0.0	-
1885	45.6	233	-	-	51.8	319	2.6	17
1886	51.2	376	-	-	48.6	192	0.2	1
1892	49.5	292	-	-	49.6	272	1.0	5
1895	50.5	392	-	-	48.0	176	1.5	1
1900	51.0	383	1.9	2	46.5	182	0.6	2
1906	43.0	141	5.8	29	49.6	396	1.7	3
1910(J)	47.1	253	7.8	40	44.1	273	1.0	3
1910(D)	47.0	254	7.4	42	45.2	271	0.3	2
1918	39.5	359	23.0	57	28.6	163	8.8	27
1922	38.0	334	29.9	142	29.2	115	2.9	12
1923	37.7	248	31.0	191	30.1	158	1.2	6
1924	45.9	400	34.0	151	18.2	40	1.9	12
1929	37.5	250	37.8	287	23.5	59	1.2	7
1931	60.9	512	31.1	52	6.9	36	1.2	3
1935	53.2	419	38.6	154	6.7	21	1.5	9
1945	39.3	202	48.8	393	9.2	12	2.6	21
1950	43.0	288	46.8	315	9.3	9	0.9	1
1951	47.8	312	49.4	295	2.6	6	0.3	0
1955	49.3	335	47.4	277	2.8	6	0.6	0
1959	48.8	353	44.6	258	6.0	6	0.6	1
1964	42.9	292	44.8	317	11.4	9	0.9	0
1966	41.4	242	48.8	364	8.6	12	1.1	0
1970	46.2	322	43.9	288	7.6	6	2.3	2
1974(F)	38.8	297	38.0	301	19.8	14	3.4	11
1974(O)	36.7	277	40.2	319	18.8	13	4.3	14
1979	44.9	339	37.8	269	14.1	11	3.2	4

Summary Results of General Elections 1832-2005 (GB) (contd.)

Election	Con %	Con MPs[1]	Lab %	Lab MPs	Lib %	Lib MPs[2]	Other %	Other MPs
1983	43.5	397	28.3	209	26.0	23	2.2	4
1987	43.3	376	31.5	229	23.1	22	2.1	6
1992	42.8	336	35.2	271	18.3	20	3.7	7
1997	31.5	165	44.3	418	17.2	46	7.0	12
2001	32.7	166	42.0	412	18.8	52	6.5	11
2005	33.2	198	36.1	355	22.6	62	8.0	13

1. Including Liberal Conservatives, 1847-59; Liberal Unionists, 1886-1910(D); National, National Liberal and National Labour, 1931-45.
2. Including both Liberal and National Liberal, 1922; Independent Liberal, 1931; SDP/Liberal Alliance, 1983-87; Liberal Democrat 1992 onwards.

Table 2.03: Votes Cast at General Elections 1832-2005 (UK)

Election	Con[1]	%	Lab	%	Lib[2]	%	Others	%	Total
1832	241,284	29.4	-	-	554,719	66.7	31,773	3.9	827,776
1835	261,269	42.6	-	-	349,868	57.4	-	-	611,137
1837	379,694	48.3	-	-	418,331	51.7	-	-	798,025
1841	306,314	50.9	-	-	273,902	46.9	13,229	2.2	593,445
1847	205,481	42.2	-	-	259,310	53.9	17,637	3.9	482,429
1852	311,481	41.4	-	-	430,882	58.4	1,541	0.2	743,904
1857	239,712	33.1	-	-	464,127	65.1	12,713	1.8	716,552
1859	193,232	34.3	-	-	372,117	65.7	151	0.0	565,500
1865	346,035	39.8	-	-	508,821	60.2	-	-	854,856
1868	903,708	38.4	-	-	1,428,776	61.5	1,157	0.1	2,333,251
1874	1,091,622	43.9	-	-	1,281,159	52.7	93,170	3.4	2,466,037
1880	1,426,351	42.0	-	-	1,836,423	55.4	96,642	2.6	3,359,416
1885	2,020,927	43.5	-	-	2,199,998	47.4	417,310	9.1	4,638,235
1886	1,520,886	51.4	-	-	1,353,581	45.0	99,696	3.6	2,974,163
1892	2,159,150	47.0	-	-	2,088,019	45.1	351,150	7.9	4,598,319
1895	1,894,772	49.1	-	-	1,765,266	45.7	206,244	5.2	3,866,282
1900	1,767,958	50.3	62,698	1.3	1,572,323	45.0	120,503	3.4	3,523,482
1906	2,422,071	43.4	321,663	4.8	2,751,057	49.4	131,300	2.4	5,626,091
1910(J)	3,104,407	46.8	505,657	7.0	2,866,157	43.5	191,179	2.7	6,667,400
1910(D)	2,420,169	46.6	371,802	6.4	2,293,869	44.2	149,398	2.8	5,235,238
1918	4,144,192	38.7	2,245,777	20.8	2,785,374	25.6	1,611,475	14.9	10,786,818
1922	5,502,298	38.5	4,237,349	29.7	4,139,460	28.8	513,223	3.0	14,392,330
1923	5,514,541	38.0	4,439,780	30.7	4,301,481	29.7	291,893	1.6	14,547,695
1924	7,854,523	46.8	5,489,087	33.3	2,928,737	17.8	367,932	2.1	16,640,279
1929	8,656,225	38.1	8,370,417	37.1	5,308,738	23.5	312,995	1.3	22,648,375
1931	13,156,790	60.7	6,649,630[3]	30.9	1,476,123	7.0	373,830	1.4	21,656,373
1935	11,755,654	53.3	8,325,491	38.0	1,443,093	6.7	472,816	2.0	21,997,054
1945	9,972,010	39.6	11,967,746	48.0	2,252,430	9.0	903,009	3.4	25,095,195
1950	12,492,404	43.4	13,266,176	46.1	2,621,487	9.1	391,057	1.4	28,771,124
1951	13,718,199	48.0	13,948,883	48.8	730,546	2.6	198,966	0.6	28,596,594
1955	13,310,891	49.7	12,405,254	46.4	722,402	2.7	321,182	1.2	26,759,729
1959	13,750,875	49.4	12,216,172	43.8	1,640,760	5.9	254,845	0.9	27,862,652
1964	12,002,642	43.4	12,205,808	44.1	3,099,283	11.2	349,415	1.3	27,657,148
1966	11,418,455	41.9	13,096,629	48.0	2,327,457	8.5	422,206	1.5	27,264,747
1970	13,145,123	46.4	12,208,758	43.1	2,117,035	7.5	873,882	3.0	28,344,798
1974(F)	11,872,180	37.9	11,645,616	37.2	6,059,519	19.3	1,762,847	5.6	31,340,162
1974(O)	10,462,565	35.8	11,457,079	39.3	5,346,704	18.3	1,922,756	6.7	29,189,104

Votes Cast at General Elections 1832-2005 (UK) (contd.)

Election	Con[1]	%	Lab	%	Lib[2]	%	Others	%	Total
1979	13,697,923	43.9	11,532,218	36.9	4,313,804	13.8	1,677,417	5.4	31,221,362
1983	13,012,316	42.4	8,456,934	27.6	7,780,949	25.4	1,420,938	4.6	30,671,137
1987	13,760,583	42.3	10,029,807	30.8	7,341,633	22.6	1,397,555	4.4	32,529,578
1992	14,093,007	41.9	11,560,484	34.4	5,999,606	17.8	1,960,977	5.8	33,614,074
1997	9,600,943	30.7	13,518,167	43.2	5,242,947	16.8	2,924,227	9.3	31,286,284
2001	8,357,615	31.7	10,724,953	40.7	4,814,321	18.3	2,470,494	9.4	26,367,383
2005	8,784,915	32.4	9,552,436	35.2	5,985,454	22.0	2,825,705	10.4	27,148,510

1. Including Liberal Conservatives, 1847-59; Liberal Unionists, 1886-1910(D); National, National Liberal and National Labour, 1931-45.
2. Including both Liberal and National Liberal, 1922; Independent Liberal, 1931; SDP/Liberal Alliance, 1983-87; Liberal Democrat 1992 onwards.
3. Including 324,893 (4.9%) votes cast for the 25 unendorsed candidates -see Table 1.26.

Table 2.04: Votes Cast at General Elections 1832-2005 (GB)

Election	Con[1]	%	Lab	%	Lib[2]	%	Others	%	Total
1832	213,254	28.9	-	-	525,706	71.1	-	-	738,960
1835	235,907	42.8	-	-	315,002	57.2	-	-	550,909
1837	353,000	48.2	-	-	379,961	51.8	-	-	732,961
1841	286,650	52.7	-	-	256,774	47.2	692	0.1	544,116
1847	194,223	43.1	-	-	253,376	56.2	2,848	0.6	450,447
1852	249,809	40.8	-	-	360,387	58.9	1,541	0.3	611,737
1857	177,971	31.0	-	-	396,192	68.9	614	0.1	574,777
1859	157,974	33.4	-	-	314,708	66.6	151	0.0	472,833
1865	304,538	40.0	-	-	457,289	60.0	-	-	761,827
1868	864,551	38.6	-	-	1,374,315	61.4	969	0.0	2,239,835
1874	1,000,006	44.6	-	-	1,241,381	55.4	2	0.0	2,241,389
1880	1,326,744	42.7	-	-	1,780,171	57.3	1,107	0.0	3,108,022
1885	1,909,424	45.6	-	-	2,169,976	51.8	107,369	2.6	4,186,769
1886	1,422,685	51.2	-	-	1,351,671	48.6	4,813	0.2	2,779,169
1892	2,079,887	49.5	-	-	2,083,692	49.6	41,567	1.0	4,205,146
1895	1,840,143	50.5	-	-	1,750,260	48.0	55,374	1.5	3,645,777
1900	1,722,344	51.0	62,698	1.9	1,569,454	46.5	19,593	0.6	3,374,089
1906	2,358,853	43.0	317,047	5.8	2,724,485	49.6	91,025	1.7	5,491,410
1910(J)	3,035,425	47.1	501,706	7.8	2,845,818	44.1	63,922	1.0	6,446,871
1910(D)	2,363,761	47.0	371,802	7.4	2,274,866	45.2	17,211	0.3	5,027,640
1918	3,854,979	39.5	2,245,777	23.0	2,785,374	28.6	861,463	8.8	9,747,593
1922	5,394,326	38.0	4,237,349	29.9	4,139,460	29.2	413,309	2.9	14,184,444
1923	5,397,380	37.7	4,439,780	31.0	4,301,481	30.1	166,796	1.2	14,305,437
1924	7,403,245	45.9	5,489,087	34.0	2,928,737	18.2	299,836	1.9	16,120,905
1929	8,301,568	37.5	8,370,417	37.8	5,208,635	23.5	257,702	1.2	22,138,322
1931	13,007,224	60.9	6,640,220[3]	31.1	1,476,123	6.9	250,777	1.2	21,374,344
1935	11,462,814	53.2	8,325,491	38.6	1,443,093	6.7	314,489	1.5	21,545,887
1945	9,579,560	39.3	11,902,287	48.8	2,252,430	9.2	641,153	2.6	24,375,430
1950	12,140,070	43.0	13,198,360	46.8	2,621,487	9.3	249,769	0.9	28,209,686
1951	13,443,271	47.8	13,886,559	49.4	730,546	2.6	73,005	0.3	28,133,381
1955	12,868,244	49.3	12,369,640	47.4	722,402	2.8	152,822	0.6	26,113,108
1959	13,305,862	48.8	12,171,802	44.6	1,637,507	6.0	171,368	0.6	27,286,539
1964	11,600,745	42.9	12,103,049	44.8	3,081,929	11.4	233,109	0.9	27,028,832
1966	11,049,826	41.4	13,024,016	48.8	2,298,348	8.6	296,320	1.1	26,668,510
1970	12,723,082	46.2	12,110,564	43.9	2,105,030	7.6	627,009	2.3	27,565,685

Votes Cast at General Elections 1832-2005 (GB) (contd.)

Election	Con[1]	%	Lab	%	Lib[2]	%	Others	%	Total
1974(F)	11,872,180	38.8	11,645,616	38.0	6,059,519	19.8	1,045,221	3.4	30,622,536
1974(O)	10,462,565	36.7	11,457,079	40.2	5,346,704	18.8	1,220,662	4.3	28,487,010
1979	13,697,923	44.9	11,532,218	37.8	4,313,804	14.1	981,530	3.2	30,525,475
1983	13,012,316	43.5	8,456,934	28.3	7,780,949	26.0	656,013	2.2	29,906,212
1987	13,760,583	43.3	10,029,807	31.5	7,341,633	23.1	667,403	2.1	31,799,426
1992	14,048,399	42.8	11,560,484	35.2	5,999,606	18.3	1,220,492	3.7	32,828,981
1997	9,591,085	31.5	13,518,167	44.3	5,242,947	17.2	2,143,323	7.0	30,495,522
2001	8,355,193	32.7	10,724,953	42.0	4,814,321	18.8	1,662,542	6.5	25,557,009
2005	8,782,197	33.2	9,552,436	36.1	5,985,454	22.6	2,110,821	8.0	26,430,908

1. Including Liberal Conservatives, 1847-59; Liberal Unionists, 1886-1910(D); National, National Liberal and National Labour, 1931-45.

2. Including both Liberal and National Liberal, 1922; Independent Liberal, 1931; SDP/Liberal Alliance, 1983-87; Liberal Democrat 1992 onwards.

3. Including 324,893 (4.9%) votes cast for the 25 unendorsed candidates -see Table 1.26.

Table 2.05: Party Votes as Percentages of Electorate 1950-2005 (UK & GB)

Party	— 1950 — UK	GB	— 1951 — UK	GB	— 1955 — UK	GB	— 1959 — UK	GB
Conservative	36.5	36.2	39.6	39.5	38.2	37.9	38.9	38.5
Labour	38.7	39.3	40.3	40.8	35.6	36.4	34.5	35.3
Liberal	7.6	7.8	2.1	2.1	2.1	2.1	4.6	4.7
Others	1.1	0.7	0.6	0.2	0.9	0.4	0.7	0.5
Non-voters	16.1[1]	15.9	17.4[1]	17.4	23.2	23.1	21.3	21.0

Party	— 1964 — UK	GB	— 1966 — UK	GB	— 1970 — UK	GB	— 1974(F) — UK	GB
Conservative	33.4	33.1	31.7	31.5	33.4	33.2	29.9	30.7
Labour	34.0	34.6	36.4	37.2	31.0	31.6	29.3	30.1
Liberal	8.6	8.8	6.5	6.6	5.4	5.5	15.2	15.6
Others	1.0	0.7	1.2	0.8	2.2	1.6	4.4	2.7
Non-voters	23	22.8	24.2	23.9	28.0	28.1	21.2	20.9

Party	— 1974(O) — UK	GB	— 1979 — UK	GB	— 1983 — UK	GB	— 1987 — UK	GB
Conservative	26.1	26.8	33.3	34.2	30.8	31.6	31.9	32.7
Labour	28.6	29.3	28.1	28.8	20.0	20.6	23.2	23.8
Liberal[2]	13.3	13.7	10.5	10.8	18.5	18.9	17.0	17.4
Others	4.8	3.1	4.1	2.4	3.4	1.6	3.2	1.6
Non-voters	27.2	27.0	24.0	23.8	27.3	27.3	24.7	24.5

Party Votes as Percentages of Electorate (contd.)

Party	— 1992 — UK	GB	— 1997 — UK	GB	— 2001 — UK	GB	— 2005 — UK	GB
Conservative	32.6	33.3	21.9	22.5	18.8	19.3	19.9	20.4
Labour	26.7	27.4	30.8	31.7	24.2	24.8	21.6	22.2
Liberal [2]	13.9	14.2	12.0	12.3	10.8	11.1	13.5	13.9
Others	4.5	2.9	6.7	5.0	5.6	3.8	6.4	4.9
Non-voters	22.3	22.1	28.6	28.5	40.6	40.9	38.6	38.7

1. Excluding electors in uncontested seats.
2. SDP/Liberal Alliance 1983-87; Liberal Democrat 1992 on.

Table 2.06: Conservative and Labour Votes as Percentages of Two-Party Votes 1945-2005 (GB)

Party	1945	1950	1951	1955	1959	1964	1966	1970	1974(F)
Conservative	45.5	47.9	49.2	51.0	52.2	48.9	45.9	51.2	50.5
Labour	54.5	52.1	50.8	49.0	47.8	51.1	54.1	48.8	49.5

Party	1974(O)	1979	1983	1987	1992	1997	2001	2005
Conservative	47.7	54.3	60.6	57.8	54.9	41.5	43.8	47.9
Labour	52.3	45.7	39.4	42.2	45.1	58.5	56.2	52.1

Table 2.07: Conservative, Labour and Liberal Votes as Percentages of Three-Party Votes 1950-2005 (GB)

Party	1950	1951	1955	1959	1964	1966	1970	1974(F)
Conservative	43.4	47.9	49.6	49.1	43.3	41.9	47.2	40.1
Labour	47.2	49.5	47.6	44.9	45.2	49.4	45.0	39.4
Liberal	9.4	2.6	2.8	6.0	11.5	8.7	7.8	20.5

Party	1974(O)	1979	1983	1987	1992	1997	2001	2005
Conservative	38.4	46.4	44.5	44.2	44.4	33.8	35.0	36.1
Labour	42.0	39.0	28.9	32.2	36.6	47.7	44.9	39.3
Liberal [1]	19.6	14.6	26.6	23.6	19.0	18.5	20.1	24.6

1. SDP/Liberal Alliance 1983-87; Liberal Democrat 1992 on.

Table 2.08: Change in Party Share of the Vote and Swing 1945-2005 (GB)

	Two-party ('Steed') swing, Con/Lab*	Total vote ('Butler') swing, Con/Lab*	Change in % share of total vote Con	Lab	Lib
1945-50	2.4	2.9	3.7	-2.0	0.1
1950-51	1.3	1.1	4.8	2.6	-6.7
1951-55	1.8	1.8	1.5	-2.0	0.2
1955-59	1.2	1.2	-0.5	-2.8	3.2
1959-64	-3.3	-3.1	-5.9	0.2	5.4
1964-66	-3.0	-2.8	-1.5	4.0	-2.8
1966-70	5.3	4.9	4.8	-4.9	-1.0
1970-Feb 1974	-0.7	-0.8	-7.4	-5.9	12.2
Feb- Oct 1974	-2.8	-2.2	-2.1	2.2	-1.0

Change in Party Share of the Vote and Swing 1945-2005 (GB) (contd.)

| | Two-party ('Steed') swing, Con/Lab* | Total vote ('Butler') swing, Con/Lab* | Change in % share of total vote | | |
			Con	Lab	Lib
Oct 1974-1979	6.6	5.3	8.2	-2.4	-4.3
1979-83	6.3	4.1	-1.4	-9.5	11.9
1983-87	-2.8	-1.7	-0.2	3.2	-2.9
1987-92	-2.9	-2.1	-0.5	3.7	-4.8
1992-97	-13.4	-10.2	-11.3	9.1	-1.1
1997-01	2.3	1.8	1.2	-2.4	1.6
2001-05	4.1	3.1	0.5	-5.8	3.8

* + = to Con; - = to Lab. For a full explanation of swing see Introductory Notes.

Table 2.09: Votes per Seat Won 1945-2005 (GB)

	C	Lab	L[1]	PC	SNP
1945	47,424	30,286	187,703	no seat	no seat
1950	42,153	41,900	291,276	no seat	no seat
1951	43,087	47,073	121,758	no seat	no seat
1955	38,413	44,656	120,400	no seat	no seat
1959	37,694	47,178	272,918	no seat	no seat
1964	39,729	38,180	342,437	no seat	no seat
1966	45,660	35,780	191,529	no seat	no seat
1970	39,513	42,051	350,838	no seat	306,802
1974 (F)	39,974	38,690	432,823	85,687	90,454
1974 (O)	37,771	35,916	411,285	55,440	76,329
1979	40,407	42,871	392,164	66,272	252,130
1983	32,777	40,464	338,302	62,655	165,988
1987	36,597	43,798	333,711	41,200	138,824
1992	41,811	42,659	299,980	38,737	209,855
1997	58,128	32,340	113,977	40,258	103,592
2001	50,332	26,031	92,583	48,973	92,863
2005	44,335	26,908	96,539	58,279	68,711

1. SDP/Liberal Alliance 1983-87; Liberal Democrat 1992 on.

Table 2.10: Seats and Votes: Major Parties at General Elections 1945-2005

| | Con | | | Lab | | | L | | |
	%seats	%votes	seats/votes	%seats	%votes	seats/votes	%seats	%votes	seats/votes
1945	32.8	39.6	0.83	61.4	48.0	1.28	1.9	9.0	0.21
1950	47.7	43.4	1.10	50.4	46.1	1.09	1.4	9.1	0.15
1951	51.3	48.0	1.07	47.2	48.8	0.97	1.0	2.6	0.38
1955	54.8	49.7	1.10	44.0	46.4	0.95	0.9	2.7	0.33
1959	57.9	49.4	1.17	41.0	43.8	0.94	0.9	5.9	0.15
1964	48.3	43.4	1.11	57.8	44.1	1.31	1.4	11.2	0.13
1966	40.1	41.9	0.96	57.8	48.0	1.20	1.9	8.5	0.22
1970	53.3	46.4	1.15	45.7	43.1	1.06	1.0	7.5	0.13
1974(F)	46.8	37.9	1.23	47.4	37.2	1.27	2.2	19.3	0.11
1974(O)	43.6	35.8	1.22	50.2	39.3	1.28	2.1	18.3	0.11
1979	53.4	43.9	1.22	42.4	36.9	1.15	1.7	13.8	0.12
1983	61.1	42.4	1.44	32.2	27.6	1.17	3.5	25.4	0.14

Seats and Votes: Major Parties at General Elections 1945-2005 (contd.)

	Con			Lab			L		
	%seats	*%votes*	*seats/votes*	*%seats*	*%votes*	*seats/votes*	*%seats*	*%votes*	*seats/votes*
1987	57.9	42.3	1.37	35.2	30.8	1.14	3.4	22.6	0.15
1992	51.6	41.9	1.23	41.6	34.4	1.21	3.1	17.8	0.17
1997	25.0	30.7	0.81	63.4	43.2	1.47	7.0	16.8	0.42
2001	25.2	31.7	0.79	62.5	40.7	1.54	7.9	18.3	0.43
2005	30.7	32.4	0.95	55.0	35.2	1.56	9.6	22.0	0.44

Table 2.11: Votes Cast for Winners and Losers 1974-2005

	Winners			Losers		
	Candidates	*Votes*	*% of Total Votes*	*Candidates*	*Votes*	*% of Total Votes*
1974 (February)						
C	297	7,279,384	23.2	326	4,592,796	14.6
Lab	301	7,151,965	22.8	322	4,493,651	14.3
L	14	312,372	1.0	503	5,747,147	18.3
PC	2	21,926	0.1	34	149,448	0.5
SNP	7	113,496	0.4	63	519,684	1.7
Others	14	406,581	1.3	252	551,712	1.8
Total	**635**	**15,285,724**	**48.8**	**1,500**	**16,054,438**	**51.2**
1974 (October)						
C	277	6,284,720	21.5	345	4,177,845	14.3
Lab	319	7,264,542	24.9	304	4,192,537	14.4
L	13	249,539	0.9	606	5,097,165	17.4
PC	3	47,492	0.2	33	118,829	0.4
SNP	11	173,655	0.6	60	665,962	2.3
Others	12	415,844	1.4	269	500,974	1.7
Total	**635**	**14,435,792**	**49.5**	**1,617**	**14,753,312**	**50.5**
1979						
C	339	9,558,212	30.6	283	4,139,711	13.3
Lab	269	6,348,058	20.3	354	5,184,160	16.6
L	11	236,118	0.8	566	4,077,686	13.1
PC	2	26,695	0.1	34	105,849	0.3
SNP	2	28,438	0.1	69	475,821	1.5
Others	12	341,912	1.1	635	698,702	2.2
Total	**635**	**16,539,433**	**53.0**	**1,941**	**14,681,929**	**47.0**
1983						
C	397	10,087,462	32.9	236	2,924,854	9.6
Lab	209	4,274,800	13.9	424	4,182,134	13.6
L[1]	23	454,019	1.5	610	7,326,930	23.9
PC	2	28,017	0.1	36	97,292	0.3
SNP	2	28,548	0.1	70	303,427	1.0
Others	17	342,837	1.1	552	620,817	2.0
Total	**650**	**15,215,683**	**49.6**	**1,928**	**15,455,454**	**50.4**

Votes Cast for Winners and Losers 1974-2005 (contd.)

	Winners			Losers		
	Candidates	*Votes*	*% of Total Votes*	*Candidates*	*Votes*	*% of Total Votes*
1987						
C	376	10,559,017	32.4	257	3,201,566	9.8
Lab	229	5,418,705	16.7	404	4,611,102	14.2
L[1]	22	411,598	1.3	611	6,930,035	21.3
PC	3	49,310	0.2	35	74,289	0.2
SNP	3	58,508	0.2	68	357,965	1.1
Others	17	405,424	1.2	300	452,059	1.4
Total	**650**	**16,902,562**	**52.0**	**1,675**	**15,627,016**	**48.0**
1992						
C	336	9,999,802	29.7	309	4,093,205	12.2
Lab	271	6,634,483	19.7	363	4,926,001	14.7
LD	20	407,131	1.2	612	5,592,475	16.6
PC	4	65,051	0.2	31	89,896	0.3
SNP	3	61,259	0.2	69	568,305	1.7
Others	17	399,700	1.2	914	776,766	2.3
Total	**651**	**17,567,426**	**52.3**	**2,298**	**16,046,648**	**47.7**
1997						
C	165	3,850,317	12.3	483	5,750,626	18.4
Lab	418	10,709,774	34.2	221	2,808,393	9.0
LD	46	1,012,771	3.2	593	4,230,176	13.5
PC	4	62,565	0.2	36	98,465	0.3
SNP	6	114,835	0.4	66	506,715	1.6
Others	20	414,780	1.3	1,666	1,726,867	5.5
Total	**659**	**16,165,042**	**51.7**	**3,065**	**15,121,242**	**48.3**
2001						
C	166	3,554,822	13.5	477	4,802,793	18.2
Lab	412	8,250,072	31.3	228	2,474,881	9.4
LD	52	1,061,620	4.0	587	3,752,701	14.2
PC	4	52,724	0.2	36	143,169	0.5
SNP	5	65,811	0.2	67	398,503	1.5
Others	20	402,787	1.5	1265	1,407,500	5.3
Total	**659**	**13,387,836**	**50.8**	**2660**	**12,979,547**	**49.2**
2005						
C	198	4,471,171	16.5	432	4,313,744	15.9
Lab	355	6,637,016	24.4	272	2,915,420	10.7
LD	62	1,284,238	4.7	564	4,701,216	17.3
PC	3	40,905	0.2	37	133,933	0.5
SNP	6	82,470	0.3	53	329,797	1.2
Others	22	402,613	1.5	1,550	1,835,987	6.8
Total	**646**	**12,918,413**	**47.6**	**2,908**	**14,230,097**	**52.4**

1. SDP/Liberal Alliance 1983-87; Liberal Democrat 1992 on.

Table 2.12: Seat Gains and Losses at General Elections 1885-2005

Election	Con net[1]	Lab net	L net[2]	Others net
1885[3]	-	-	-	-
1886	44	-	-44	•
1892	-49	-	51	-2
1895	90	-	-89	-1
1900	3	2	-4	-1
1906	-211	25	185	1
1910(J)	103	-4	-98	-1
1910(D)	•	2	-4	2
1918[3]	-	-	-	-
1922	-18	67	-39	-10
1923	-88	47	42	-1
1924	155	-42	-114	1
1929	-140	126	14	•
1931	217	-215	6	-8
1935	-84	94	-12	2
1945[4]	-187	199	-8	-4
1950[5]	11	-8	2	-5
1951	22	-19	-3	•
1955[6]	11	-10	•	-1
1959	23	-23	•	•
1964	-56	56	2	-2
1966	-51	48	2	1
1970	67	-60	-7	•
1974(F)[7]	-14	3	2	9
1974(O)	-20	19	-2	3
1979	55	-40	-3	-12
1983[8]	7	-5	-2	•
1987	-17	21	-5	1
1992	-41	42	-2	1
1997[9]	-178	146	28	4
2001	1	-5	6	-1
2005[10]	33	-47	11	3

• No overall gain or loss.

1. Including Liberal Unionists 1886-1910(D); National, National Liberal and National Labour, 1931-45.
2. Including both Liberal and National Liberals in 1922; Independent Liberals in 1931; SDP/Liberal Alliance 1983-87; Liberal Democrat 1992 on.
3. Boundary changes. Calculation of gains and losses not applicable.
4. Boundary changes. Calculations are based on the 593 constituencies with either unchanged boundaries or minor changes only.
5. Boundary changes. Calculations are based on the 88 constituencies with either unchanged boundaries or minor changes only.
6. Boundary changes. Calculations are based on the 454 constituencies with either unchanged boundaries or minor changes only.
7. Boundary changes. Calculations are based on the 322 constituencies with either unchanged boundaries or minor changes only.
8. Boundary changes. Calculations are based on the 109 constituencies with either unchanged boundaries or minor changes only.
9. Boundary changes. Calculations are based on the 165 constituencies with unchanged boundaries together with the notional 1992 results for the 494 'new' constituencies. See Introductory Notes.
10. Boundary changes in Scotland. Calculations are based on notional 1997 results in the 59 constituencies in Scotland. See Introductory notes.

Table 2.13: Seats Which Changed Hands at General Elections 1950-2005

	1950	1951	1955	1959	1964	1966	1970	1974(F)	1974(O)	1979	1983	1987	1992	1997[2]	2001	2005[3]
Con from																
L[1]	0	2	0	1	0	0	5	2	2	3	2	6	2	0	2	5
Lab	10	21	11	28	5	0	68	1	0	51	6	6	1	0	5	31
DP	0	0	0	0	0	0	1	0	0	0	0	0	0	0	0	0
Irish LP	1	0	1	0	0	0	0	0	0	0	0	0	0	0	0	0
Ind	2	0	0	0	0	0	0	0	0	0	0	0	0	0	1	0
Ind Con	0	0	0	0	0	0	1	0	0	0	0	0	0	0	0	0
Ind L	1	0	0	0	0	0	0	0	0	0	0	0	0	0	0	0
SNP	0	0	0	0	0	0	0	0	0	7	0	0	0	0	1	0
Lab from																
Con	1	0	1	5	58	47	6	11	17	6	0	22	40	144	1	0
L	0	2	0	0	2	2	2	0	1	1	1	2	3	2	0	0
PC	0	0	0	0	0	0	1	0	0	1	0	0	0	0	1	0
SNP	0	0	0	0	0	0	1	0	0	2	0	2	0	0	0	0
Ind	0	1	0	0	0	0	0	0	0	0	0	1	0	0	0	0
Ind Con	0	0	0	0	1	0	0	0	2	0	0	0	0	0	0	0
Ind Lab	1	0	0	0	0	0	0	0	0	0	0	0	0	0	0	0
SCLP	0	0	0	0	0	0	0	0	0	2	0	0	0	0	0	0
L from																
Con	2	0	0	1	3	3	0	2	1	0	1	3	4	30	7	3
Lab	0	1	0	0	0	1	0	2	0	0	0	0	0	0	1	12
Ind Con	0	0	0	0	1	0	0	0	0	0	0	0	0	0	0	0
PC	0	0	0	0	0	0	0	0	0	0	0	0	0	0	0	1
UDUP from																
UU	0	0	0	0	0	0	0	0	0	2	0	0	0	0	3	4
Irish LP from																
Con	0	1	0	0	0	0	0	0	0	0	0	0	0	0	0	0

Seats Which Changed Hands at General Elections 1950–2005 (contd.)

	1950	1951	1955	1959	1964	1966	1970	1974(F)	1974(O)	1979	1983	1987	1992	1997[2]	2001	2005[3]
PC from																
Con	0	0	0	0	0	0	0	0	0	0	0	1	0	0	0	0
Lab	0	0	0	0	0	0	0	2	1	0	0	0	0	0	1	0
L	0	0	0	0	0	0	0	0	0	0	0	0	1	0	0	0
Prot U from																
Con	0	0	0	0	0	0	1	0	0	0	0	0	0	0	0	0
Rep LP from																
Con	0	0	0	0	0	1	0	0	0	0	0	0	0	0	0	0
SF from																
DUP	0	0	0	0	0	0	0	0	0	0	0	0	0	1	0	0
N	0	0	2	0	0	0	0	0	0	0	0	0	0	0	0	0
SDLP	0	0	0	0	0	0	0	0	0	0	0	0	0	1	2	1
UU	0	0	0	0	0	0	0	0	0	0	0	0	0	0	0	0
SDLP from																
UU	0	0	0	0	0	0	0	0	0	0	0	1	0	0	0	1
SNP from																
Con	0	0	0	0	0	0	0	4	4	0	0	3	0	3	0	0
Lab	0	0	0	0	0	0	1	2	0	0	0	0	0	0	0	2
Unity from																
Con	0	0	0	0	0	0	1	0	0	0	0	0	0	0	0	0
UU from																
Unity	0	0	0	0	0	0	0	1	0	0	0	0	0	0	0	0
Ind Soc	0	0	0	0	0	0	0	1	0	0	0	0	0	0	0	0
UDUP	0	0	0	0	0	0	0	0	0	0	0	0	0	1	0	0
UKUP	0	0	0	0	0	0	0	0	0	0	0	0	0	0	1	0
Ind Lab from																
Lab	0	0	0	0	0	0	1	1	0	0	0	0	0	0	0	0

Seats Which Changed Hands at General Elections 1950–2005 (contd.)

	1950	1951	1955	1959	1964	1966	1970	1974(F)	1974(O)	1979	1983	1987	1992	1997[2]	2001	2005[3]
Ind Rep from																
UUUC	0	0	0	0	0	0	0	0	1	0	0	0	0	0	0	0
UKUP from																
UPUP	0	0	0	0	0	0	0	0	0	0	0	0	0	1	0	0
Ind from																
Con	0	0	0	0	0	0	0	0	0	0	0	0	0	1	0	0
Lab	0	0	0	0	0	0	0	0	0	0	0	0	0	0	1	0
Respect from																
Lab	0	0	0	0	0	0	0	0	0	0	0	0	0	0	0	1
No label from																
Lab	0	0	0	0	0	0	0	0	0	0	0	0	0	0	0	1
TOTAL	**18**	**28**	**15**	**35**	**70**	**54**	**89**	**29**	**29**	**74**	**10**	**47**	**51**	**184**	**30**	**62**

1. Includes SDP/Liberal Alliance 1983-87; Liberal Democrat 1992 onwards throughout.
2. Change figures based on notional 1992 results in new constituencies.
3. Change figures based on notional 1997 results in Scotland.

Table 2.14: Votes per Candidate in Contested Seats 1832-2005

| | —— Con[1] —— | | —— Lab —— | | —— L[2] —— | | —Nat— |
	Cands	Votes per seat	Cands	Votes per seat	Cands	Votes per seat	Scotland & Wales
Election								
1832	284	850	-	-	527	1,053	-	-
1835	286	914	-	-	384	911	-	-
1837	363	1,046	-	-	395	1,059	-	-
1841	286	1,071	-	-	275	996	-	-
1847	209	983	-	-	257	1,009	-	-
1852	301	1,035	-	-	393	1,096	-	-
1857	203	1,181	-	-	331	1,402	-	-
1859	198	976	-	-	282	1,320	-	-
1865	264	1,311	-	-	355	1,433	-	-
1868	345	2,619	-	-	479	2,983	-	-
1874	382	2,858	-	-	437	2,932	-	-
1880	463	3,081	-	-	458	4,010	-	-
1885	592	3,414	-	-	558	3,943	-	-
1886	445	3,418	-	-	409	3,309	-	-
1892	566	3,815	-	-	519	4,023	-	-
1895	456	4,155	-	-	436	4,049	-	-
1900	406	4,355	15	4,180	380	4,138	-	-
1906	543	4,461	50	6,433	509	5,405	-	-
1910(J)	575	5,399	78	6,483	510	5,620	-	-
1910(D)	476	5,084	53	7,015	432	5,310	-	-
1918	404	10,258	350	6,417	394	7,069	-	-
1922	440	12,505	410	10,335	475	8,715	-	-
1923	501	11,007	424	10,471	446	9,645	-	-
1924	518	15,163	505	10,869	333	8,795	-	-
1929	586	14,772	569	14,711	513	10,348	3	1,307
1931	527	24,965	510[3]	13,038	112[4]	13,180	7	3,286
1935	557	21,105	539	15,446	161	8,963	9	3,561
1945	617	16,162	601	19,913	306	7,361	15	3,107
1950	617	20,247	617	21,501	475	5,519	10	2,729
1951	613	22,379	617	22,608	109	6,702	6	3,037
1955	624	21,332	620	20,008	110	6,567	13	4,402
1959	625	22,001	621	19,672	216	7,596	25	3,972
1964	630	19,052	628	19,436	365	8,491	38	3,515
1966	629	18,153	622	21,056	311	7,484	43	4,408
1970	628	20,932	625	19,534	332	6,377	101	4,770
1974(F)	623	19,056	623	18,693	517	11,721	106	7,590
1974(O)	622	16,821	623	18,390	619	8,638	107	9,401
1979	622	22,022	623	18,511	577	7,476	107	5,951
1983	633	20,557	633	13,360	633	12,292	110	4,157
1987	633	21,739	633	15,845	633	11,598	109	4,955
1992	645	21,850	634	18,234	632	9,493	107	7,332
1997	648	14,816	639	21,155	639	8,205	112	6,987
2001	643	12,998	640	16,758	639	7,534	112	5,895
2005	630	13,944	627	15,235	626	9,561	112	5,242

Votes per Candidate in Contested Seats 1832-2005 (contd.)

1. Including Liberal Conservatives, 1847-59; Liberal Unionists, 1886-1910(D); National, National Liberal and National Labour, 1931-45.
2. Including both Liberal and National Liberal, 1922; Independent Liberal, 1931; SDP/Liberal Alliance, 1983-87; Liberal Democrat 1992 onwards.
3. Including 24 unendorsed.
4. Including Independent Liberals.

Table 2.15: Unopposed Returns 1832-2005

Election	Total Seats	C	Lab	L	N	Others	Total	%
1832	658	66	-	109	-	14	189	28.7
1835	658	121	-	154	-	0	275	41.8
1837	658	121	-	115	-	0	236	35.9
1841	658	212	-	113	-	12	337	51.2
1847	656	213	-	136	-	18	367	55.9
1852	654	160	-	95	-	0	255	39.0
1857	654	148	-	176	-	4	328	50.2
1859	654	196	-	183	-	0	379	58.0
1865	658	142	-	161	-	0	303	46.0
1868	658	91	-	121	-	0	212	32.2
1874	652	125	-	52	10	0	187	28.7
1880	652	58	-	41	10	0	109	16.7
1885	670	10	-	14	19	0	43	6.4
1886	670	118	-	40	66	0	224	33.4
1892	670	40	-	13	9	1	63	9.4
1895	670	132	-	11	46	0	189	28.2
1900	670	163	0	22	58	0	243	36.3
1906	670	13	0	27	73	1	114	17.0
1910(J)	670	19	0	1	55	0	75	11.2
1910(D)	670	72	3	35	53	0	163	24.3
1918	707	41	11	27	1	27	107	15.1
1922	615	42	4	10	1	0	57	9.3
1923	615	35	3	11	1	0	50	8.1
1924	615	16	9	6	1	0	32	5.2
1929	615	4	0	0	3	0	7	1.1
1931	615	56	6[1]	5	0	0	67	10.9
1935	615	26	13	0	0	1	40	6.5
1945	640	1	2	0	0	0	3	0.5
1950	625	2	0	0	0	0	2	0.3
1951	625	4	0	0	0	0	4	0.6
1955	630	0	0	0	0	0	0	-
1959	630	0	0	0	0	0	0	-
1964	630	0	0	0	0	0	0	-
1966	630	0	0	0	0	0	0	-
1970	630	0	0	0	0	0	0	-
1974(F)	635	0	0	0	0	0	0	-
1974(O)	635	0	0	0	0	0	0	-
1979	635	0	0	0	0	0	0	-
1983	650	0	0	0	0	0	0	-

Unopposed Returns 1832-2005 (contd.)

Election	Total Seats	C	Lab	L	N	Others	Total	%
1987	650	0	0	0	0	0	0	-
1992	651	0	0	0	0	0	0	-
1997	659	0	0	0	0	0	0	-
2001	659	0	0	0	0	0	0	-
2005	646	0	0	0	0	0	0	-

1. Including one unendorsed.

Table 2.16: Forfeited Deposits at General Elections 1918-2005

Election	Con	Lab	L^1	Com	NF	PC	SNP	Others	$Total^2$	% of total opposed candidates
1918	3	6	44	-				108	161	10.6
1922	1	7	32	1	-	-	-	11	52	3.8
1923	0	17	8	0	-	-	-	2	27	1.9
1924	1	28	30	1	-	-	-	8	68	4.9
1929	18	35	25	21	-	1	2	11	113	6.6
1931	5	21	6	21	-	1	2	29	85	6.9
1935	1	16	40	0	-	1	5	18	81	6.2
1945	6	2	76	12	-	6	6	74	182	10.8
1950	5	0	319	97	-	6	3	31	461	24.7
1951	3	1	66	10	-	4	1	11	96	7.0
1955	3	1	60	15	-	7	1	13	100	7.1
1959	2	1	55	17	-	14	3	24	116	7.6
1964	5	8	52	36	-	21	12	52	186	10.6
1966	9	3	104	57	-	18	10	36	237	13.9
1970	10	6	184	58	10	25	43	72	408	22.2
1974(F)	8	25	23	43	54	26	7	135	321	15.0
1974(O)	28	13	125	29	90	26	0	131	442	19.6
1979	3	22	303	38	303	29	29	274	1,001	38.9
1983	5	119	11	35	60	32	53	424	739	28.7
1987	0	0	1	19	-	25	1	243	289	12.4
1992	4	1	11	4	14	20	0	847	901	30.6
1997	8	0	13	3	6	15	0	1,548	1,593	42.8
2001	5	0	1	6	5	5	0	1,155	1,177	41.7
2005	5	0	1	6	13	8	0	1,352	1,385	39.0

From the General Election of 1918 until October 1, 1985, a candidate forfeited the deposit of £150 if he failed to poll more than one-eighth of the total votes cast, exclusive of spoilt papers. In the case of the two-member constituencies which existed until 1950, the number of votes was deemed to be the number of good ballot papers counted. The money from forfeited deposits goes to the Treasury but in the case of the University constituencies (where a candidate had to poll more than one-eighth of the first preference votes) the deposit was forfeited to the University. In the Combined Scottish Universities, the only three-member constituency, the requirement was that a candidate must poll more than one-eighth of the first preference votes divided by three. On October 1, 1985, the deposit was raised to £500 but the threshold was lowered to one-twentieth of the total votes cast, exclusive of spoilt papers.

Where a candidate is nominated at a General Election in more than one constituency not more than one of the deposits can be returned irrespective of the number of votes polled. Eight deposits were forfeited in Ireland in 1918 owing to this rule. Until 1950, the deposit was not returned to a successful candidate until he had taken the Oath as a Member of Parliament and, especially in 1918, Sinn Fein MPs must have forfeited their deposits through refusing to take their seats in the House of Commons.

Forfeited Deposits at General Elections 1918-2005 (contd.)

1. SDP/Liberal Alliance 1983-87; Liberal Democrat 1992 on.
2. Throughout this table, forfeited deposits due to multiple candidatures or failure to take the Oath have been ignored.

Table 2.17: Single Member Seats Won on a Minority Vote 1885-2005

Election	C	Lab	L	Others	Total	% of seats
1885	8	0	9	5	22	51.2
1886	0	0	0	0	0	-
1892	6	0	1	3	10	31 3
1895	5	0	8	2	15	51 7
1900	2	0	1	1	4	50.0
1906	11	2	9	5	27	58.7
1910(J)	8	0	21	1	30	65.2
1910(D)	1	0	10	2	13	76.5
1918	50	17	21	9	97	37.6
1922	89	54	28	3	174	74.0
1923	90	65	46	2	203	79.6
1924	80	33	7	4	124	54 4
1929	151	118	40	1	310	65.5
1931	21	4	8	1	34	30 1
1935	32	17	7	2	58	37.9
1945	92	71	2	9	174	51.3
1950	106	76	5	0	187	36.7
1951	25	14	0	0	39	31.0
1955	25	11	1	0	37	26.2
1959	47	31	2	0	80	31.1
1964	154	71	7	0	232	53.2
1966	131	43	11	0	185	46.7
1970	68	48	6	2	124	27.9
1974(F)	234	150	9	15	408	68.3
1974(O)	224	131	11	14	380	59.8
1979	107	83	6	10	206	32.6
1983	165	141	15	15	336	51.7
1987	142	109	19	13	283	43.5
1992	125	103	17	15	260	39.9
1997	152	105	38	18	313	47.5
2001	134	141	37	21	333	50.5
2005	143	215	46	22	426	65.9

Table 2.18: Single Member Seats Won on a Majority of the Electorate 1918-2005

Election	C	Lab	L	Others	Total	% of contested seats
1918	15	0	3	16	34	6.0
1922	7	8	1	0	16	3.0
1923	0	7	1	0	8	1.5
1924	41	6	2	1	50	9.2
1929	0	26	0	0	26	4.6
1931	204	10	9	20	243	46.6
1935	25	20	1	3	49	9.0
1945	0	80	0	0	80	13.4
1950	45	106	1	0	152	24.4
1951	84	128	2	0	214	34.5
1955	53	52	1	0	106	16.8
1959	53	54	0	0	107	16.8
1964	2	52	0	0	54	8.6
1966	1	54	0	0	55	8.7
1970	0	20	0	0	20	3.2
1974(F)	0	22	0	0	22	3.5
1974(O)	0	10	0	0	10	1.6
1979	5	12	0	0	17	2.7
1983	0	1	0	0	1	0.2
1987	3	12	0	0	15	2.3
1992	16	18	0	0	34	5.2
1997	0	14	0	0	14	2.1
2001	0	0	0	0	0	-
2005	0	0	0	0	0	-

Table 2.19: Liberals and Nationalists in Second Place 1950-1979 (GB)

Election	L	PC	SNP
1950	17	0	0
1951	9	0	0
1955	11	1	1
1959	26	1	1
1964	55	0	1
1966	26	1	3
1970	26	8	9
1974(F)	145	7	17
1974(O)	102	6	42
1979	82	1	13

Table 2.20: Finishing Order of the Political Parties 1983-2005 (GB)

	1st	*2nd*	*3rd*	*4th*
1983				
Conservative	397	180	54	2
Labour	209	132	282	10
Lib/SDP	23	313	290	7
SNP	2	7	5	58
PC	2	1	2	33
1987				
Conservative	376	210	42	4
Labour	229	149	249	5
Lib/SDP	22	260	330	20
SNP	3	13	8	47
PC	3	1	1	33
1992				
Conservative	336	257	35	1
Labour	271	192	158	10
LD	20	154	388	67
SNP	3	36	28	5
PC	4	2	5	24
1997				
Conservative	165	386	76	13
Labour	418	102	115	4
LD	46	104	427	62
SNP	6	44	17	5
PC	4	4	4	28
2001				
Conservative	166	353	81	32
Labour	412	119	106	3
LD	52	108	428	49
SNP	5	43	11	13
PC	4	12	5	18
2005				
Conservative	198	262	120	42
Labour	355	140	130	2
LD	62	187	341	35
SNP	6	19	15	18
PC	3	8	3	23

Table 3.01: The Conservative Vote 1832-2005[1]

Election	Candidates	Unopposed Returns	MPs Elected	Forfeited Deposits	Total votes	% of GB total	% of UK total
1832	350	66	175	-	241,284	28.9	29.4
1835	407	121	273	-	261,269	42.8	42.6
1837	484	121	314	-	379,694	48.2	48.3
1841	498	212	367	-	306,314	52.7	50.9
1847	422	213	325	-	205,481	43.1	42.2
1852	461	160	330	-	316,718	40.8	41.4
1857	351	148	264	-	239,712	31.0	33.1
1859	394	196	298	-	193,232	33.4	34.3
1865	406	142	289	-	346,035	40.0	39.8
1868	436	91	271	-	903,318	38.6	38.4
1874	507	125	350	-	1,091,708	44.6	43.9
1880	521	58	237	-	1,426,351	42.7	42.0
1885	602	10	249	-	2,020,927	45.6	43.5
1886	563	118	393	-	1,520,886	51.2	51.4
1892	606	40	313	-	2,159,150	49.5	47.0
1895	588	132	411	-	1,894,772	50.5	49.1
1900	569	163	402	-	1,767,958	51.0	50.3
1906	556	13	156	-	2,422,071	43.0	43.4
1910(J)	594	19	272	-	3,104,407	47.1	46.8
1910(D)	548	72	271	-	2,420,169	47.0	46.6
1918	445	41	382	3	4,144,192	39.5	38.7
1922	482	42	344	1	5,502,298	38.0	38.5
1923	536	35	258	0	5,514,541	37.7	38.0
1924	534	16	412	1	7,854,523	45.9	46.8
1929	590	4	260	18	8,656,225	37.5	38.1
1931	583	61	522	5	13,156,790	60.9	60.7
1935	583	26	429	1	11,755,654	53.2	53.3
1945	618	1	210	6	9,972,010	39.3	39.6
1950	619	2	298	5	12,492,404	43.0	43.4
1951	617	4	321	3	13,718,199	47.8	48.0
1955	624	0	345	3	13,310,891	49.3	49.7
1959	625	0	365	2	13,750,875	48.8	49.4
1964	630	0	304	5	12,002,642	42.9	43.4
1966	629	0	253	9	11,418,455	41.4	41.9
1970	628	0	330	10	13,145,123	46.2	46.4
1974(F)	623	0	297	8	11,872,180	38.8	37.9
1974(O)	622	0	277	28	10,462,565	36.7	35.8
1979	622	0	339	3	13,697,923	44.9	43.9
1983	633	0	397	5	13,012,316	43.5	42.4
1987	633	0	376	0	13,760,583	43.3	42.3
1992	645	0	336	4	14,093,007	42.8	41.9
1997	648	0	165	8	9,600,943	31.5	30.7
2001	643	0	166	5	8,357,615	32.7	31.7
2005	630	0	198	5	8,784,915	33.2	32.4

1. Including Liberal Conservative 1847-59; Liberal Unionist 1886-1910(O); National, National Liberal and National Labour 1931-45.

Table 3.02: The Labour Vote 1900-2005

Election	Candidates	Unopposed Returns	MPs Elected	Forfeited Deposits	Total votes	% of GB total	% of UK total
1900	15 [1]	0	2	-	62,698	1.9	1.3
1906	50	0	29	-	321,663	5.8	4.8
1910(J)	78	0	40	-	505,657	7.8	7.0
1910(D)	56	3	42	-	371,802	7.4	6.4
1918	361	11	57	6	2,245,777	23.0	20.8
1922	414	4	142	7	4,237,349	29.9	29.7
1923	427	3	191	17	4,439,780	31.0	30.7
1924	514	9	151	28	5,489,087	34.0	33.3
1929	569	0	287	35	8,370,417	37.8	37.1
1931 [2]	516	6	52	21	6,649,630	31.1	30.9
1935	552	13	154	16	8,325,491	38.6	38.0
1945	603	2	393	2	11,967,746	48.8	48.0
1950	617	0	315	0	13,266,176	46.8	46.1
1951	617	0	295	1	13,948,883	49.4	48.8
1955	620	0	277	1	12,405,254	47.4	46.4
1959	621	0	258	1	12,216,172	44.6	43.8
1964	628	0	317	8	12,205,808	44.8	44.1
1966	622	0	364	3	13,096,629	48.8	48.0
1970	625	0	288	6	12,208,758	43.9	43.1
1974(F)	623	0	301	25	11,645,616	38.0	37.2
1974(O)	623	0	319	13	11,457,079	40.2	39.2
1979	623	0	269	22	11,532,218	37.8	36.9
1983	633	0	209	119	8,456,934	28.3	27.6
1987	633	0	229	0	10,029,807	31.5	30.8
1992	634	0	271	1	11,560,484	35.2	34.4
1997	639	0	418	0	13,518,167	44.3	43.2
2001	640	0	412	0	10,724,953	42.0	40.7
2005	627	0	355	0	9,552,436	36.1	35.2

1. J. Keir Hardie is counted twice in this total. He contested both Preston and Merthyr Tydfil and was elected for the latter.
2. Including 25 unendorsed candidates (see Table 1.26, footnote 3) of whom six (including one unopposed) were elected, one deposit was forfeited and the total votes polled were 324,893 (4.9%).

Table 3.03: The Liberal Vote 1832-2005[1]

Election	Candidates	Unopposed Returns	MPs Elected	Forfeited Deposits	Total votes	% of GB total	% of UK total
1832	636	109	441	-	554,719	71.1	66.7
1835	538	154	385	-	349,868	57.2	57.4
1837	510	115	344	-	418,331	51.8	51.7
1841	388	113	271	-	273,902	47.2	46.9
1847	393	136	292	-	259,311	56.2	53.9
1852	488	95	324	-	430,882	58.9	58.4
1857	507	176	377	-	464,127	68.9	65.1
1859	465	183	356	-	372,117	66.6	65.7
1865	516	161	369	-	508,821	60.0	60.2
1868	600	121	387	-	1,428,776	61.4	61.5
1874	489	52	242	-	1,281,159	55.4	52.7
1880	499	41	352	-	1,836,423	57.3	55.4
1885	572	14	319	-	2,199,998	51.8	47.4
1886	449	40	192	-	1,353,581	48.6	45.0
1892	532	13	272	-	2,088,019	49.6	45.1
1895	447	11	177	-	1,765,266	48.0	45.7
1900	402	22	183	-	1,572,323	46.5	45.0
1906	536	27	399	-	2,751,057	49.6	49.4
1910(J)	511	1	274	-	2,866,157	44.1	43.5
1910(D)	467	35	272	-	2,293,869	45.2	44.2
1918	421	27	163	44	2,785,374	28.5	25.6
1922	485	10	115	32	4,139,460	29.2	28.8
1923	457	11	158	8	4,301,481	30.1	29.7
1924	339	6	40	30	2,928,737	18.2	17.8
1929	513	0	59	25	5,308,738	23.5	23.5
1931	117	5	36	6	1,476,123	6.9	7.0
1935	161	0	21	40	1,443,093	6.7	6.7
1945	306	0	12	76	2,252,430	9.2	9.0
1950	475	0	9	319	2,621,487	9.3	9.1
1951	109	0	6	66	730,546	2.6	2.6
1955	110	0	6	60	722,402	2.8	2.7
1959	216	0	6	55	1,640,760	6.0	5.9
1964	365	0	9	52	3,099,283	11.4	11.2
1966	311	0	12	104	2,327,457	8.6	8.5
1970	332	0	6	184	2,117,035	7.6	7.5
1974(F)	517	0	14	23	6,059,519	19.8	19.3
1974(O)	619	0	13	125	5,346,704	18.8	18.3
1979	577	0	11	303	4,313,804	14.1	13.8
1983	633	0	23	11	7,780,949	26.0	25.4
1987	633	0	27	1	7,341,633	23.1	22.6
1992	632	0	20	11	5,999,606	18.3	17.8
1997	639	0	46	13	5,242,947	17.2	16.8
2001	639	0	52	1	4,814,321	18.8	18.3
2005	626	0	62	1	5,985,454	22.6	22.0

1. Including both Liberal and National Liberal 1922; Independent Liberal 1931; SDP/Liberal Alliance 1983-87; Liberal Democrat 1992 onwards.

Table 3.04: The Scottish National Party Vote 1929-2005

Election	Candidates	MPs Elected	Forfeited Deposits	Total votes	% of Scottish total
1929	2	0	2	3,313	0.2
1931	5	0	2	20,954	1.0
1935	8	0	5	29,517	1.3
1945	8	0	6	30,595	1.2
1950	3	0	3	9,708	0.4
1951	2	0	1	7,299	0.3
1955	2	0	1	12,112	0.5
1959	5	0	3	21,738	0.8
1964	15	0	12	64,044	2.4
1966	23	0	10	128,474	5.0
1970	65	1	43	306,802	11.4
1974(F)	70	7	7	633,180	21.9
1974(O)	71	11	0	839,617	30.4
1979	71	2	29	504,259	17.3
1983	72	2	53	331,975	11.8
1987	71	3	1	416,473	14.0
1992	72	3	0	629,564	21.5
1997	72	6	0	621,550	22.1
2001	72	5	0	464,314	20.1
2005	59	6	0	412,267	17.7

Table 3.05: The Plaid Cymru Vote 1929-2005

Election	Candidates	MPs Elected	Forfeited Deposits	Total votes	% of Welsh total
1929	1	0	1	609	0.0
1931	2	0	1	2,050	0.2
1935	1	0	1	2,534	0.3
1945	7	0	6	16,017	1.2
1950	7	0	6	17,580	1.2
1951	4	0	4	10,920	0.7
1955	11	0	7	45,119	3.1
1959	20	0	14	77,571	5.2
1964	23	0	21	69,507	4.8
1966	20	0	18	61,071	4.3
1970	36	0	25	175,016	11.5
1974(F)	36	2	26	171,374	10.8
1974(O)	36	3	26	166,321	10.8
1979	36	2	29	132,544	8.1
1983	38	2	32	125,309	7.8
1987	38	3	25	123,599	7.3
1992	35	4	20	154,947	8.9
1997	40	4	15	161,030	9.9
2001	40	4	5	195,893	14.3
2005	40	3	8	174,838	12.6

Table 3.06: The Social Democratic Party Vote 1983-1987

Election	Candidates	MPs Elected	Forfeited Deposits	Total votes	% of UK total
1983	311	6	6	3,570,834	11.6
1987	306	5	0	3,168,183	9.7

Table 3.07: The Liberal Party Vote 1983-1987

Election	Candidates	MPs Elected	Forfeited Deposits	Total votes	% of UK total
1983	322	17	5	4,210,115	13.7
1987	327	22	1	4,173,450	12.8

Table 3.08: The Green Party Vote 1979-2005[1]

Election	Candidates	MPs Elected	Forfeited Deposits	Total votes	% of UK total
1979	53	0	53	39,918	0.1
1983	108	0	108	53,848	0.2
1987	133	0	133	89,753	0.3
1992	256	0	256	171,927	0.5
1997	95	0	95	63,991	0.2
2001	145	0	135	166,477	0.6
2005	203	0	179	283,414	1.0

1. The Ecology Party formed in February 1974 changed its name to the Green Party in September 1985. The party fought just 3 seats in February 1974 and 4 in October 1974.

Table 3.09: The National Front Vote 1970-1992

Election	Candidates	MPs Elected	Forfeited Deposits	Total votes	% of UK total
1970	10	0	10	11,449	0.0
1974(F)	54	0	54	76,865	0.2
1974(O)	90	0	90	113,843	0.4
1979	303	0	303	191,719	0.6
1983	60	0	60	27,065	0.1
1987	0	0	0	-	-
1992	14	0	14	4,750	0.0

Table 3.10: The British National Party Vote 1992-2005

Election	Candidates	MPs Elected	Forfeited Deposits	Total votes	% of UK total
1992	13	0	13	7,005	0.0
1997	57	0	54	35,832	0.1
2001	33	0	28	47,129	0.2
2005	119	0	85	192,745	0.7

Table 3.11: The United Kingdom Independence Party Vote 1997-2005

Election	Candidates	MPs Elected	Forfeited Deposits	Total votes	% of UK total
1997	193	0	192	105,722	0.3
2001	428	0	422	390,563	1.5
2005	496	0	458	605,973	2.2

Table 3.12: Vote for Parties in Northern Ireland 1974(F)-2005

The Ulster Unionist Party Vote 1974-2005

Election	Candidates	MPs Elected	Forfeited Deposits	Total votes	% of NI total
1974(F)					
Anti-Assembly	7	7	0	232,103	32.3
Pro-Assembly	7	0	2	94,301	13.1
1974 (O)	7	6	0	256,065	36.5
1979	11	5	0	254,578	36.6
1983	16	11	1	259,952	34.0
1987	12	9	0	276,230	37.8
1992	13	9	0	271,049	34.5
1997	16	10	1	258,349	32.7
2001	17	6	0	216,839	26.8
2005	18	1	2	127,414	17.8

The Ulster Democratic Unionist Party Vote 1974-2005

Election	Candidates	MPs Elected	Forfeited Deposits	Total votes	% of NI total
1974(F)	2	1	0	58,656	8.2
1974 (O)	2	1	0	59,451	8.5
1979	5	3	2	70,975	10.2
1983	14	3	3	152,749	20.0
1987	4	3	0	85,642	11.7
1992	7	3	0	103,039	13.1
1997	9	2	0	107,348	13.6
2001	14	5	0	181,999	22.5
2005	18	9	0	241,856	33.7

The Social Democratic and Labour Party Vote 1974-2005

Election	Candidates	MPs Elected	Forfeited Deposits	Total votes	% of NI total
1974(F)	12	1	4	160,437	22.4
1974(O)	9	1	1	154,193	22.0
1979	9	1	3	126,325	18.2
1983	17	1	7	137,012	17.9
1987	13	3	0	154,087	21.1
1992	13	4	0	184,445	23.5
1997	18	3	3	190,814	24.1
2001	18	3	2	169,865	21.0
2005	18	3	2	125,626	17.5

Vote for Parties in Northern Ireland 1974(F)-2005 (contd.)

The Sinn Fein Party Vote 1983-2005

Election	Candidates	MPs Elected	Forfeited Deposits	Total votes	% of NI total
1983	14	1	7	102,701	13.4
1987	14	1	4	83,389	11.4
1992	14	0	5	78,291	10.0
1997	17	2	4	126,921	16.1
2001	18	4	4	175,933	21.7
2005	18	5	4	174,530	24.3

The Alliance Party Vote 1974-2005

Election	Candidates	MPs Elected	Forfeited Deposits	Total votes	% of NI total
1974(F)	3	0	2	22,660	3.2
1974(O)	5	0	1	44,644	6.4
1979	12	0	8	82,892	11.9
1983	12	0	6	61,275	8.0
1987	16	0	5	72,671	10.0
1992	16	0	5	68,665	8.7
1997	17	0	6	62,972	8.0
2001	10	0	5	28,999	3.6
2005	12	0	5	28,291	3.9

Table 4.01: Electorate and Turnout at General Elections 1832-2005

	Total Electorate	Electorate in uncontested seats	% of Total	Age of Register in mths[1]	Turnout%[2]
1832					
England	609,772	132,859	21.8	-	68.1
Wales	41,763	30,385	72.8	-	76.2
Scotland	64,447	14,047	21.8	-	85.0
Ireland	90,068	25,314	28.1	-	73.9
Universities	6,888	4,815	69.9	-	82.2
United Kingdom	**812,938**	**207,420**	**25.5**	**4**	**70.4**
1835					
England	625,255	263,517	42.1	-	65.1
Wales	42,426	29,427	69.4	-	75.1
Scotland	72,778	23,744	32.6	-	70.9
Ireland	98,402	42,494	43.2	-	57.1
Universities	6,915	6,915	100.0	-	-
United Kingdom	**845,776**	**366,097**	**43.3**	**5**	**65.0**
1837					
England	741,374	234,711	31.7	-	64.0
Wales	49,706	27,800	55.9	-	71.7
Scotland	84,302	31,704	37.6	-	68.0
Ireland	122,073	57,822	47.4	-	55.0
Universities	7,209	5,109	70.9	-	44.7
United Kingdom	**1,004,664**	**357,146**	**35.6**	**12**	**63.6**
1841					
England	777,560	394,005	50.7	-	64.1
Wales	54,653	43,429	79.5	-	68.7
Scotland	83,632	47,611	56.9	-	62.2
Ireland	94,065	49,632	52.8	-	57.0
Universities	7,469	7,469	100.0	-	-
United Kingdom	**1,017,379**	**542,146**	**53.3**	**11**	**63.4**
1847					
England	828,819	489,058	59.0	-	57.3
Wales	55,251	45,044	81.5	-	65.1
Scotland	88,792	56,520	63.7	-	51.1
Ireland	124,825	66,113	53.0	-	29.2
Universities	8,827	-	-	-	59.1
United Kingdom	**1,106,514**	**656,735**	**59.4**	**12**	**53.4**
1852					
England	858,081	375,324	43.8	-	57.7
Wales	54,858	41,669	76.0	-	74.5
Scotland	98,967	54,232	54.8	-	45.5
Ireland	163,546	54,880	33.6	-	62.3
Universities	9,237	5,763	62.4	-	46.5
United Kingdom	**1,184,689**	**531,868**	**44.9**	**11**	**57.9**

Electorate and Turnout at General Elections 1832-2005 (contd.)

	Total Electorate	*Electorate in uncontested seats*	*% of Total*	*Age of Register in mths[1]*	*Turnout%[2]*
1857					
England	878,803	432,596	49.2	-	57.3
Wales	55,686	44,889	80.6	-	68.1
Scotland	100,206	60,049	59.9	-	66.3
Ireland	191,045	72,977	38.2	-	61.8
Universities	9,790	8,090	82.6	-	59.1
United Kingdom	**1,235,530**	**618,601**	**50.1**	**8**	**58.9**
1859					
England	900,128	512,747	57.0	-	61.9
Wales	56,033	50,078	89.4	-	73.1
Scotland	105,608	93,737	88.8	-	65.6
Ireland	200,242	134,147	67.0	-	73.2
Universities	9,889	9,889	100.0	-	-
United Kingdom	**1,271,900**	**800,598**	**62.9**	**9**	**63.7**
1865					
England	970,096	413,250	42.6	-	62.0
Wales	61,656	53,542	86.8	-	76.0
Scotland	105,069	63,484	60.4	-	70.7
Ireland	202,683	119,709	59.1	-	59.2
Universities	10,900	5,184	48.7	-	84.5
United Kingdom	**1,350,404**	**655,169**	**48.5**	**12**	**62.5**
1868					
England	1,880,368	313,183	16.7	-	67.6
Wales	127,385	53,303	41.8	-	74.8
Scotland	231,376	87,798	37.9	-	74.1
Ireland	223,400	149,095	66.7	-	67.2
Universities	22,184	10,785	48.6	-	88.4
United Kingdom	**2,484,713**	**614,164**	**24.7**	**4**	**68.5**
1874					
England	2,097,206	495,141	23.6	-	65.8
Wales	137,143	41,805	30.5	-	71.3
Scotland	271,240	62,512	23.0	-	70.9
Ireland	222,622	40,117	18.0	-	64.0
Universities	24,931	24,931	100.0	-	-
United Kingdom	**2,753,142**	**664,506**	**24.1**	**6**	**66.4**
1880					
England	2,338,809	291,245	12.5	-	71.3
Wales	149,841	48,668	32.5	-	78.3
Scotland	293,581	53,675	18.3	-	80.0
Ireland	229,204	34,953	15.2	-	67.3
Universities	28,615	14,733	51.5	-	80.5
United Kingdom	**3,040,050**	**443,274**	**14.6**	**8**	**72.2**

Electorate and Turnout at General Elections 1832-2005 (contd.)

	Total Electorate	Electorate in uncontested seats	% of Total	Age of Register in mths[1]	Turnout%[2]
1885					
England	4,094,674	42,595	1.0	-	81.9
Wales	282,242	33,095	11.7	-	82.2
Scotland	560,580	30,462	0.1	-	82.0
Ireland	737,965	146,461	19.9	-	75.0
Universities	32,569	25,709	78.9	-	77.2
United Kingdom	**5,708,030**	**278,322**	**4.9**	**4**	**81.2**
1886					
England	4,094,674	1,265,691	30.9	-	74.1
Wales	282,242	107,350	38.0	-	74.5
Scotland	560,580	80,772	14.4	-	72.3
Ireland	737,965	493,550	66.9	-	79.8
Universities	32,569	25,835	79.3	-	55.8
United Kingdom	**5,708,030**	**1,973,198**	**34.6**	**11½**	**74.2**
1892					
England	4,478,524	301,868	6.7	-	78.7
Wales	314,647	40,010	12.7	-	75.6
Scotland	589,520	-	-	-	78.3
Ireland	740,536	171,499	23.2	-	67.7
Universities	37,314	32,962	88.3	-	56.2
United Kingdom	**6,160,541**	**546,339**	**89.0**	**11½**	**77.4**
1895					
England	4,620,320	1,195,625	25.9	-	79.2
Wales	322,784	19,296	6.0	-	79.3
Scotland	616,178	35,714	5.8	-	76.3
Ireland	732,046	442,807	60.5	-	72.7
Universities	39,191	39,191	100.0	-	-
United Kingdom	**6,330,519**	**1,732,633**	**27.4**	**12**	**78.4**
1900					
England	4,929,485	1,647,537	33.4	-	76.0
Wales	340,290	114,552	33.7	-	76.4
Scotland	661,748	33,260	5.0	-	75.3
Ireland	757,849	524,739	69.2	-	60.9
Universities	41,563	41,563	100.0	-	-
United Kingdom	**6,730,935**	**2,361,651**	**35.1**	**14½**	**75.1**
1906					
England	5,416,537	227,095	4.2	-	83.6
Wales	387,535	148,487	38.3	-	82.6
Scotland	728,725	7,464	1.0	-	80.9
Ireland	686,661	522,612	76.1	-	82.1
Universities	45,150	11,290	25.0	-	67.0
United Kingdom	**7,264,608**	**916,948**	**12.6**	**6**	**83.2**

Electorate and Turnout at General Elections 1832-2005 (contd.)

	Total Electorate	*Electorate in uncontested seats*	*% of Total*	*Age of Register in mths[1]*	*Turnout%[2]*
1910(J)					
England	5,774,892	54,348	0.9	-	87.7
Wales	425,744	-	-	-	84.9
Scotland	762,184	-	-	-	84.7
Ireland	683,767	420,304	61.5	-	80.3
Universities	48,154	19,060	39.6	-	71.3
United Kingdom	**7,694,741**	**493,712**	**6.4**	**6**	**86.8**
1910(D)					
England	5,774,892	1,025,512	17.8	-	82.1
Wales	425,744	123,423	29.0	-	78.3
Scotland	779,012	90,057	11.6	-	81.8
Ireland	683,767	419,489	61.4	-	74.8
Universities	46,566	40,496	87.9	-	73.1
United Kingdom	**7,709,981**	**1,698,977**	**22.0**	**16 ½ [3]**	**81.6**
1918[4]					
England	16,021,600	2,023,222	12.6	-	55.7
Wales	1,170,974	367,641	31.4	-	65.9
Scotland	2,205,383	216,015	9.8	-	55.1
Ireland	1,926,274	474,778	24.6	-	69.5
Universities	68,091	-	-	-	60.2
United Kingdom	**21,392,322**	**3,081,656**	**14.4**	**5**	**57.2**
1922					
England	16,726,739	1,272,920	7.6	-	72.8
Wales	1,235,579	111,898	9.1	-	79.4
Scotland	2,231,532	82,053	3.7	-	70.4
N. Ireland	608,877	447,468	73.5	-	77.2
Universities	71,729	32,355	45.1	-	65.9
United Kingdom	**20,874,456**	**1,946,694**	**9.3**	**5**	**73.0**
1923					
England	17,079,822	951,223	5.6	-	71.1
Wales	1,258,973	166,044	13.2	-	77.3
Scotland	2,250,826	105,500	4.7	-	67.9
N. Ireland	615,320	404,818	65.8	-	76.5
Universities	78,120	34,109	43.6	-	72.6
United Kingdom	**21,283,061**	**1,661,694**	**7.8**	**6**	**71.1**
1924					
England	17,471,109	611,975	3.5	-	77.4
Wales	1,287,543	301,355	23.4	-	80.0
Scotland	2,279,893	72,258	3.2	-	75.1
N. Ireland	610,064	87,744	14.4	-	66.7
Universities	82,379	3,104	3.8	-	66.9
United Kingdom	**21,730,988**	**1,076,436**	**5.0**	**4½**	**77.0**

Electorate and Turnout at General Elections 1832-2005 (contd.)

	Total Electorate	Electorate in uncontested seats	% of Total	Age of Register in mths[1]	Turnout%[2]
1929[5]					
England	23,424,580	129,401	0.6	-	76.6
Wales	1,598,509	-	-	-	82.4
Scotland	2,940,456	-	-	-	73.5
N. Ireland	771,946	199,989	25.9	-	63.8
Universities	119,257	3,361	2.8	-	65.8
United Kingdom	**28,854,748**	**332,751**	**1.2**	**6**	**76.3**
1931					
England	24,423,766	1,660,748	6.8	-	76.1
Wales	1,625,118	251,865	15.5	-	79.3
Scotland	2,992,433	291,440	9.7	-	77.4
N. Ireland	773,302	521,178	67.4	-	74.5
Universities	137,742	97,011	70.4	-	69.8
United Kingdom	**29,952,361**	**2,822,242**	**9.4**	**5**	**76.4**
1935					
England	25,618,571	811,794	3.2	-	70.7
Wales	1,669,793	529,638	31.7	-	76.4
Scotland	3,115,917	42,079	1.4	-	72.6
N. Ireland	805,220	403,947	50.2	-	72.0
Universities	164,948	30,663	18.6	-	57.9
United Kingdom	**31,374,449**	**1,818,121**	**5.8**	**5½**	**71.1**
1945					
England	27,045,729	21,325	0.1	-	73.4
Wales	1,798,199	39,652	2.2	-	75.7
Scotland	3,343,120	-	-	-	69.0
N. Ireland	835,980	68,752	8.2	-	67.4
Universities	217,363	-	-	-	53.3
United Kingdom	**33,240,391**	**129,729**	**0.4**	**5**	**72.8**
1950					
England	28,374,288	-	-	-	84.4
Wales	1,802,356	-	-	-	84.8
Scotland	3,370,190	-	-	-	80.9
N. Ireland	865,421	140,501	16.2	-	77.4
Great Britain	33,546,834	-	-	-	84.1
United Kingdom	**34,412,255**	**140,501**	**0.4**	**8½**	**83.9**
1951					
England	28,813,343	-	-	-	82.7
Wales	1,812,664	-	-	-	84.4
Scotland	3,421,419	-	-	-	81.2
N. Ireland	871,905	292,271	33.5	-	79.9
Great Britain	34,047,426	-	-	-	82.6
United Kingdom	**34,919,331**	**292,271**	**0.8**	**11**	**82.6**

Electorate and Turnout at General Elections 1832-2005 (contd.)

	Total Electorate	Electorate in uncontested seats	% of Total	Age of Register in mths[1]	Turnout%[2]
1955					
England	28,790,285	-	-	-	76.9
Wales	1,801,217	-	-	-	79.6
Scotland	3,387,536	-	-	-	75.1
N. Ireland	873,141	-	-	-	74.1
Great Britain	33,979,038	-	-	-	76.9
United Kingdom	**34,852,179**	-	-	7½	**76.8**
1959					
England	29,303,126	-	-	-	78.9
Wales	1,805,686	-	-	-	82.6
Scotland	3,413,732	-	-	-	78.1
N. Ireland	874,760	-	-	-	65.9
Great Britain	34,522,544	-	-	-	79.0
United Kingdom	**35,397,304**	-	-	12	**78.7**
1964					
England	29,804,627	-	-	-	77.0
Wales	1,805,454	-	-	-	80.1
Scotland	3,393,421	-	-	-	77.6
N. Ireland	890,552	-	-	-	71.7
Great Britain	35,003,502	-	-	-	77.2
United Kingdom	**35,894,054**	-	-	12	**77.1**
1966					
England	29,894,141	-	-	-	75.9
Wales	1,800,925	-	-	-	79.0
Scotland	3,359,891	-	-	-	76.0
N. Ireland	902,288	-	-	-	66.1
Great Britain	35,054,957	-	-	-	76.1
United Kingdom	**35,957,245**	-	-	5½	**75.8**
1970[6]					
England	32,737,025	-	-	-	71.4
Wales	1,958,778	-	-	-	77.4
Scotland	3,629,017	-	-	-	74.1
N. Ireland	1,017,193	-	-	-	76.6
Great Britain	38,324,820	-	-	-	71.9
United Kingdom	**39,342,013**	-	-	8	**72.0**
1974(F)[7]					
England	33,077,571	-	-	-	79.0
Wales	1,993,516	-	-	-	80.0
Scotland	3,655,621	-	-	-	79.0
N. Ireland	1,027,155	-	-	-	69.9
Great Britain	38,726,708	-	-	-	79.1
United Kingdom	**39,753,863**	-	-	4½	**78.8**

Electorate and Turnout at General Elections 1832-2005 (contd.)

	Total Electorate	Electorate in uncontested seats	% of Total	Age of Register in mths[1]	Turnout%[2]
1974(O)[7]					
England	33,341,371	-	-	-	72.6
Wales	2,008,284	-	-	-	76.6
Scotland	3,686,792	-	-	-	74.8
N. Ireland	1,036,523	-	-	-	67.7
Great Britain	39,036,447	-	-	-	73.0
United Kingdom	**40,072,970**	-	-	12	**72.8**
1979[7]					
England	34,211,471	-	-	-	75.9
Wales	2,061,109	-	-	-	79.4
Scotland	3,795,865	-	-	-	76.8
N. Ireland	1,027,204	-	-	-	67.7
Great Britain	40,068,445	-	-	-	76.2
United Kingdom	**41,095,649**	-	-	7	**76.0**
1983[7]					
England	35,143,479	-	-	-	72.5
Wales	2,113,855	-	-	-	76.1
Scotland	3,886,899	-	-	-	72.7
N. Ireland	1,048,766	-	-	-	72.9
Great Britain	41,144,233	-	-	-	72.7
United Kingdom	**42,192,999**	-	-	8	**72.7**
1987[7]					
England	35,987,776	-	-	-	75.4
Wales	2,151,352	-	-	-	78.9
Scotland	3,952,465	-	-	-	75.1
N. Ireland	1,089,160	-	-	-	67.0
Great Britain	42,091,593	-	-	-	75.5
United Kingdom	**43,180,753**	-	-	8	**75.3**
1992[8]					
England	36,071,067	-	-	-	78.0
Wales	2,194,218	-	-	-	79.7
Scotland	3,885,131	-	-	-	75.5
N. Ireland	1,124,900	-	-	-	69.8
Great Britain	42,150,416	-	-	-	77.9
United Kingdom	**43,275,316**	-	-	6	**77.7**
1997[8]					
England	36,516,012	-	-	-	71.4
Wales	2,203,059	-	-	-	73.5
Scotland	3,949,112	-	-	-	71.3
N. Ireland	1,177,969	-	-	-	67.1
Great Britain	42,668,183	-	-	-	71.5
United Kingdom	**43,846,152**	-	-	7	**71.4**

Electorate and Turnout at General Elections 1832-2005 (contd.)

	Total Electorate	Electorate in uncontested seats	% of Total	Age of Register in mths[1]	Turnout%[2]
2001[9]					
England	36,991,780	-	-	-	59.1
Wales	2,236,143	-	-	-	61.4
Scotland	3,984,306	-	-	-	58.1
N. Ireland	1,191,009	-	-	-	68.0
Great Britain	43,212,229	-	-	-	59.1
United Kingdom	**44,403,238**	-	-	-[10]	**59.4**
2005[9]					
England	37,041,396	-	-	-	61.3
Wales	2,224,650	-	-	-	62.6
Scotland	3,839,900	-	-	-	60.8
N. Ireland	1,139,993	-	-	-	62.9
Great Britain	43,105,946	-	-	-	61.3
United Kingdom	**44,245,939**	-	-	-[10]	**61.4**

1. This figure is based on the qualifying date in England and Wales. The qualifying date in the other parts of the United Kingdom sometimes varied by a few weeks from that in England and Wales.
2. This figure makes allowance, prior to 1950, for the multi-member seats. See Introductory Notes.
3. In Scotland the election was contested on the November 1910 Register which had a qualifying date of July 31.
4. Those who had served in the war were enfranchised at 19 years of age. Women were enfranchised at 30 years of age.
5. Extension of the franchise to women at 21 years of age.
6. Extension of the franchise to persons at 18 years of age.
7. Estimated figures, see Introductory Notes and Table 4.07. The formula used was number of "dated names" multiplied by 12/364 for February 1974; 236/364 for October 1974 etc.
8. These figures are based on a combination of estimates (as above) and the exact 'on the day' electorate as supplied by a number of Returning Officers.
9. Figures as supplied by Returning Officers for 'on the day' electorate.
10. Under the Representation of the People Act 2000 electors are able to register at any time of the year. Each local authority publishes a monthly list of changes to take account of house moves, deaths, and other amendments. In practice, applications to be on the register need to be received anything from 5 to 8 weeks before an election. This means that when a General Election is called it has usually been too late to apply to vote. The Electoral Administration Act 2006 will allow applications to register to vote closer to the election date.

Table 4.02: Unadjusted and Adjusted Turnout at General Elections 1950-1997*

	Unadjusted Turnout		Adjusted Turnout	
	GB	UK	GB	UK
1950	84.1	83.9	87.7	87.5
1951	82.6	82.6	89.3	89.2
1955	76.9	76.8	79.5	79.5
1959	79.0	78.7	85.4	85.0
1964	77.2	77.1	83.4	83.3
1966	76.1	75.8	77.4	77.1
1970	71.9	72.0	75.0	75.1
1974(F)	79.1	78.8	79.8	79.5

Unadjusted and Adjusted Turnout at General Elections 1950-1997* (contd.)

	Unadjusted Turnout		Adjusted Turnout	
	GB	*UK*	*GB*	*UK*
1974(O)	73.0	72.8	78.8	78.7
1979	76.2	76.0	78.8	78.6
1983	72.7	72.7	75.8	75.9
1987	75.5	75.3	78.8	78.6
1992	77.9	77.7	79.9	79.7
1997	71.5	71.4	73.9	73.9

*   For an explanation of these calculations see the entry under 'Electorate' in the Introductory Notes. This adjustment is no longer relevant following the introduction of 'rolling registration'.

Table 4.03: The Electorate 1945-2006

Year	Total Electorate	Service voters qualification	Full age attainers[1]
ENGLAND			
1945[2]	27,544,167	2,602,934	-
1946	28,865,697	955,918	-
1947	29,376,680	451,951	-
1948	29,715,892	268,138	-
1949	28,371,842	121,724	-
1950	28,408,683	157,261	-
1951	28,813,384	215,403	220,882
1952	28,896,772	269,101	225,306
1953	28,904,032	271,175	213,443
1954	28,923,119	276,609	200,483
1955	29,018,827	289,542	229,113
1956	29,117,160	292,370	234,764
1957	29,173,270	300,946	230,576
1958	29,237,876	293,711	236,924
1959	29,303,126	282,814	244,756
1960	29,415,941	289,451	231,749
1961	29,469,255	269,531	237,341
1962	29,589,260	223,226	227,295
1963	29,684,814	194,386	256,941
1964	29,804,374	192,211	283,200
1965	30,025,849	195,915	293,310
1966	30,185,780	196,583	293,698
1967	30,290,803	194,008	304,896
1968	30,570,603	190,401	399,448
1969	30,819,095	177,872	359,693
1970[3]	32,960,554	122,349	379,169
1971	33,186,051	79,385	432,397
1972	33,316,464	90,956	431,396
1973	33,412,961	87,435	428,833
1974	33,492,353	86,064	428,656
1975	33,755,747	104,057	424,285
1976	33,928,554	99,511	456,757
1977	34,084,807	95,255	461,341

The Electorate 1945-2006 (contd.)

Year	Total Electorate	Service voters qualification	Full age attainers[1]
ENGLAND			
1978	34,279,940	164,766	479,897
1979	34,611,408	208,255	504,984
1980	34,831,958	206,111	507,794
1981	35,068,122	205,743	585,568
1982	35,363,733	212,321	629,028
1983	35,569,726	234,301	617,759
1984	35,800,362	237,609	605,954
1985	35,937,374	237,428	570,649
1986	36,158,417	235,466	575,955
1987	36,393,203	236,549	593,024
1988	36,448,414	232,262	576,745
1989	36,364,782	231,683	542,196
1990	36,388,575	225,460	522,100
1991	36,302,099	229,483	466,137
1992	36,435,873	231,229	456,738
1993	36,411,280	223,185	426,673
1994	36,455,151	210,971	412,610
1995	36,544,929	192,593	395,356
1996	36,626,853	178,944	413,485
1997	36,806,467	171,054	432,063
1998	36,885,805	167,216	430,906
1999	36,947,525	160,922	418,813
2000	36,994,211	n/a	390,000
2001	37,101,328	130,622	379,665
2002[6]	37,296,327	n/a	396,090
2003	37,179,095	44,838	409,247
2004	36,972,519	27,575	390,664
2005	37,043,608	18,937	392,536
2006	37,151,991	17,871	412,661
WALES			
1945[2]	1,824,517	146,597	-
1946	1,871,665	59,341	-
1947	1,893,824	26,134	-
1948	1,913,969	15,866	-
1949	1,802,124	5,610	-
1950	1,797,984	7,482	-
1951	1,812,676	10,927	12,719
1952	1,813,666	13,895	12,844
1953	1,813,088	14,616	11,986
1954	1,814,300	14,548	11,746
1955	1,815,011	15,412	13,794
1956	1,810,769	15,504	13,656
1957	1,807,892	16,731	13,217
1958	1,808,422	16,379	13,540
1959	1,805,686	15,943	13,932
1960	1,803,777	15,920	13,715

The Electorate 1945-2006 (contd.)

Year	Total Electorate	Service voters qualification	Full age attainers[1]
WALES			
1961	1,801,781	15,035	13,216
1962	1,804,483	11,699	13,341
1963	1,805,495	9,734	14,722
1964	1,805,495	9,846	15,516
1965	1,813,203	10,230	15,438
1966	1,816,565	10,217	15,635
1967	1,817,616	10,390	16,081
1968	1,827,670	10,285	20,331
1969	1,842,335	9,863	19,587
1970[3]	1,971,629	5,764	22,180
1971	1,990,094	3,738	25,230
1972	1,997,400	4,298	24,304
1973	2,005,749	4,089	23,647
1974	2,016,741	3,901	23,999
1975	2,032,966	4,705	24,271
1976	2,046,444	4,767	26,153
1977	2,055,172	4,860	26,176
1978	2,065,019	7,222	27,585
1979	2,083,772	9,290	28,629
1980	2,098,552	9,129	28,363
1981	2,115,093	9,204	34,789
1982	2,127,935	9,961	36,719
1983	2,138,385	10,856	35,546
1984	2,148,484	11,264	34,931
1985	2,142,609	11,379	32,320
1986	2,160,147	11,569	34,694
1987	2,175,168	12,101	34,814
1988	2,180,269	12,518	34,233
1989	2,194,625	12,970	32,391
1990	2,207,542	13,095	30,456
1991	2,207,283	13,574	26,753
1992	2,218,551	14,399	27,408
1993	2,222,624	14,165	25,707
1994	2,222,091	13,460	25,642
1995	2,220,290	12,266	23,839
1996	2,217,893	11,409	25,566
1997	2,222,533	11,019	27,516
1998	2,230,452	11,109	25,977
1999	2,227,571	11,159	27,148
2000	2,232,474	n/a	27,150
2001	2,238,211	9,064	26,910
2002[6]	2,235,666	n/a	25,462
2003	2,225,599	4,284	25,814
2004	2,219,973	2,859	23,590
2005	2,233,467	2,185	25,136
2006	2,236,808	1,157	25,200

The Electorate 1945-2006 (contd.)

Year	Total Electorate	Service voters qualification	Full age attainers[1]
SCOTLAND			
1945[2]	3,451,935	323,230	-
1946	3,584,289	115,431	-
1947	3,614,201	54,583	-
1948	3,642,497	31,006	-
1949	3,370,320	10,831	-
1950	3,404,101	15,052	-
1951	3,421,433	22,388	26,903
1952	3,413,792	28,151	24,079
1953	3,408,777	28,928	23,457
1954	3,407,253	30,079	21,804
1955	3,414,592	31,861	27,054
1956	3,410,718	32,408	26,951
1957	3,410,152	34,315	24,827
1958	3,407,801	33,303	25,033
1959	3,413,732	32,128	25,414
1960	3,414,572	31,488	24,414
1961	3,402,449	30,364	24,681
1962	3,404,172	25,474	23,992
1963	3,397,839	21,064	24,983
1964	3,393,391	21,432	27,583
1965	3,389,908	21,795	25,348
1966	3,385,710	21,503	25,833
1967	3,374,151	21,209	26,396
1968	3,387,905	20,782	35,691
1969	3,398,392	19,650	31,406
1970[3]	3,659,107	12,347	47,231
1971	3,685,283	7,585	49,234
1972	3,691,007	8,955	49,479
1973	3,688,186	8,907	49,029
1974	3,704,631	8,327	50,641
1975	3,733,232	10,053	49,488
1976	3,764,194	9,867	53,654
1977	3,786,051	9,289	49,709
1978	3,809,091	15,240	52,672
1979	3,837,019	19,828	51,973
1980	3,860,551	19,572	58,285
1981	3,885,462	19,910	64,720
1982	3,913,385	20,829	70,260
1983	3,934,220	23,175	68,572
1984	3,957,276	23,890	68,636
1985	3,967,943	24,696	65,940
1986	3,986,654	24,762	63,739
1987	3,994,893	25,300	61,965
1988	3,967,377	24,802	60,254
1989	3,932,911	24,623	58,618
1990	3,936,704	24,581	52,260

The Electorate 1945-2006 (contd.)

Year	Total Electorate	Service voters qualification	Full age attainers[1]
SCOTLAND			
1991	3,914,590	25,220	47,275
1992	3,928,996	25,475	47,732
1993	3,931,429	24,681	45,786
1994	3,947,157	23,431	44,475
1995	3,961,566	22,099	44,065
1996	3,963,072	19,797	44,873
1997	3,984,406	18,984	48,064
1998	3,992,502	20,208	47,516
1999	4,011,450	18,686	51,691
2000	3,992,034	18,226	47,413
2001	4,001,018	17,705	48,313
2002[6]	3,966,801	16,289	47,188
2003	3,887,059	3,067	48,640
2004	3,857,997	2,100	47,031
2005	3,857,631	1,707	45,790
2006	3,861,207	1,576	47,504
NORTHERN IRELAND			
1945[2]	851,417	25,821	-
1946	864,709	10,879	-
1947	865,558	6,484	-
1948	874,342	5,095	-
1949	865,421	1,388	-
1950	865,364	2,768	-
1951	871,905	4,008	4,107
1952	873,596	6,609	4,017
1953	874,958	5,096	3,834
1954	874,701	4,348	3,858
1955	877,051	5,887	3,876
1956	875,384	5,178	4,031
1957	873,987	4,415	4,074
1958	872,647	5,573	4,080
1959	874,739	4,633	4,223
1960	880,202	5,382	4,392
1961	880,149	6,184	3,702
1962	883,693	5,354	3,556
1963	888,490	4,916	3,877
1964	891,043	5,532	4,258
1965	899,427	5,186	4,462
1966	906,634	4,942	4,333
1967	909,841	- [4]	- [4]
1968	916,866	3,810	4,607
1969	926,549	3,516	4,404
1970[3]	1,025,215	1,728	15,529
1971	1,033,801	1,433	12,922
1972	1,033,608	1,282	12,606

The Electorate 1945-2006 (contd.)

Year	Total Electorate	Service voters qualification	Full age attainers[1]
NORTHERN IRELAND			
1973	1,032,034	1,211	12,096
1974	1,041,886	1,227	15,227
1975	1,041,117	1,497	15,978
1976	1,033,240	1,123	15,511
1977	1,032,914	885	15,968
1978	1,033,702	1,507	16,152
1979	1,040,506	1,861	16,804
1980	1,049,466	1,783	15,739
1981	1,053,332	1,776	16,472
1982	1,057,263	2,268	18,197
1983	1,061,185	2,797	17,997
1984	1,077,605	3,157	20,135
1985	1,082,609	3,196	18,543
1986	1,087,399	3,397	17,780
1987	1,103,111	3,344	20,384
1988	1,109,011	3,346	20,212
1989	1,120,508	3,438	21,995
1990	1,130,602	3,358	22,042
1991	1,132,811	3,412	20,728
1992	1,141,466	3,456	20,083
1993	1,153,204	3,393	17,955
1994	1,162,335	3,132	17,460
1995	1,169,423	2,770	16,790
1996	1,176,927	2,366	17,150
1997	1,190,198	2,224	18,440
1998	1,188,034	1,972	18,378
1999	1,202,339	1,995	18,587
2000	1,204,721	n/a	16,889
2001	1,205,097	n/a	16,977
2002[6]	1,196,970	n/a	17,890
2003[7]	1,071,600	n/a	8,875
2004	1,067,564	n/a	5,953
2005	1,045,537	n/a	9,952
2006	1,153,409	n/a	7,998
GREAT BRITAIN			
1945[2]	32,820,619	3,072,761	-
1946	34,321,651	1,130,690	-
1947	34,884,705	532,668	-
1948	35,272,358	315,010	-
1949	33,544,286	138,165	-
1950	33,610,768	179,795	-
1951	34,047,493	248,718	260,504
1952	34,124,230	311,147	262,229
1953	34,125,897	314,719	248,886
1954	34,144,672	321,236	234,033

The Electorate 1945-2006 (contd.)

Year	Total Electorate	Service voters qualification	Full age attainers[1]
GREAT BRITAIN			
1955	34,248,430	336,815	269,961
1956	34,338,647	340,282	275,371
1957	34,391,314	351,992	268,620
1958	34,454,099	343,393	275,497
1959	34,522,544	330,885	284,102
1960	34,634,290	336,859	269,878
1961	34,673,485	314,930	275,238
1962	34,797,915	260,399	264,628
1963	34,886,085	225,184	296,646
1964	35,003,260	223,489	326,299
1965	35,228,960	227,696	334,096
1966	35,388,055	228,303	335,166
1967	35,482,570	225,607	347,373
1968	35,786,178	221,468	455,470
1969	36,059,822	207,385	410,686
1970[3]	38,591,290	140,460	448,580
1971	38,861,428	90,708	506,861
1972	39,004,871	104,209	505,179
1973	39,106,896	100,431	501,509
1974	39,213,725	98,292	503,296
1975	39,521,945	118,815	498,044
1976	39,739,192	114,145	536,564
1977	39,926,030	109,404	537,226
1978	40,154,050	187,228	560,154
1979	40,532,199	237,373	585,586
1980	40,791,061	234,812	594,442
1981	41,068,677	234,857	685,077
1982	41,405,053	243,111	736,007
1983	41,642,331	268,332	721,877
1984	41,906,122	272,763	709,521
1985	42,047,926	273,503	668,909
1986	42,305,218	271,797	676,388
1987	42,563,264	273,950	689,803
1988	42,596,060	269,582	671,232
1989	42,492,318	269,276	633,205
1990	42,532,821	263,136	604,816
1991	42,423,972	268,277	540,165
1992	42,583,420	271,103	531,878
1993	42,565,333	262,031	498,166
1994	42,624,399	247,862	482,727
1995	42,726,785	226,958	463,260
1996	42,807,818	210,150	483,924
1997	43,013,406	201,057	507,643
1998	43,108,759	198,533	504,399
1999	43,186,546	195,767	497,652
2000	43,218,719	n/a	464,563

The Electorate 1945-2006 (contd.)

Year	Total Electorate	Service voters qualification	Full age attainers[1]
GREAT BRITAIN			
2001	43,340,557	157,391	454,888
2002[6]	43,498,794	n/a	468,740
2003	43,291,753	52,189	483,701
2004	43,050,489	32,534	461,285
2005	43,134,706	22,829	463,462
2006	43,250,006	20,604	485,365
UNITED KINGDOM			
1945[2]	33,672,036	3,098,582	-
1946	35,186,360	1,141,569	-
1947	35,750,263	539,152	-
1948	36,146,700	320,105	-
1949	34,409,707	139,553	-
1950	34,476,132	182,563	-
1951	34,919,398	252,726	264,611
1952	34,997,826	317,756	266,246
1953	35,000,855	319,815	252,720
1954	35,019,373	325,584	237,891
1955	35,125,481	342,702	273,837
1956	35,214,031	345,460	279,402
1957	35,265,301	356,407	272,694
1958	35,326,746	348,966	279,577
1959	35,397,283	335,518	288,325
1960	35,514,492	342,241	274,270
1961	35,553,634	321,114	278,940
1962	35,681,608	265,753	268,184
1963	35,774,575	230,100	300,523
1964	35,894,303	229,021	330,557
1965	36,128,387	232,882	338,558
1966	36,294,689	233,245	339,499
1967	36,392,411	225,607[5]	347,373[5]
1968	36,703,044	225,278	460,077
1969	36,986,371	210,901	415,090
1970[3]	39,616,505	142,188	464,109
1971	39,895,229	92,141	519,783
1972	40,038,479	105,491	517,785
1973	40,138,930	101,642	513,605
1974	40,255,611	99,519	518,523
1975	40,563,062	120,312	514,022
1976	40,772,432	115,268	552,075
1977	40,958,944	110,289	553,194
1978	41,187,752	188,735	576,306
1979	41,572,705	239,234	602,390
1980	41,840,527	236,595	610,181
1981	42,122,009	236,633	701,549
1982	42,462,316	245,379	754,204

The Electorate 1945-2006 (contd.)

Year	Total Electorate	Service voters qualification	Full age attainers[1]
UNITED KINGDOM			
1983	42,703,516	271,129	739,874
1984	42,983,727	275,920	729,656
1985	43,130,535	276,699	687,452
1986	43,392,617	275,194	694,168
1987	43,666,375	277,294	710,187
1988	43,705,071	272,928	691,444
1989	43,612,826	272,714	655,200
1990	43,663,423	266,494	626,858
1991	43,556,783	271,689	560,893
1992	43,724,886	274,559	551,961
1993	43,718,537	265,424	516,121
1994	43,786,734	250,994	500,187
1995	43,896,208	229,728	480,050
1996	43,984,745	212,516	501,074
1997	44,203,604	203,281	526,083
1998	44,296,793	200,505	522,777
1999	44,388,885	197,762	516,239
2000	44,423,440	n/a	481,452
2001	44,545,654	n/a	471,865
2002[6]	44,695,764	n/a	486,630
2003	44,363,353	n/a	492,576
2004	44,118,053	n/a	467,238
2005	44,180,243	n/a	473,414
2006	44,403,415	n/a	493,363

1. From 1951-69 this figure relates to the number of persons attaining full age (21) after the qualifying date for the Register and before June 16 (April 14 in N. Ireland) who were able to vote at elections where polling took place after October 1. From 1970 those attaining full age during the currency of the Register had their date of birth given in the Register and they could vote from that date.

2. The register published on October 15. In subsequent years until 2002 the Register came into effect on 16 February.

3. Extension of franchise to persons at 18 years of age.

4. Figures not available.

5. Excluding figures for Northern Ireland which are not available.

6. From 2002 onwards the figures refer to the Register published on 1 December of the previous year. The Representation of the People Act 2000 allowed those with a service qualification to register at their home address in the usual way. A fall in the number of 'service voters' followed.

7. The fall in electorate in Northern Ireland followed the introduction of an individual as opposed to household-based registration system. This system also made the identification of 'categories' of electors redundant.

Sources:

England and Wales; *Registrar-General's Statistical Reviews of England and Wales, Part 2, Tables.* 1945-1973.

Electoral Statistics (Office of Population Censuses and Surveys/National Statistics), 1974 onwards.

Scotland; *Registrar-General for Scotland, Annual Report, Part 2, Population and Vital Statistics.*

Northern Ireland; Ministry of Home Affairs, 1945-72; Chief Electoral Officer for Northern Ireland 1973 onwards.

Table 4.04: Overseas Electors 1987-2005

The Representation of the People Act 1985 made provision for British citizens who are resident outside the U.K. to qualify as 'overseas electors' in the constituency for which they were last registered for a period of 5 years after they leave. The Representation of the People Act 1989 extended the qualifying period to 20 years and enfranchised those who went abroad before they were old enough to register as electors.

Year	England	Wales	Scotland	N. Ireland	Total
1987	9,980	250	800	70	11,100
1988	1,868	52	165	7	2,092
1989	1,662	36	132	6	1,836
1990	1,122	29	79	7	1,237
1991	31,175	910	2,172	197	34,454
1992	29,146	895	1,750	151	31,942
1993	20,123	644	1,256	108	22,131
1994	16,920	529	1,012	91	18,552
1995	16,326	502	1,027	79	17,934
1996	16,258	491	1,055	82	17,886
1997	21,362	658	1,466	97	23,583
1998	15,590	457	1,180	88	17,315
1999	12,273	352	978	74	13,677
2000	n/a	n/a	837	n/a	
2001	11,661	303	972	n/a	12,936
2002	8,746	244	766	n/a	9,756
2003	7,613	237	681	n/a	8,531
2004	8,630	261	754	n/a	9,645
2005	17,347	436	1,192	n/a	18,975

Table 4.05: Voluntary Patients in Mental Hospitals 1984-2000

The Representation of the People Act 1983 made provision for voluntary patients in mental hospitals to register for an address other than that of the hospital. Since the Representation of the People Act 2000 only a tiny number of electors are identified in this category.

Year	England	Wales	Scotland	N. Ireland	Total
1984	-	-	807	-	-
1985	3,057	325	235	295	3,912
1986	2,412	272	201	-	-
1987	1,966	221	458	225	2,870
1988	1,776	275	521	164	2,736
1989	1,441	168	317	216	2,142
1990	984	169	338	148	1,639
1991	883	164	523	91	1,661
1992	1,127	226	885	149	2,387
1993	1,056	165	674	76	1,971
1994	716	108	425	62	1,311
1995	622	100	363	66	1,151
1996	477	90	398	55	1,020
1997	568	98	510	19	1,195
1998	468	61	305	30	864
1999	380	29	309	25	743
2000	905	16	215	n/a	1,136

Table 4.06: Electorate Calculator*

This calendar shows the number of days the Electoral Register has been in force from its publication on February 16 each year since 1955. For Leap Years February 29 becomes Day 13 and all following consecutive numbers should be increased by one. Since the introduction of rolling registration in 2001 this calculator is no longer relevant.

February	March	April	May	June	July	August	September	October	November	December	January	February
16-0	1-13	1-44	1-74	1-105	1-135	1-166	1-197	1-227	1-258	1-288	1-319	1-350
17-1	2-14	2-45	2-75	2-106	2-136	2-167	2-198	2-228	2-259	2-289	2-320	2-351
18-2	3-15	3-46	3-76	3-107	3-137	3-168	3-199	3-229	3-260	3-290	3-321	3-352
19-3	4-16	4-47	4-77	4-108	4-138	4-169	4-200	4-230	4-261	4-291	4-322	4-353
20-4	5-17	5-48	5-78	5-109	5-139	5-170	5-201	5-231	5-262	5-292	5-323	5-354
21-5	6-18	6-49	6-79	6-110	6-140	6-171	6-202	6-232	6-263	6-293	6-324	6-355
22-6	7-19	7-50	7-80	7-111	7-141	7-172	7-203	7-233	7-264	7-294	7-325	7-356
23-7	8-20	8-51	8-81	8-112	8-142	8-173	8-204	8-234	8-265	8-295	8-326	8-357
24-8	9-21	9-52	9-82	9-113	9-143	9-174	9-205	9-235	9-266	9-296	9-327	9-358
25-9	10-22	10-53	10-83	10-114	10-144	10-175	10-206	10-236	10-267	10-297	10-328	10-359
26-10	11-23	11-54	11-84	11-115	11-145	11-176	11-207	11-237	11-268	11-298	11-329	11-360
27-11	12-24	12-55	12-85	12-116	12-146	12-177	12-208	12-238	12-269	12-299	12-330	12-361
28-12	13-25	13-56	13-86	13-117	13-147	13-178	13-209	13-239	13-270	13-300	13-331	13-362
	14-26	14-57	14-87	14-118	14-148	14-179	14-210	14-240	14-271	14-301	14-332	14-363
	15-27	15-58	15-88	15-119	15-149	15-180	15-211	15-241	15-272	15-302	15-333	15-364
	16-28	16-59	16-89	16-120	16-150	16-181	16-212	16-242	16-273	16-303	16-334	
	17-29	17-60	17-90	17-121	17-151	17-182	17-213	17-243	17-274	17-304	17-335	
	18-30	18-61	18-91	18-122	18-152	18-183	18-214	18-244	18-275	18-305	18-336	
	19-31	19-62	19-92	19-123	19-153	19-184	19-215	19-245	19-276	19-306	19-337	
	20-32	20-63	20-93	20-124	20-154	20-185	20-216	20-246	20-277	20-307	20-338	
	21-33	21-64	21-94	21-125	21-155	21-186	21-217	21-247	21-278	21-308	21-339	
	22-34	22-65	22-95	22-126	22-156	22-187	22-218	22-248	22-279	22-309	22-340	
	23-35	23-66	23-96	23-127	23-157	23-188	23-219	23-249	23-280	23-310	23-341	
	24-36	24-67	24-97	24-128	24-158	24-189	24-220	24-250	24-281	24-311	24-342	
	25-37	25-68	25-98	25-129	25-159	25-190	25-221	25-251	25-282	25-312	25-343	
	26-38	26-69	26-99	26-130	26-160	26-191	26-222	26-252	26-283	26-313	26-344	
	27-39	27-70	27-100	27-131	27-161	27-192	27-223	27-253	27-284	27-314	27-345	
	28-40	28-71	28-101	28-132	28-162	28-193	28-224	28-254	28-285	28-315	28-346	
	29-41	29-72	29-102	29-133	29-163	29-194	29-225	29-255	29-286	29-316	29-347	
	30-42	30-73	30-103	30-134	30-164	30-195	30-226	30-256	30-287	30-317	30-348	
	31-43		31-104		31-165	31-196		31-257		31-318	31-349	

* For an explanation of the use of this calendar see the entry under 'Electorate' in the Introductory Notes.

Table 5.01: Principal Changes in Electoral Law and Practice 1832-2006

Date[1]

June 1832   *Representation of the People Act* (known as the 'First Reform Act'). Modest reform of electoral law, extension of the franchise and re-distribution of seats.

August 1867   *Representation of the People Act* (sometimes called the 'Second Reform Act'). Extension of the franchise and re-distribution of seats.

July 1868   *Parliamentary Elections Act*. Removed the trial of election petitions from a House of Commons committee to the Courts.

July 1872   *Ballot Act*. Introduced voting by secret ballot.

August 1883   *Corrupt and Illegal Practices Prevention Act*. Placed a maximum limit on election expenses incurred by candidates.

December 1884   *Representation of the People Act* (sometimes called the 'Third Reform Act'). Extension of the franchise and re-distribution of seats.

February 1918   *Representation of the People Act*. Abolition of property qualification for voting. Women enfranchised at age 30 and over. Charges of Returning Officers no longer to be paid by candidates. All polls at General Elections to be held on the same day. Postal and proxy voting introduced for servicemen. Candidates required to lodge £150 deposit on nomination which was forfeited if they failed to poll more than one eighth of the total votes cast. Candidates entitled to free postage on their election addresses or leaflets. Redistribution of seats.

March 1922   *Irish Free State (Agreement) Act*. No further writs to be issued for constituencies in Ireland other than Northern Ireland.

October 1924   First use of radio for broadcasts by the party leaders during a General Election campaign.

July 1926   *Re-Election of Ministers Act (1919) Amendment Act*. Removed the necessity for Ministers of the Crown to seek re-election on accepting office.

July 1928   *Representation of the People (Equal Franchise) Act*. Women enfranchised at age 21 and over. Male and female adult suffrage achieved.

July 1948   *Representation of the People Act*. All plural voting and university constituencies abolished. Extension of postal voting to civilians. Limit on the number of cars which candidates could use on polling day. Redistribution of seats.

December 1949   *Electoral Registers Act*. Persons coming of age between November and June each year to be included in the electoral register, marked by the symbol 'Y' and eligible to vote at any election from October onwards.

October 1951   First use of television for broadcasts by the party leaders during a General Election campaign.

December 1958   *Representation of the People (Amendment Act)*. Removal of the restriction on the number of cars which candidates could use on polling day.

July 1963   *Peerage Act*. Peers allowed to disclaim Peerages for life and thus become eligible for membership of the House of Commons.

April 1969   *Representation of the People Act*. Extension of the franchise to persons at age 18 and over. Close of poll extended from 9.00 p.m. to 10.00 p.m.

July 1981   *Representation of the People Act*. Disqualified convicted persons serving sentences of more than 12 months in the British Islands or the Republic of Ireland from nomination to or membership of the House of Commons.

Principal Changes In The Electoral System 1832-2006 (contd.)

July 1985	*Representation of the People Act.* Extended the franchise to British citizens who are resident outside the UK to qualify as 'overseas electors' in the constituency for which they were last registered for a period of 5 years. Extended absent voting to holidaymakers and raised the deposit to £500 but reduced the threshold to one-twentieth of the total votes cast.
July 1989	*Representation of the People Act.* Extended period during which British citizens could qualify as 'overseas electors' from 5 to 20 years.
November 1998	*Registration of Political Parties Act.* Required political parties to register names to prevent attempts to confuse the electorate.
March 2000	*Representation of the People Act.* Introduced 'rolling' registration enabling electors to be added to or deleted from the Register at any time of the year. Relaxed rules governing qualification for registration, and introduced postal voting 'on demand'. Required registration officers to compile an edited version of the electoral register omitting those who asked for their names to be excluded.
November 2000	*Political Parties, Elections and Referendums Act.* Established an independent Electoral Commission with wide-ranging functions, including the regulation of political parties, their registration, expenditure and funding; the conduct of elections and referendums; and the encouragement and evaluation of innovations in electoral arrangements.
May 2002	*Electoral Fraud (Northern Ireland) Act.* Introduced individual as opposed to household registration with those wishing to register required to provide personal identification information and to produce photographic identification when subsequently voting at a polling station.
July 2006	*Electoral Administration Act.* Introduced measures to simplify electoral law and improve the way in which elections are conducted, including extending the registration period; reducing the age for parliamentary candidates to 18; establishing new elections offences; and requiring voters to sign for ballot papers at polling stations.

1. The dates given are those on which the Acts came into force but frequently major changes in election law were not effective until the Dissolution of the Parliament then in being or until the coming into force of a Statutory Instrument.

Table 5.02: General Election Timetable 1832-1910

Year	Parliament Dissolved[1]	First Nomination	First Contest	Last Contest[2]	Parliament Assembled
1832	December 3	December 8	December 10	Jan 8 (1833)	January 29
1835	Dec 29 (1834)	January 5	January 6	February 6	February 19
1837	July 17	July 22	July 24	August 18	November 15
1841	June 23	June 28	June 29	July 22	August 19
1847	July 23	July 28	July 29	August 26	November 18
1852	July 1	July 6	July 7	July 31	November 4
1857	March 21	March 26	March 27	April 24	April 30
1859	April 23	April 27	April 28	May 18	May 31
1865	July 6	July 10	July 11	July 24	Feb 1 (1866)
1868	November 11	November 16	November 17	December 7	December 10
1874	January 26	January 29	January 31	February 17	March 5
1880	March 24	March 30	March 31	April 27	April 29
1885	November 18	November 23	November 24	December 18	Jan 12 (1886)
1886	June 26	June 30	July 1	July 27	August 5
1892	June 28	July 1	July 4	July 26	August 4
1895	July 8	July 12	July 13	August 7	August 12
1900	September 25	September 28	October 1	October 24	December 3
1906	January 8	January 11	January 12	February 8	February 13
1910(J)	January 10	January 14	January 15	February 10	February 15
1910(D)	November 28	December 2	December 3	December 19	Jan 31 (1911)

Between 1705 and 1832 General Elections took place in the following years. The dates given are those of the first and last elections to each Parliament. 1705 (May 7-June 6); 1708 (April 30-July 7); 1710 (October 2-November 16); 1713 (August 22-November 12); 1715 (January 22-March 9); 1722 (March 19-May 9); 1727 (August 14-October 17); 1734 (April 22-June 6); 1741 (April 30-June 11); 1747 (June 26-August 4): 1754 (April 13-May 20); 1761 (March 25-May 5); 1768 (March 16-May 6); 1774 (October 5-November 10); 1780 (September 6-October 18); 1784 (March 30-May 10); 1790 (June 16-July 28); 1796 (May 25-June 29); 1802 (July 5-August 28); 1806 (October 29-December 17); 1807 (May 4-June 9); 1812 (October 5-November 10); 1818 (June 15-July 25); 1820 (March 6-April 14); 1826 (June 7-July 12); 1830 (July 29-September 1); 1831 (April 28-June 1).

1. The Septennial Act of 1715 fixed the duration of a Parliament at seven years.

2. The length of time between the first and last contested election is somewhat distorted by the fact that it was usual for the polling in the University constituencies and in Orkney and Shetland to be held a week or so after the other constituencies had completed polling. If University constituencies and Orkney and Shetland are excluded, the last polls were held on the following dates: 1832—January 1, 1833; 1835—January 27; 1837—August 18; 1841—July 22; 1847—August 18; 1852— July 28; 1857—April 24; 1859—May 18; 1865—July 24; 1868—November 30; 1874—February 17; 1880—April 14; 1885—December 9; 1886— July 17; 1892—July 19; 1895—July 29; 1900—October 15; 1906—January 29; 1910(J)—January 31; 1910(D)—December 19.

Table 5.03: General Election Timetable 1918-2005

Year	Election Date Announced[1]	Parliament Dissolved[2]	Nominations Closed	Polling Day[3]	Parliament Assembled
1918	November 14	November 25	December 4	Saturday, December 14[4]	February 4 (1919)
1922	October 23	October 26	November 4	Wednesday, November 15	November 20
1923	November 13	November 16	November 26	Thursday, December 6	January 8 (1924)
1924	October 9	October 9	October 18	Wednesday, October 29	December 2
1929	April 24	May 10	May 20	Thursday, May 30	June 25
1931	October 6	October 7	October 16	Tuesday, October 27	November 3
1935	October 23	October 25	November 4	Thursday, November 14	November 26
1945	May 23	June 15	June 25	Thursday, July 5[5]	August 1
1950	January 11	February 3	February 13	Thursday, February 23	March 1
1951	September 19	October 5	October 15	Thursday, October 25	October 31
1955	April 15	May 6	May 16	Thursday, May 26	June 7
1959	September 8	September 18	September 28	Thursday, October 8	October 20
1964	September 15	September 25	October 5	Thursday, October 15	October 27
1966	February 28	March 10	March 21	Thursday, March 31	April 18
1970	May 18	May 29	June 8	Thursday, June 18	June 29
1974(F)	February 7	February 8	February 18	Thursday, February 28	March 6
1974(O)	September 18	September 20	September 30	Thursday, October 10	October 22
1979	March 29	April 7	April 23	Thursday, May 3	May 9
1983	May 9	May 13	May 23	Thursday, June 9	June 15
1987	May 11	May 18	May 27	Thursday, June 11	June 17
1992	March 11	March 16	March 25	Thursday, April 9	April 27
1997	March 17	April 8	April 16	Thursday, May 1	May 7
2001	May 8	May 14	May 22	Thursday, June 7	June 13
2005	April 5	April 11	April 19	Thursday, May 5	May 11

108

General Election Timetable 1918-1997 (contd.)

1. The method of informing the country of a Dissolution has been as follows:

   Announcement made by the Leader of the House of Commons: General Election of 1918.

   Announcement by the Prime Minister in the House of Commons: General Elections of 1923, 1924, 1929, 1931, 1935.

   Official announcement issued to the press during a parliamentary recess: General Elections of 1922, 1945, 1950, 1959, 1964, 1974(O).

   Official announcement issued to the press during a parliamentary session: General Elections of 1966, 1970, 1974(F), 1979, 1983, 1987.

   Broadcast (sound radio) by the Prime Minister during a parliamentary recess: General Elections of 1951 and 1955.

   Live announcement by the Prime Minister in Downing Street during a parliamentary session: General Elections of 1992, 1997 and 2005. In 2001 the PM announced the calling of the election to an audience of school children in London.

2. The Parliament Act of 1911 fixed the duration of a Parliament at five years.

3. The date of polling did not apply to the University constituencies (where the poll remained open for five days), Orkney and Shetland (where the poll remained open for two days until 1929), or in a few cases where polling in a constituency was postponed due to the death of a candidate after the close of nominations.

4. The counting of votes did not take place until December 28 as the ballot papers of His Majesty's Forces serving on the Western Front (who had been allowed to vote by post) had to be collected and dispatched to Britain.

5. Due to the appointed polling day falling during the local holiday week in several constituencies, polling was delayed in twenty-two constituencies until July 12 and in one constituency until July 19. The counting of votes did not take place until July 26 as the ballot papers of His Majesty's Forces serving in certain countries overseas (who had been allowed to vote by post) had to be collected and dispatched to Britain by air.

Table 5.04: Absent Voters 1924-1945[1]

	1924	1929	1931	1935	1945
ENGLAND	160,141	169,338	166,511	158,282	1,044,761
WALES	6,701	7,907	8,542	8,326	55,487
SCOTLAND	15,082	18,796	18,426	17,444	168,574
N. IRELAND	2,277	1,965	2,135	1,924	12,298
UNITED KINGDOM	**184,201**	**198,006**	**195,614**	**185,976**	**1,281,120**

1. Statistics of absent voters were not compiled until the General Election of 1924. The above figures give the number of electors on the absent voters list at each election. This list contained the names of civilian and service voters eligible to vote by post plus a small number of proxy voters. There are no statistics available of the number of absent voters who actually voted.

Source: Returns of Election Expenses (Home Office).

Table 5.05: Postal Ballot Papers 1945-2005

	No of postal ballot papers issued	No of covering envelopes returned before close of poll	Number rejected[1]	No of ballot papers included at the start of the count
1945[2]				
ENGLAND	1,037,298	882,762	11,911	870,851
WALES	54,434	45,763	726	45,037
SCOTLAND	121,336	99,797	1,688	98,109
N. IRELAND	6,451	4,366	34	4,332
UNITED KINGDOM	**1,219,519**	**1,032,688**	**14,359**	**1,018,329**
1950				
ENGLAND	410,126	386,884	7,879	379,005
WALES	23,916	22,500	815	21,685
SCOTLAND	49,444	46,150	2,084	44,066
N. IRELAND	24,231	22,504	913	21,591
UNITED KINGDOM	**507,717**	**478,038**	**11,691**	**466,347**
1951				
ENGLAND	688,427	627,415	10,618	616,797
WALES	38,819	34,986	862	34,124
SCOTLAND	79,294	71,367	2,029	69,338
N. IRELAND	25,337	23,199	884	22,315
UNITED KINGDOM	**831,877**	**756,967**	**14,393**	**742,574**
1955				
ENGLAND	489,248	435,097	8,506	426,591
WALES	30,412	26,596	711	25,885
SCOTLAND	53,341	45,854	1,485	44,369
N. IRELAND	21,999	19,357	609	18,748
UNITED KINGDOM	**595,000**	**526,904**	**11,311**	**515,593**
1959				
ENGLAND	585,776	520,551	10,922	509,629
WALES	34,054	29,532	848	28,684
SCOTLAND	55,739	48,204	1,481	46,723
N. IRELAND	17,258	13,944	421	13,523
UNITED KINGDOM	**692,827**	**612,231**	**13,672**	**598,559**

Postal Ballot Papers 1945-2005 (contd.)

	No of postal ballot papers issued	No of covering envelopes returned before close of poll	Number rejected[1]	No of ballot papers included at the start of the count
1964				
ENGLAND	692,674	614,344	12,818	601,526
WALES	39,286	34,343	1,094	33,249
SCOTLAND	68,184	59,376	1,841	57,535
N. IRELAND	18,757	15,864	538	15,326
UNITED KINGDOM	**818,901**	**723,927**	**16,291**	**707,636**
1966				
ENGLAND	505,637	433,708	11,338	422,370
WALES	33,966	28,677	1,129	27,548
SCOTLAND	55,486	46,711	1,695	45,016
N. IRELAND	22,392	18,910	803	18,107
UNITED KINGDOM	**617,481**	**528,006**	**14,965**	**513,041**
1970				
ENGLAND	599,638	525,842	10,820	515,022
WALES	41,088	35,919	1,017	34,902
SCOTLAND	62,656	53,603	1,550	52,053
N. IRELAND	27,867	24,310	932	23,378
UNITED KINGDOM	**731,249**	**639,674**	**14,319**	**625,355**
1974(F)[3]				
ENGLAND	606,468	530,583	13,098	517,485
WALES	45,004	35,152	1,377	33,775
SCOTLAND	62,261	54,278	1,391	52,887
N. IRELAND	29,708	25,067	307	24,760
UNITED KINGDOM	**743,441**	**645,080**	**16,173**	**628,907**
1974(O)[4]				
ENGLAND	882,433	718,240	20,516	697,724
WALES	59,970	48,714	2,014	46,700
SCOTLAND	90,136	73,190	1,875	71,315
N. IRELAND	42,592	35,180	814	34,366
UNITED KINGDOM	**1,075,131**	**875,324**	**25,219**	**850,105**
1979				
ENGLAND	680,930	572,835	17,953	554,882
WALES	56,647	48,095	2,105	45,990
SCOTLAND	76,917	65,082	1,965	63,117
N. IRELAND	32,841	28,880	900	27,980
UNITED KINGDOM	**847,335**	**714,892**	**22,923**	**691,969**
1983				
ENGLAND	622,013	529,243	16,017	513,226
WALES	46,862	40,001	1,892	38,109
SCOTLAND	54,017	43,593	1,461	42,132
N. IRELAND	34,712	30,797	710	30,087
UNITED KINGDOM	**757,604**	**643,634**	**20,080**	**623,554**

Postal Ballot Papers 1945-2005 (contd.)

	No of postal ballot papers issued	No of covering envelopes returned before close of poll	Number rejected[1]	No of ballot papers included at the start of the count
1987				
ENGLAND	792,412	683,399	20,270	663,129
WALES	56,093	48,221	2,193	46,028
SCOTLAND	64,077	54,354	1,857	52,497
N. IRELAND	35,366	32,375	967	31,408
UNITED KINGDOM	**947,948**	**818,349**	**25,287**	**793,062**
1992				
ENGLAND	693,238	593,590	17,139	575,160
WALES	47,644	40,043	1,995	38,048
SCOTLAND	66,607	56,355	1,759	54,596
N. IRELAND	27,585	24,907	572	24,335
UNITED KINGDOM	**835,074**	**714,895**	**21,465**	**692,139**
1997[5]				
ENGLAND	797,649	648,576	21,981	627,214
WALES	47,691	39,325	2,097	37,228
SCOTLAND	62,025	49,817	1,765	48,052
N. IRELAND	29,840	26,648	528	26,120
UNITED KINGDOM	**937,205**	**764,366**	**26,371**	**738,614**
2001[6]				
ENGLAND	1,507,345	1,193,780	23,795	1,169,985
WALES	110,900	91,395	4,533	86,862
SCOTLAND	108,699	90,405	2,446	87,959
N.IRELAND	31,111	26,493	415	26,078
UNITED KINGDOM	**1,758,055**	**1,402,073**	**31,189**	**1,370,884**
2005[6]				
ENGLAND	4,739,753	3,626,321	86,170	3,486,848
WALES	283,032	221,340	10,220	211,244
SCOTLAND	312,036	238,488	4,917	242,738
N. IRELAND	27,680	23,890	1,238	22,962
UNITED KINGDOM	**5,362,501**	**4,110,039**	**102,545**	**3,963,792**

Statistics of postal voting were not compiled until the General Election of 1945. Prior to 1945, the only General Election in which there must have been a substantial number of postal votes was that of 1918. Between the wars only members of His Majesty's Forces serving in the U.K. and a few civilians could vote by post. The Representation of the People Act 1949 considerably increased the categories of those eligible to vote by post. The Representation of the People Act 1985 extended postal voting to anyone who could not reasonably be expected to vote in person and this allowed people going on holiday to apply for a postal or proxy vote. The Representation of the People Act 2000 introduced postal voting 'on demand' which allowed any elector to apply for a postal vote.

1. Number of cases in which the covering envelope or its contents were marked "empty", "rejected", "declaration rejected" or "vote rejected". This figure was not always available in later years and therefore the number of ballot papers included in the count plus the number rejected do not always sum to the number returned before the close of poll.

2. These figures relate only to Service voters. In addition, a total of 1,381 civilian postal voters had their ballot papers included in constituency counts.

3. Columns 2-4 are exclusive of the figures for Abertillery, Ashford, Bassetlaw, Bath, Bedwellty, Ebbw Vale, Monmouth and Pontypool. The Returning Officers failed to make the statutory return to the Home Office.

Postal Ballot Papers 1945-2005 (contd.)

4. Columns 2-4 are exclusive of the figures for Devizes and Northwich. The Returning Officers failed to make the statutory return to the Home Office.

5. Columns 2-4 exclude 12 constituencies in England which did not submit postal ballot details.

6. Not all constituencies were able to provide complete data.

Sources: 1945:House of Commons Papers, 1945-46 (22) xx, 609.
         1950-1997: Returns compiled by the Home Office and, as appropriate, the
         Scottish Office and the Northern Ireland Office.
         2001-2005: compiled by the authors on behalf of the Electoral Commission.

Table 5.06: Postal Ballot Papers (Summary) 1945-2005

	Issued Postal Ballot papers as % of total electorate	Number returned as % of No. issued	Number rejected as % of No. returned	No. of Postal Ballot Papers included at the start of the count as % of total poll
1945[1]	3.7	84.7	1.4	4.2
1950	1.5	94.2	2.4	1.6
1951	2.4	91.0	1.9	2.6
1955	1.7	88.6	2.1	1.9
1959	2.0	88.4	2.2	2.1
1964	2.3	88.4	2.3	2.6
1966	1.7	85.5	2.8	1.9
1970	1.9	87.5	2.2	2.2
1974(F)	1.9	87.8	2.5	2.0
1974(O)	2.7	81.7	2.9	2.9
1979	2.1	84.4	3.2	2.2
1983	1.8	85.0	3.1	2.0
1987	2.2	86.3	3.1	2.4
1992	1.9	85.6	3.0	2.3
1997	2.1	81.6	3.5	2.4
2001	4.0	79.8	2.2	5.2
2005	12.1	78.6	2.5	15.0

Table 5.07: Spoilt Ballot Papers 1880-2005*

	Want of official mark	Voting for more than one candidate	Writing or mark by which voter could be identified	Unmarked or void for uncertainty	Total	Average per constit.
1880						
ENGLAND	-	-	-	-	7,905	31
WALES	-	-	-	-	531	19
SCOTLAND	-	-	-	-	1,797	33
IRELAND	-	-	-	-	1,551	27
UNITED KINGDOM	**-**	**-**	**-**	**-**	**11,784**[1]	**29**
1924						
ENGLAND & WALES	1,997	4,418	8,334	9,415	24,164	49
SCOTLAND	864	436	1,647	3,038	5,985	88
N. IRELAND	24	507	298	626	1,455	146
UNITED KINGDOM	**2,885**	**5,361**	**10,279**	**13,079**	**31,604**	**54**
1950						
SCOTLAND	1,849	986	1,136	1,295	5,266	74
1951						
SCOTLAND	1,193	646	1,254	1,574	4,667	66
1955						
SCOTLAND	921	671	1,158	1,841	4,591	65
1959						
SCOTLAND	927	796	878	1,615	4,216	59
1964						
ENGLAND	1,750	12,289	5,358	12,087	31,484	62
WALES	234	1,137	275	921	2,567	71
SCOTLAND	823	1,063	887	1,929	4,702	66
N. IRELAND	19	997	267	1,037	2,320	193
UNITED KINGDOM	**2,826**	**15,486**	**6,787**	**15,974**	**41,073**	**65**
1966						
ENGLAND	1,203	8,847	7,145	21,913	39,108	77
WALES	198	1,036	309	1,737	3,280	91
SCOTLAND	652	852	790	2,894	5,188	73
N. IRELAND	8	784	281	1,250	2,323	194
UNITED KINGDOM	**2,061**	**11,519**	**8,525**	**27,794**	**49,899**	**79**
1970						
ENGLAND	1,414	10,406	6,588	14,809	33,217	65
WALES	78	1,547	258	635	2,518	70
SCOTLAND	623	1,208	354	1,251	3,436	48
N. IRELAND	3	983	341	849	2,176	181
UNITED KINGDOM	**2,118**	**14,144**	**7,541**	**17,544**	**41,347**	**66**

Spoilt Ballot Papers 1880-2005* (contd.)

	Want of official mark	Voting for more than one candidate	Writing or mark by which voter could be identified	Unmarked or void for uncertainty	Total	Average per constit.
1974(F)						
ENGLAND	2,063	8,651	6,386	15,108	32,208	62
WALES	197	1,134	255	585	2,171	60
SCOTLAND	824	657	333	1,403	3,217	45
N. IRELAND	92	1,772	346	2,446	4,656	388
UNITED KINGDOM	**3,176**	**12,214**	**7,320**	**19,542**	**42,252**[2]	**67**
1974(O)						
ENGLAND	2,095	8,543	4,599	9,892	25,129	49
WALES	225	1,201	214	502	2,142	60
SCOTLAND	582	983	196	869	2,630	37
N. IRELAND	36	2,765	1,000	4,004	7,805	650
UNITED KINGDOM	**2,938**	**13,492**	**6,009**	**15,267**	**37,706**[3]	**59**
1979						
ENGLAND	2,034	63,622	5,064	26,640	97,360	189
WALES	293	5,081	307	3,964	9,645	268
SCOTLAND	804	852	316	1,359	3,331	47
N. IRELAND	151	2,960	114	4,287	7,512	626
UNITED KINGDOM	**3,282**	**72,515**	**5,801**	**36,250**	**117,848**[4]	**186**
1983						
ENGLAND	1,698	21,551	3,875	12,666	39,790	76
WALES	166	3,042	190	686	4,084	107
SCOTLAND	709	639	564	965	2,877	40
N. IRELAND	246	2,706	64	1,337	4,353	256
UNITED KINGDOM	**2,819**	**27,938**	**4,693**	**15,654**	**51,104**	**79**
1987						
ENGLAND	1,463	9,770	4,093	11,987	27,213	52
WALES	76	1,374	158	653	2,261	60
SCOTLAND	599	381	485	1,055	2,520	35
N. IRELAND	270	2,691	240	1,650	4,851	285
UNITED KINGDOM	**2,408**	**14,216**	**4,976**	**15,345**	**36,945**	**57**
1992						
ENGLAND	1,381	10,325	4,283	14,033	30,022	57
WALES	123	1,114	263	882	2,382	63
SCOTLAND	660	441	442	1,043	2,586	36
N. IRELAND	429	2,658	20	1,629	4,736	279
UNITED KINGDOM	**2,593**	**14,538**	**5,008**	**17,587**	**39,726**	**61**
1997						
ENGLAND	1,238	·22,098	3,933	57,731	85,169[5]	161
WALES	124	1,068	225	1,109	2,526	63
SCOTLAND	482	475	262	1,374	2,593	36
N. IRELAND	325	1,593	1	1,201	3,120	173
UNITED KINGDOM	**2,169**	**25,234**	**4,421**	**61,415**	**93,408**[5]	**142**

Spoilt Ballot Papers 1880-2005* (contd.)

	Want of official mark	Voting for more than one candidate	Writing or mark by which voter could be identified	Unmarked or void for uncertainty	Total	Average per constit.
2001[6]						
ENGLAND	1,486	16,372	3,366	63,123	85,542	162
WALES	142	1,041	136	1,870	3,191	80
SCOTLAND	686	939	214	2,395	4,234	59
N. IRELAND	234	4,238	44	2,522	7,038	391
UNITED KINGDOM	**2,548**	**22,590**	**3,700**	**69,910**	**100,005**	**152**
2005[6]						
ENGLAND	2,025	14,376	3,438	48,402	70,587	133
WALES	181	1,070	109	1,986	3,616	90
SCOTLAND	397	1,245	783	2,902	4,669	79
N. IRELAND	426	4,121	127	1,492	6,166	343
UNITED KINGDOM	**2,971**	**20,595**	**4,439**	**54,377**	**85,038**	**129**

* With the exceptions of the General Elections of 1880 and 1924, statistics relating to spoilt ballot papers were not compiled (except in Scotland from 1950) until the General Election of 1964.

1. No returns from ten constituencies in England and seven in Ireland.

2. No returns from two constituencies in England.

3. No return from one constituency in England.

4. The increased number of spoilt ballot papers in England and Wales at this election was due to local elections being held on the same day and electors being asked to mark two ballot papers.

5. Two English constituencies did not subdivide rejected ballot papers into categories. The totals are correct, but the U.K. and England rows do not sum to that total. The increased number of spoilt ballot papers in England at this election was due to local elections being held on the same day and electors being asked to mark two ballot papers.

6. A number of constituencies either did not provide full data or did not sub-divide rejected ballot papers into categories. The General Election coincided with local elections in most of non-metropolitan England.

Sources: 1880: House of Commons Papers, 1881 (25), lxxiv, 285
1924: House of Commons Papers, 1926 (49) xxii, 619
1950-1997: Returns compiled by the Home Office and, as appropriate, the Scottish Office and the Northern Ireland Office.
2001-2005: compiled by the authors on behalf of the Electoral Commission.

Table 5.08: Polling Districts and Stations 1950-2005

Election	Polling Districts[1]	Polling Stations[2]
1950	25,304	48,243
1951	26,348	48,212
1955	27,797	49,510
1959	28,951	49,817
1964	30,255	49,637
1966	30,470	49,565
1970	30,864	49,687
1974(F)	31,287	48,631
1974(O)	31,171	48,384
1979	33,086	48,035
1983	34,247	46,903
1987	35,042	46,566
1992	34,589	45,303
1997	36,275	45,397
2001	36,736	44,939
2005	n/a	42,179

1. Each constituency is divided into a number of polling districts by the local authority (in Scotland by the Returning Officer).

2. Each constituency polling district is further divided into a number of polling stations for the accommodation of electors. A separate room or separate booth may contain a separate polling station, or several polling stations may be constructed in the same room or booth. A Presiding Officer and clerks are appointed and separate equipment is provided for each polling station.

Source: Returns of Election Expenses (Home Office).

Table 5.09: Candidates' Expenses 1885-2005

Election	Agents[1] £	Clerks[2] £	Printing[3] £	Meetings[4] £	Rooms[5] £	Miscellaneous[6] £	Personal Expenses[7] £	Total[8] £	Average[9] £
1885	220,150	103,119	284,190	28,080	35,517	62,729	56,502	790,287	610
1886	123,523	64,635	201,077	13,630	18,794	35,276	28,213	485,148	544
1892	192,874	98,999	310,379	19,627	29,709	60,033	49,437	761,058	614
1895	151,177	82,500	259,248	13,786	24,090	47,194	40,001	617,996	624
1900	148,245	78,605	274,061	15,831	24,265	44,683	41,422	627,112	730
1906	196,656	130,051	418,596	30,456	46,137	71,670	65,355	958,921	827
1910(J)	195,177	146,100	469,949	43,946	54,232	93,020	65,801	1,068,225	861
1910(D)	156,611	104,915	335,160	33,446	39,627	71,272	49,929	790,960	769
1918									
1922	131,783	171,604	465,182	50,113	52,000	81,773	65,620	1,018,075	707
1923	124,631	167,296	436,411	58,529	52,647	82,334	60,492	982,340	679
1924	111,407	148,746	415,684	60,657	50,614	78,736	55,321	921,165	645
1929	138,148	188,043	577,344	68,221	66,852	106,715	68,184	1,213,507	701
1931	76,729	101,993	298,544	40,373	36,823	61,922	37,721	654,105	506
1935	83,699	107,020	340,493	41,628	40,484	68,047	40,722	722,093	536
1945	98,064	82,417	623,774	51,804	42,525	110,672	63,960	1,073,216	638
1950	90,536	65,321	714,870	67,415	53,893	114,057	64,032	1,170,124	626
1951	74,877	52,297	589,979	52,095	45,581	80,039	51,150	946,018	688
1955	78,808	51,923	557,055	37,333	42,096	85,205	52,257	904,677	642
1959	80,722	55,910	669,688	36,672	46,729	100,490	61,008	1,051,219	684
1964	85,616	51,683	824,085	40,950	51,578	104,665	70,626	1,229,203	700
1966	82,856	46,449	762,706	33,046	49,461	96,228	66,136	1,136,882	666
1970	86,061	50,480	1,046,373	30,296	50,759	128,827	73,184	1,465,980	798
1974(F)	102,996	49,926	1,591,994	37,517	64,043	162,184	87,747	2,096,407	982
1974(O)	103,010	46,528	1,748,728	41,585	67,164	161,499	92,714	2,261,228	1,004

Candidates' Expenses 1885–2005 (contd.)

Election	Agents[1] £	Clerks[2] £	Printing[3] £	Meetings[4] £	Rooms[5] £	Miscellaneous[6] £	Personal Expenses[7] £	Total[8] £	Average[9] £
1979	175,874	65,799	2,873,765	58,796	93,682	289,525	131,817	3,689,258	1,432
1983	285,916	101,756	4,887,627	100,230	185,753	584,037	169,469	6,314,788	2,449
1987	326,927	107,974	6,612,952	88,652	260,756	641,913	266,547	8,305,721	3,572
1992	405,324	123,455	8,680,793	101,241	321,477	801,117	345,739	10,779,146	3,655
1997	455,416	123,218	10,577,643	102,851	405,358	1,264,719	415,754	13,344,959	3,584
2001	289,740	100,644	10,076,829	63,637	356,654	997,794	306,560	11,885,785 *	3,581

Election	Personal† £	Payments by candidate £	Payments by agent £	Petty expenditure £	Unpaid claims £	Disputed claims £	Incurred prior to becoming a candidate £	Notional expenditure incurred £	Incurred for purpose other than election £	Total £	Average £
2005[10]	204,651	235,974	10,453,064	149,961	22,938	32,337	577,348	2,856,947	51,391	14,171,960	3,988

Note: † Not included in total expenses.

  * Total includes an extra £484.88. One candidate declared only the total amount spent, without giving detailed figures under the prescribed headings.

A limit on the amount a candidate could spend on an election campaign was first introduced by the Corrupt and Illegal Practices Prevention Act, 1883. It fixed the legal maximum in a borough constituency at £350 where the number of electors on the register did not exceed 2,000. In boroughs with an electorate of over 2,000 the limit was £380 plus an additional £30 for each complete 1,000 electors above 2,000. In counties, the limit was £650 where the electorate did not exceed 2,000 and £710 in constituencies with over 2,000 electors plus an additional £60 for every complete 1,000 electors above 2,000.

The following is a summary of subsequent changes:

1918   Borough constituencies—5d per elector; county constituencies—7d (reduced to 6d in 1929). Personal expenses and the fee, if any, paid to an election agent up to a maximum of £50 in a borough and £75 in a county were excluded from the limit.

1949   Borough constituencies—£450 plus 1½d per elector; county constituencies—£450 plus 2d per elector. Personal expenses excluded from the limit. [In Northern Ireland until 1957 expenditure was limited to 2d per elector with personal expenses and election agent's fee (up to a maximum of £50 in a borough and £75 in a county) excluded from the limit.]

1969   Borough constituencies —£750 plus one shilling (5p) for every eight electors; county constituencies—£750 plus one shilling (5p) for every six electors. Personal expenses excluded from the limit.

Candidates' Expenses 1885–2005 (contd.)

1974   Borough constituencies—£1,075 plus 6p for every eight electors; county constituencies—£1,075 plus 6p for every six electors. Personal expenses excluded from the limit.

1978   Borough constituencies —£1,750 plus 1½p per elector; county constituencies—£1,750 plus 2p per elector. Personal expenses excluded from the limit.

1982   Borough constituencies—£2,700 plus 2.3p per elector; county constituencies—£2,700 plus 3.1p per elector. Personal expenses excluded from the limit.

1986   Borough constituencies—£3,240 plus 2.8p per elector; county constituencies—£3,240 plus 3.7p per elector. Personal expenses excluded from the limit.

1987   Borough constituencies—£3,370 plus 2.9p per elector; county constituencies—£3,370 plus 3.8p per elector. Personal expenses excluded from the limit.

1992   Borough constituencies—£4,330 plus 3.7p per elector; county constituencies—£4,330 plus 4.9p per elector. Personal expenses excluded from the limit.

1997   Borough constituencies—£4,965 plus 4.2p per elector; county constituencies—£4,965 plus 5.6p per elector. Personal expenses excluded from the limit.

2001   Borough constituencies—£5,483 plus 4.6p per elector; county constituencies—£5,483 plus 6.2p per elector. Personal expenses excluded from the limit.

2005   Borough constituencies—£7,150 plus 5.0p per elector; county constituencies—£7,150 plus 7.0p per elector. Personal expenses excluded from the limit.

Prior to 1918, candidates also paid the expenses of the Returning Officers (see Table 5.10) and these charges have not been included in the above totals.

1. Fees paid to election agents, sub-agents and polling agents.

2. Payments for clerks and messengers.

3. The expenses of printing, of advertising, of publishing, issuing and distributing addresses and notices, and of stationery, postage, telegrams.

4. Expenses of holding public meetings, including payments to speakers.

5. Cost of hire of committee rooms.

6. All expenses in respect of miscellaneous matters not included in the previous columns.

7. The personal expenses of the candidate.

Candidates' Expenses 1885-2005 (contd.)

8. This figure has not always been complete owing to the fact that at most elections a small number of candidates have failed to lodge a return of their expenses. The total expenditure at the General Elections of 1886, 1895, 1900, 1910(D), 1922, 1923, 1924, 1931 and 1935 were substantially reduced due to the high proportion of uncontested seats. The expenses of unopposed candidates were either nil or very small.

9. Average expenditure per candidate to nearest £. This figure is distorted for some elections due to the number of uncontested seats.

10. Electoral Commission introduced a new reporting category.

Source: Returns of Election Expenses (Home Office). Electoral Commission 2001 and 2005.

Table 5.10: Returning Officers' Expenses 1832-2005

This table shows the costs incurred by Returning Officers in the conduct of General Elections. The figures from 1918 onwards are probably a slight overestimate of the actual expenses of each election as the cost of by-elections falling within the same financial year (April 1 to March 31) are included in the totals, separate figures not being published by the Treasury. This distortion may however be offset by the fact that disputes sometimes arise between Returning Officers and the Treasury as to expenses and as a result some payments to Returning Officers are delayed and would not be included in the figures for the financial year which included the General Election. Returning Officers' expenses include the administrative costs of the election, printing, etc. Prior to 1918 these charges were paid by the candidates (the total charges in each constituency being divided equally among the candidates) in addition to their own election expenses (see Table 5.09). In 1991 responsibility for accounting relating to Parliamentary elections in the United Kingdom was transferred from the Treasury to the Home Departments (Statutory Instrument 1991, no. 1728). Because both the 1992 and 1997 general election campaigns straddled two financial years, the figures given cover the periods 1991-3 and 1996-8.

Election	Returning Officers' expenses	Average per constit.[1]	Election	Returning Officers' expenses	Average per constit.[1]
	£	£		£	£
1832	56,441	141	1923	324 566	528
1835	Not available	-	1924	339,028	551
1837	Not available	-	1929	422,244	687
1841	31,621[2]	111	1931	305,945	497
1847	Not available	-	1935	314,500	511
1852	48,978	123	1945	667,999	1,044
1857	35,566	89	1950	806,974	1,291
1859	Not available	-	1951	850,657	1,361
1865	47,320	118	1955	996,560	1,582
1868	95,130	226	1959	1,147,856	1,822
1874	140,976	339	1964	1,698,286	2,696
1880	130,813	314	1966	1,551,496	2,463
1885	235,907	352	1970	2,078,165	3,299
1886	138,938	207	1974(F) &		
1892	197,542	295	1974(O)	6,349,362	4,999
1895	156,742	234	1979	7,115,539	11,206
1900	150,279	224	1983	12,139 634	18,676
1906	206,335	308	1987	14,741 334	22,679
1910(J)	227,557	340	1992	22,703,801	34,875
1910(D)	187,753	280	1997	29,764,513	45,166
1918	490,716	694[3]	2001	36 million	c54,600
1922	280,138	456	2005	46 million	c71,200

The total cost to the taxpayer of a General Election is however considerably greater than figures given would suggest. It is not possible to estimate the cost of diverting civil servants, local government staff, police officers, etc. from their normal duties to election work. A proportion of the annual cost (which since 1958 has been borne by ratepayers/council tax payers but partly recovered from government grants) of compiling the electoral register should also be allowed for in any attempt to estimate the cost of an election . The Home Office estimated the cost of compiling the 1997-98 register as £40 million (Hansard, 7 July 1997, col. 366w). A further expenditure is the free delivery of the election address of each candidate, poll-cards and postal ballot papers. Since 1964, the Post Office has been able to recover this cost from the Treasury and figures supplied by the Treasury/Home Departments' Accounting Officers give their costs as: 1964—£990,275; 1966—£1,118,193; 1970—£1,648,854; 1974(F)—£2,895,853; 1974(O)- £3,331,459; 1979—£6,668,614; 1983—£11,281,228; 1987—£12,152,497; 1992—£18,011,749; 1997—£23,359,582. 2001—20.2 million; 2005—no figure available.

Returning Officers' Expenses 1832-2005 (contd.)

1. This figure is distorted for several elections prior to 1955 due to the number of uncontested constituencies in which expenses would be low.

2. England and Wales only.

3. The high expenditure at this election was probably due to the considerable increase in the number of polling stations and the purchase of new ballot-boxes and other equipment.

Sources: Prior to 1868, House of Commons papers as listed in earlier editions of this book.
1868-1910: Returns of Election Expenses (Home Office)
1918: House of Commons Debates (1921),142,c. 1893
1922-66: Finance Accounts of the United Kingdom
1970-87: Consolidated Fund and National Loans Fund Accounts (Supplementary Statements)
1992-97: Reports of Accounting Officers on Returning Officers' expenses.
2001 & 2005: Estimates only derived from Electoral Commission sources.

Table 5.11: Polling Postponed by Death of a Candidate 1918-2005

Since 1918 when polling at a General Election took place on the same date in all constituencies (except in the Universities) the death of a candidate after nomination and prior to the day of election caused a postponement of the election. This has only occurred at seven General Elections. Following the 2005 case, the Electoral Administration Act 2006 allows for an election to continue in certain circumstances even if a candidate dies.

1918   F.A. Lucas the Conservative candidate for Lambeth, Kennington died three days before polling.

1923   C.F. White the Liberal candidate and former MP for Derbyshire, Western died two days before polling.

1929   H. Yates the Labour candidate for Warwickshire, Rugby died three days before polling.

1945   W. Windsor the Labour candidate and former MP for Kingston upon Hull, Central died six days before polling.

1950   E.L. Fleming the Conservative candidate for Manchester, Moss Side (and former MP for Manchester, Withington) died six days before polling.

1951   F. Collindridge the Labour candidate and former MP for Barnsley died nine days before polling.

2005   Ms J. Harrison the Liberal Democrat candidate for Staffordshire South died five days before polling.

Table 5.12: Electoral Administration – Miscellaneous Information

POLLING DAYS

The polling at a General Election has been on a Thursday since 1935. Prior to that it was a Tuesday in 1931; a Wednesday in 1922 and 1924; a Thursday in 1923 and 1929; a Saturday in 1918.

By-elections are now normally held on a Thursday but in 1958 the Pontypool by-election was held on a Monday; in 1965 the Saffron Walden poll was held on a Tuesday; in 1978 (because the Returning Officer wished to avoid a clash with the television coverage of the opening match in the World Cup football competition) the Hamilton by-election was held on a Wednesday; in 1956 the Newport by-election was held on a Friday; in 1951 the Harrow, West by-election was held on a Saturday.

POLLING HOURS

The hours of poll for a General Election were, with one minor exception, standardised in the United Kingdom from 1885. From 1885 to 1913 polling took place between 8 a.m. and 8 p.m. on one day; from 1913 to 1950 the hours of poll could be extended by one hour in the morning and/or the evening on request of any of the candidates; from 1950 to 1970 the hours of poll were 7 a.m. to 9 p.m.; and since February 1970 polling has taken place between 7 a.m. and 10 p.m. Voting over two days was retained for Orkney and Shetland until 1926. More detailed information may be found in Appendix 5 of the fifth (1989) edition of this book.

Electoral Administration – Miscellaneous Information (contd.)

POSTAL VOTES

The Representation of the People Act 2000 made it easier for people to obtain absent votes. Activity by both local authorities and the political parties has led to considerable increases in the issue and inclusion in the count of postal votes.

Pre Representation of the People Act 2000

The previous record for the largest number of postal ballot papers issued and included in a count is held by Fermanagh and South Tyrone. At the General Election of 1974(O) the number issued was 9,911 (13.9% of the electorate) of which 8,979 (14.2% of the total poll) were included in the count.

If Northern Ireland is excluded, Cambridge holds the record. At the General Election of 1992, which took place during the University Easter vacation, the number of postal ballot papers issued was 5,560 (8.0% of the electorate) of which 5,085 (10.1% of the total poll) were included in the count. Prior to that the record was held by Devon North at the General Election of 1974(O). There the number issued was 4,109 (5.6% of the electorate) of which 3,298 (5.6% of the total poll) were included in the count.

Glasgow, Bridgeton holds the record for the smallest postal vote. At the General Election of 1950 there were only 115 postal ballot-papers issued and 91 counted. At the General Election of 1966 the number issued increased to 127 but the number included in the count fell to a record low figure of 87.

Post Representation of the People Act 2000

The record for the largest number of postal votes issued and included in the count is held by Rushcliffe. In 2005 31,872 ballot papers (39.9% of the electorate) were issued; of these 26,163 (46.5% of all valid votes cast) were included in the count. The record for the largest proportion of the electorate to be issued with postal votes is held by Newcastle-upon-Tyne North with 45.4% (also in 2005). The same constituency also holds the record for postal votes as a proportion of all votes cast (56.0%).

An early sign of the impact of the new legislation came in Stevenage in 2001. 25,510 electors (36.5% of the total) were issued with a postal vote. Postal votes made up some 43% of all vosts cast.

SPOILT BALLOT PAPERS

Since statistics relating to spoilt ballot-papers were first compiled for the United Kingdom in 1964, the record for the highest number of spoilt papers is held by Belfast, West. At the General Election of 1979, 2,283 were rejected of which 1,913 were unmarked or void for uncertainty.

If Northern Ireland is excluded, the highest number of spoilt papers was at Cardiff, West at the General Election of 1979 when the total was 2,253. Of this number, 2,123 were unmarked or void for uncertainty many of them having the word 'Conservative' written across them. This seat was being defended by the Speaker and there was no Conservative candidate.

The lowest number of spoilt papers was at Edinburgh, Leith at the General Election of 1974(O) when only nine were rejected. The official Return of Election Expenses for the General Election of 1992 records that no ballot papers were rejected in the count at either Bosworth or East Berkshire.

Table 6.01: Parliamentary Boundary Commissions 1831-2005

Until the creation of permanent Boundary Commissions in 1944, reviews of boundaries were undertaken from time to time by ad hoc Commissions and the following list gives the relevant dates of each report but it should be noted that irrespective of the date the boundary changes were implemented (by Act or Statutory Instrument) they did not come into effect until the Dissolution of the Parliament then in being.

Permanent Boundary Commissions (for England, Wales, Scotland and Northern Ireland) were created in 1944 and prior to the 1945 election they carried out a review of twenty abnormally large constituencies in England. Initial reports were published between September and December 1947 and the First Periodical Reports appeared between August and November 1954. The original rules laid down that each Commission must report not less than three or more than seven years from the date of their previous report but this was altered in 1958 to between ten and fifteen years. The Second Periodical Reports were published in June 1969 and the Third Periodical Reports between November 1982 and February 1983. The Boundary Commissions Act 1992 changed the interval between reports to 'not less than eight or more than 12' years and the Fourth Periodical Reports were published between February and June 1995. The Fifth Periodical Reports were published from February 2005.

Commenced review	Date of report	Date of Act or SI	Length of time (months)
ENGLAND			
August 8, 1831	February 10, 1832	July 11, 1832	11
August 16, 1867	February 5, 1868	July 13, 1868	11
December 5, 1884	February 10, 1885 & April 22, 1885	June 25, 1885	6
May 14, 1917	September 27, 1917	February 6, 1918	9
October 26, 1944	March 29, 1945	June 11, 1945	8
January 31, 1946[1]	October 24, 1947	July 30, 1948	30
July 28, 1953	November 10, 1954	January 5, 1955 & February 1, 1955	18
February 16, 1965	April 21, 1969	November 11, 1970	69
February 17, 1976	February 1, 1983	March 16, 1983	85
February 21, 1991	June 6, 1995	June 28, 1995	52
February 22, 2000	October 31, 2006		
WALES			
August 8, 1831	February 10, 1832	July 11, 1832	11
August 16, 1867	February 5, 1868	July 13, 1868	11
December 5, 1884	February 10, 1885	June 25, 1885	6
May 14, 1917	September 27, 1917	February 6, 1918	9
January 31, 1946[1]	November 17, 1947	July 30, 1948	30
July 28, 1953	November 10, 1954	February 1, 1955	18
February 16, 1965	May 19, 1969	November 11, 1970	69
February 16, 1981	January 25, 1983	March 16, 1983	25
November 9, 1993	February 15, 1995	April 11, 1995	17
December 16, 2002	December 14, 2005	April 25, 2006	40
SCOTLAND			
November 8, 1831	February 21, 1832	July 17, 1832	8
December 5, 1884	February 10, 1885	June 25, 1885	6
May 16, 1917	September 28, 1917	February 6, 1918	9
January 31, 1946[1]	November 5, 1947	July 30, 1948	30
July 27, 1953	August 23, 1954	January 5, 1955	17
February 16, 1965	April 24, 1969	November 11, 1970	69

Parliamentary Boundary Commissions 1831-2005 (contd.)

Commenced review	Date of report	Date of Act or SI	Length of time (months)
SCOTLAND contd.			
February 16, 1978	February 18, 1983	March 16, 1983	61
February 16, 1992	February 16, 1995	April 11, 1995	38
June 29, 2001	December 14, 2004	February 10, 2005	44
NORTHERN IRELAND			
January 31, 1946[1]	September 4, 1947	July 30, 1948	30
January ?, 1954[2]	November 10, 1954	Not applicable[3]	-
February 16, 1965	June 10, 1969	November 11, 1970	69
February 16, 1976	October 27, 1982	December 22, 1982	70
March 19, 1993	June 20, 1995	November 23, 1995	32
May 16, 2003			

1. The membership of the Commissions was published in *The Times* on January 4, 1946 and they held their first meeting on January 31 when it was announced that a review would now commence. No official notice of the commencement of the review was published in the *London Gazette*.
2. No official notice of the commencement of the review was published in the *Belfast Gazette* and when the report was published it did not give the January date.
3. The report recommended no change.

Table 6.02: Electoral Quotas 1946-2005

In considering boundary changes, the Boundary Commissions apply an electoral quota which is a figure obtained by dividing the total electorate by the number of constituencies existing at the time the Commissions begin their reviews. So far as practicable each constituency should have an electorate close to the electoral quota but the length of time between the start of the reviews, the reports and final approval by Parliament means that the quota may have altered considerably. Until 1965 the quota was calculated for Great Britain as a whole but since then it has been related to each part of the United Kingdom. The following table shows the electoral quota used by each Commission.

Commenced review	Effective from General Election	Electoral Quota			
		England	Wales	Scotland	N. Ireland
1946	1950	57,697	57,697	57,697	71,457
1953[1]	1955	55,670	55,670	55,670	72,913
1965	1974(F)	58,759	50,367	47,745	74,952
1976[2]	1983	65,753	58,753	53,649	61,206
1991[3]	1997	69,281	58,525	54,569	67,852
2000[4]	2005[5]	-	-	69,934	-
	n/a	69,934	55,640	-	60,969

1. 1954 in Northern Ireland.
2. 1978 in Scotland and 1981 in Wales.
3. 1992 in Scotland and 1993 in Wales and Northern Ireland.
4. 2001 in Scotland; 2002 in Wales; 2003 in Northern Ireland.
5. Scotland only. The review implemented the Scotland Act 1998 which reduced the number of Scottish Westminster constituencies by requiring the Boundary Commission to adopt the quota for England in its calculations.

Table 6.03: Constituency Boundary Changes 1945-2005

Election	Unchanged	%	Minor changes	%	Major changes	%
1945[1]	562	87.8	31	4.8	47	7.4
1950[2]	80	12.8	8	1.3	537	85.9
1951[3]	584	93.4	41	6.6	0	-
1955[2]	382	60.6	72	11.4	176	28.0
1959[3]	615	97.6	15	2.4	0	-
1964[3]	566	89.8	64	10.2	0	-
1974(F)[2]	210	33.1	109	17.2	316	49.7
1983[2]	66	10.4	43	6.8	526	82.8
1987[3]	556	85.5	92	14.2	2	0.3
1992[4]	550	84.6	98	15.1	2	0.3
1997[2]	165	25.3	76	11.7	410	63.0
2001[3]	643	97.6	16	2.4	0	-
2005[5]	590	89.5	1	0.2	68	10.3

1. Review of 20 abnormally large constituencies and the creation of an additional 25 seats.
2. Review of all constituency boundaries.
3. Review of certain constituencies to bring the boundaries into line with changes which had taken place in local government boundaries.
4. Review of certain constituencies to bring the boundaries into line with changes which had taken place in local government boundaries and the creation of one additional seat.
5. Review of all constituency boundaries in Scotland.

As regards what constitutes a major or minor change, the figures in each category prior to 1974 are based on the Commissioners' reports but modified as a result of information from other sources. Since 1974 it has been possible to obtain the number of electors involved in each change and only changes involving less than 5% of the electorate have been classed as minor. Boundary changes involving no electors have been classed as unchanged. With the limited information available prior to 1974 it is possible that some minor changes should have been classed as major or unchanged so the figures for the redistributions of 1950 and 1955 should be treated with caution.

Table 6.04: Seats in the House of Commons 1832-2005

	1832-1868[1]	1868-1885[2]	1885-1918[3]	1918-1922[4]	1922-1945[5]	1945-1950[6]	1950-1955[7]	1955-1974(F)[8]	1974(F)-1983[9]	1983-1987[10]	1992[11]	1997[12]-2001	2005[15]
London Boroughs	18	22	59	62	62	62	43	42	92	84	84	74	74
English Boroughs	304	263	166	193	193	216	248	247	212	194	195	200	200
English Counties	142	170	231	230	230	232	215	222	212	245	245	255	255
ENGLAND	**464**	**455**	**456**	**485**	**485**	**510**	**506**	**511**	**516**	**523**	**524**	**529**	**529**
Welsh Boroughs	15	16	12	11	11	11	10	10	10	6	6	6	6
Welsh Counties	17	17	22	24	24	24	26	26	26	32	32	34	34
WALES	**32**	**33**	**34**	**35**	**35**	**35**	**36**	**36**	**36**	**38**	**38**	**40**	**40**
Scottish Burghs	23	26	31	33	33	33	32	32	29	29	29	28	19
Scottish Counties	30	32	39	38	38	38	39	39	42	43	43	44	40
SCOTLAND	**53**	**58**	**70**	**71**	**71**	**71**	**71**	**71**	**71**	**72**	**72**	**72**	**59**
Irish Boroughs	39	39	16	21	4	4	4	4	4	4	4	4	4
Irish Counties	64	64	85	80	8	8	8	8	8	13	13	14	14
IRELAND[13]	**103**	**103**	**101**	**101**	**12**	**12**	**12**	**12**	**12**	**17**	**17**	**18**	**18**
UNIVERSITIES[14]	**6**	**9**	**9**	**15**	**12**	**12**	**0**	**0**	**0**	**0**	**0**	**0**	**0**
UNITED KINGDOM	**658**	**658**	**670**	**707**	**615**	**640**	**625**	**630**	**635**	**650**	**651**	**659**	**646**

1. Representation of the People Acts (England and Wales/Scotland/Ireland), 1832. In 1844 Sudbury (2 seats) was disfranchised reducing the number of Members to 656. In 1852 St. Albans (2 seats) was disfranchised reducing the number of Members to 654. By the Appropriation of Seats (Sudbury and St. Albans) Act, 1861 two of these seats were allocated immediately to Birkenhead and Lancashire, Southern, and the remaining two seats were given to Yorkshire, West Riding from the Dissolution of Parliament in 1865. The number of Members was thus restored to 656 in 1861 and 658 in 1865.

2. Representation of the People Acts (England and Wales/Scotland/Ireland), 1868. In 1870 Beverley (2 seats), Bridgwater (2 seats), Cashel (1seat) and Sligo (1 seat) were disfranchised reducing the number of Members to 652. In June 1885, Macclesfield (2 seats) and Sandwich (2 seats) were disfranchised reducing the number of Members to 648.

3. Redistribution of Seats Act, 1885.

4. Representation of the People Act, 1918.

5. Government of Ireland Act, 1920.

6. House of Commons (Redistribution of Seats) Act, 1944.

7. Representation of the People Act, 1948.

8. Statutory Instruments, 1955, Nos. 2-31 and 165-186.

Seats in the House of Commons 1832-2005 (contd.)

9. Statutory Instruments, 1970, Nos. 1674,1675,1678,1680.
10. Statutory Instruments, 1982, No. 183; 1983, Nos. 417, 418, 422.
11. Statutory Instrument, 1990, No. 1307.
12. Statutory Instruments, 1995, Nos. 1036, 1037, 1626, 2992.
13. The whole of Ireland until 1922, thereafter Northern Ireland only.
14. The University seats were divided as follows: 1832-68—England 4; Ireland 2. 1868-1918—England 5; Scotland 2; Ireland 2. 1918-50—England 7; Wales 1; Scotland 3; Ireland (until 1922) 4; Northern Ireland (from 1922) 1.
15. Statutory Instrument, 2005, No. 250.

Table 7.01: Members Elected at General Elections 1832-2005

Election	C[1]	%	Lab	%	L[2]	%	Others	%	Total	Overall majority[3]
1832	175*	26.6		-	441	67.0	42	6.4	658	L 225
1835	273*	41.5	-	-	385	58.5	-	-	658	L 113
1837	314	47.7	-	-	344*	52.3	-	-	658	L 29
1841	367	55.8	-	-	271*	41.2	20	3.0	658	C 77
1847	325	49.5	-	-	292*	44.5	39	6.0	656	None
1852	330	50.5	-	-	324*	49.5	-	-	654	C 7
1857	264	40.4	-	-	377	57.6	13	2.0	654	L 100
1859	298	45.6	-	-	356*	54.4	-	-	654	L 59
1865	289	43.9	-	-	369*	56.1	-	-	658	L 81
1868	271	41.2	-	-	387*	58.8	-	-	658	L 115
1874	350	53.7	-	-	242*	37.1	60	9.2	652	C 49
1880	237	36.3	-	-	352*	54.0	63	9.7	652	L 51
1885	249	37.2	-	-	319*	47.6	102	15.2	670	None
1886	393*	58.7	-	-	192	28.7	85	12.6	670	C 116
1892	313	46.7	-	-	272	40.6	85	12.7	670	None
1895	411	61.4	-	-	177*	26.4	82	12.2	670	C 153
1900	402	60.0	2	0.3	183*	27.3	83	12.4	670	C 135
1906	156*	23.3	29	4.3	399	59.6	86	12.8	670	L 129
1910(J)	272*	40.6	40	6.0	274	40.9	84	12.5	670	None
1910(D)	271*	40.4	42	6.3	272	40.6	85	12.7	670	None
1918	382*	54.0	57	8.1	163	23.1	105	14.8	707	Co 283[4]
1922	344	55.9	142	23.1	115*	18.7	14	2.3	615	C 74
1923	258	41.9	191	31.1	158*	25.7	8	1.3	615	None
1924	412	67.0	151	24.6	40*	6.5	12	1.9	615	C 210
1929	260*	42.3	287	46.7	59	9.6	9	1.4	615	None
1931	522*	84.9	52[5]	8.5	36[6]	5.8	5	0.8	615	Nat 492
1935	429*	69.8	154	25.0	21	3.4	11	1.8	615	Nat 242
1945	210*	32.8	393	61.4	12	1.9	25	3.9	640	Lab 147
1950	298*	47.7	315	50.4	9	1.4	3	0.5	625	Lab 6
1951	321	51.3	295	47.2	6	1.0	3	0.5	625	C 16
1955	345*	54.8	277	44.0	6	0.9	2	0.3	630	C 59
1959	365	57.9	258	41.0	6	0.9	1	0.2	630	C 99
1964	304*	48.3	317	50.3	9	1.4	-	-	630	Lab 5
1966	253	40.1	364*	57.8	12	1.9	1	0.2	630	Lab 97
1970	330	52.3	288*	45.7	6	1.0	6	1.0	630	C 31
1974(F)	297*	46.8	301	47.4	14	2.2	23	3.6	635	None
1974(O)	277*	43.6	319	50.2	13	2.1	26	4.1	635	Lab 4
1979	339	53.4	269*	42.4	11	1.7	16	2.5	635	C 44
1983	397	61.1	209	32.2	23	3.5	21	3.2	650	C 144
1987	376*	57.9	229	35.2	22	3.4	23	3.5	650	C 101
1992	336	51.6	271	41.6	20	3.1	24	3.7	651	C 21
1997	165	25.0	418	63.4	46	7.0	30*	4.6	659	Lab 178
2001	166	25.2	412	62.5	52	7.9	29*	4.4	659	Lab 166
2005	198	30.7	355	55.0	62	9.6	31*	4.8	646	Lab 65

* Including the Speaker.

1. Including Liberal Conservatives, 1847-59; Liberal Unionists, 1886-1910(D); National, National Liberal and National Labour, 1931-45.

2. Including both Liberal and National Liberal, 1922; Independent Liberal, 1931; SDP/Liberal Alliance, 1983-87; Liberal Democrat 1992 onwards.

130

Members Elected at General Elections 1832-2005 (contd.)

3. This figure represents the majority of the Government over all other parties combined. The Speaker has been excluded when calculating the majority.
4. Theoretical majority. 73 Sinn Fein members did not take their seats.
5. Including 6 unendorsed.
6. Of this total, 4 Liberals opposed the National Government and are counted with the Opposition in calculating the overall majority.

Table 7.02: Candidates at General Elections 1832-2005

Election	C[1]	%	Lab	%	L[2]	%	Others	%	Total	Cands per seat
1832	350	33.8	-	-	636	61.3	51	4.9	1,037	1.6
1835	407	43.1	-	-	538	56.9	-	-	945	1.4
1837	484	48.7	-	-	510	51.3	-	-	994	1.5
1841	498	54.4	-	-	388	42.3	30	3.3	916	1.4
1847	422	48.0	-	-	393	44.7	64	7.3	879	1.3
1852	461	48.4	-	-	488	51.2	4	0.4	953	1.5
1857	351	40.0	-	-	507	57.6	21	2.4	878	1.3
1859	394	45.8	-	-	465	54.1	1	0.1	860	1.3
1865	406	44.0	-	-	516	56.0	-	-	922	1.4
1868	436	42.0	-	-	600	57.7	3	0.3	1,039	1.6
1874	507	46.9	-	-	489	45.3	84	7.8	1,080	1.7
1880	521	47.2	-	-	499	45.3	83	7.5	1,103	1.7
1885	602	45.0	-	-	572	42.7	164	12.3	1,338	2.0
1886	563	50.5	-	-	449	40.3	103	9.2	1,115	1.7
1892	606	46.5	-	-	532	40.8	165	12.7	1,303	1.9
1895	588	49.8	-	-	447	37.9	145	12.3	1,180	1.8
1900	569	51.6	15	1.4	402	36.5	116	10.5	1,102	1.6
1906	556	43.7	50	3.9	536	42.1	131	10.3	1,273	1.9
1910(J)	594	45.2	78	5.9	511	38.9	132	10.0	1,315	2.0
1910(D)	548	46.0	56	4.7	467	39.2	120	10.1	1,191	1.8
1918	445	27.4	361	22.3	421	25.9	396	24.4	1,623	2.3
1922	482	33.4	414	28.7	485	33.7	60	4.2	1,441	2.3
1923	536	37.1	427	29.5	457	31.6	26	1.8	1,446	2.4
1924	534	37.4	514	36.0	339	23.7	41	2.9	1,428	2.3
1929	590	34.1	569	32.9	513	29.7	58	3.3	1,730	2.8
1931	583	45.1	516[3]	39.9	117[4]	9.1	76	5.9	1,292	2.1
1935	583	43.2	552	41.0	161	11.9	52	3.9	1,348	2.2
1945	618	36.7	603	35.8	306	18.2	156	9.3	1,683	2.6
1950	619	33.2	617	33.0	475	25.4	157	8.4	1,868	3.0
1951	617	44.8	617	44.8	109	8.0	33	2.4	1,376	2.2
1955	624	44.3	620	44.0	110	7.8	55	3.9	1,409	2.2
1959	625	40.7	621	40.4	216	14.1	74	4.8	1,536	2.4
1964	630	35.9	628	35.7	365	20.8	134	7.6	1,757	2.8
1966	629	36.9	622	36.4	311	18.2	145	8.5	1,707	2.7
1970	628	34.2	625	34.0	332	18.1	252	13.7	1,837	2.9
1974(F)	623	29.2	623	29.2	517	24.2	372	17.4	2,135	3.4
1974(O)	622	27.6	623	27.7	619	27.5	388	17.2	2,252	3.5
1979	622	24.1	623	24.2	577	22.4	754	29.3	2,576	4.1
1983	633	24.6	633	24.6	633	24.6	679	26.2	2,578	4.0
1987	633	27.2	633	27.2	633	27.2	426	18.4	2,325	3.6

Candidates at General Elections 1832-2005 (contd.)

Election	C[1]	%	Lab	%	L[2]	%	Others	%	Total	Cands per seat
1992	645	21.9	634	21.5	632	21.4	1,038	35.2	2,949	4.5
1997	648	17.4	639	17.2	639	17.2	1,798	48.3	3,724	5.7
2001	643	19.4	640	19.3	639	19.3	1,397	42.1	3,319	5.0
2005	630	17.7	627	17.6	626	17.6	1,671	47.0	3,554	5.5

1. Including Liberal Conservatives, 1847-59; Liberal Unionists, 1886-1910(D); National, National Liberal and National Labour, 1931-45.
2. Including both Liberal and National Liberal, 1922; Independent Liberal, 1931; SDP/Liberal Alliance, 1983-87; Liberal Democrat 1992 onwards.
3. Including 25 unendorsed.
4. Including Independent Liberals.

Table 7.03: Number of Candidates per Single Member Seat 1885-2005

	One	Two	Three	Four	Five	Six	Seven	Eight	Nine	Ten	Eleven	Total Seats
1885	35	538	39	4	0	0	0	0	0	0	0	616
1886	212	400	4	0	0	0	0	0	0	0	0	616
1892	57	527	30	2	0	0	0	0	0	0	0	616
1895	181	406	29	0	0	0	0	0	0	0	0	616
1900	229	379	7	1	0	0	0	0	0	0	0	616
1906	108	462	45	1	0	0	0	0	0	0	0	616
1910(J)	69	501	46	0	0	0	0	0	0	0	0	616
1910(D)	153	446	16	1	0	0	0	0	0	0	0	616
1918	101	311	211	36	10	1	0	0	0	0	0	670
1922	48	293	212	22	1	0	0	0	0	0	0	576
1923	41	280	254	1	0	0	0	0	0	0	0	576
1924	30	318	223	5	0	0	0	0	0	0	0	576
1929	5	98	447	26	0	0	0	0	0	0	0	576
1931	54	409	99	14	0	0	0	0	0	0	0	576
1935	34	389	146	7	0	0	0	0	0	0	0	576
1945	3	259	291	42	6	0	0	0	0	0	0	601
1950	2	113	405	100	5	0	0	0	0	0	0	625
1951	4	495	122	4	0	0	0	0	0	0	0	625
1955	0	489	133	8	0	0	0	0	0	0	0	630
1959	0	373	238	19	0	0	0	0	0	0	0	630
1964	0	194	379	53	4	0	0	0	0	0	0	630
1966	0	234	349	44	2	1	0	0	0	0	0	630
1970	0	185	328	103	13	1	0	0	0	0	0	630
1974(F)	0	38	370	191	32	3	1	0	0	0	0	635
1974(O)	0	0	346	238	44	7	0	0	0	0	0	635
1979	0	3	173	300	118	28	12	0	1	0	0	635
1983	0	0	251	250	99	31	12	5	1	0	1	650
1987	0	0	351	236	51	11	1	0	0	0	0	650
1992	0	0	103	253	183	81	23	7	0	1	0	651
1997	0	0	18	134	176	165	101	35	23	7	0	659
2001	0	0	45	198	208	134	49	20	5	0	0	659
2005	0	0	21	136	215	128	92	34	17	2	0[1]	646

1. Fifteen candidates stood in Sedgefield.

Table 7.04: Women Members Elected at General Elections 1918-2005

Election	C	Lab	L¹	Com	NF	PC	SNP	Others	Total	% of total MPs
1918	0	0	0	-	-	-	-	1[2]	1	0.1
1922	1	0	1	0	-	-	-	0	2	0.3
1923	3	3	2	0	-	-	-	0	8	1.3
1924	3	1	0	0	-	-	-	0	4	0.7
1929	3	9	1	0	-	0	0	1	14	2.3
1931	13	0	1	0	-	0	0	1	15	2.4
1935	6	1	1	0	-	0	0	1	9	1.5
1945	1	21	1	0	-	0	0	1	24	3.8
1950	6	14	1	0	-	0	0	0	21	3.4
1951	6	11	0	0	-	0	0	0	17	2.7
1955	10	14	0	0	-	0	0	0	24	3.8
1959	12	13	0	0	-	0	0	0	25	4.0
1964	11	18	0	0	-	0	0	0	29	4.6
1966	7	19	0	0	-	0	0	0	26	4.1
1970	15	10	0	0	0	0	0	1[3]	26	4.1
1974(F)	9	13	0	0	0	0	1	0	23	3.6
1974(O)	7	18	0	0	0	0	2	0	27	4.3
1979	8	11	0	0	0	0	0	0	19	3.0
1983	13	10	0	0	0	0	0	0	23	3.5
1987	17	21	2	0	0	0	1	0	41	6.3
1992	20	37	2	0	0	0	1	0	60	9.2
1997	13	101	3	0	0	0	2	1	120	18.2
2001	14	95	5	0	0	0	0	4	126	17.9
2005	17	98	10	0	0	0	0	3	128	19.8

1. SDP/Liberal Alliance 1983-87; Liberal Democrat 1992 onwards.
2. Countess Markievicz (SF) who was elected for Dublin, St. Patrick's. She did not take her seat in the House of Commons.
3. Miss B.J. Devlin (Mid-Ulster—Unity).

Table 7.05: Women Candidates at General Elections 1918-2005

Election	C	Lab	L[1]	Com	NF	PC	SNP	Others	Total	Candidates
1918	1	4	4	-	-	-	-	8	17	1.0
1922	5	10	16	0	-	-	-	2	33	2.3
1923	7	14	12	0	-	-	-	1	34	2.4
1924	12	22	6	0	-	-	-	1	41	2.9
1929	10	30	25	3	-	0	0	1	69	4.0
1931	16	36[2]	5	2	-	0	1	2	62	4.8
1935	19	33	11	0	-	0	0	4	67	5.0
1945	14	41	20	2	-	1	0	9	87	5.2
1950	29[3]	42	45	9	-	0	0	2	127[3]	6.8
1951	25	41	11	0	-	0	0	0	77	5.6
1955	33	43	14	1	-	1	0	0	92	6.5
1959	28	36	16	1	-	0	0	0	81	5.3
1964	24	33	24	4	-	1	0	4	90	5.1
1966	21	30	20	6	-	0	0	4	81	4.7
1970	26	29	23	6	1	0	10	4	99	5.4
1974(F)	33	40	40	3	3	2	8	14	143	6.7
1974(O)	30	50	49	2	5	1	8	16	161	7.1
1979	31	52	52	4	36	1	6	34	216	8.4
1983	40	78	75	5	6	6	9	61	280	10.9
1987	46	92	106	4	0	9	6	66	329	14.2
1992	63	138	143	1	1	7	15	205	571	19.3
1997	69	157	140	0	0	7	15	284	672	18.0
2001	92	149	139	0	1	7	16	232	636	19.2
2005	122	166	144	1	0	4	13	270	720	20.3

1. SDP/Liberal Alliance 1983-87; Liberal Democrat 1992 onwards.

2. Including 6 unendorsed.

3. Miss Florence Horsbrugh (C) is counted twice in this total. She was defeated at Midlothian and Peeblesshire but subsequently elected for Manchester, Moss Side where polling had been postponed due to the death of the Conservative candidate.

133

Table 7.06: Ethnic Minority Members Elected at General Elections 1979-2005

Election	C	Lab	L	Total
1979	0	0	0	0
1983	0	0	0	0
1987	0	4	0	4
1992	1	5	0	6
1997	0	9	0	9
2001	0	12	0	12
2005	2	13	0	15

Table 7.07: Ethnic Minority Candidates at General Elections 1979-2005 (Main Parties Only)

Election	C	Lab	L	Total
1979	2	1	2	5
1983	4	6	8	18
1987	6	14	9	29
1992	8	9	5	22
1997	9	13	17	39
2001	16	21	29	66
2005	41	32	40	113

Table 7.08: Women Members of Parliament – Miscellaneous Information

The first woman to be elected to the House of Commons was Countess Markievicz (Sinn Fein) on December 28, 1918. She did not take her seat.

The first woman to take her seat in the House of Commons was Nancy Astor (Con) on December 1, 1919.

The youngest woman to be elected to the House of Commons was Bernadette Devlin (Unity) who was twenty-one years of age when elected on April 18, 1969.

Irene Ward (Con) was a member of the House of Commons longer than any other woman. She was first elected for Wallsend in 1931 and was defeated in 1945. In 1950 she was elected for Tynemouth and retired in February 1974(F).

Barbara Castle (Lab) holds the record for the longest period of continuous service by a woman. First elected for Blackburn in 1945, she retired in 1979.

Margaret Thatcher (Con) was elected for Finchley in 1959 and retired in 1992.

Betty Boothroyd (Lab), was elected the first woman Speaker of the House in 1992.

Angela (Lab) and Maria Eagle (Lab) were the first twin sisters to be elected to the House of Commons in 1997.

Table 8.01: Ministers Defeated 1918-2005

Election[1]	Ministry at Dissolution	Cabinet Ministers	Ministers not in the Cabinet	Law Officers	Junior Ministers[2]
1918	COALITION	0	0	0	0
1922	CONSERVATIVE	1	0	1	4
1923	CONSERVATIVE	2	2	1	2
1924	LABOUR	1	0	0	7
1929	CONSERVATIVE	1	0	2	5
1931	NATIONAL[3]	0	0	1	3
1935	NATIONAL	2	0	0	0
1945	NATIONAL[4]	5	8	0	19
1950	LABOUR	1	0	1	5
1951	LABOUR	0	0	0	2
1955	CONSERVATIVE	0	0	0	0
1959	CONSERVATIVE	0	0	0	2
1964	CONSERVATIVE	2	1	0	3
1966	LABOUR	0	0	0	0
1970	LABOUR	1	3	0	10
1974(F)	CONSERVATIVE	1	0	0	2
1974(O)	LABOUR	0	0	0	0
1979	LABOUR	1	0	0	7
1983	CONSERVATIVE	0	0	0	2
1987	CONSERVATIVE	0	0	1	4
1992	CONSERVATIVE	2	2	0	5
1997	CONSERVATIVE	7	7	1	20
2001	LABOUR	0	0	0	1
2005	LABOUR	0	0	0	5

1. At by-elections the following Ministers were defeated:
   Sir A.S.T. Griffith-Boscawen (C), Minister of Agriculture and Fisheries (Dudley, 1921).
   T.A. Lewis (L), Lord Commissioner of the Treasury (Glamorgan, Pontypridd, 1922).
   Sir A.S.T. Griffith-Boscawen (C), Minister of Health (Surrey, Mitcham, 1923).
   J.W. Hills (C), Financial Secretary to the Treasury (Liverpool, Edge Hill, 1923).
   Hon. G.F. Stanley (C), Under-Secretary of State for the Home Department (Willesden, East, 1923).
   P.C. Gordon Walker (Lab), Secretary of State for Foreign Affairs (Leyton, 1965).
   With the exception of Sir A.S.T. Griffith-Boscawen who, after his defeat at Dudley in 1921, retained office and was elected at another by-election one month later, all defeated Ministers subsequently resigned office.
2. Including the Treasurer, Comptroller and Vice-Chamberlain of H.M. Household.
3. The defeated members of the former Labour Government were:-
   Cabinet Ministers, 13; Ministers not in the Cabinet, 1; Junior Ministers, 20.
4. The defeated members of the former Coalition Government were:-
   Ministers not in the Cabinet, 10; Law Officers, 1; Junior Ministers, 14.

Table 8.02: Seats Vacant at Dissolution 1886-2005

1886	No seat vacant	1950	Deptford (Lab)
1892	Essex, Epping (C)		Durham, Chester-le-Street (Lab)
	Lambeth, Norwood (C)		Islington, North (Lab)
	Pembroke & Haverfordwest Boroughs (C)		Manchester, Ardwick (Lab)
	Swansea Town (L)		Rotherham (Lab)
1895	No seat vacant		Sheffield, Hillsborough (Lab)
			Sheffield, Park (Lab)
1900	Armagh, South (N)	1951	Droylsden (Lab)
1906	Cambridge University (C)		Lanarkshire, Lanark (C)
	Montgomeryshire (L)		Lincolnshire, Grantham (C)
1910(J)	Ipswich (L)	1955	Glasgow, Pollok (C)
	Kensington, South (C)		Kent, Gravesend (Lab)
	Liverpool, Exchange (L)		Norwich, South (C)
	Middlesex, Uxbridge (C)	1959	Birmingham, Sparkbrook (Lab)
	Portsmouth (L)		Kensington, South (C)
	Tipperary, Mid (N)		Lancashire, Clitheroe (C)
1910(D)	Carmarthenshire, Western (L)		Midlothian (Lab)
	Kerry, East (Ind N)		Nottingham, North (Lab)
	Lancashire, Clitheroe (Lab)		Yorkshire, Richmond (C)
1918	Belfast, North (C)	1964	Ashton-under-Lyne (Lab)
	Cork, North-East (Ind N)		Bebington (C)
	Fulham (C)		Berkshire, Newbury (C)
	Staffordshire, Western (C)		Blackpool, South (C)
	Surrey, Kingston (C)		Cheshire, Runcorn (C)
	Surrey, Reigate (Nat P)		Edinburgh, Pentlands (C)
1922	Roxburghshire and Selkirkshire (Co L)		Norfolk, North (Lab)
			Northamptonshire, Kettering (Lab)
1923	Ayrshire and Bute, Kilmarnock (L)		Renfrewshire, West (NL& C)
	Glasgow, Central (C)		Salford, West (Lab)
	University of Wales (NL)		Shoreditch and Finsbury (Lab)
	Warwickshire, Warwick & Leamington (C)		Southgate (C)
1924	London University (C)		Surrey, Woking (C)
1929	Buckinghamshire, Aylesbury (C)		Westmorland(C)
	Cambridge University (C)	1966	Birmingham, Edgbaston (C)
	Carlisle (C)		Cornwall, Falmouth & Camborne (Lab)
	Lancashire, Ince (Lab)	1970	Northumberland, Morpeth (Lab)
	Nottinghamshire, Mansfield (Lab)		Twickenham (C)
	Preston (one seat) (C)	1974(F)	Worcestershire, South (C)
	Willesden, East (C)	1974(O)	Newcastle upon Tyne, East (Lab)
	Yorkshire, Thirsk and Malton (C)		Swansea, East (Lab)
1931	Gateshead[1] (Lab)	1979	Abingdon (C)
	Yorkshire, Hemsworth (Lab)		Batley and Morley (Lab)
1935	Derbyshire, Clay Cross (Lab)		Chipping Barnet (C)
	Essex, Harwich (NL)		Derbyshire, North-East (Lab)
	Hammersmith, North (Lab)	1983	Cardiff, North-West (C)
	Holborn[1] (C)		Rhondda (Lab)
	Lancashire, Farnworth (C)	1987	Deptford (Lab)
	Roxburghshire and Selkirkshire (C)		Kirkcaldy (Lab)
1945	Antrim (one seat) (C)	1992	No seat vacant
	Bradford, East (C)	1997	Don Valley (Lab)
	Bristol, North (NL)		Meriden (C)
	Cardiganshire (L)	2001	No seat vacant
	Hythe (C)	2005	No seat vacant
	Wednesbury (Lab)		
	Yorkshire, Rother Valley (Lab)		

1. Member died on the day of Dissolution

Table 8.03: The Weather on Polling Day 1918-2005

Election	Weather
1918	Rain over the whole country with thunderstorms in the North.
1922	Quiet weather with low temperatures. Fog in many places.
1923	Fog in central England and Southern Scotland but fine elsewhere.
1924	Wet and very windy.
1929	Fine in the North but cloudy in the South.
1931	Unsettled in Scotland and Northern Ireland but fine elsewhere.
1935	Unsettled with strong winds in the West and South-West.
1945	Clear and fair.
1950	Sunny and mild until evening then heavy rain.
1951	Light fog and frost in the morning but clearing and remaining generally fair.
1955	Generally fine and sunny but with some showers in the evening.
1959	A dry autumn day.
1964	Rain over much of the country.
1966	Mild day with only a trace of rain anywhere except in the North of Scotland.
1970	Fine everywhere.
1974(F)	Some rain in all parts of the country but especially in the South West.
1974(O)	Cloudy with showers in some parts but few instances of heavy rain.
1979	Fair. The only appreciable rain was reported from Scotland and the West Country.
1983	Cloudy with light showers in most areas. Warm.
1987	Generally cool. Frequent showers, sometimes heavy with thunderstorms in many areas but mainly dry and sunny in western districts.
1992	A fine, sunny day. Cloudier in Scotland with some showers in the far north.
1997	Sunny and dry throughout the country. Warm away from south facing coasts.
2001	Cloudy and wet at times in North and East. Drier and sunnier in South and West.
2005	Cloud and patchy rain across much of the country. Mostly dry in southern England.

Sources: 1918-35 and 1983-87 Meteorological Office; 1945-79 Nuffield College studies of British General Elections; 1992-2005 press reports.

Table 8.04: The First Result 1918-2005

Since 1918 when polling in all constituencies at a General Election took place on the same day, there has always been keen competition between Returning Officers to provide the first result declared. The following constituencies provided the first result of each General Election. From 1950 the actual time of declaration is given. The record for the quickest count is held by Sunderland South – 41 minutes in 2001.

Election	Constituency	Election	Constituency
1918	Salford, North	1964	Cheltenham (10.00 p.m.)
1922	Wallasey	1966	Cheltenham (10.04 p.m.)
1923	Manchester, Exchange	1970	Guildford (11.10 p.m.)
1924	Salford, South	1974(F)	Guildford (11.10 p.m.)
1929	Oxford	1974(O)	Guildford (11.10 p.m.)
1931	Hornsey	1979	Glasgow Central (11.34 p.m.)
1935	Cheltenham	1983	Torbay (11.10 p.m.)
1945	Salford, South	1987	Torbay (11.02 p.m.)
1950	Salford, West (10.45 p.m.)	1992	Sunderland South (11.06 p.m.)
1951	Salford, West (10.21 p.m.)	1997	Sunderland South (10.46 p.m.)
1955	Cheltenham (10.08 p.m.)	2001	Sunderland South (10.41 p.m.)
	Salford, West (10.08 p.m.)	2005	Sunderland South (10.43 p.m.)
1959	Billericay (9.57 p.m.)		

Note: Close of poll extended in 1970 from 9.00 p.m, to 10.00 p.m.

Sources: The Press Association, *The Times*, local newspapers, ITN.

Table 8.05: The Overnight Results 1950-2005

Since 1950 an increasing number of constituencies have commenced counting immediately after polling finished instead of waiting until the next morning. The following is a summary of the strength of the parties and of gains and losses when all the overnight counts had been completed.

| | —— State of Parties —— | | | | —— Party Gains and Losses —— | | | | | | | |
| | *Total* | | | | | C | | Lab | | L | | Others | |
Election	*Results*	*C*	*Lab*	*L*	*Others*	+	-	+	-	+	-	+	-
1950	264	102	163	1	0	-	-	-	-	-	-	-	-
1951	319	145	175	2	1	11	1	0	12	1	0	1	0
1955	357	176	179	2	0	9	0	0	8	0	0	0	1
1959	388	205	180	3	0	21	4	3	21	1	0	0	0
1964	430	181	247	2	0	4	49	52	4	0	2	0	1
1966	461	151	304	5	1	0	43	42	1	2	1	1	0
1970	418	188	227	2	1	54	6	9	51	0	3	1	4
1974(F)	442	177	255	5	5	2	12	10	5	2	1	4	0
1974(O)	493	185	294	5	9	1	21	20	1	0	2	5	2
1979	514	258	245	7	4	52	6	11	47	0	1	0	9
1983	572	352	199	17	4	8	1	1	6	1	3	0	0
1987	595	348	225	16	6	12	27	25	6	2	8	4	2
1992	618	321	269	16	12	2	43	43	1	3	2	1	3
1997	606	145	412	39	10	0	173	143	0	27	1	4	0
2001	625	161	406	47	11	8	8	2	8	8	1	2	3
2005	619	195	353	59	12	36	3	0	47	16	5	4	1

Table 8.06: Reasons for Holding General Elections 1832-2005

1832	To elect a new Parliament subsequent to the passing of the First (Electoral) Reform Act.
1835	Viscount Melbourne resigned as Prime Minister and was succeeded by Sir Robert Peel who immediately asked for a Dissolution.
1837	Death of William IV.
1841	Request by the Prime Minister after a defeat in the House of Commons.
1847	Request by the Prime Minister for a Dissolution on Parliament nearing the end of its statutory term of seven years.
1852	Lord John Russell resigned as Prime Minister after a defeat in the House of Commons. He was succeeded by the Earl of Derby who four months later requested a Dissolution .
1857	Request by the Prime Minister for a Dissolution after a defeat in the House of Commons.
1859	Request by the Prime Minister for a Dissolution after a defeat in the House of Commons.
1865	Request by the Prime Minister for a Dissolution on Parliament nearing the end of its statutory term of seven years.
1868	To elect a new Parliament subsequent to the passing of the Second (Electoral) Reform Act.
1874	Request by the Prime Minister for a Dissolution on Parliament nearing the end of its statutory term of seven years.
1880	Request by the Prime Minister for a Dissolution on Parliament nearing the end of its statutory term of seven years.
1885	Resignation of the Liberal Government and request for a Dissolution after a defeat in the House of Commons on an amendment to the Finance Bill. The Marquess of Salisbury formed a minority Conservative Government but within five months he requested a Dissolution.
1886	Resignation of the Liberal Government and request for a Dissolution after a defeat in the House of Commons on the Irish Home Rule Bill.
1892	Request by the Prime Minister for a Dissolution on Parliament nearing the end of its statutory term of seven years.
1895	Resignation of the Liberal Government after a defeat in the House of Commons on the issue of the supply of cordite to the Army. The Marquess of Salisbury formed a minority Conservative Government and immediately requested a Dissolution.
1900	Request by the Prime Minister for a Dissolution to obtain a renewal of the electors' confidence in the Government at a time when it appeared that the South African War was drawing to a close.
1906	Resignation of the Conservative Government after a series of defeats in by-elections and internal disputes over tariff reform. Sir Henry Campbell-Bannerman formed a minority Liberal Government and immediately requested a Dissolution.
1910(J)	Request by the Prime Minister for a Dissolution after the House of Lords had rejected the Finance Bill.
1910(D)	Request by the Prime Minister for a Dissolution after a Constitutional Conference of Liberal and Conservative members had failed to agree on proposals to limit the power of the House of Lords.
1918	End of World War 1. Parliament should have been dissolved in 1915 but its life was extended due to the war.
1922	David Lloyd George resigned as Prime Minister of a Coalition Government and Andrew Bonar Law formed a Conservative Government and immediately asked for a Dissolution.
1923	Andrew Bonar Law resigned as Prime Minister and was succeeded by Stanley Baldwin who within six months asked for a Dissolution to obtain a mandate for tariff reforms.
1924	Resignation of the Labour Government and request for a Dissolution after a defeat in the House of Commons on the issue of the Government's decision not to prosecute J.R. Campbell, editor of a Communist Party journal, under the Incitement to Mutiny Act.

Reasons for Holding General Elections 1832-2005 (contd.)

1929	Request by the Prime Minister for a Dissolution on Parliament nearing the end of its statutory term of five years.
1931	Resignation of the Labour Government and formation of a National Government by James Ramsay MacDonald who six weeks later asked for a Dissolution in order to obtain a new mandate.
1935	Request by the Prime Minister for a Dissolution on Parliament nearing the end of its statutory term of five years.
1945	End of War in Europe. Parliament should have been dissolved in 1940 but its life was extended due to the war.
1950	Request by the Prime Minister for a Dissolution on Parliament nearing the end of its statutory term of five years.
1951	Request by the Prime Minister for a Dissolution to obtain a renewal of the electors' confidence in the Government and an adequate parliamentary majority.
1955	Sir Winston Churchill resigned as Prime Minister and was succeeded by Sir Anthony Eden who immediately asked for a Dissolution.
1959	Request by the Prime Minister for a Dissolution on Parliament nearing the end of its statutory term of five years.
1964	Request by the Prime Minister for a Dissolution on Parliament nearing the end of its statutory term of five years.
1966	Request by the Prime Minister for a Dissolution to obtain a renewal of the electors' confidence in the Government and an adequate parliamentary majority.
1970	Request by the Prime Minister for a Dissolution on Parliament nearing the end of its statutory term of five years.
1974(F)	Request by the Prime Minister for a Dissolution to obtain a renewal of the electors' confidence in the Government on the eve of a strike by the National Union of Mineworkers.
1974(O)	Request by the Prime Minister for a Dissolution to obtain a renewal of the electors' confidence in the Government and an overall parliamentary majority.
1979	Resignation of the Labour Government and a request for a Dissolution following a defeat in the House of Commons on a motion of no confidence.
1983	Request by the Prime Minister for a Dissolution on Parliament nearing the end of its statutory term of five years.
1987	Request by the Prime Minister for a Dissolution on Parliament nearing the end of its statutory term of five years.
1992	Request by the Prime Minister for a Dissolution on Parliament nearing the end of its statutory term of five years.
1997	Request by the Prime Minister for a Dissolution on Parliament nearing the end of its statutory term of five years.
2001	Request by the Prime Minister for a Dissolution on Parliament nearing the end of its statutory term of five years.
2005	Request by the Prime Minister for a Dissolution on Parliament nearing the end of its statutory term of five years.

Parliamentary By-Elections

Table 9.01: Parliamentary By-Elections 1945-2006 (GB)

No.	Constituency	Date	Result	% Maj GE	% turn GE	% turn BE	turn % chng	% Con GE	% Con BE	Con % chng	% Lab GE	% Lab BE	Lab % chng	% Lib GE	% Lib BE	Lib % chng	% Nat GE	% Nat BE	Nat % chng	Con/Lab swing[1]	Con/Lib swing[1]	Lab/Lib swing[1]
	1945-50 Parliament																					
1	Smethwick	1.10.45	Lab held	31.8	72.4	65.4	-7.0	34.1	31.2	-2.9	65.9	68.8	2.9							-2.9		
2	Ashton-under-Lyme	2.10.45	Lab held	12.8	78.6	70.5	-8.1	43.6	35.0	-8.6	56.4	54.1	-2.3		10.9	10.9				-3.2	-9.8	-6.6
3	Edinburgh East	3.10.45	Con held	19.1	69.4	51.0	-18.4	37.3	38.4	1.1	56.4	61.6	5.2				6.3		-6.3	-2.1		
4	Monmouth	30.10.45	Con held	3.8	72.0	66.7	-5.3	51.9	52.7	0.8	48.1	47.3	-0.8							0.8		
5	City of London	31.10.45	Con held	67.8	63.9	51.6	-12.3	78.8	75.0	-3.8				11.0	25.0	14.0						
6	Bromley	14.11.45	Con held	10.9	70.9	60.6	-10.3	45.0	49.6	4.6	34.1	39.1	5.0	20.9	11.3	-9.6				-0.2	7.1	7.3
7	Bournemouth	15.11.45	Con held	33.8	71.2	56.5	-14.7	55.5	46.8	-8.7	21.7	33.7	12.0	22.8	19.5	-3.3				-10.4	-2.7	7.7
8	Kensington South	20.11.45	Con held	50.9	67.9	36.8	-31.1	69.8	81.7	11.9	18.9		-18.9	11.3	18.3	7.0				15.4	2.5	-13.0
9	Tottenham North	13.12.45	Lab held	43.6	70.3	39.5	-30.8	28.2	36.4	8.2	71.8	63.6	-8.2							8.2		
10	Preston	31.1.46	Lab held	4.5	80.2	64.9	-15.3	41.8	44.4	2.6	46.3	55.6	9.3	6.1		-6.1				-3.4	4.4	7.7
11	Ayrshire South	7.2.46	Lab held	22.6	75.0	69.0	-6.0	38.7	36.4	-2.3	61.3	63.6	2.3							-2.3		
12	Glasgow Cathcart	12.2.46	Con held	17.6	67.6	55.6	-12.0	58.8	52.5	-6.3	41.2	37.1	-4.1					10.4	10.4	-1.1		
13	Heywood & Radcliffe	21.2.46	Lab held	2.0	76.4	75.6	-0.8	49.0	49.5	0.5	51.0	50.5	-0.5							0.5		
14	Hemsworth	22.2.46	Lab held[2]	62.8	80.8			18.6			81.4											
15	Combined English Universities*	13.3.46	Con x Ind	n/a	50.0	42.1	-7.9															
16	Ogmore	4.6.46	Lab held	58.4	75.6	33.1	-42.5	18.0		-18.0	76.4	70.6	-5.8				5.6	29.4	23.8	-6.1		
17	Bexley	22.7.46	Lab held	27.1	76.7	61.2	-15.5	29.8	47.5	17.7	56.9	52.5	-4.4	13.3		-13.3				11.1	15.5	4.5
18	Pontypool	23.7.46	Lab held	54.6	77.0	64.8	-12.2	22.7	26.8	4.1	77.3	73.2	-4.1							4.1		
19	Battersea North	25.7.46	Lab held	47.8	70.9	55.4	-15.5	26.1	29.6	3.5	73.9	68.9	-5.0							4.3		
20	Glasgow Bridgeton	29.8.46	ILP held	33.6	58.2	53.3	-4.9	33.6	21.6	-12.0		28.0	28.0							-20.0		
21	Bermondsey, Rotherhithe	19.11.46	Lab held	58.2	68.1	50.9	-17.2	20.9	9.7	-11.2	79.1	65.0	-14.1		25.3	25.3				1.5	-18.3	-19.7
22	Paddington North	20.11.46	Lab held	24.1	71.0	53.9	-17.1	37.1	43.2	6.1	61.2	55.6	-5.6							5.9		
23	Combined Scottish Universities*	21.11.46	Con x Ind	n/a	51.6	50.7	0.9															
24	Aberdeen South	26.11.46	Con held	4.5	71.9	65.5	-6.4	46.8	54.8	8.0	42.3	45.2	2.9	10.9		-10.9				2.6	9.5	6.9
25	Aberdare	5.12.46	Lab held	68.6	76.1	65.7	-10.4	15.7	11.7	-4.0	84.3	68.3	-16.0					20.0	20.0	6.0		
26	Kilmarnock	5.12.46	Lab held	18.8	76.1	68.4	7.7	40.6	32.5	-8.1	59.4	59.7	0.3					7.8	7.8	-4.2		
27	Normanton	11.2.47	Lab held	68.6	79.9	54.6	-25.3	15.7	17.8	2.1	84.3	79.8	-4.5							3.3		
28	Jarrow	7.5.47	Lab held	32.0	76.0	73.4	-2.6	34.0	37.5	3.5	66.0	59.3	-6.7							5.1		
29	Liverpool Edge Hill	11.9.47	Lab held	29.8	66.1	62.7	-3.4	35.1	42.6	7.5	64.9	52.1	-12.8		4.4	4.4				10.2	1.6	-8.6
30	Islington West	25.9.47	Lab held	47.6	60.1	51.4	-8.7	26.2	26.6	0.4	73.8	57.2	-16.6		16.0	16.0				8.5	-7.8	-16.3
31	Gravesend	26.11.47	Lab held	17.2	74.5	77.3	2.8	35.3	48.2	12.9	52.5	51.8	-0.7	12.2		-12.2				6.8	12.6	5.8
32	Howdenshire	27.11.47	Con held	26.8	71.1	67.0	-4.1	56.0	64.0	8.0	29.2	25.5	-3.7	14.8	10.5	-4.3				5.9	6.2	0.3
33	Edinburgh East	27.11.47	Lab held	19.1	69.4	63.0	-6.4	37.3	34.3	-3.0	56.4	50.6	-5.8		10.1	10.1	6.3	5.0	-1.3	1.4	-6.6	-8.0
34	Epsom	4.12.47	Con held	12.2	74.6	70.5	-4.1	50.0	61.0	11.0	37.8	31.5	-6.3	12.2	7.5	-4.7				8.7	7.9	-0.8
35	Glasgow Camlachie	28.1.48	Con x Lab	15.4	65.0	56.8	-8.2	42.3	43.7	1.4	57.7	42.1	-15.6							8.5		-8.4
36	Paisley	18.2.48	Lab held	22.9	73.9	76.0	2.1	32.7	43.2	10.5	55.6	56.8	1.2	10.0		-10.0				4.7	10.3	5.6
37	Wigan	4.3.48	Lab held	36.4	80.4	81.4	1.0	31.8	35.7	3.9	68.2	59.0	-9.2							6.6		
38	Croydon North	11.3.48	Lab held	1.0	73.2	74.8	1.6	41.1	54.0	12.9	40.1	34.6	-5.5	18.8	9.4	-9.4				8.2	11.2	3.0
39	Brigg	24.3.48	Lab held	17.8	74.6	77.1	2.5	41.1	45.4	4.3	58.9	54.6	-4.3							4.3		
40	Southwark Central	29.4.48	Lab held	43.8	62.6	48.7	-13.9	28.1	34.6	6.5	71.9	65.4	-6.5							6.5		
41	Glasgow Gorbals	30.9.48	Lab held	60.0	56.8	50.0	-6.8	20.0	28.6	8.6	80.0	54.5	-25.5							17.1		
42	Stirling & Falkirk	7.10.48	Lab held	12.2	71.5	72.9	1.4	43.9	42.8	-1.1	56.1	49.0	-7.1					8.2	8.2	3.0		
43	Edmonton	13.11.48	Lab held	39.2	69.0	62.7	-6.3	29.0	46.6	17.6	68.2	53.4	-14.8							16.2		
44	Glasgow Hillhead	25.11.48	Con held	24.9	65.8	56.7	-9.1	58.5	68.4	9.9	33.6	31.6	-2.0	7.9		-7.9				6.0	8.9	3.0

Parliamentary By-Elections 1945-2006 (GB) (contd.)

	Date	Result	% Maj GE	% turn GE	% turn BE	turn % chng	% Con GE	% Con BE	Con % chng	% Lab GE	% Lab BE	Lab % chng	% Lib GE	% Lib BE	Lib % chng	% Nat GE	% Nat BE	Nat % chng	Con/Lab swing	Con/Lib swing	Lab/Lib swing
1945-50 Parliament																					
45 Batley & Morley	17.2.49	Lab held	29.7	80.7	81.3	0.6	28.4	40.7	12.3	58.1	59.3	1.2	13.5		-13.5				5.6	12.9	7.4
46 Hammersmith S	24.2.49	Lab held	16.0	65.7	60.6	-5.1	42.0	47.2	5.2	58.0	52.8	-5.2							5.2		
47 St. Pancras North	10.3.49	Lab held	29.1	71.0	65.1	-5.9	34.7	39.5	4.8	63.8	57.5	-6.3							5.6		
48 Sowerby	16.3.49	Lab held	19.9	81.9	80.7	-1.2	30.9	46.9	16.0	50.8	53.1	2.3	18.3		-18.3				6.9	17.2	10.3
49 Leeds West	21.7.49	Lab held	31.5	75.2	65.1	-10.1	27.6	44.8	17.2	59.1	55.2	-3.9	13.3		-13.3				10.6	15.3	4.7
50 Bradford South	8.12.49	Lab held	19.4	76.7	74.4	-2.3	33.1	42.4	9.3	52.5	51.3	-1.2	14.4		-14.4				5.3	11.9	6.6
Average over Parliament				70.9	61.9	-8.7	37.4	42.3	3.5	57.9	53.4	-3.9	13.6	13.0	-2.7	6.1	13.5	8.9	3.8	5.0	-0.0
1950-51 Parliament																					
1 Sheffield Neepsend	5.4.50	Lab held	45.6	83.8	62.9	-20.9	27.2	26.8	-0.4	72.8	70.9	-1.9							0.7		
2 Dunbartonshire W	25.4.50	Lab held	1.5	85.5	83.4	-2.1	47.8	49.6	1.8	49.3	50.4	1.1							0.4		
3 Brighouse & Spenborough	4.5.50	Lab held	4.4	88.0	85.4	-2.6	47.8	49.5	1.7	52.2	50.5	-1.7							1.7		
4 Leicester NE	28.9.50	Lab held	23.2	85.8	63.0	-22.8	33.3	42.1	8.8	56.5	57.9	1.4	9.5		-9.5				3.7	9.2	5.5
5 Glasgow Scotstoun	25.10.50	Con held	0.5	84.6	73.7	-10.9	46.5	50.8	4.3	46.0	47.3	1.3	4.9		-4.9				1.5	4.6	3.1
6 Oxford	2.11.50	Con held	6.2	84.9	69.3	-15.6	46.9	57.5	10.6	40.7	42.5	1.8	11.6		-11.6				4.4	11.1	6.7
7 Birmingham Handsworth	16.11.50	Con held	11.3	83.1	63.2	-19.9	50.5	60.7	10.2	39.2	38.1	-1.1	10.3		-10.3				5.7	10.3	4.6
8 Bristol SE	30.11.50	Lab held	35.8	85.0	61.1	-23.9	26.8	35.2	8.4	62.6	56.7	-5.9	9.5	8.1	-1.4				7.2	4.9	-2.3
9 Abertillery	30.11.50	Lab held	74.2	84.6	71.1	-13.5	12.9	13.5	0.6	87.1	86.5	-0.6							0.6		
10 Bristol West	15.2.51	Con held	28.9	82.4	53.6	-28.8	58.9	81.4	22.5	30.0	18.6	-11.4	11.1		-11.1				17.0	16.8	-0.1
11 Ormskirk	5.4.51	Con held	32.6	83.9	64.7	-19.2	66.3	71.5	5.2	33.7	26.5	-7.2							6.2		
12 Harrow West	21.4.51	Lab held	29.1	86.7	68.0	-18.7	58.6	72.0	13.4	29.5	28.0	-1.5	11.9		-11.9				7.5	12.7	5.2
13 Woolwich East	14.6.51	Lab held	28.5	83.3	66.8	-16.5	33.0	39.3	6.3	61.5	60.7	-0.8	3.5		-3.5				3.6	4.9	1.4
14 Westhoughton	21.6.51	Lab held	24.6	88.2	76.5	-11.7	37.7	39.6	1.9	62.3	60.4	-1.9							1.9		
Average over Parliament				85.0	68.8	-16.2	42.4	49.3	6.8	51.7	49.6	-2.0	9.0	8.1	-8.0				4.4	9.3	3.0
1951-55 Parliament																					
1 Bournem'th E & Christchurch	6.2.52	Con held	38.2	80.8	63.8	-17.0	63.3	61.8	-1.5	25.1	23.4	-1.7	11.6	10.1	-1.5				0.1	0.0	-0.1
2 Southport	6.2.52	Con held	35.4	77.7	61.0	-16.7	60.2	62.0	1.8	24.8	28.5	3.7	15.0	9.5	-5.5				-1.0	3.7	4.6
3 Leeds South East	7.2.52	Lab held	21.0	84.4	55.7	-28.7	39.5	36.8	-2.7	60.5	63.2	2.7							-2.7		
4 Dundee East	17.7.52	Lab held	7.6	87.2	71.5	-15.7	46.2	35.6	-10.6	53.8	56.3	2.5					7.4	7.4	-6.6		
5 Cleveland	23.10.52	Lab held	9.6	85.1	71.4	-13.7	45.2	45.9	0.7	54.8	54.1	-0.7							0.7		
6 Wycombe	4.11.52	Con held	3.4	86.2	83.9	-2.3	51.7	52.0	0.3	48.3	48.0	-0.3							0.3		
7 Birmingham Small Heath	27.11.52	Lab held	32.5	77.2	46.6	-30.6	30.9	33.0	2.1	63.4	67.0	3.6	5.7		-5.7				-0.8	3.9	4.7
8 Farnworth	27.11.52	Lab held	18.4	86.8	71.0	-15.8	40.8	40.1	-0.7	59.2	59.9	0.7							-0.7		
9 Canterbury	12.2.53	Con held	30.1	80.1	49.2	-30.9	61.1	67.1	6.0	31.0	32.9	1.9	7.9		-7.9				2.1	7.0	4.9
10 Isle of Thanet	12.3.53	Con held	23.2	78.0	58.7	-19.3	61.6	61.3	-0.3	38.4	38.7	0.3							-0.3		
11 Barnsley	31.3.53	Lab held	52.4	77.2	57.9	-19.3	17.3	27.1	9.8	69.7	72.9	3.2	13.0		-13.0				3.3	11.4	8.1
12 Stoke-on-Trent N	31.3.53	Lab held	42.8	83.8	50.5	-33.3	28.6	24.5	-4.1	71.4	75.5	4.1							-4.1		
13 Hayes &Harlington	1.4.53	Lab held	29.6	82.2	45.0	-37.2	35.2	36.1	0.9	64.8	63.9	-0.9							0.9		
14 Sunderland South	13.5.53	Con x Lab	0.6	82.2	72.7	-9.5	49.7	48.6	-1.1	50.3	46.1	-4.2		5.3	5.3				1.6	-3.2	-4.8
15 Abingdon	30.6.53	Con held	11.0	80.0	75.9	-4.1	55.5	53.2	-2.3	44.5	39.7	-4.8		7.1	7.1				1.3	-4.7	-6.0
16 Birmingham Edgbaston	2.7.53	Con held	28.6	76.1	50.2	-25.9	64.3	67.6	3.3	35.7	32.4	-3.3							3.3		

Parliamentary By-Elections 1945-2006 (GB) (contd.)

	Date	Result	% Maj GE	% turn GE	turn BE	turn % chng	% Con GE	% Con BE	Con % chng	% Lab GE	% Lab BE	Lab % chng	% Lib GE	% Lib BE	Lib % chng	% Nat GE	% Nat BE	Nat % chng	Con/Lab swing	Con/Lib swing	Lab/Lib swing
17 Broxtowe	17.9.53	Lab held	45.4	84.1	63.5	-20.6	27.3	25.9	-1.4	72.7	74.1	1.4	-	-	-	-	-	-	-1.4	-	-
18 Crosby	12.11.53	Con held	41.8	79.8	62.5	-17.3	70.9	68.1	-2.8	29.1	27.6	-1.5	-	-	-	-	-	-	-0.7	-	-
19 Ormskirk	12.11.53	Con held	34.8	78.7	54.1	-24.6	67.4	65.4	-2.0	32.6	34.6	2.0	-	-	-	-	-	-	-2.0	-	-
20 Holborn & St. Pancras South	19.11.53	Lab held	4.4	73.7	56.2	-17.5	45.8	45.6	-0.2	50.2	52.1	1.9	4.0	2.3	-1.7	-	-	-	-1.1	0.8	1.8
21 Paddington N	3.12.53	Lab held	11.4	81.0	60.3	-20.7	44.3	45.3	1.0	55.7	53.8	-1.9	-	-	-	-	-	-	1.5	-	-
22 Ilford North	3.2.54	Con held	17.5	84.8	45.4	-39.4	55.5	59.8	4.3	38.0	32.3	-5.7	6.5	7.9	1.4	-	-	-	5.0	1.5	-3.6
23 Harwich	11.2.54	Con held	17.8	78.8	58.8	-20.0	58.9	59.1	0.2	41.1	40.9	-0.2	-	-	-	-	-	-	0.2	-	-
24 Hull, Haltemprice	11.2.54	Con held	16.2	82.8	45.7	-37.1	58.1	61.8	3.7	41.9	38.2	-3.7	-	-	-	-	-	-	3.7	-	-
25 Bournemouth W	18.2.54	Con held	31.0	77.7	45.1	-32.6	65.5	69.7	4.2	34.5	30.3	-4.2	-	-	-	-	-	-	4.2	-	-
26 Arundel &Shoreham	9.3.54	Con held	34.8	78.0	54.2	-23.8	67.4	68.5	1.1	32.6	31.5	-1.1	-	-	-	-	-	-	1.1	-	-
27 Harrogate	11.3.54	Con held	41.2	78.7	55.3	-23.4	70.6	70.8	0.2	29.4	29.2	-0.2	-	-	-	-	-	-	0.2	-	-
28 Edinburgh East	8.4.54	Lab held	8.2	83.8	61.8	-22.0	45.9	42.4	-3.5	54.1	57.6	3.5	-	-	-	-	-	-	-3.5	-	-
29 Motherwell	14.4.54	Lab held	14.6	84.7	70.5	-14.2	42.7	39.3	-3.4	57.3	56.4	-0.9	-	-	-	-	-	-	-1.3	-	-
30 Croydon East	30.9.54	Con held	17.6	84.2	57.5	-26.7	58.8	56.6	-2.2	41.2	35.4	-5.8	-	8.0	8.0	-	-	-	1.8	-5.1	-6.9
31 Shoreditch & Finsbury	21.10.54	Lab held	45.2	73.2	40.7	-32.5	27.4	21.8	-5.6	72.6	78.2	5.6	-	-	-	-	-	-	-5.6	-	-
32 Wakefield	21.10.54	Lab held	16.6	85.3	68.6	-16.7	41.7	41.9	0.2	58.3	58.1	-0.2	-	-	-	-	-	-	0.2	-	-
33 Aldershot	28.10.54	Con held	20.6	77.8	58.7	-19.1	60.3	60.1	-0.2	39.7	39.9	0.2	-	-	-	-	-	-	-0.2	-	-
34 Aberdare	28.10.54	Lab held	63.1	86.1	69.7	-16.4	15.4	14.5	-0.9	78.5	69.5	-9.0	-	-	-	6.1	16.0	9.9	4.1	-	-
35 Sutton & Cheam	4.11.54	Con held	25.6	81.7	55.6	-26.1	62.8	66.5	3.7	37.2	33.5	-3.7	-	-	-	-	-	-	3.7	-	-
36 Morpeth	4.11.54	Lab held	43.8	85.5	73.0	-12.5	28.1	28.7	0.6	71.9	71.3	-0.6	-	-	-	-	-	-	0.6	-	-
37 Liverpool W Derby	18.11.54	Lab held	3.2	80.3	58.9	-21.4	51.6	53.2	1.6	48.4	46.8	-1.6	-	-	-	-	-	-	1.6	-	-
38 Inverness	21.12.54	Con held	29.0	69.3	49.2	-20.1	64.5	41.4	-23.1	35.5	22.6	-12.9	-	36.0	36.0	-	-	-	-5.1	-29.6	-24.5
39 Norfolk South	13.1.55	Con held	9.0	82.4	66.6	-15.8	54.5	51.5	-3.0	45.5	48.5	3.0	-	-	-	-	-	-	-3.0	-	-
40 Orpington	20.1.55	Con held	25.4	82.0	55.4	-26.6	62.7	65.8	3.1	37.3	34.2	-3.1	-	-	-	-	-	-	3.1	-	-
41 Twickenham	25.1.55	Con held	24.2	81.3	47.3	-34.0	62.1	64.0	1.9	37.9	36.0	-1.9	-	-	-	-	-	-	1.9	-	-
42 Edinburgh North	27.1.55	Con held	17.6	80.0	46.4	-33.6	58.8	59.4	0.6	41.2	40.6	-0.6	-	-	-	-	-	-	0.6	-	-
43 Stockport South	3.2.55	Con held	8.4	84.2	64.6	-19.6	54.2	54.3	0.1	45.8	45.7	-0.1	-	-	-	-	-	-	0.1	-	-
44 Wrexham	17.3.55	Lab held	26.8	84.8	62.4	-22.4	34.8	30.8	-4.0	61.6	57.9	-3.7	-	-	-	3.6	11.3	7.7	-0.1	-	-
Average over Parliament				81.1	58.9	-22.2	50.2	49.7	-0.6	48.1	47.3	-0.8	9.1	10.8	2.0	4.9	11.6	8.3	0.2	-1.3	-2.0
1955-59 Parliament																					
1 Gateshead W	7.12.55	Lab held	30.6	72.5	42.3	-30.2	34.7	33.5	-1.2	65.3	66.5	1.2	-	-	-	-	-	-	-1.2	-	-
2 Greenock	8.12.55	Lab held	2.8	77.9	75.3	-2.6	48.6	46.3	-2.3	51.4	53.7	2.3	-	-	-	-	-	-	-2.3	-	-
3 Torquay	15.12.55	Con held	35.0	75.5	62.6	-12.9	60.4	51.0	-9.4	25.4	25.2	-0.2	14.2	23.8	9.6	-	-	-	-4.6	-9.5	-4.9
4 Blaydon	2.2.56	Lab held	33.0	80.7	56.5	-24.2	33.5	30.1	-3.4	66.5	69.9	3.4	-	-	-	-	-	-	-3.4	-	-
5 Leeds NE	9.2.56	Con held	22.8	73.1	39.9	-33.2	61.4	63.2	1.8	38.6	36.8	-1.8	-	-	-	-	-	-	1.8	-	-
6 Hereford	14.2.56	Con held	28.4	78.8	61.5	-17.3	51.8	44.3	-7.5	23.4	19.3	-4.1	24.8	36.4	11.6	-	-	-	-1.7	-9.6	-7.9
7 Gainsborough	14.2.56	Con held	11.6	76.8	61.9	-14.9	55.8	40.8	-15.0	44.2	37.6	-6.6	-	21.6	21.6	-	-	-	-4.2	-18.3	-14.1
8 Taunton	14.2.56	Con held	12.6	85.5	75.0	-10.5	52.1	50.8	-1.3	39.5	49.2	9.7	8.4	-	-8.4	-	-	-	-5.5	3.6	9.1
9 Walthamstow W	1.3.56	Lab held	31.4	72.5	52.0	-20.5	34.3	20.2	-14.1	65.7	64.7	-1.0	-	14.7	14.7	-	-	-	-6.6	-14.4	-7.9
10 Tonbridge	7.6.56	Con held	20.8	75.5	60.6	-14.9	60.4	52.0	-8.4	39.6	48.0	8.4	-	-	-	-	-	-	-8.4	-	-
11 Newport	6.7.56	Lab held	7.4	81.6	72.1	-9.5	46.3	39.9	-6.4	53.7	56.3	2.6	-	-	-	-	-	-	-4.5	-	-
12 Chester le Street	27.9.56	Lab held	52.6	79.6	64.9	-14.7	23.7	19.2	-4.5	76.3	80.8	4.5	-	-	-	-	3.8	3.8	-4.5	-	-
13 Chester, City of	15.11.56	Con held	25.1	77.9	71.5	-6.4	56.7	51.7	-5.0	31.6	36.2	4.6	11.7	12.1	0.4	-	-	-	-4.8	-2.7	2.1
14 Melton	19.12.56	Con held	21.8	80.9	56.5	-24.4	60.9	53.3	-7.6	39.1	46.7	7.6	-	-	-	-	-	-	-7.6	-	-
15 Lewisham N	14.2.57	Lab x Con	8.0	77.9	70.8	-7.1	54.0	46.5	-7.5	46.0	49.5	3.5	-	-	-	-	-	-	-5.5	-	-

Parliamentary By-Elections 1945-2006 (GB) (contd.)

	Date	Result	% Maj GE	% turn GE	% turn BE	turn % chng	% Con GE	% Con BE	Con % chng	% Lab GE	% Lab BE	Lab % chng	% Lib GE	% Lib BE	Lib % chng	% Nat GE	% Nat BE	Nat % chng	Con/Lab swing	Con/Lib swing	Lab/Lib swing
16 Wednesbury	28.2.57	Lab held	20.8	72.9	60.0	-12.9	39.6	28.0	-11.6	60.4	62.1	1.7	-	-	-	-	-	-	-6.7	-	-
17 Carmarthen	28.2.57	Lab x Lib	6.8	85.1	87.5	2.4	-	-	-	42.7	47.3	4.6	49.5	41.2	-8.3	7.8	11.5	3.7	-	-	6.5
18 Bristol West	7.3.57	Con held	50.6	74.6	61.1	-13.5	75.3	70.2	-5.1	24.7	29.8	5.1	-	-	-	-	-	-	-5.1	-	-
19 Warwick & Leamington	7.3.57	Con held	29.0	78.8	77.9	-0.9	64.5	52.3	-12.2	35.5	47.7	12.2	-	-	-	-	-	-	-12.2	-	-
20 Beckenham	21.3.57	Con held	38.0	76.5	64.7	-11.8	69.0	62.9	-6.1	31.0	37.1	6.1	-	-	-	-	-	-	-6.1	-	-
21 Newcastle upon Tyne North	21.3.57	Con held	27.6	77.6	64.1	-13.5	63.8	60.2	-3.6	36.2	39.8	3.6	-	-	-	-	-	-	-3.6	-	-
22 Edinburgh South	29.5.57	Con held	35.0	77.2	65.8	-11.4	67.5	45.6	-21.9	32.5	30.9	-1.6	-	23.5	23.5	-	-	-	-10.2	-22.7	-12.6
23 East Ham North	30.5.57	Lab held	18.2	74.9	57.3	-17.6	40.9	29.4	-11.5	59.1	56.3	-2.8	-	-	-	-	-	-	-4.4	-	-
24 Hornsey	30.5.57	Con held	23.0	76.3	63.0	-13.3	60.2	53.5	-6.7	37.2	46.5	9.3	-	-	-	-	-	-	-8.0	-	-
25 Dorset North	27.6.57	Con held	19.7	82.2	75.8	-6.4	52.1	45.1	-7.0	15.5	18.3	2.8	32.4	36.1	3.7	-	-	-	-4.9	-5.4	-0.5
26 Gloucester	12.9.57	Lab held	1.8	80.9	71.0	-9.9	49.1	28.6	-20.5	50.9	51.3	0.4	-	20.1	20.1	-	-	-	-10.5	-20.3	-9.9
27 Ipswich	24.10.57	Lab held	5.8	80.5	75.6	-4.9	47.1	32.7	-14.4	52.9	45.8	-7.1	-	21.5	21.5	-	-	-	-3.7	-18.0	-14.3
28 Leicester SE	28.11.57	Con held	28.4	78.5	56.4	-22.1	64.2	61.0	-3.2	35.8	39.0	3.2	-	-	-	-	-	-	-3.2	-	-
29 Liverpool Garston	5.12.57	Con held	27.0	71.0	49.7	-21.3	63.5	49.2	-14.3	36.5	35.6	-0.9	-	-	-	-	-	-	-6.7	-	-
30 Rochdale	12.2.58	Lab x Con	3.0	82.8	80.2	-2.6	51.5	19.8	-31.7	48.5	44.7	-3.8	-	35.5	35.5	-	-	-	-14.0	-33.6	-19.7
31 Glasgow Kelvingrove	13.3.58	Lab x Con	10.8	67.6	60.5	-7.1	55.4	41.6	-13.8	44.6	48.0	3.4	-	15.2	15.2	-	-	-	-8.6	-14.8	-8.1
32 Torrington	27.3.58	Lib x Con	30.2	69.2	80.6	11.4	65.1	37.4	-27.7	34.9	24.6	-10.3	-	38.0	38.0	-	-	-	-8.7	-32.9	-24.2
33 Islington North	15.5.58	Lab held	20.6	64.7	35.6	-29.1	39.7	29.3	-10.4	60.3	67.7	7.4	-	-	-	-	-	-	-8.9	-	-
34 Ealing South	12.6.58	Lab held	28.6	77.9	64.5	-13.4	59.5	50.3	-9.2	30.9	32.5	1.6	9.6	17.2	7.6	-	-	-	-5.4	-8.4	-3.0
35 St. Helens	12.6.58	Lab held	28.6	73.5	54.6	-18.9	35.7	35.3	-0.4	64.3	64.7	0.4	-	-	-	-	-	-	-0.4	-	-
36 Wigan	12.6.58	Lab held	32.2	80.3	70.3	-10.0	32.2	26.5	-5.7	64.4	71.0	6.6	-	-	-	-	-	-	-6.2	-	-
37 Weston-super-Mare	12.6.58	Con held	25.4	73.8	72.2	-1.6	62.7	49.3	-13.4	37.3	26.2	-11.1	-	24.5	24.5	-	-	-	-1.2	-19.0	-17.8
38 Argyll	12.6.58	Con held	35.2	66.6	67.1	0.5	67.6	46.8	-20.8	32.4	25.7	-6.7	-	27.5	27.5	-	-	-	-7.1	-24.2	-17.1
39 Morecambe & Lonsdale	6.11.58	Con held	42.4	74.4	63.8	-10.6	71.2	65.3	-5.9	28.8	34.7	5.9	-	-	-	-	-	-	-5.9	-	-
40 Chichester	6.11.58	Con held	41.6	71.8	51.7	-20.1	70.8	70.9	0.1	29.2	29.1	-0.1	-	-	-	-	-	-	0.1	-	-
41 Pontypool	10.11.58	Lab held	45.8	77.1	61.7	-15.4	27.1	21.5	-5.6	72.9	68.5	-4.4	-	-	-	-	10.0	10.0	-0.6	-	-
42 Aberdeenshire E	20.11.58	Con held	37.0	59.8	65.9	6.1	68.5	48.6	-19.9	31.5	27.1	-4.4	-	24.3	24.3	-	-	-	-7.8	-22.1	-14.4
43 Shoreditch & Finsbury	27.11.58	Lab held	47.0	61.6	24.9	-36.7	26.5	24.0	-2.5	73.5	76.0	2.5	-	-	-	-	-	-	-2.5	-	-
44 Southend West	29.1.59	Con held	43.4	74.1	42.9	-31.2	64.2	55.6	-8.6	20.8	20.2	-0.6	15.0	24.2	9.2	-	-	-	-4.0	-8.9	-4.9
45 Harrow East	19.3.59	Con held	8.8	82.6	68.9	-13.7	54.4	52.8	-1.6	45.6	46.2	0.6	-	-	-	-	-	-	-1.1	-	-
46 Norfolk South West	25.3.59	Lab held	0.6	82.6	75.2	-7.4	49.7	46.4	-3.3	50.3	51.0	0.7	-	-	-	-	-	-	-2.0	-	-
47 Galloway	9.4.59	Con held	33.8	69.1	72.7	3.6	66.9	50.4	-16.5	33.1	23.9	-9.2	-	25.7	25.7	-	-	-	-3.7	-	-17.5
48 Penistone	11.6.59	Lab held	24.6	80.0	65.0	-15.0	37.7	35.9	-1.8	62.3	64.1	1.8	-	-	-	-	-	-	-1.8	-	-
49 Whitehaven	18.6.59	Lab held	16.0	83.8	79.2	-4.6	42.0	41.4	-0.6	58.0	58.6	0.6	-	-	-	-	-	-	-0.6	-	-
Average over Parliament				**76.1**	**63.5**	**-12.6**	**52.9**	**44.0**	**-8.9**	**44.5**	**45.6**	**1.1**	**20.7**	**25.4**	**15.9**	**7.8**	**8.4**	**5.8**	**-5.0**	**-15.6**	**-9.0**
1959-64 Parliament																					
1 Brighouse & Spenborough	17.3.60	Con x Lab	0.2	85.5	82.4	-3.1	49.9	50.8	0.9	50.1	49.2	-0.9	-	-	-	-	-	-	0.9	-	-
2 Harrow West	17.3.60	Con held	41.8	79.2	61.6	-17.6	70.9	55.7	-15.2	29.1	18.2	-10.9	-	21.4	21.4	-	-	-	-2.2	-18.3	-16.2
3 Edinburgh North	19.5.60	Con held	28.0	73.9	53.8	-20.1	64.0	54.2	-9.8	36.0	30.3	-5.7	-	15.5	15.5	-	-	-	-2.1	-12.7	-10.6
4 Bolton East	16.11.60	Con held	5.6	80.9	68.2	-12.7	52.8	37.8	-15.0	47.2	36.2	-11.0	-	24.8	24.8	-	-	-	-2.0	-19.9	-17.9

Parliamentary By-Elections 1945-2006 (GB) (contd.)

No.	Constituency	Date	Result	% Maj GE	% turn GE	% turn BE	turn % chng	% Con GE	% Con BE	Con % chng	% Lab GE	% Lab BE	Lab % chng	% Lib GE	% Lib BE	Lib % chng	% Nat GE	% Nat BE	Nat % chng	Con/Lab swing[1]	Con/Lib swing[1]	Lab/Lib swing[1]
5	Bedfordshire Mid	16.11.60	Con held	11.4	84.5	71.1	-13.4	46.8	45.4	-1.4	35.4	29.2	-6.2	17.8	24.8	7.0	–	–	–	2.4	-4.2	-6.6
6	Tiverton	16.11.60	Con held	30.4	80.7	68.4	-12.3	55.6	45.7	-9.9	25.2	17.6	-7.6	19.2	36.7	17.5	–	–	–	-1.2	-13.7	-12.6
7	Petersfield	16.11.60	Con held	39.6	73.6	53.6	-20.0	60.9	54.4	-6.5	21.3	16.6	-4.7	17.8	29.0	11.2	–	–	–	-0.9	-8.9	-8.0
8	Ludlow	16.11.60	Con held	20.6	76.2	63.6	-12.6	60.3	46.4	-13.9	39.7	26.3	-13.4	–	27.3	27.3	–	–	–	-0.2	-20.6	-20.4
9	Carshalton	16.11.60	Con held	23.5	82.5	54.2	-28.3	54.0	51.7	-2.3	30.5	20.7	-9.8	15.5	27.6	12.1	–	–	–	3.8	-7.2	-11.0
10	Ebbw Vale	17.11.60	Lab held	62.0	85.8	76.1	-9.7	19.0	12.7	-6.3	81.0	68.8	-12.2	–	11.5	11.5	–	7.0	7.0	3.0	-8.9	-11.9
11	Blyth	24.11.60	Lab held	49.2	82.6	54.1	-28.5	25.4	21.6	-3.8	74.6	68.9	-5.7	–	–	–	–	–	–	0.9	–	–
12	Worcester	16.3.61	Con held	15.4	79.3	64.2	-15.1	57.7	39.7	-18.0	42.3	30.2	-12.1	–	30.1	30.1	–	–	–	-3.0	-24.1	-21.1
13	Cambridgeshire	16.3.61	Con held	15.8	78.0	62.4	-15.6	57.9	45.9	-12.0	42.1	30.1	-12.0	–	24.0	24.0	–	–	–	0.0	-18.0	-18.0
14	High Peak	16.3.61	Con held	12.0	82.7	72.5	-10.2	46.0	37.4	-8.6	34.0	32.1	-1.9	20.0	30.5	10.5	–	–	–	-3.4	-9.6	-6.2
15	Colchester	16.3.61	Con held	15.7	82.4	64.9	-17.5	51.6	47.2	-4.4	35.9	33.1	-2.8	12.5	19.7	7.2	–	–	–	-0.8	-5.8	-5.0
16	Birmingham Small Heath	23.3.61	Lab held	14.8	65.7	42.6	-23.1	42.6	28.8	-13.8	57.4	59.2	1.8	–	12.0	12.0	–	–	–	-7.8	-12.9	-5.1
17	Warrington	20.4.61	Lab held	12.6	76.9	56.7	-20.2	43.7	31.6	-12.1	56.3	55.9	-0.4	–	12.5	12.5	–	–	–	-5.9	-12.3	-6.5
18	Paisley	20.4.61	Lab held	14.6	78.9	68.1	-10.8	42.7	13.2	-29.5	57.3	45.4	-11.9	–	41.4	41.4	–	–	–	-8.8	-35.5	-26.7
19	Bristol SE	4.5.61	Lab held	12.4	81.4	56.7	-24.7	43.8	30.5	-13.3	56.2	69.5	13.3	–	–	–	–	–	–	-13.3	–	–
20	Manchester Moss Side	7.11.61	Con held	24.6	69.2	46.7	-22.5	62.3	41.2	-21.1	37.7	25.8	-11.9	–	27.8	27.8	–	–	–	-4.6	-24.5	-19.9
21	Fife East	8.11.61	Con held	39.8	75.2	67.3	-7.9	69.9	47.5	-22.4	30.1	26.4	-3.7	–	26.1	26.1	–	–	–	-9.4	-24.3	-14.9
22	Oswestry	8.11.61	Con held	27.9	74.2	60.8	-13.4	55.9	40.8	-15.1	28.0	28.0	0.0	16.1	28.4	12.3	–	–	–	-7.6	-13.7	-6.2
23	Glasgow Bridgeton	16.11.61	Lab held	26.8	68.5	41.9	-26.6	36.6	20.7	-15.9	63.4	57.5	-5.9	–	–	–	–	18.7	18.7	-5.0	–	–
24	Lincoln	8.3.62	Lab held	10.2	84.2	75.0	-9.2	44.9	30.2	-14.7	55.1	50.5	-4.6	–	18.2	18.2	–	–	–	-5.1	-16.5	-11.4
25	Blackpool North	13.3.62	Con held	36.2	74.8	55.2	-19.6	57.8	38.3	-19.5	21.6	26.4	4.8	20.6	35.3	14.7	–	–	–	-12.2	-17.1	-5.0
26	Middlesbrough E	14.3.62	Lab held	23.0	76.2	52.2	-24.0	38.5	14.8	-23.7	61.5	60.5	-1.0	–	22.9	22.9	–	–	–	-11.4	-23.3	-12.0
27	Orpington	14.3.62	Lib x Con	34.4	82.8	80.3	-2.5	56.6	34.7	-21.9	22.2	12.4	-9.8	21.2	52.9	31.7	–	–	–	-6.1	-26.8	-20.8
28	Pontefract	22.3.62	Lab held	52.8	84.3	63.3	-21.0	23.6	19.4	-4.2	76.4	77.3	0.9	–	–	–	–	–	–	-2.6	–	–
29	Stockton-on-Tees	5.4.62	Lab held	7.4	83.9	81.5	-2.4	46.3	27.8	-18.5	53.7	45.3	-8.4	–	26.9	26.9	–	–	–	-5.1	-22.7	-17.7
30	Derby North	17.4.62	Lab held	2.2	76.7	60.5	-16.2	47.2	22.5	-24.7	49.4	46.0	-3.4	–	25.4	25.4	–	–	–	-10.7	-25.1	-14.4
31	Montgomeryshire	15.5.62	Lib held	10.8	83.8	85.1	1.3	31.3	21.9	-9.4	26.6	20.6	-6.0	42.1	51.3	9.2	–	6.2	6.2	-1.7	-9.3	-7.6
32	Middlesbrough W	6.6.62	Lab x Con	19.5	84.5	72.2	-12.3	54.9	33.7	-21.2	35.4	39.7	4.3	9.7	25.8	16.1	–	–	–	-12.8	-18.7	-5.9
33	Derbyshire West	6.6.62	Con held	22.6	81.9	79.4	-2.5	61.3	36.1	-25.2	38.7	27.3	-11.4	–	32.5	32.5	–	–	–	-6.9	-28.9	-22.0
34	West Lothian	14.6.62	Lab held	20.6	77.9	71.1	-6.8	39.7	11.4	-28.3	60.3	50.9	-9.4	–	14.4	14.4	–	23.3	23.3	-9.5	-21.4	-11.9
35	Leicester NE	12.7.62	Lab held	3.8	78.4	60.8	-17.6	48.1	24.2	-23.9	51.9	41.6	-10.3	–	34.3	34.3	–	–	–	-6.8	-29.1	-22.3
36	Dorset South	22.11.62	Lab x Con	15.1	78.8	70.2	-8.6	49.8	31.8	-18.0	34.7	33.5	-1.2	15.5	21.6	6.1	–	–	–	-8.4	-12.1	-3.7
37	Norfolk Central	22.11.62	Con held	15.5	79.9	60.2	-19.7	50.3	37.7	-12.6	34.8	37.0	2.2	14.9	25.3	10.4	–	–	–	-7.4	-11.5	-4.1
38	Northamptonshire S	22.11.62	Con held	14.0	82.7	69.0	-13.7	57.0	41.2	-15.8	43.0	38.6	-4.4	–	20.2	20.2	–	–	–	-5.7	-18.0	-12.3
39	Chippenham	22.11.62	Con held	21.1	80.2	68.0	-12.2	52.1	36.9	-15.2	31.0	29.1	-1.9	16.9	34.0	17.1	–	–	–	-6.7	-16.2	-9.5
40	Glasgow Woodside	22.11.62	Lab x Con	6.1	75.2	54.7	-20.5	49.2	30.1	-19.1	43.1	36.1	-7.0	7.7	22.7	15.0	–	11.1	11.1	-6.1	-17.1	-11.0
41	Colne Valley	21.3.63	Lab x Con	14.4	84.1	78.9	-5.2	29.9	15.4	-14.5	44.3	44.4	0.1	25.8	39.5	13.7	–	–	–	-7.3	-14.1	-6.8
42	Rotherham	28.3.63	Lab held	25.6	78.9	56.3	-22.6	37.2	28.4	-8.8	62.8	69.3	6.5	–	–	–	–	–	–	-7.7	–	–
43	Swansea East	28.3.63	Lab held	45.5	80.1	55.9	-24.2	22.0	7.3	-14.7	67.5	61.2	-6.3	–	26.3	26.3	10.5	5.2	-5.3	-4.2	-20.5	-16.3
44	Leeds South	20.6.63	Lab held	27.6	79.0	60.5	-18.5	31.0	20.1	-10.9	58.6	63.0	4.4	10.4	16.9	6.5	–	–	–	-7.7	-8.7	-1.1
45	Deptford	4.7.63	Lab held	23.8	69.3	44.1	-25.2	38.1	19.2	-18.9	61.9	58.3	-3.6	–	22.5	22.5	–	–	–	-7.7	-20.7	-13.1
46	West Bromwich	4.7.63	Lab held	14.8	72.5	55.2	-17.3	42.6	23.6	-19.0	57.4	58.8	1.4	–	17.6	17.6	–	–	–	-10.2	-18.3	-8.1
47	Stratford	15.8.63	Con held	37.0	76.9	69.4	-7.5	68.5	43.5	-25.0	31.5	34.1	2.6	–	21.0	21.0	–	–	–	-13.8	-23.0	-9.2
48	Bristol South East	20.8.63	Lab held	12.4	81.4	42.2	-39.2	43.8	–	–	56.2	79.7	23.5	–	20.3	20.3	–	–	–	–	–	–
49	Luton	7.11.63	Lab x Con	10.2	82.5	74.0	-8.5	55.1	39.5	-15.6	44.9	48.0	3.1	–	11.4	11.4	–	–	–	-9.4	-13.5	-4.2
50	Kinross & Perth-shire West	7.11.63	Con held	51.4	71.0	76.1	5.1	68.2	57.4	-10.8	16.8	15.2	-1.6	–	19.5	19.5	15.0	7.3	-7.7	-4.6	-15.2	-10.6

Parliamentary By-Elections 1945-2006 (GB) (contd.)

	Date	Result	% Maj GE	% turn GE	% turn BE	turn % chng	% Con GE	% Con BE	Con % chng	% Lab GE	% Lab BE	Lab % chng	% Lib GE	% Lib BE	Lib % chng	% Nat GE	% Nat BE	Nat % chng	Con/Lab swing	Con/Lib swing	Lab/Lib swing
51 Dundee West	21.11.63	Lab held	1.3	82.9	71.6	-11.3	48.3	39.4	-8.9	49.6	50.6	1.0					7.4	7.4	-5.0		
52 St. Marylebone	5.12.63	Con held	40.9	65.5	44.2	-21.3	64.5	54.9	-9.6	23.6	31.8	8.2	11.9	13.3	1.4				-8.9	-5.5	3.4
53 Manchester Openshaw	5.12.63	Lab held	20.4	76.0	46.1	-29.9	39.8	29.2	-10.6	60.2	65.9	5.7							-8.2		
54 Sudbury & Woodbridge	5.12.63	Con held	20.0	81.1	70.5	-10.6	53.0	49.6	-3.4	33.0	37.0	4.0	14.0	13.4	-0.6				-3.7	-1.4	2.3
55 Dumfriesshire	12.12.63	Con held	43.8	77.4	71.6	-5.8	58.4	40.9	-17.5	41.6	38.5	-3.1		10.9	10.9		9.7	9.7	-7.2	-14.2	-7.0
56 Winchester	14.5.64	Con held	43.6	76.7	68.7	-8.0	67.3	52.2	-15.1	23.7	34.6	10.9		13.2	13.2				-13.0	-14.2	-1.2
57 Rutherglen	14.5.64	Lab x Con	4.2	85.8	74.6	-3.8	52.1	44.5	-7.6	47.9	55.5	7.6							-7.6		
58 Bury St. Edmunds	14.5.64	Con held	17.4	78.6	74.6	-4.0	58.7	49.0	-9.7	41.3	43.5	2.2		7.5	7.5				-6.0	-8.6	-2.7
59 Devizes	14.5.64	Con held	9.5	79.2	75.8	-3.4	51.4	46.8	-4.6	41.9	42.9	1.0		10.3	10.3				-2.8	-7.5	-4.7
60 Faversham	4.6.64	Lab held	0.6	83.8	74.8	-9.0	49.7	44.1	-5.6	50.3	55.1	4.8							-5.2		
61 Liverpool Scotland	11.6.64	Lab held	23.6	62.5	42.0	-20.5	38.2	25.7	-12.5	61.8	74.3	12.5							-12.5		
Average over Parliament				78.5	64.0	-14.5	49.1	35.4	-13.7	44.8	42.8	-1.9	17.3	23.6	16.9	12.8	10.7	7.8	-5.7	-16.0	-10.3
1964-66 Parliament																					
1 Leyton	21.1.65	Con x Lab	16.8	70.2	57.7	-12.5	33.5	42.8	9.3	50.3	42.4	-7.9	16.2	14.0	-2.2				8.6	5.8	-2.9
2 Nuneaton	21.1.65	Lab held	23.7	80.1	60.8	-19.3	29.1	34.9	5.8	52.8	49.0	-3.8	18.1	16.1	-2.0				4.8	3.9	-0.9
3 Altrincham & Sale	4.2.65	Con held	18.8	81.2	62.0	-19.2	46.8	50.0	3.2	28.0	29.0	1.0	25.2	19.4	-5.8				1.1	4.5	3.4
4 East Grinstead	4.2.65	Con held	26.2	78.0	64.5	-13.5	53.2	55.0	1.8	19.8	13.5	-6.3	27.0	31.5	4.5				4.1	-1.4	-5.4
5 Salisbury	4.2.65	Con held	13.9	78.6	69.1	-9.5	48.3	48.2	-0.1	34.4	37.4	3.0	17.3	12.9	-4.4				-1.6	2.2	3.7
6 Saffron Walden	23.3.65	Con held	12.0	82.4	76.1	-6.3	49.4	48.6	-0.8	37.4	39.5	2.1	13.2	11.9	-1.3				-1.5	0.3	1.7
7 Roxburghshire etc	24.3.65	Lib x Con	3.9	82.2	82.2	0.0	42.8	38.6	-4.2	15.8	11.3	-4.5	38.9	49.2	10.3	2.5		-2.5	0.2	-7.3	-7.4
8 Abertillery	1.4.65	Lab held	71.8	75.5	63.2	-12.3	14.1	14.3	0.2	85.9	79.0	-6.9					6.7	6.7	3.6		
9 Birmingham Hall Green	6.5.65	Con held	20.8	75.8	52.4	-23.4	52.6	54.8	2.2	31.8	28.8	-3.0	15.6	16.4	0.8				2.6	0.7	-1.9
10 Hove	22.7.65	Con held	36.8	69.6	58.5	-11.1	68.4	62.2	-6.2	31.6	20.6	-11.0		16.9	16.9				2.4	-11.6	-14.0
11 Cities of London & Westminster	4.11.65	Con held	27.7	59.7	41.8	-17.9	58.3	59.5	1.2	30.6	32.9	2.3	11.1	6.3	-4.8				-0.5	3.0	3.6
12 Erith & Crayford	11.11.65	Lab held	20.6	79.6	72.0	-7.6	32.5	37.4	4.9	53.1	55.4	2.3	14.4	7.2	-7.2				1.3	6.1	4.8
13 Hull North	27.1.66	Lab held	2.5	77.2	76.3	-0.9	40.8	40.8	0.0	43.3	52.2	8.9	15.9	6.3	-9.6				-4.5	4.8	9.3
Average over Parliament				76.2	64.4	-11.8	43.8	45.2	1.3	39.6	37.8	-1.8	19.4	17.3	-0.4	2.5	6.7	2.1	1.6	0.9	-0.5
1966-70 Parliament																					
1 Carmarthen	14.7.66	PC x Lab	20.1	83.0	74.9	-8.1	11.6	7.1	-4.5	46.2	33.1	-13.1	26.1	20.8	-5.3	16.1	39.0	22.9	4.3	0.4	-3.9
2 Nuneaton	9.3.67	Lab held	22.3	79.7	66.1	-13.6	31.6	32.7	1.1	53.9	42.1	-11.8	14.5	17.6	3.1				6.5	-1.0	-7.5
3 Rhondda West	9.3.67	Lab held	68.3	80.3	82.2	1.9	7.8	4.3	-3.5	76.1	49.0	-27.1		1.9	1.9	8.7	39.9	31.2	11.8	-2.7	-14.5
4 Glasgow Pollok	9.3.67	Con x Lab	4.8	79.0	75.7	-3.3	47.6	36.9	-10.7	52.4	31.2	-21.2		1.9	1.9		28.2	28.2	5.3	-6.3	-11.6
5 Honiton	16.3.67	Con held	27.8	78.6	72.6	-6.0	54.5	57.0	2.5	26.7	20.4	-6.3	18.8	22.6	3.8				4.4	-0.7	-5.1
6 Brierley Hill	27.4.67	Con held	2.4	79.0	68.0	-11.0	51.2	53.8	2.6	48.8	36.2	-12.6		10.0	10.0				7.6	-3.7	-11.3
7 Cambridge	21.9.67	Con x Lab	2.1	80.0	65.7	-14.3	43.4	51.6	8.2	45.5	36.6	-8.9	11.1	12.8	1.7				8.6	3.3	-5.3
8 Walthamstow W	21.9.67	Con x Lab	36.3	71.0	54.0	-17.0	24.8	37.0	12.2	61.1	36.7	-24.4	14.1	22.9	8.8				18.3	1.7	-16.6
9 Leicester South W	2.11.67	Con x Lab	17.4	74.0	57.5	-16.5	41.3	51.6	10.3	58.7	35.9	-22.8		12.5	12.5				16.6	-1.1	-17.7
10 Manchester Gorton	2.11.67	Lab held	20.2	72.6	72.4	-0.2	39.9	44.5	4.6	60.1	45.9	-14.2		5.9	5.9				9.4	-0.6	-10.1
11 Hamilton	2.11.67	SNP x Lab	42.4	73.3	73.7	0.4	28.8	12.5	-16.3	71.2	41.5	-29.7					46.0	46.0	6.7		
12 Derbyshire W	23.11.67	Con held	12.4	83.4	64.5	-18.9	49.6	56.6	7.0	37.2	18.4	-18.8	13.2	19.8	6.6				12.9	0.2	-12.7

Parliamentary By-Elections 1945-2006 (GB) (contd.)

	Date	Result	% Maj GE	% turn GE	% turn BE	turn % chng	% Con GE	% Con BE	Con % chng	% Lab GE	% Lab BE	Lab % chng	% Lib GE	% Lib BE	Lib % chng	% Nat GE	% Nat BE	Nat % chng	Con/Lab swing	Con/Lib swing	Lab/Lib swing
13 Kensington S	15.3.68	Con held	45.3	58.1	40.0	-18.1	65.1	75.4	10.3	19.8	8.6	-11.2	15.1	12.6	-2.5				10.8	6.4	-4.4
14 Acton	28.3.68	Con x Lab	15.4	73.9	59.7	-14.2	42.3	48.6	6.3	57.7	33.9	-23.8		11.4	11.4				15.1	-2.6	-17.6
15 Dudley	28.3.68	Con x Lab	18.2	73.9	63.5	-10.4	40.9	58.1	17.2	59.1	34.0	-25.1		7.9	7.9				21.2	4.7	-16.5
16 Meriden	28.3.68	Con x Lab	7.2	85.7	66.0	-19.7	46.4	64.8	18.4	53.6	35.2	-18.4							18.4		
17 Warwick & Leamington	28.3.68	Con held	15.5	78.9	58.5	-20.4	51.6	68.3	16.7	36.1	16.5	-19.6	12.3	15.2	2.9				18.2	6.9	-11.3
18 Oldham West	13.6.68	Con x Lab	22.4	70.9	54.7	-16.2	38.8	46.5	7.7	61.2	33.6	-27.6		6.7	6.7				17.7	0.5	-17.2
19 Sheffield Brightside	13.6.68	Lab held	54.6	66.2	49.8	-16.4	21.3	34.8	13.5	75.9	55.1	-20.8							17.2		
20 Nelson & Colne	27.6.68	Con x Lab	12.3	80.9	74.2	-6.7	37.0	48.9	11.9	49.3	38.4	-10.9		9.0	9.0				11.4	1.5	-10.0
21 Caerphilly	18.7.68	Lab held	59.7	76.7	75.9	-0.8	14.6	10.4	-4.2	74.3	45.6	-28.7		3.6	3.6	11.1	40.4	29.3	12.3	-3.9	-16.2
22 Bassetlaw	31.10.68	Lab held	23.2	73.4	68.0	-5.4	38.4	47.9	9.5	61.6	49.7	-11.9							10.7		
23 New Forest	7.11.68	Con held	24.5	74.2	55.9	-18.3	51.2	66.3	15.1	26.7	13.8	-12.9	22.1	19.9	-2.2				14.0	8.7	-5.4
24 Brighton Pavilion	27.3.69	Con held	16.2	70.3	45.1	-25.2	58.1	70.6	12.5	41.9	18.6	-23.3		10.8	10.8				17.9	0.8	-17.1
25 Walthamstow East	27.3.69	Con x Lab	5.6	80.1	51.2	-28.9	42.3	63.1	20.8	47.9	36.9	-11.0	9.8		-9.8				15.9	15.3	-0.6
26 Weston-super-Mare	27.3.69	Con held	23.3	78.5	60.8	-17.7	52.1	65.7	13.6	28.8	14.6	-14.2	19.1	19.7	0.6				13.9	6.5	-7.4
27 Chichester	22.5.69	Con held	32.1	73.2	53.4	-19.8	57.2	74.2	17.0	25.1	12.2	-12.9	17.7	13.6	-4.1				15.0	10.6	-4.4
28 Birmingham Ladywood	26.6.69	Lib x Lab	35.2	59.7	51.9	-7.8	17.4	16.8	-0.6	58.9	25.5	-33.4	23.7	54.3	30.6				16.4	-15.6	-32.0
29 Islington North	30.10.69	Lab held	28.7	54.2	32.8	-21.4	30.7	38.9	8.2	59.4	49.2	-10.2	9.9	10.2	0.3				9.2	4.0	-5.3
30 Paddington North	30.10.69	Lab held	26.1	66.4	46.3	-20.1	32.3	48.3	16.0	58.4	51.7	-6.7	9.3		-9.3				11.4	12.7	1.3
31 Newcastle-u-Lyme	30.10.69	Lab held	23.6	79.9	72.3	-7.6	38.2	43.9	5.7	61.8	46.1	-15.7		6.4	6.4				10.7	-0.4	-11.1
32 Swindon	30.10.69	Con x Lab	24.6	73.5	69.8	-3.7	36.7	41.8	5.1	61.3	40.5	-20.8		15.3	15.3				13.0	-5.1	-18.1
33 Glasgow Gorbals	30.10.69	Lab held	50.3	61.7	58.5	-3.2	22.8	18.6	-4.2	73.1	53.4	-19.7	16.8	17.8	1.0		25.0	25.0	7.8	5.3	-9.0
34 Louth	4.12.69	Con held	9.4	75.0	44.7	-30.3	46.3	57.9	11.6	36.9	19.9	-17.0							14.3		
35 Wellingborough	4.12.69	Con x Lab	4.8	86.5	69.6	-16.9	47.6	54.4	6.8	52.4	39.8	-12.6							9.7		
36 Bridgwater	12.3.70	Con held	6.3	80.2	70.3	-9.9	44.4	55.5	11.1	38.1	31.9	-6.2	17.5	12.6	-4.9				8.7	8.0	-0.7
37 Ayrshire South	19.3.70	Lab held	34.4	75.1	76.3	1.2	32.8	25.6	-7.2	67.2	54.0	-13.2					20.4	20.4	3.0		
Average over Parliament				**74.6**	**62.1**	**-12.6**	**38.9**	**45.7**	**6.8**	**52.0**	**34.7**	**-17.3**	**15.9**	**14.5**	**4.2**	**12.0**	**34.1**	**29.0**	**12.0**	**2.0**	**-10.4**
1970-Feb 1974 Parliament																					
1 St.Marylebone	22.10.70	Con held	32.8	59.6	35.3	-24.3	62.1	63.4	1.3	29.3	27.0	-2.3	8.6	6.2	-2.4				1.8	1.9	0.0
2 Enfield West	19.11.70	Con held	31.7	71.2	49.9	-21.3	57.9	57.3	-0.6	26.2	26.0	-0.2	12.8	12.3	-0.5				-0.2	-0.1	0.2
3 Liverpool Scotland	1.4.71	Lab held	49.6	50.7	37.7	-13.0	25.2	18.4	-6.8	74.8	71.3	-3.5							-1.7		
4 Arundel & Shoreham	1.4.71	Con held	37.9	72.0	53.1	-18.9	60.8	64.1	3.3	22.9	20.9	-2.0	16.3	14.7	-1.6				2.7	2.5	-0.2
5 Southampton Itchen	27.5.71	Con held	67.2	54.2	50.1	-4.1		31.6	31.6		55.4	55.4		5.4	5.4				-10.1		
6 Bromsgrove	27.5.71	Lab x Con	17.0	76.6	67.0	-9.6	58.5	41.4	-17.1	41.5	51.6	10.1							-13.6		
7 Goole	27.5.71	Lab held	20.4	69.5	55.6	-13.9	39.8	31.1	-8.7	60.2	68.9	8.7							-8.7		
8 Hayes & Harlington	17.6.71	Lab held	16.5	67.2	42.3	-24.9	41.2	25.3	-15.9	57.7	74.7	17.0							-16.5		
9 Greenwich	8.7.71	Lab held	21.0	64.0	39.2	-24.8	36.3	28.0	-8.3	57.3	66.7	9.4	6.4		-6.4				-8.9	-0.9	7.9
10 Stirling & Falkirk	19.9.71	Lab held	15.9	73.1	60.0	-13.1	34.8	18.9	-15.9	50.7	46.5	-4.2				14.5	34.6	20.1	-5.9		
11 Widnes	23.9.71	Lab held	15.4	68.8	45.4	-23.4	42.3	30.9	-11.4	57.7	69.1	11.4	14.6	10.7	-3.9				-11.4	-1.8	6.7
12 Macclesfield	30.9.71	Con held	18.8	76.4	75.6	-0.8	52.1	44.7	-7.4	33.3	42.7	9.4		2.4	2.4				-8.4	-2.4	8.7
13 Merthyr Tydfil	13.4.72	Lab x Ind L	23.2	77.9	79.5	1.6	9.8	7.4	-2.4	28.7	48.5	19.8				9.6	37.0	27.4	-11.1		
14 Southwark	4.5.72	Lab held	39.1	48.2	32.1	-16.1	28.2	18.1	-10.1	67.3	79.3	12.0							-11.1		
15 Kingston upon Thames	4.5.72	Con held	24.9	69.2	53.6	-15.6	56.6	52.3	-4.3	31.7	31.0	-0.7	11.7	11.3	-0.4				-1.8	-2.0	-0.2
16 Rochdale	26.10.72	Lib x Lab	11.2	72.8	69.1	-3.7	28.0	17.7	-10.3	41.6	31.1	-10.5	30.4	42.3	11.9				0.1	-11.1	-11.2

Parliamentary By-Elections 1945-2006 (GB) (contd.)

	Date	Result	% Maj GE	% turn GE	% turn BE	turn % chng	% Con GE	% Con BE	Con % chng	% Lab GE	% Lab BE	Lab % chng	% Lib GE	% Lib BE	Lib % chng	% Nat GE	% Nat BE	Nat % chng	Con/Lab swing¹	Con/Lib swing¹	Lab/Lib swing¹
17 Uxbridge	7.12.72	Con held	7.6	74.9	54.3	-20.6	49.3	39.9	-9.4	41.7	36.6	-5.1	9.0	10.3	1.3	-	-	-	-2.2	-5.4	-3.2
18 Sutton & Cheam	7.12.72	Lib x Con	30.8	67.6	56.3	-11.3	58.1	31.9	-26.2	27.3	8.7	-18.6	14.6	53.6	39.0	-	-	-	-3.8	-32.6	-28.8
19 Lincoln	1.3.73	D Lab x Lab	12.0	74.5	72.6	-1.9	39.0	17.5	-21.5	51.0	23.3	-27.7	-	-	-	-	-	-	3.1	-	-
20 Chester-le-Street	1.3.73	Lab held	43.2	73.7	72.3	-1.4	28.4	8.4	-20.0	71.6	53.0	-18.6	-	38.6	38.6	-	-	-	-0.7	-29.3	-28.6
21 Dundee East	1.3.73	Lab held	5.9	76.1	70.6	-5.5	42.4	25.2	-17.2	48.3	32.7	-15.6	-	8.3	8.3	8.9	30.2	21.3	-0.8	-12.8	-12.0
22 West Bromwich	24.5.73	Lab held	10.4	62.2	43.6	-18.6	44.8	25.4	-19.4	55.2	53.2	-2.0	-	-	-	-	-	-	-8.7	-	-
23 Westhoughton	24.5.73	Lab held	10.8	76.9	63.4	-13.5	44.6	42.3	-2.3	55.4	57.0	1.6	-	-	-	-	-	-	-2.0	-	-
24 Manchester Exchange	27.6.73	Lab held	40.7	57.0	43.7	-13.3	27.8	7.1	-20.7	68.5	55.3	-13.2	-	36.5	36.5	-	-	-	-3.8	-28.6	-24.9
25 Isle of Ely	26.7.73	Lib x Con	19.8	71.9	65.8	-6.1	59.9	35.0	-24.9	40.1	26.7	-13.4	-	38.3	38.3	-	-	-	-5.8	-31.6	-25.9
26 Ripon	26.7.73	Lib x Con	34.7	73.7	64.3	-9.4	60.7	40.5	-20.2	26.2	13.9	-12.3	13.1	43.5	30.4	-	-	-	-4.0	-25.3	-21.4
27 Hove	8.11.73	Con held	37.4	66.8	62.4	-4.4	68.7	47.8	-20.9	31.3	11.6	-19.7	-	37.3	37.3	-	-	-	-0.6	-29.1	-28.5
28 Berwick upon Tweed	8.11.73	Lib x Con	23.3	73.7	75.0	1.3	50.7	39.7	-11.0	27.4	19.8	-7.6	21.9	39.9	18.0	-	-	-	-1.7	-14.5	-12.8
29 Edinburgh North	8.11.73	Con held	15.7	70.1	51.7	-18.7	52.8	34.7	-14.1	37.1	24.0	-13.1	10.1	18.4	8.3	-	18.9	18.9	-0.5	-11.2	-10.7
30 Glasgow Govan	8.11.73	SNP x Lab	31.8	63.3	51.7	-11.6	28.2	11.7	-16.5	60.0	38.2	-21.8	-	8.2	8.2	10.3	41.9	31.6	2.7	-12.4	-15.0
Average over Parliament				68.5	56.5	-11.9	44.4	32.3	-12.2	45.6	42.2	-3.4	14.1	23.1	13.4	10.8	32.5	23.9	-4.1	-13.0	-10.5
Feb-Oct 1974 Parliament																					
1 Newham South	23.6.74	Lab held	51.3	63.2	25.9	-37.3	12.2	11.1	-1.1	66.1	62.7	-3.4	14.8	12.5	-2.3	-	-	-	1.2	0.6	-0.5
Oct 1974-1979 Parliament																					
1 Woolwich West	26.6.75	Con x Lab	8.5	73.9	62.3	-11.6	38.6	48.8	10.2	47.1	42.1	-5.0	14.3	5.3	-9.0	-	-	-	7.6	9.6	2.0
2 Coventry NW	4.3.76	Lab held	20.3	75.2	72.9	-2.3	31.6	37.4	5.8	51.9	47.7	-4.2	15.7	11.3	-4.4	-	-	-	5.0	5.1	0.1
3 Carshalton	11.3.76	Con held	7.5	74.3	60.5	-13.8	45.4	51.7	6.3	37.9	27.5	-10.4	16.7	15.0	-1.7	-	-	-	8.4	4.0	-4.4
4 Wirral	11.3.76	Con held	19.2	75.5	55.5	-20.0	50.8	66.8	16.0	31.6	20.3	-11.3	17.6	11.4	-6.2	-	-	-	13.7	11.1	-2.6
5 Rotherham	24.6.76	Lab held	42.5	65.5	46.8	-18.7	22.1	34.7	12.6	64.6	50.7	-13.9	13.3	7.8	-5.5	-	-	-	13.3	9.1	-4.2
6 Thurrock	15.7.76	Lab held	31.2	68.6	54.1	-14.5	24.4	35.4	11.0	55.6	45.3	-10.3	20.0	12.2	-7.8	-	-	-	10.7	9.4	-1.3
7 Newcastle upon Tyne Central	4.11.76	Lab held	55.3	58.4	41.0	-17.4	16.5	19.7	3.2	71.8	47.6	-24.2	11.7	29.0	17.3	-	-	-	13.7	-7.1	-20.8
8 Walsall North	4.11.76	Con x Lab	33.4	66.6	51.5	-15.1	26.1	43.4	17.3	59.5	31.6	-27.9	13.4	3.2	-10.2	-	-	-	22.6	13.8	-8.9
9 Workington	4.11.76	Con x Lab	23.7	75.8	74.2	-1.6	32.3	48.2	15.9	56.0	45.6	-10.4	11.7	6.2	-5.5	-	-	-	13.2	10.7	-2.5
10 Cambridge	2.12.76	Con held	5.2	69.6	49.2	-20.4	41.2	51.0	9.8	36.0	26.0	-10.0	21.1	18.3	-2.8	-	-	-	9.9	6.3	-3.6
11 City of London & Westminster S	24.2.77	Con held	20.8	53.2	39.6	-13.6	51.7	59.1	7.4	30.9	19.7	-11.2	14.9	9.8	-5.1	-	-	-	9.3	6.3	-3.1
12 Birmingham Stechford	31.3.77	Con x Lab	29.8	64.1	58.8	-5.3	27.8	43.4	15.6	57.6	38.0	-19.6	14.6	8.0	-6.6	-	-	-	17.6	11.1	-6.5
13 Ashfield	28.4.77	Con x Lab	41.1	74.7	59.7	-15.0	22.3	43.1	20.8	63.4	42.5	-20.9	14.3	9.6	-4.7	-	-	-	20.9	12.8	-8.1
14 Grimsby	28.4.77	Lab held	15.2	69.4	70.2	0.8	31.9	45.7	13.8	47.1	46.9	-0.2	20.6	6.7	-13.9	-	-	-	7.0	13.9	6.9
15 Saffron Walden	7.7.77	Con held	13.4	78.1	64.8	-13.3	43.7	55.7	12.0	26.0	14.6	-11.5	30.3	25.2	-5.1	-	-	-	11.7	8.6	-3.2
16 Birmingham Ladywood	18.8.77	Lab held	42.4	56.9	42.6	-14.3	22.1	28.4	6.3	64.5	53.1	-11.4	13.4	4.9	-8.5	-	-	-	8.9	7.4	-1.5
17 Bournemouth E	24.11.77	Con held	26.5	70.5	42.6	-27.9	51.7	63.4	11.7	21.0	15.3	-5.7	25.2	13.4	-11.8	-	-	-	8.7	11.8	3.1
18 Ilford North	2.3.78	Con x Lab	1.6	74.5	69.1	-5.4	40.9	50.3	9.4	42.5	38.0	-4.5	16.6	5.0	-11.6	-	-	-	7.0	10.5	3.6
19 Glasgow Garscadden	13.4.78	Lab held	38.0	70.8	69.1	-1.7	12.9	18.5	5.6	50.9	45.4	-5.5	5.0	-	-5.0	31.2	32.9	1.7	5.6	5.3	-0.3
20 Lambeth Central	20.4.78	Lab held	33.9	52.6	44.5	-8.1	26.2	34.4	8.2	60.1	49.4	-10.7	12.5	5.3	-7.2	-	-	-	9.5	7.7	-1.8

Parliamentary By-Elections 1945-2006 (GB) (contd.)

	Date	Result	% Maj GE	% turn GE	turn BE	turn % chng	% Con GE	% Con BE	Con % chng	% Lab GE	% Lab BE	Lab % chng	% Lib GE	% Lib BE	Lib % chng	% Nat GE	% Nat BE	Nat % chng	Con/Lab swing[1]	Con/Lib swing[1]	Lab/Lib swing[1]
21 Epsom & Ewell	27.4.78	Con held	27.5	73.7	54.9	-18.8	54.1	63.6	9.5	19.3	16.5	-2.8	26.6	12.8	-13.8	-	-	-	6.2	11.7	5.5
22 Wycombe	27.4.78	Con held	15.5	74.3	59.0	-15.3	46.3	60.0	13.7	30.8	28.5	-2.3	19.4	7.4	-12.0	-	-	-	8.0	12.9	4.9
23 Hamilton	31.6.78	Lab held	38.0	77.2	72.1	-5.1	9.5	13.0	3.5	47.5	51.0	3.5	4.0	2.6	-1.4	39.0	33.4	-5.6	0.0	2.5	2.5
24 Manchester Moss Side	13.7.78	Lab held	12.8	62.9	51.6	-11.3	34.3	40.6	6.3	47.1	46.4	-0.7	17.6	9.2	-8.4	-	-	-	3.5	7.4	3.9
25 Penistone	13.7.78	Lab held	30.2	74.7	59.8	-14.9	24.0	32.9	8.9	54.2	45.5	-8.7	21.8	21.6	-0.2	-	-	-	8.8	4.6	-4.3
26 Berwick & E Lothian	26.9.78	Lab held	5.7	83.0	71.2	-11.8	37.6	40.2	2.6	43.3	47.4	4.1	5.9	3.6	-2.3	13.2	8.8	-4.4	-0.8	2.5	3.2
27 Pontefract & Castleford	26.11.78	Lab held	54.2	71.2	48.9	-22.3	16.2	27.3	11.1	70.4	65.8	-4.6	12.3	6.9	-5.4	-	-	-	7.9	8.3	0.4
28 Clitheroe	1.3.79	Con held	16.8	78.6	62.8	-15.8	48.0	65.0	17.0	31.2	28.4	-2.8	20.8	6.6	-14.2	-	-	-	9.9	15.6	5.7
29 Knutsford	1.3.79	Con held	24.6	76.8	57.2	-19.6	51.0	67.1	16.1	22.6	15.6	-7.0	26.4	15.8	-10.6	-	-	-	11.6	13.4	1.8
30 Liverpool Edge Hill	29.3.79	Lib x Lab	24.6	61.2	57.2	-4.0	20.8	9.4	-11.4	51.9	23.8	-28.1	27.3	64.1	36.8	-	-	-	8.4	-24.1	-32.5
Average over Parliament				**70.1**	**57.5**	**-12.6**	**33.4**	**43.3**	**9.9**	**46.5**	**37.2**	**-9.3**	**16.8**	**12.4**	**-4.9**	**27.8**	**25.0**	**-2.8**	**9.6**	**7.4**	**-2.2**
1979-83 Parliament																					
1 Manchester Cen.	27.9.79	Lab held	48.7	63.7	33.6	-30.1	22.1	12.0	-10.1	70.8	70.7	-0.1	5.3	14.2	8.9	-	-	-	-5.0	-9.5	-4.5
2 Hertfordshire SW	13.12.79	Con held	27.0	79.7	48.3	-31.4	54.7	45.9	-8.8	27.7	27.7	0.0	16.2	23.6	7.4	-	-	-	-4.4	-8.1	-3.7
3 Southend East	13.3.80	Con held	27.0	70.1	62.5	-7.6	56.1	36.8	-19.3	29.1	35.6	6.5	13.1	25.1	12.0	-	-	-	-12.9	-15.7	-2.8
4 Glasgow Central	26.6.80	Lab held	56.1	59.5	42.8	-16.7	16.4	8.8	-7.6	72.5	60.8	-11.7	-	-	-	11.1	26.3	15.2	2.1	-	-
5 Warrington	16.7.81	Lab held	32.9	71.3	67.0	-4.3	28.8	7.1	-21.7	61.7	48.4	-13.3	9.0	42.4	33.4	-	-	-	-4.2	-27.6	-23.4
6 Croydon NW	22.10.81	Lib x Con	9.3	72.5	62.8	-9.7	49.4	30.5	-18.9	40.1	26.0	-14.1	10.5	40.0	29.5	-	-	-	-2.4	-24.2	-21.8
7 Crosby	26.11.81	SDP x Con	31.5	75.2	69.3	-5.9	56.9	39.8	-17.1	25.4	9.5	-15.9	15.2	49.0	33.8	-	-	-	-0.6	-25.5	-24.9
8 Glasgow Hillhead	25.3.82	SDP x Con	6.6	75.7	76.4	0.7	41.0	26.6	-14.4	34.4	25.9	-8.5	14.4	33.4	19.0	10.1	11.3	1.2	-3.0	-16.7	-13.8
9 Beaconsfield	27.4.82	Con held	41.5	76.9	53.9	-22.3	61.7	61.8	0.1	20.2	10.4	-9.8	17.1	26.8	9.7	-	-	-	5.0	-4.8	-9.8
10 Mitcham & Mordern	3.6.82	Con x Lab	1.3	75.3	48.5	-28.4	43.9	43.4	-0.5	45.2	24.4	-20.8	8.9	29.4	20.5	-	-	-	10.2	-10.5	-20.7
11 Coatbridge & Airdrie	24.6.82	Lab held	33.4	75.3	56.3	-19.0	27.5	26.2	-1.3	60.9	55.1	-5.8	-	8.2	8.2	11.6	10.5	-1.1	2.3	-4.8	-7.0
12 Gower	16.9.82	Lab held	22.7	80.8	65.4	-15.4	30.5	22.1	-8.4	53.2	43.5	-9.7	9.1	25.1	16.0	7.2	8.7	1.5	0.7	-12.2	-12.9
13 Peckham	28.10.82	Lab held	31.7	57.7	38.0	-19.7	28.1	12.4	-15.7	59.8	50.3	-9.5	7.7	32.9	25.2	-	-	-	-3.1	-20.5	-17.4
14 Birmingham Northfield	28.10.82	Lab x Con	0.3	70.6	55.0	-15.6	45.4	35.6	-9.8	45.1	36.3	-8.8	8.1	26.1	18.0	-	-	-	-0.5	-13.9	-13.4
15 Glasgow Queen's Pk	2.12.82	Lab held	40.4	68.3	47.0	-21.3	24.1	12.0	-12.1	64.5	56.0	-8.5	-	9.4	9.4	9.7	20.0	10.3	-1.8	-10.8	-9.0
16 Bermondsey	24.2.83	Lib x Lab	38.7	59.3	57.7	-1.6	24.9	5.5	-19.4	63.6	26.1	-37.5	6.8	57.7	50.9	-	-	-	9.1	-35.2	-44.2
17 Darlington	24.3.83	Lab held	2.1	78.4	80.0	1.6	43.4	34.9	-8.5	45.5	39.5	-6.0	10.2	24.5	14.3	-	-	-	-1.3	-11.4	-10.2
Average over Parliament				**71.2**	**56.7**	**-14.5**	**38.5**	**27.1**	**-11.4**	**48.2**	**38.0**	**-10.2**	**10.8**	**29.2**	**19.8**	**9.9**	**15.4**	**5.4**	**-0.6**	**-15.7**	**-14.9**
1983-87 Parliament																					
1 Penrith & the Border	28.7.83	Con held	30.9	73.1	55.7	-17.4	58.8	46.0	-12.8	13.3	7.4	-5.9	27.9	44.6	16.7	-	-	-	-3.5	-14.8	-11.3
2 Chesterfield	1.3.84	Lab held	15.7	81.2	76.9	-4.3	32.4	15.2	-17.3	48.1	46.5	-1.7	19.5	34.7	15.1	-	-	-	-7.8	-16.2	-8.4
3 Cynon Valley	3.5.84	Lab held	35.4	73.4	65.7	-7.7	14.2	7.4	-6.8	56.0	58.8	2.7	20.6	19.9	-0.7	9.2	11.0	1.8	-4.8	-3.1	1.8
4 Surrey SW	3.5.84	Con held	27.6	74.5	61.7	-12.8	59.7	49.3	-10.4	8.2	6.7	-1.5	32.1	43.3	11.2	-	-	-	-4.5	-10.8	-6.4
5 Stafford	3.5.84	Con held	26.5	76.5	65.6	-10.9	51.2	40.4	-10.9	23.7	27.4	3.6	24.7	31.8	7.0	-	-	-	-7.3	-9.0	-1.7
6 Portsmouth S	14.6.84	SDP x Con	24.6	67.3	54.5	-12.8	50.0	34.3	-15.8	22.6	26.5	3.9	25.4	37.6	12.1	-	-	-	-9.8	-14.0	-4.2
7 Enfield Southgate	13.12.84	Con held	34.7	69.6	50.6	-19.0	58.1	49.6	-8.5	17.9	11.9	-6.0	23.4	35.6	12.2	-	-	-	-1.3	-10.4	-9.1
8 Brecon & Radnor	4.7.85	Lib x Con	23.2	80.1	79.4	-0.7	48.2	27.7	-20.5	25.0	34.4	9.3	24.4	35.8	11.4	1.7	1.1	-0.6	-15.0	-16.0	-1.0
9 Tyne Bridge	5.12.85	Lab held	31.3	61.5	38.1	-23.4	25.2	11.1	-14.1	56.5	57.8	1.3	18.3	29.7	11.4	-	-	-	-7.7	-12.8	-5.1
10 Fulham	10.4.86	Lab x Con	12.2	76.1	70.8	-5.3	46.2	34.9	-11.3	34.0	44.4	10.4	18.3	18.7	0.5	-	-	-	-10.9	-5.9	5.0
11 Ryedale	8.5.86	Lib x Con	28.7	71.8	67.3	-4.5	59.2	41.3	-17.9	10.3	8.4	-1.9	30.5	50.3	19.8	-	-	-	-8.0	-18.9	-10.9

Parliamentary By-Elections 1945-2006 (GB) (contd.)

	Date	Result	% Maj GE	% turn GE	% turn BE	turn % chng	% Con GE	% Con BE	Con % chng	% Lab GE	% Lab BE	Lab % chng	% Lib GE	% Lib BE	Lib % chng	% Nat GE	% Nat BE	Nat % chng	Con/Lab swing[1]	Con/Lib swing[1]	Lab/Lib swing[1]
12 West Derbyshire	8.5.86	Con held	28.8	77.4	71.9	-5.5	55.9	39.5	-16.4	17.1	19.8	2.7	27.1	39.4	12.3				-9.6	-14.4	-4.8
13 Newcastle-u-Lyme	17.7.86	Lab held	5.5	77.3	62.0	-15.3	36.4	19.1	-17.3	41.9	40.7	-1.2	21.6	38.8	17.2				-8.1	-17.3	-9.2
14 Knowsley North	13.11.86	Lab held	44.4	69.5	57.0	-12.5	20.1	6.3	-13.8	64.5	56.3	-8.2	14.8	34.6	19.7				-2.8	-16.8	-14.0
15 Greenwich	26.2.87	SDP x Lab	3.5	67.7	68.4	0.7	34.8	11.2	-23.6	38.2	33.8	-4.4	25.1	53.0	27.9				-9.6	-25.8	-16.2
16 Truro	12.3.87	Lib held	19.2	79.6	70.3	-9.3	38.1	31.6	-6.6	4.5	7.1	2.6	57.3	60.4	3.1				-4.6	-4.8	-0.3
Average over Parliament				73.5	63.5	-10.0	43.0	29.1	-14.0	30.1	30.5	0.4	25.7	38.0	12.3	5.5	6.1	0.6	-7.2	-13.2	-6.0
1987-92 Parliament																					
1 Kensington	14.7.88	Con held	14.3	64.7	51.6	-13.1	47.5	41.6	-5.9	33.2	38.1	4.9	17.2	10.8	-6.4				-5.4	0.3	5.7
2 Glasgow Govan	10.11.88	SNP x Lab	52.5	73.4	60.2	-13.2	11.9	7.3	-4.6	64.8	36.9	-27.9	12.3	4.1	-8.2	10.4	48.8	38.4	11.7	1.8	-9.9
3 Epping Forest	15.12.88	Con held	41.5	76.3	49.0	-27.3	60.9	39.5	-21.4	18.4	18.7	0.3	19.4	25.9	6.5				-10.9	-14.0	-3.1
4 Richmond (Yorks)	23.2.89	Con held	34.2	72.1	64.4	-7.7	61.2	37.2	-24.0	11.8	4.9	-6.9	27.0	22.0	-5.0				-8.6	-9.5	-1.0
5 Pontypridd	23.2.89	Lab held	36.8	76.2	62.2	-14.0	19.5	13.5	-6.0	56.3	53.4	-3.0	18.9	3.9	-15.0	5.3	25.3	20.0	-1.6	4.5	6.1
6 Vale of Glamorgan	4.5.89	Lab x Con	12.1	79.3	70.7	-8.6	46.8	36.3	-10.5	34.7	48.9	14.2	16.7	4.2	-12.5	1.8	3.5	1.7	-12.4	1.0	13.4
7 Glasgow Central	15.6.89	Lab held	51.5	65.6	52.8	-12.8	13.0	7.6	-5.4	64.5	54.6	-9.9	10.5	1.5	-9.0	9.9	30.2	20.2	2.3	1.8	-0.4
8 Vauxhall	15.6.89	Lab held	21.2	64.0	44.4	-19.6	29.0	18.8	-10.2	50.2	52.8	2.6	18.2	17.5	-0.7				-6.4	-4.8	1.7
9 Staffordshire Mid	22.3.90	Lab x Con	25.9	79.4	77.5	-1.9	50.6	32.3	-18.3	24.7	49.1	24.4	23.2	11.2	-12.0				-21.4	-3.2	18.2
10 Bootle	24.5.90	Lab held	46.8	72.9	50.6	-22.3	20.1	9.1	-11.0	66.9	75.4	8.5	13.0	9.0	-4.0				-9.8	-3.5	6.3
11 Knowsley South	27.9.90	Lab held	42.9	74.1	33.4	-40.7	21.6	15.2	-6.4	64.5	68.8	4.3	13.9	8.5	-5.4				-5.4	-0.5	4.9
12 Eastbourne	18.10.90	LD x Con	30.2	75.6	60.7	-14.9	59.9	40.9	-19.0	8.8	5.0	-3.8	29.7	50.8	21.1				-7.6	-20.1	-12.5
13 Bootle	8.11.90	Lab held	46.8	72.9	39.7	-33.2	20.1	9.2	-10.9	66.9	78.4	11.5	13.0	7.9	-5.1				-11.2	-2.9	8.3
14 Bradford North	8.11.90	Lab held	3.3	72.7	53.4	-19.3	39.5	16.8	-22.7	42.8	51.7	8.9	17.7	25.3	7.6				-15.8	-15.2	0.7
15 Paisley North	29.11.90	Lab held	68.7	73.5	53.7	-19.8	15.8	14.8	-1.0	55.5	44.0	-11.5	15.8	8.3	-7.5	12.9	29.4	16.5	5.3	3.3	-2.0
16 Paisley South	29.11.90	Lab held	41.1	75.3	55.0	-20.3	14.7	13.4	-1.3	56.2	46.1	-10.1	15.1	9.8	-5.3	14.0	27.5	13.5	4.4	2.0	-2.4
17 Ribble Valley	7.3.91	LD x Con	39.5	79.2	71.2	-8.0	60.9	38.5	-22.4	17.7	9.4	-8.3	21.4	48.5	27.1				-7.1	-24.8	-17.7
18 Neath	4.4.91	Lab held	47.3	78.8	63.7	-15.1	16.1	8.6	-7.5	63.4	51.8	-11.6	14.1	5.8	-8.3	6.4	23.4	17.0	2.1	0.4	-1.7
19 Monmouth	16.5.91	Lab x Con	19.8	80.8	75.8	-5.0	47.5	34.0	-13.5	27.7	39.3	11.6	24.0	24.8	0.8	0.8	0.6	-0.2	-12.6	-7.2	5.4
20 Liverpool Walton	4.7.91	Lab held	43.2	73.6	56.7	-16.9	14.4	2.9	-11.5	64.4	53.1	-11.3	21.2	36.0	14.8				-0.1	-13.2	-13.1
21 Hemsworth	7.11.91	Lab held	49.8	75.7	42.6	-33.1	17.2	10.5	-6.7	67.0	66.3	-0.7	15.8	20.1	4.3				-3.0	-5.5	-2.5
22 Kincardine &Deeside	7.11.91	LD x Con	4.4	75.2	64.6	-10.6	40.7	30.6	-10.1	15.9	7.7	-8.2	36.3	49.0	12.7	6.5	11.1	4.6	-1.0	-11.4	-10.5
23 Langbaurgh	7.11.91	Lab x Con	3.3	78.8	65.3	-13.5	41.7	39.1	-2.6	38.4	42.9	4.5	19.9	16.1	-3.8				-3.6	0.6	4.2
Average over Parliament				74.4	57.4	-17.0	33.5	22.5	-11.0	44.1	43.4	-0.8	18.9	18.3	-0.6	7.6	22.2	14.6	-5.1	-5.2	-0.1
1992-97 Parliament																					
1 Newbury	6.5.93	LD x Con	18.6	82.8	71.3	-11.5	55.9	26.9	-29.0	6.0	2.0	-4.0	37.3	65.1	27.8				-12.5	-28.4	-15.9
2 Christchurch	29.7.93	LD x Con	39.9	80.7	74.2	-6.5	63.5	31.4	-32.1	12.1	2.7	-9.4	23.6	62.2	38.6				-11.4	-35.4	-24.0
3 Rotherham	5.5.94	Lab held	40.2	71.7	43.7	-28.0	23.7	9.9	-13.8	63.9	55.6	-8.3	12.3	29.7	17.4				-2.8	-15.6	-12.9
4 Barking	9.6.94	Lab held	17.8	70.0	38.3	-31.7	33.9	10.4	-23.5	51.6	72.1	20.5	14.5	12.0	-2.5				-22.0	-10.5	11.5
5 Eastleigh	9.6.94	LD x Con	23.3	82.9	58.7	-24.2	51.3	24.7	-26.6	20.7	27.6	6.9	28.0	44.3	16.3				-16.8	-21.5	-4.7
6 Newham NE	9.6.94	Lab held	27.8	60.3	34.8	-25.5	30.5	14.6	-15.9	58.3	74.9	16.6	11.2	4.2	-7.0				-16.3	-4.5	11.8
7 Bradford South	9.6.94	Lab held	9.3	75.6	44.2	-31.4	38.4	17.8	-20.6	47.6	55.3	7.7	13.7	23.9	10.2				-14.2	-15.4	-1.3
8 Dagenham	9.6.94	Lab held	16.0	70.7	37.0	-33.7	36.3	9.9	-26.4	52.3	72.0	19.7	11.4	8.4	-3.0				-23.1	-11.7	11.4
9 Monklands East	30.6.94	Lab held	43.3	75.0	70.2	-4.8	16.0	2.3	-13.7	61.3	49.8	-11.5	4.6	2.6	-2.0	18.0	44.9	26.9	-1.1	-5.9	-4.8
10 Dudley West	15.12.94	Lab x Con	8.1	82.1	47.0	-35.1	48.8	18.8	-30.1	40.7	68.8	28.1	10.5	7.6	-2.9				-29.1	-13.6	15.5
11 Islwyn	16.2.95	Lab held	59.5	81.4	45.1	-36.3	14.9	3.9	-11.0	74.3	69.2	-5.1	5.7	10.6	4.9	3.9	12.7	8.8	-3.0	-8.0	-5.0
12 Perth & Kinross	25.5.95	SNP x Con	4.2	76.9	62.0	-14.9	40.2	21.4	-18.8	12.5	22.9	10.4	11.4	11.8	0.4	36.0	40.4	4.4	-14.6	-9.6	5.0

Parliamentary By-Elections 1945-2006 (GB) (contd.)

	Date	Result	% Maj GE	% turn GE	% turn BE	turn % chng	% Con GE	% Con BE	Con % chng	% Lab GE	% Lab BE	Lab % chng	% Lib GE	% Lib BE	Lib % chng	% Nat GE	% Nat BE	Nat % chng	Con/Lab swing[1]	Con/Lib swing[1]	Lab/Lib swing[1]
13 Littleborough & Saddleworth	27.7.95	LD x Con	8.4	81.6	64.4	-17.2	44.2	23.6	-20.6	19.9	33.8	13.9	35.9	38.5	2.6	-	-	-	-17.3	-11.6	5.7
14 Hemsworth	1.2.96	Lab held	52.2	75.9	39.5	-36.4	18.6	8.8	-9.8	70.8	71.9	1.1	10.5	6.9	-3.6	-	-	-	-5.5	-3.1	2.4
15 Staffordshire SE	11.4.96	Lab x Con	12.5	82.0	59.6	-22.4	50.7	28.5	-22.2	38.2	60.1	21.9	9.6	4.7	-4.9	-	-	-	-22.1	-8.7	13.4
16 Barnsley East	12.12.96	Lab held	63.0	72.9	33.6	-39.3	14.2	7.3	-6.9	77.2	76.4	-0.8	8.6	8.4	-0.2	-	-	-	-3.1	-3.4	-0.3
17 Wirral South	27.2.97	Lab x Con	16.3	82.3	73.0	-9.3	50.8	34.4	-16.4	34.6	52.6	18.0	13.1	10.1	-3.0	-	-	-	-17.2	-6.7	10.5
Average over Parliament				**76.8**	**52.7**	**-24.0**	**37.2**	**17.3**	**-19.8**	**43.6**	**51.0**	**7.4**	**15.4**	**20.6**	**5.2**	**19.3**	**32.7**	**13.4**	**-13.6**	**-12.5**	**1.1**
1997-2001 Parliament																					
1 Uxbridge	31.7.97	Con held	1.7	72.4	55.5	-16.9	43.6	51.1	7.5	41.8	39.3	-2.5	10.9	5.6	-5.3	-	-	-	5.0	6.4	1.4
2 Paisley South	6.11.97	Lab held	34.1	69.1	42.9	-26.2	8.7	7.0	-1.7	57.5	44.1	-13.4	9.4	11.0	1.6	23.4	32.5	9.1	5.9	-1.7	-7.5
3 Beckenham	20.11.97	Con held	9.1	74.3	43.6	-30.7	42.5	41.2	-1.3	33.4	37.4	4.0	18.1	18.4	0.3	-	-	-	-2.7	-0.8	1.9
4 Winchester	20.11.97	LD held	0.0	78.3	68.7	-9.6	42.1	28.4	-13.7	10.5	1.7	-8.8	42.1	68.0	25.9	-	-	-	-2.5	-19.8	-17.4
5 Leeds Central	10.6.99	Lab held	55.9	54.2	19.6	-34.6	13.7	12.3	-1.4	69.6	48.2	-21.4	11.3	30.8	19.5	-	-	-	10.0	-10.5	-20.5
6 Eddisbury	22.7.99	Con held	2.4	75.6	51.5	-24.1	42.5	44.8	2.3	40.1	40.2	0.1	13.2	13.8	0.6	-	-	-	1.1	0.8	-0.3
7 Hamilton South	23.9.99	Lab held	48.0	71.1	41.3	-29.8	8.6	7.2	-1.4	65.6	36.9	-28.7	5.1	3.3	-1.8	17.6	34.0	16.4	13.7	0.2	-13.5
8 Wigan	23.9.99	Lab held	51.7	67.7	25.1	-42.6	16.9	18.0	1.1	68.6	59.6	-9.0	10.0	13.3	3.3	-	-	-	5.1	-1.1	-6.2
9 Kensington & Chelsea	25.11.99	Con held	25.7	54.7	29.8	-24.9	53.6	56.4	2.8	28.0	22.0	-6.0	15.3	9.4	-5.9	-	-	-	4.4	4.4	0.0
10 Ceredigion	3.2.00	PC held	17.3	73.9	45.6	-28.3	14.9	16.5	1.6	24.3	14.4	-9.9	16.5	23	6.5	41.6	42.8	1.2	5.8	-2.5	-8.2
11 Romsey	4.5.00	LD x Con	16.6	76.4	55.5	-20.9	46.0	42.0	-4	18.6	3.7	-14.9	29.4	50.6	21.2	-	-	-	5.5	-12.6	-18.1
12 Tottenham	22.6.00	Lab held	53.6	56.9	25.4	-31.5	15.7	16.0	0.3	69.3	53.5	-15.8	10.8	19.1	8.3	-	-	-	8.1	-4.0	-12.1
13 Preston	23.11.00	Lab held	38.9	65.8	29.6	-36.2	21.9	25.0	3.1	60.8	45.7	-15.1	14.7	16.2	1.5	-	-	-	9.1	0.8	-8.3
14 West Bromwich W.	23.11.00	Lab held[3]	42.0	54.4	27.6	-26.8	-	-	-				7.2	8.1	0.9	-	-	-	-	-	-5.5
15 Glasgow Anniesland	23.11.00	Lab held	44.7	63.8	38.4	-25.4	11.5	10.9	-0.6	61.8	51.7	-10.1	5.1	3.2	-1.9	17.1	21.0	3.9	4.8	-0.8	-5.5
16 Falkirk West	21.12.00	Lab held	35.9	72.6	36.2	-36.4	12.1	8.3	-3.8	59.3	43.5	-15.8				23.4	39.9	16.5	6.0	-1.0	-7.0
Average over Parliament			**29.9**	**67.6**	**39.8**	**-27.8**	**26.3**	**25.7**	**-0.6**	**47.3**	**36.1**	**-11.2**	**14.6**	**19.6**	**5.0**	**24.6**	**34.0**	**9.4**	**5.3**	**-2.8**	**-8.1**
2001-2005 Parliament																					
1 Ipswich	22.11.01	Lab held	20.8	57.0	40.2	-16.8	30.5	28.4	-2.1	51.3	43.4	-7.9	15.2	22.4	7.2	-	-	-	2.9	-4.7	-7.6
2 Ogmore	14.2.02	Lab held	48.0	58.2	35.9	-22.3	11.1	7.5	-3.6	62.0	52.0	-10.0	12.8	8.7	-4.1	14.0	20.8	6.8	3.2	0.3	-7.1
3 Brent East	18.9.03	LD x Lab	45.0	51.9	36.2	-15.7	18.2	16.1	-2.1	63.2	33.8	-29.4	10.6	39.1	28.5	-	-	-	13.7	-15.3	-29.0
4 Birmingham, Hodge Hill	15.7.04	Lab held	43.9	47.9	37.9	-10.0	20.0	17.3	-2.7	63.9	36.5	-27.4	8.1	34.2	26.1	-	-	-	12.4	-14.4	-26.8
5 Leicester South	15.7.04	LD x Lab	31.4	58.0	41.5	-16.5	23.1	19.7	-3.4	54.5	29.3	-25.2	17.2	34.9	17.7	-	-	-	10.9	-10.6	-21.5
6 Hartlepool	30.9.04	Lab held	38.3	55.8	45.8	-10.0	20.9	9.7	-11.2	59.1	40.7	-18.4	15.0	34.2	19.2	-	-	-	3.6	-15.2	-18.8
Average over Parliament			**37.9**	**54.8**	**39.6**	**-15.2**	**20.6**	**16.5**	**-4.2**	**59.0**	**39.3**	**-19.7**	**13.2**	**28.9**	**15.8**	**14.0**	**20.8**	**6.8**	**7.8**	**-10.0**	**-18.5**

Parliamentary By-Elections 1945-2006 (GB) (contd.)

	Date	Result	% Maj GE	% turn GE	% turn BE	turn % chng	% Con GE	% Con BE	Con % chng	% Lab GE	% Lab BE	Lab % chng	% Lib GE	% Lib BE	Lib % chng	% Nat GE	% Nat BE	Nat % chng	Con/ Lab swing¹	Con/ Lib swing¹	Lab/ Lib swing¹
2005 Parliament																					
1 Cheadle	14.7.05	LD held	8.5	69.7	55.2	-14.5	40.4	42.4	.2	8.8	4.6	-4.2	48.9	52.2	3.3	-	-	-	3.1	-0.7	-3.8
2 Livingston	29.9.05	Lab held	29.5	58.5	38.6	-19.9	10.1	6.8	-3.3	51.1	41.8	-9.3	15.4	14.8	-0.6	21.6	32.7	11.1	3.0	-1.4	-4.4
3 Dunfermline & West Fife	9.2.06	LD x Lab	27.3	59.9	48.7	-11.2	10.3	7.8	-2.5	47.4	30.6	-16.8	20.2	35.8	15.6	18.9	21.0	2.1	7.2	-9.1	-16.2
4 Blaenau Gwent	29.6.06	Ind held	25.9	66.1	51.7	-14.4	2.3	3.7	1.4	32.3	37.0	4.7	4.3	5.4	1.1	2.4	6.5	4.1	-1.7	0.2	1.8
5 Bromley & Chislehurst	29.6.06	Con held	28.9	64.9	40.5	-24.4	51.1	40.0	-11.1	22.2	6.6	-15.6	20.3	37.8	17.5	-	-	-	2.3	-14.4	-16.6
Average over Parliament (to 29.6.2006)			**24.0**	**63.8**	**46.9**	**-16.9**	**22.8**	**20.1**	**-2.7**	**32.4**	**24.1**	**-8.2**	**21.8**	**29.2**	**7.4**	**14.3**	**20.1**	**5.8**	**2.8**	**-5.1**	**-7.8**

* Previous election conducted using STV in multi-member seat.

1. Positive figure = swing to first named party; negative figure = swing to second named party. For a full explanation of swing see Introductory Notes.
2. Unopposed.
3. Sitting (Labour) MP contested as 'The Speaker' in 1997.

Table 10.01: Seat Gains and Losses at By-Elections 1885-2005

From	C^1 net	Lab net	L^2 net	Others net
1885-86	2	-	-1	-1
1886-92	-20	-	19	1
1892-95	4	-	-4	•
1895-1900	-11	-	10	1
1900-06	-25	3	17	5
1906-10(J)	11	3	-16	2
1910(J)-10(D)	•	•	•	•
1910(D)-18	13	-5	-10	2
1918-22	-10	13	-6	3
1922-23	-3	2	2	-1
1923-24	1	•	-1	•
1924-29	-16	12	4	•
1929-31	3	-2	-1	•
1931-35	-9	10	-1	•
1935-45	-28	12	•	16
1945-50	4	-1	•	-3
1950-51	•	•	•	•
1951-55	1	-1	•	•
1955-59	-2	4	•	-2
1959-64	-5	4	1	•
1964-66	•	-1	1	•
1966-70	11	-15	1	3
1970-74(F)	-5	•	5	•
1974(F)-74(O)	•	•	•	•
1974(O)-79	6	-6	1	-1
1979-83	-3	1	4	-2
1983-87	-4	•	4	•
1987-92	-7	3	3	1
1992-97	-8	3	4	1
1997-2001	-1	•	1	•
2001-05	•	-2	2	•

• No overall gain or loss

1. Including Liberal Unionists 1886-1910(D); National, National Liberal and National Labour 1931-45.

2. Including both Liberal and National Liberal in 1922: Independent Liberal in 1931; SDP/Liberal Alliance 1983-87; Liberal Democrat 1992 onwards.

Table 10.02: Seats Which Changed Hands at By-Elections 1950-2005

	1950 -51	1951 -55	1955 -59	1959 -64	1964 -66	1966 -70	1970 -74(F)	1974(F) -74(O)	1974(O) -1979	1979 -83	1983 -87	1987 -92	1992 -97	1997 -2001	2001 -05
C from															
Lab	0	1	0	1	1	12	0	0	5	0	0	0	0	0	0
Ind C	0	0	2	0	0	0	0	0	0	0	0	0	0	0	0
ENP	0	0	0	0	0	0	0	0	1	0	0	0	0	0	0
Ind SDP	0	0	0	0	0	0	0	0	0	1	0	0	0	0	0
Lab from															
C	0	0	3	6	0	0	1	0	0	1	1	4	3	0	0
L	0	0	1	0	0	0	0	0	0	0	0	0	0	0	0
Ind Lab	0	0	0	0	0	0	2	0	0	0	0	0	0	0	0
L¹ from															
C	0	0	1	1	1	0	4	0	0	3	3	3	4	1	0
Lab	0	0	0	0	0	1	1	0	1	0	0	0	0	0	2
Ind Lab	0	0	0	0	0	0	0	0	0	1	1	0	0	0	0
PC from															
Lab	0	0	0	0	0	1	0	0	0	0	0	0	0	0	0
SNP from															
Con	0	0	0	0	0	0	0	0	0	0	0	0	1	0	0
Lab	0	0	0	0	0	1	1	0	0	0	1	1	0	0	0
UNITY from															
C	0	0	0	0	0	1	0	0	0	0	0	0	0	0	0
IND C from															
SF	0	0	1	0	0	0	0	0	0	0	0	0	0	0	0
IND LAB from															
Lab	0	0	0	0	0	0	1	0	0	0	0	0	0	0	0
UKUP from															
UPUP	0	0	0	0	0	0	0	0	0	0	0	0	1	0	0
DUP from															
UU	0	0	0	0	0	0	0	0	0	0	0	0	0	1	0
TOTAL	0	1	8	8	2	16	10	0	7	6	5	8	9	2	2

1. Includes SDP/Liberal Alliance 1983-87; Liberal Democrat 1992 onwards, throughout

Table 10.03: Contested and Uncontested By-Elections 1832-2005

From	Contested	%	Uncontested	%	Total[1]	% of total seats
1832-35	35	60.3	23	39.7	58	8.8
1835-37	47	52.8	42	47.2	89	13.5
1837-41	49	46.7	56	53.3	105	16.0
1841-47	62	26.8	169	73.2	231	35.1
1847-52	73	42.4	99	57.6	172	26.2
1852-57	98	45.0	120	55.0	218	33.3
1857-59	24	26.7	66	73.3	90	13.8
1859-65	102	46.2	119	53.8	221	33.8
1865-68	45	31.9	96	68.1	141	21.4
1868-74	104	59.1	72	40.9	176	26.7
1874-80	123	63.7	70	36.3	193	29.6
1880-85	99	51.3	94	48.7	193	29.6
1885-86	15	39.5	23	60.5	38	5.7
1886-92	102	57.0	77	43.0	179	26.7
1892-95	53	51.5	50	48.5	103	15.4
1895-1900	79	69.9	34	30.1	113	16.9
1900-06	81	71.1	33	28.9	114	17.0
1906-10(J)	68	68.0	32	32.0	100	14.9
1910(J)-10(D)	10	47.6	11	52.4	21	3.1
1910(D)-18	115	46.6	132	53.4	247[2]	36.9
1918-22	78	72.2	30	27.8	108	15.3
1922-23	16	100.0	0	-	16	2.6
1923-24	9	90.0	1	10.0	10	1.6
1924-29	61	96.8	2	3.2	63	10.2
1929-31	33	91.7	3	8.3	36	5.9
1931-35	50	80.6	12	19.4	62	10.1
1935-45	150	68.5	69	31.5	219[3]	35.6
1945-50	51	98.1	1	1.9	52	8.1
1950-51	15	93.8	1	6.2	16	2.6
1951-55	45	93.8	3	6.2	48	7.7
1955-59	52	100.0	0	-	52	8.3
1959-64	62	100.0	0	-	62	9.8
1964-66	13	100.0	0	-	13	2.1
1966-70	38	100.0	0	-	38	6.0
1970-74(F)	30	100.0	0	-	30	4.8
1974(F)-74(O)	1	100.0	0	-	1	0.2
1974(O)-79	30	100.0	0	-	30	4.7
1979-83	20	100.0	0	-	20	3.1
1983-87	31	100.0	0	-	31	4.8
1987-92	24	100.0	0	-	24	3.7
1992-97	18	100.0	0	-	18	2.8
1997-2001	16	100.0	0	-	17	2.6
2001-05	6	100.0	0	-	6	0.9
TOTAL	**2,233**	**59.2**	**1,540**	**40.8**	**3,774**	

1 Prior to 1926, by-elections could occur through MPs seeking re-election after appointment to certain ministerial and other offices. This considerably increased the number of by-elections during the period.

2 From the outbreak of the First World War on August 4, 1914 until the Dissolution in 1918 there were 29 contested and 89 uncontested by-elections. The three major parties observed a truce during the war by nominating candidates only for seats which they had previously held. Twenty members of the House of Commons were killed or died on active service.

3 From the outbreak of the Second World War on September 3, 1939 until the Dissolution in 1945 there were 75 contested and 66 uncontested by-elections. The three major parties observed a truce during the war by nominating candidates only for seats which they had previously held. Twenty-three members of the House of Commons were killed or died on active service.

Table 10.04: Forfeited Deposits at By-Elections 1918-2005

From	Con	Lab	L¹	Com	NF	PC	SNP	Others	Total	% of total opposed candidates
1918-22	1	0	2	1	-	-	-	8	12	6.2
1922-23	0	1	1	0	-	-	-	2	4	9.5
1923-24	0	0	2	0	-	-	-	0	2	8.0
1924-29	0	5	10	0	-	0	1	4	20	11.1
1929-31	0	0	2	6	-	0	1	2	11	11.8
1931-35	0	0	3	5	-	0	2	6	16	12.0
1935-45	0	1	2	3	-	0	2	43	51	14.1
1945-50	3	1	9	2	-	0	4	16	35	24.3
1950-51	0	0	1	1	-	0	0	3	5	14.3
1951-55	0	0	7	1	-	1	1	4	14	13.2
1955-59	0	0	1	1	-	3	0	12	17	12.3
1959-64	2	1	8	6	-	3	4	37	61	27.0
1964-66	0	1	4	0	-	1	0	10	16	32.7
1966-70	4	2	12	6	1	0	0	23	48	34.0
1970-74(F)	4	2	9	1	4	0	0	29	49	40.8
1974(F)-(O)	1	0	0	0	1	0	0	1	3	60.0
1974(O)-79	1	0	20	1	18	0	1	65	106	60.2
1979-83	6	2	2	3	5	1	2	80	101	67.3
1983-87	1	3	0	1	2	2	0	72	81	50.9
1987-92	2	2	4	2	4	1	0	116	131	61.2
1992-97	3	2	2	1	2	0	0	94	104	65.4
1997-2001	0	2	2	0	2	0	0	73	140	56.4
2001-05	0	0	0	0	2	0	0	42	67	65.7

1. SDP/Liberal Alliance 1983-87; Liberal Democrat 1992 onwards.

Table 10.05: Candidates at By-Elections 1885-2005

From	C	Lab	L	Com	ILP	N	NF	PC	SNP	Others	Total
1885-86	15	-	33	-	-	5	-	-	-	2	55
1886-92	151	-	98	-	-	29	-	-	-	11	289
1892-95	63	-	75	-	3	15	-	-	-	5	161
1895-1900	103	-	67	-	4	19	-	-	-	7	200
1900-06	93	7	70	-	0	19	-	-	-	12	201
1906-10(J)	72	13	66	-	0	22	-	-	-	17	190
1910(J)-10(D)	11	2	15	-	0	3	-	-	-	0	31
1910(D)-18	151	20	126	-	2	38	-	-	-	58	395
1918-22	76	56	69	1	0	0	-	-	-	21	223
1922-23	14	12	12	0	0	0	-	-	-	4	42
1923-24	10	8	7	0	0	0	-	-	-	1	26
1924-29	60	56	59	1	0	0	-	0	1	5	182
1929-31	32	31	14	7	1	1	-	0	3	7	96
1931-35	55	48	19	6	4	1	-	0	4	8	145
1935-45	176	98	20	4	11	0	-	3	7	112	431
1945-50	51	48	14	3	4	1	-	2	4	18	145
1950-51	16	14	1	1	2	0	-	0	0	2	36
1951-55	48	45	8	1	0	0	-	2	1	4	109
1955-59	50	50	19	1	3	1	-	3	0	11	138
1959-64	61	62	50	6	1	0	-	3	6	37	226
1964-66	13	13	12	0	0	0	0	1	0	10	49
1966-70	38	37	27	6	0	0	1	3	4	25	141
1970-74(F)	30	30	19	1	0	0	5	1	4	30	120
1974(F)-74(O)	1	1	1	0	0	0	1	0	0	1	5
1974(O)-79	30	30	29	1	0	0	18	0	3	65	176
1979-83	17	17	16	3	0	0	5	1	4	87	150
1983-87	16	16	16	1	0	0	2	2	0	106	159
1987-92	24	23	23	2	0	0	4	3	5	120	204
1992-97	18	17	17	1	0	0	2	1	2	104	162
1997-2001	16	16	16	0	0	0	2	1	4	85	140
2001-05	6	6	6	0	0	0	2	1	0	46	67

Table 10.06: Women Elected at By-Elections 1918-2005

From	C	Lab	L¹	Com	NF	PC	SNP	Others	Total	% of MPs elected
1918-22	1²	0	1³	0	-	-	-	0	2	1.9
1922-23	1	0	0	0	-	-	-	0	1	6.3
1923-24	0	0	0	0	-	-	-	0	0	-
1924-29	1	4	1	0	-	0	0	0	6	9.5
1929-31	0	2	0	0	-	0	0	0	2	5.6
1931-35	0	0	0	0	-	0	0	0	0	-
1935-45	3	3	0	0	-	0	0	0	6	2.7
1945-50	1	1	0	0	-	0	0	0	2	3.8
1950-51	0	0	0	0	-	0	0	0	0	-
1951-55	2	2	0	0	-	0	0	0	4	8.3
1955-59	2	2	0	0	-	0	0	0	4	7.7
1959-64	1	0	0	0	-	0	0	0	1	1.6
1964-66	0	0	0	0	-	0	0	0	0	-
1966-70	0	0	0	0	0	0	1	1⁴	2	5.3
1970-74(F)	0	1	0	0	0	0	1	0	2	6.7
1974(F)-(O)	0	0	0	0	0	0	0	0	0	-
1974(O)-79	0	1	0	0	0	0	0	0	1	3.3
1979-83	1	2	1	1	0	0	0	0	4	20.0
1983-87	1	2	2	0	0	0	0	0	5	16.1
1987-92	0	3	0	0	0	0	0	0	3	12.5
1992-97	0	3	1	0	0	0	1	0	5	27.8
1997-2001	1	0	1	0	0	0	0	0	2	11.8
2001-05	0	0	1	0	0	0	0	0	1	16.7

1. SDP/Liberal Alliance 1983-87; Liberal Democrat 1992 onwards.
2. Viscountess Astor, the first woman to sit in the House of Commons. She was returned for Plymouth, Sutton at a by-election on November 15, 1919. The by-election was caused by the succession of her husband to the Peerage.
3. Mrs. Margaret Wintringham, the first Liberal woman to be elected. She was returned for Lincolnshire, Louth at a by-election on September 22, 1921. The by-election was caused by the death of her husband.
4. Miss B.J. Devlin (Mid-Ulster—Unity).

Table 10.07: Women Candidates at By-Elections 1918-2005

From	C	Lab	L¹	Com	NF	PC	SNP	Others	Total	% of total candidates
1918-22	1	2	1	0	-	-	-	0	4	1.8
1922-23	1	0	0	0	-	-	-	0	1	2.4
1923-24	0	0	0	0	-	-	-	0	0	-
1924-29	3	7	2	0	-	0	0	0	12	6.6
1929-31	1	3	2	1	-	0	1	1	9	9.4
1931-35	0	4	0	0	-	0	0	1	5	3.4
1935-45	5	4	2	1	-	0	0	13	25	5.8
1945-50	1	1	0	0	-	0	1	3	6	4.1
1950-51	0	0	1	0	-	0	0	0	1	2.8
1951-55	3	5	0	0	-	0	0	0	8	7.3
1955-59	4	3	2	0	-	1	0	1	11	8.0
1959-64	4	1	0	0	-	0	0	1	6	2.7
1964-66	0	0	2	0	-	0	0	0	2	4.1
1966-70	1	3	3	1	0	0	1	1	10	7.1
1970-74(F)	0	3	0	0	0	0	1	3	7	5.8
1974(F)-(O)	0	0	0	0	0	0	0	0	0	-
1974(O)-79	1	2	3	0	3	0	2	6	17	9.7
1979-83	2	3	1	0	0	0	0	6	12	8.0
1983-87	2	6	3	1	0	1	0	8	21	13.2
1987-92	1	6	4	0	0	0	0	21	32	15.7
1992-97	3	4	4	1	0	1	2	12	27	16.7
1997-2001	5	2	5	0	0	0	1	9	22	15.7
2001-05	1	0	5	0	0	0	0	4	10	14.9

1. SDP/Liberal Alliance 1983-87; Liberal Democrat 1992 onwards.

Table 10.08: Reasons for By-Elections 1832-2005

Cause of by-election	Total	%
Death	1,240	32.9
Resignation (including resignations following appointment as Lord Chancellor and elevation to the Peerage)	1,068	28.2
Ministerial (appointments to Ministerial officewhich required re-election)	678	18.0
Succession to the Peerage	228	6.1
Elevation to the Peerage (including Life Peerages and those summoned to the House of Lords in one of their fathers' Peerages)	221	5.9
Elections declared void following petitions	193	5.1
Members seeking re-election (for various reasons) in their constituency[1]	51	1.4
Acceptance of an appointment which did not disqualify but necessitated re-election	36	1.0
Members elected for more than one constituency declining the seats they did not wish to represent[1]	26	0.7
Members disqualified from sitting in the House of Commons[1]	16	0.4
Expulsion from the House of Commons[1]	8	0.2
Bankruptcy[1]	3	0.1
Creation of additional seats in the House of Commons during a Parliament	2	0.1
Unseated for voting in the House of Commons before taking the Oath[1]	2	0.1
Lunacy[1]	1	0.0
TOTAL	**3,773**	

1. For a detailed list see *Chronology of British Parliamentary By-Elections 1833-1987* by F.W.S. Craig (Chichester, 1987).

Table 10.09: Notable By-Election Turnovers

The ebb and flow of political support between General Elections was dramatically shown by the following by-election results:

Kent, Dartford (27/3/20). A Coalition majority of 9,370 at the previous (1918) General Election was turned into a Labour majority of 9,048.

Fulham, East (25/10/33). A Conservative majority of 14,521 at the previous (1931) General Election was turned into a Labour majority of 4,840.

Kent, Orpington (14/3/62). A Conservative majority of 14,760 at the previous (1959) General Election was turned into a Liberal majority of 7,855.

Leyton (21/1/65). A Labour majority of 7,926 at the previous (1964) General Election was turned into a Conservative majority of 205.

Walthamstow, West (21/9/67). A Labour majority of 8,725 at the previous (1966) General Election was turned into a Conservative majority of 62.

Dudley (28/3/68). A Labour majority of 10,022 at the previous (1966) General Election was turned into a Conservative majority of 11,656.

Warwickshire, Meriden (28/3/68). A Labour majority of 4,581 at the previous (1966) General Election was turned into a Conservative majority of 15,263.

Birmingham, Ladywood (26/6/69). A Labour majority of 5,315 at the previous (1966) General Election was turned into a Liberal majority of 2,713.

Swindon (30/10/69). A Labour majority of 10,443 at the previous (1966) General Election was turned into a Conservative majority of 478.

Worcestershire, Bromsgrove (27/5/71). A Labour majority of 1,868 at the previous (1970) General Election was turned into a Conservative majority of 10,874.

Rochdale (26/10/72). A Labour majority of 5,171 at the previous (1970) General Election was turned into a Liberal majority of 5,093.

Sutton and Cheam (7/12/72). A Conservative majority of 12,696 at the previous (1970) General Election was turned into a Liberal majority of 7,417.

Isle of Ely (26/7/73). A Conservative majority of 9,606 at the previous (1970) General Election was turned into a Liberal majority of 1,470.

Yorkshire, Ripon (26/7/73). A Conservative majority of 12,064 at the previous (1970) General Election was turned into a Liberal majority of 946.

Northumberland, Berwick-upon-Tweed (8/11/73). A Conservative majority of 7,145 at the previous (1970) General Election was turned into a Liberal majority of 57.

Walsall, North (4/11/76). A Labour/Co-operative majority of 15,885 at the previous (October 1974) General Election was turned into a Conservative majority of 4,379.

Workington (4/11/76). A Labour majority of 9,551 at the previous (October 1974) General Election was turned into a Conservative majority of 1,065.

Birmingham, Stechford (31/3/77). A Labour majority of 11,923 at the previous (October 1974) General Election was turned into a Conservative majority of 1,949.

Ashfield (28/4/77). A Labour majority of 22,915 at the previous (October 1974) General Election was turned into a Conservative majority of 264.

Ilford, North (2/3/78). A Labour majority of 778 at the previous (October 1974) General Election was turned into a Conservative majority of 5,497.

Liverpool, Edge Hill (29/3/79). A Labour majority of 6,171 at the previous (October 1974) General Election was turned into a Liberal majority of 8,133.

Crosby (26/11/81). A Conservative majority of 19,272 at the previous (1979) General Election was turned into a Social Democratic Party majority of 5,289.

Bermondsey (24/2/83). A Labour majority of 19,338 at the previous (1979) General Election was turned into a Liberal majority of 9,319.

Notable By-Election Turnovers (contd.)

Portsmouth, South (14/6/84). A Conservative majority of 12,335 at the previous (1983) General Election was turned into a Social Democratic Party majority of 1,341.

Ryedale (8/5/86). A Conservative majority of 16,142 at the previous (1983) General Election was turned into a Liberal majority of 4,940.

Mid Staffordshire (22/3/90). A Conservative majority of 14,654 at the previous (1987) General Election was turned into a Labour majority of 9,449.

Eastbourne (18/10/90). A Conservative majority of 16,923 at the previous (1987) General Election was turned into a Liberal Democrat majority of 4,550.

Ribble Valley (7/3/91). A Conservative majority of 19,528 at the previous (1987) General Election was turned into a Liberal Democrat majority of 4,601.

Newbury (6/5/93). A Conservative majority of 12,357 at the previous (1992) General Election was turned into a Liberal Democrat majority of 22,055.

Christchurch (29/7/93). A Conservative majority of 23,015 at the previous (1992) General Election was turned into a Liberal Democrat majority of 16,427.

Eastleigh (9/6/94). A Conservative majority of 17,702 at the previous (1992) General Election was turned into a Liberal Democrat majority of 9,239.

Dudley West (15/12/94). A Conservative majority of 5,789 at the previous (1992) General Election was turned into a Labour majority of 20,694.

Romsey (4/5/2000). A Conservative majority of 8,585 at the previous (1997) General Election was turned into a Liberal Democrat majority of 3,311.

Brent East (18/9/2003). A Conservative majority of 13,047 at the previous (2001) General Election was turned into a Liberal Democrat majority of 1,118.

Dunfermline & West Fife (9/2/06). A Labour majority of 11,562 at the previous (2005) General Election was turned into a Liberal Democrat majority of 1,800.

Nationalists

The Scottish National Party and Plaid Cymru have each gained surprise victories at by-elections:

At Lanarkshire, Motherwell on April 12, 1945, Robert McIntyre (SNP) won the seat from Labour with a majority of 617 votes. The Labour majority at the previous (1935) General Election had been 430 over a Conservative but at the by-election McIntyre had a straight fight with Labour due to the electoral truce which existed during the war. The constituency had not previously been contested by a Scottish Nationalist.

At Lanarkshire, Hamilton on November 2, 1967, Winifred Ewing (SNP) won the seat from Labour with a majority of 1,799. The Labour majority at the previous (1966) General Election had been 16,576 in a straight-fight with a Conservative. The Scottish National Party had not contested the seat since 1959 when their candidate had forfeited his deposit.

At Glasgow, Govan on November 8, 1973, Mrs. Margo Macdonald (SNP) won the seat from Labour with a majority of 571. The Labour majority at the previous (1970) General Election had been 7,142 and the SNP candidate had forfeited his deposit.

At Glasgow Govan on November 10, 1988, Jim Sillars (SNP) won the seat from Labour with a majority of 3,554. The Labour majority at the previous (1987) General Election had been 19,509 and the SNP candidate finished fourth.

At Carmarthenshire, Carmarthen on July 14, 1966, Gwynfor Evans (PC) won the seat from Labour with a majority of 2,436. The Labour majority at the previous (1966) General Election had been 9,233 in a four-cornered contest in which Evans had secured third place.

European Parliament Elections

Table 11.01: European Parliament Election 1979 (7 June)

	Total votes	%	Candidates	Elected
ENGLAND				
C	5,817,992	53.4	66	54
L	1,444,204	13.3	66	0
Lab	3,536,261	32.5	66	12
Others	86,310	0.8	21	0
Total	**10,884,767**		**219**	**66**
WALES				
C	259,729	36.6	4	1
L	67,962	9.6	4	0
Lab	294,978	41.5	4	3
PC	83,399	11.7	4	0
Others	4,008	0.6	2	0
Total	**710,076**		**18**	**4**
SCOTLAND				
C	430,772	33.7	8	5
L	178,433	14.0	8	0
Lab	421,968	33.0	8	2
SNP	247,836	19.4	8	1
Others	-	-	-	-
Total	**1,279,009**		**32**	**8**
NORTHERN IRELAND [1]				
UDUP	170,688	29.8	1	1
UPNI	3,712	0.6	1	0
UU	125,169	21.9	2	1
Others	38,198	6.7	1	0
(Total 'Loyalist')	*(337,767)*	*(59.0)*	*(5)*	*(2)*
APNI	39,026	6.8	1	0
L	932	0.2	1	0
Rep	4,418	0.8	2	0
SDLP	140,622	24.6	1	1
Others	49,474	8.6	3	0
Total	**572,239**		**13**	**3**
GREAT BRITAIN				
C	6,508,493	50.6	78	60
L	1,690,599	13.1	78	0
Lab	4,253,207	33.0	78	17
PC	83,399	0.6	4	0
SNP	247,836	1.9	8	1
Others	90,318	0.7	23	0
Total	**12,873,852**		**269**	**78**
UNITED KINGDOM				
C	6,508,493	48.4	78	60
L	1,690,599	12.6	78	0
Lab	4,253,207	31.6	78	17
PC	83,399	0.6	4	0
SNP	247,836	1.8	8	1
Others	662,557	4.9	36 [2]	3 [3]
Total	**13,446,091**		**282**	**81**

European Parliament Election 1979 (7 June) (contd.)

1. Elections were conducted using the Single Transferable Vote system of proportional represetation. Figures given are for first preference votes.
2. Including all candidates in Northern Ireland and 5 UACM, 3 EP, 1 EFP, 1 IMG, 1 MK, 1 WR and 1 EFP.
3. The three members for the Northern Ireland constituency (1 SDLP, 1 UDUP, 1 UU).

Table 11.02: European Parliament Election 1984 (14 June)

	Total votes	*%*	*Candidates*	*Elected*
ENGLAND				
C	4,879,964	43.7	66	42
Lab	3,963,213	35.5	66	24
L	1,206,908	10.8	33	0
SDP	1,035,998	9.3	33	0
(Total L/SDP)	*(2,242,906)*	*(20.1)*	*(66)*	*(0)*
Others	88,705	0.8	24	0
Total	**11,174,788**		**222**	**66**
WALES				
C	214,086	25.4	4	1
Lab	375,982	44.5	4	3
L	61,756	7.3	2	0
SDP	85,191	10.1	2	0
(Total L/SDP)	*(146,947)*	*(17.4)*	*(4)*	*(0)*
PC	103,031	12.2	4	0
Others	4,266	0.5	1	0
Total	**844,312**		**17**	**4**
SCOTLAND				
C	332,771	25.7	8	2
Lab	526,066	40.7	8	5
L	89,481	6.9	4	0
SDP	112,301	8.7	4	0
(Total L/SDP)	*(201,782)*	*(15.6)*	*(8)*	*(0)*
SNP	230,594	17.8	8	1
Others	2,560	0.2	1	0
Total	**1,293,773**		**33**	**8**
NORTHERN IRELAND[1]				
UDUP	230,251	33.6	1	1
UPUP	20,092	2.9	1	0
UU	147,169	21.5	1	1
(Total 'Loyalist')	*(397,512)*	*(58.0)*	*(3)*	*(2)*
APNI	34,046	5.0	1	0
NIEP	2,172	0.3	1	0
SDLP	151,399	22.1	1	1
SF	91,476	13.3	1	0
TWP	8,712	1.3	1	0
Total	**685,317**		**8**	**3**

European Parliament Election 1984 (14 June) (contd.)

	Total votes	%	Candidates	Elected
GREAT BRITAIN				
C	5,426,821	40.8	78	45
Lab	4,865,261	36.5	78	32
L	1,358,145	10.2	39	0
SDP	1,233,490	9.3	39	0
(Total L/SDP)	*(2,591,635)*	*(19.5)*	*(78)*	*(0)*
PC	103,031	0.8	4	0
SNP	230,594	1.7	8	1
Others	95,531	0.7	26	0
Total	**13,312,873**		**272**	**78**
UNITED KINGDOM				
C	5,426,821	38.8	78	45
Lab	4,865,261	34.8	78	32
L	1,358,145	9.7	39	0
SDP	1,233,490	8.8	39	0
(Total L/SDP)	*(2,591,635)*	*(18.5)*	*(78)*	*(0)*
PC	103,031	0.7	4	0
SNP	230,594	1.6	8	1
Others	780,848	5.6	34 [2]	3 [3]
Total	**13,998,190**		**280**	**81**

1. Elections were conducted using the Single Transferable Vote system of proportional representation. Figures given are for first preference votes.
2. Including all candidates in Northern Ireland and 15 EP, 1 CNP and 1 WR.
3. The three members for the Northern Ireland constituency (1 SDLP, 1 UDUP, 1 UU).

Table 11.03: European Parliament Election 1989 (15 June)

	Total votes	%	Candidates	Elected
ENGLAND				
C	4,790,290	37.2	66	32
Lab	5,052,668	39.2	66	34
L	848,020	6.6	66	0
SDP	72,733	0.6	15	0
Green	2,078,144	16.1	66	0
Others	39,938	0.3	24	0
Total	**12,881,793**		**303**	**66**
WALES				
C	209,313	23.5	4	0
Lab	436,730	48.9	4	4
L	28,785	3.2	4	0
SDP	3,153	0.4	1	0
PC	115,062	12.9	4	0
Green	99,546	11.1	4	0
Total	**892,589**		**21**	**4**

European Parliament Election 1989 (15 June) (contd.)

	Total votes	%	Candidates	Elected
SCOTLAND				
C	331,495	20.9	8	0
Lab	664,263	41.9	8	7
L	68,056	4.2	8	0
SNP	406,686	25.6	8	1
Green	115,028	7.2	8	0
Others	1,357	0.1	2	0
Total	**1,586,885**		**42**	**8**
NORTHERN IRELAND[1]				
UDUP	160,110	29.9	1	1
UU	118,785	22.2	1	1
(Total 'Loyalist')	*(278,895)*	*(52.1)*	*(2)*	*(2)*
APNI	27,905	5.2	1	0
C	25,789	4.8	1	0
SDLP	136,335	25.5	1	1
SF	48,914	9.1	1	0
TWP	5,590	1.0	1	0
Green	6,569	1.2	1	0
LRG	3,540	0.7	1	0
LP '87	1274	0.2	1	0
Total	**534,811**		**10**	**3**
GREAT BRITAIN				
C	5,331,098	34.7	78	32
Lab	6,153,661	40.1	78	45
L	944,861	6.2	78	0
PC	115,062	0.8	4	0
SNP	406,686	2.6	8	1
Green	2,292,718	14.9	78	0
SDP	75,886	0.5	16	0
Others	41,295	0.3	26	0
Total	**15,361,267**		**366**	**78**
UNITED KINGDOM				
C	5,331,098	33.5	78	32
Lab	6,153,661	38.7	78	45
L	944,861	5.9	78	0
PC	115,062	0.7	4	0
SNP	406,686	2.6	8	1
Green	2,292,718	14.4	78	0
SDP	75,886	0.5	16	0
Others	576,106	3.6	36[2]	3[3]
Total	**15,896,078**		**376**	**81**

1. Elections were conducted using the Single Transferable Vote system of proportional representation. Figures given are for first preference votes.
2. Including all candidates in Northern Ireland.
3. The three members for the Northern Ireland constituency (1 SDLP, 1 UDUP, 1 UU).

Table 11.04: European Parliament Election 1994 (9 June)

	Total votes	%	Candidates	Elected
ENGLAND				
C	3,913,547	30.5	71	18
Lab	5,587,177	43.5	71	51
L	2,367,650	18.4	71	2
Green	451,834	3.5	71	0
Others	526,539	4.1	162	0
Total	**12,846,747**		**446**	**71**
WALES				
C	138,323	14.6	5	0
Lab	530,749	55.9	5	5
L	82,426	8.7	5	0
PC	162,478	17.1	5	0
Green	19,413	2.0	5	0
Others	16,689	1.8	10	
Total	**950,078**		**35**	**5**
SCOTLAND				
C	216,669	14.5	8	0
Lab	635,955	42.5	8	6
L	107,811	7.2	8	0
SNP	487,237	32.6	8	2
Green	23,314	1.6	8	0
Others	24,911	1.7	16	0
Total	**1,586,885**		**56**	**8**
NORTHERN IRELAND[1]				
UDUP	163,246	29.2	1	1
UU	133,459	23.8	1	1
(Total 'Loyalist')	*(296,705)*	*(53.0)*	*(2)*	*(2)*
APNI	23,157	4.1	1	0
C	5,583	1.0	1	0
SDLP	161,992	28.9	1	1
SF	55,215	9.9	3	0
TWP	2,543	0.5	1	0
UIM	7,858	1.4	1	0
NLP	2,291	0.4	3	0
Others	4,523	0.8	4	0
Total	**559,867**		**17**	**3**
GREAT BRITAIN				
C	4,268,539	27.9	84	18
Lab	6,753,881	44.2	84	62
L	2,557,887	16.7	84	2
PC	162,478	1.1	5	0
SNP	487,237	3.2	8	2
Green	494,561	3.2	84	0
Others	568,139	3.7	188	0
Total	**15,292,722**		**537**	**84**

European Parliament Election 1994 (9 June) (contd.)

	Total votes	%	Candidates	Elected
UNITED KINGDOM				
C	4,268,539	26.9	84	18
Lab	6,753,881	42.6	84	62
L	2,557,887	16.1	84	2
PC	162,478	1.0	5	0
SNP	487,237	3.1	8	2
Green	494,561	3.1	84	0
Others	1,128,006	7.1	205[2]	3[3]
Total	**15,852,589**		**554**	**87**

1. Elections were conducted using the Single Transferable Vote system of proportional representation. Figures given are for first preference votes.
2. Including all candidates in Northern Ireland and 84 NLP, 23 UKIP and 20 Lib.
3. The three members for the Northern Ireland constituency (1 SDLP, 1 UDUP, 1 UU).

Table 11.05: European Parliament Election 1999 (10 June)

	Total votes	%	Lists/Cands	Elected
ENGLAND[1]				
C	3,240,276	38.6	9	33
Lab	2,320,640	27.7	9	24
L	1,118,295	13.3	9	9
Green	552,090	6.6	9	2
UKIP	663,804	7.9	9	3
Others	492,413	5.9	57 lists	0
Total	**8,387,518**			**71**
WALES[1]				
C	142,631	22.8	1	1
Lab	199,690	31.9	1	2
L	51,283	8.2	1	0
PC	185,235	29.6	1	2
Green	16,146	2.6	1	0
UKIP	19,702	3.1	1	0
Others	11,738	1.9	3 lists	0
Total	**626,425**			**5**
SCOTLAND[1]				
C	195,296	19.8	1	2
Lab	283,490	28.7	1	3
L	96,971	9.8	1	1
SNP	268,528	27.2	1	2
Green	57,142	5.8	1	0
SSP	39,720	4.0	1	0
UKIP	12,549	1.3	1	0
Others	34,614	3.5	5 lists	0
Total	**988,310**			**8**

European Parliament Election 1999 (contd.)

	Total votes	%	Lists/Cands	Elected
NORTHERN IRELAND [2]				
UDUP	192,762	28.4	1	1
UU	119,507	17.6	1	1
PUP	22,494	3.3	1	0
UKUP	20,283	3.0	1	0
(Total 'Loyalist')	*(355,046)*	*(52.3)*	*(4)*	*(2)*
APNI	14,391	2.1	1	0
SDLP	190,731	28.1	1	1
SF	117,643	17.3	1	0
NLP	998	0.1	1	0
Total	**678,809**		**8**	**3**
GREAT BRITAIN				
C	3,578,203	35.8	11	36
Lab	2,803,820	28.0	11	29
L	1,266,549	12.7	11	10
PC	185,235	1.9	1	2
SNP	268,528	2.7	1	2
Green	625,378	6.3	11	2
UKIP	696,055	7.0	11	3
Others	578,485	5.8	65 lists	0
Total	**10,002,253**			**84**
UNITED KINGDOM				
C	3,578,203	33.5	11	36
Lab	2,803,820	26.3	11	29
L	1,266,549	11.9	11	10
PC	185,235	1.7	1	2
SNP	268,528	2.5	1	2
Green	625,378	5.9	11	2
UKIP	696,055	6.5	11	3
Others	1,257,294	11.8	n/a	3 [3]
Total	**10,681,062**			**87**

1. Elections in Great Britain were conducted using a regional list system of proportional representation. There were 9 regions in England, with Scotland and Wales each forming a single region. The data for Great Britain gives the number of regions in which each party fielded a list of candidates.

2. Elections were conducted using the Single Transferable Vote system of proportional representation. Figures given are for first preference votes.

3. The three members for the Northern Ireland constituency (1 SDLP, 1 UDUP, 1 UU).

Table 11.06: European Parliament Election 2004 (10 June)

	Total votes	%	Lists/Cands	Elected
ENGLAND [1]				
C	4,010,288	27.9	9	24
Lab	3,110,008	21.7	9	15
L	2,202,033	15.3	9	11
Green	915,827	6.4	9	2
UKIP	2,485,263	17.3	9	12
Others	1,640,681	11.4	45 lists	0
Total	**14,364,100**			**64**
WALES[1]				
C	177,771	19.4	1	1
Lab	297,810	32.5	1	2
L	96,116	10.5	1	0
PC	159,888	17.4	1	1
Green	32,761	3.6	1	0
UKIP	96,677	10.5	1	0
Others	56,663	6.2	4 lists	0
Total	**917,686**			**4**
SCOTLAND[1]				
C	209,028	17.8	1	2
Lab	310,865	26.4	1	2
L	154,178	13.1	1	1
SNP	231,505	19.7	1	2
Green	79,695	6.8	1	0
SSP	61,356	5.2	1	0
UKIP	78,828	6.7	1	0
Others	51,362	4.4	4 lists	0
Total	**1,176,817**			**7**
NORTHERN IRELAND [2]				
UDUP	175,761	32.0	1	1
UU	91,164	16.6	1	1
(Total 'Loyalist')	*(266,925)*	*(48.6)*	*(2)*	*(2)*
SDLP	87,559	15.9	1	0
SF	144,541	26.3	1	1
Ind	36,270	6.6	1	0
Soc.Env.All	9,172	1.7	1	0
Green	4,810	0.9	1	0
Total	**549,277**		**7**	**3**
GREAT BRITAIN				
C	4,397,087	26.7	11	27
Lab	3,718,683	22.6	11	19
L	2,452,327	14.9	11	12
PC	159,888	1.0	1	1
SNP	231,505	1.4	1	2
Green	1,028,283	6.3	11	2
UKIP	2,660,768	16.2	11	12
Others	1,810,062	11.0	54 lists	0
Total	**16,458,603**			**75**

European Parliament Election 2004 (contd.)

	Total votes	%	Lists/Cands	Elected
UNITED KINGDOM				
C	4,397,087	25.9	11	27
Lab	3,718,683	21.9	11	19
L	2,452,327	14.4	11	12
PC	159,888	0.9	1	1
SNP	231,505	1.4	1	2
Green	1,033,093	6.1	11	2
UKIP	2,660,768	15.6	11	12
Others	2,354,529	13.8	n/a	3 [3]
Total	**1,700,780**			**78**

1. Elections in Great Britain were conducted using a regional list system of proportional representation. There were 9 regions in England, with Scotland and Wales each forming a single region. The data for Great Britain gives the number of regions in which each party fielded a list of candidates. Boundary changes reduced the number of seats for England from 71 in 1999 to 64. Scotland and Wales each lost 1 seat compared with 1999.
2. Elections were conducted using the Single Transferable Vote system of proportional representation. Figures given are for first preference votes.
3. The three members for the Northern Ireland constituency (1 SDLP, 1 UDUP, 1 UU).

Table 12.01: Summary Results of European Parliament Elections 1979-2004

UK Election	Con %	Con MEPs	Lab %	Lab MEPs	Lib %	L MEPs	Other %	Other MEPs
1979	48.4	60	31.6	17	12.6	0	7.3	4
1984	38.8	45	34.8	32	18.5	0	7.9	4
1989	33.5	32	38.7	45	5.9	0	21.8	4
1994	26.9	18	42.6	62	16.1	2	14.3	5
1999	33.5	36	26.3	29	11.9	10	28.4	12
2004	25.9	27	21.9	19	14.4	12	37.9	20

GB Election	Con %	Con MEPs	Lab %	Lab MEPs	Lib %	L MEPs	Other %	Other MEPs
1979	50.6	60	33.0	17	13.1	0	3.2	1
1984	40.8	45	36.5	32	19.5	0	3.2	1
1989	34.7	32	40.1	45	6.2	0	19.1	1
1994	27.9	18	44.2	62	16.7	2	11.2	2
1999	35.8	36	28.0	29	12.7	10	23.5	9
2004	26.7	27	22.6	19	14.9	12	35.8	17

Table 12.02: Votes Cast at European Parliament Elections 1979-2004

UK

Election	C	%	Lab	%	L	%	Others	%	Total
1979	6,508,493	48.4	4,253,207	31.6	1,690,599	12.6	993,792	7.3	13,446,091
1984	5,426,821	38.8	4,865,261	34.8	2,591,635	18.5	1,114,473	7.9	13,998,190
1989	5,331,098	33.5	6,153,661	38.7	944,861	5.9	3,466,458	21.8	15,896,078
1994	4,268,539	26.9	6,753,881	42.6	2,557,887	16.1	2,272,282	14.3	15,852,589
1999	3,578,203	33.5	2,803,820	26.3	1,266,549	11.9	3,032,490	28.4	10,681,062
2004	4,397,087	25.9	3,718,683	21.9	2,452,327	14.4	6,439,783	37.9	17,007,880

GB

Election	C	%	Lab	%	L	%	Others	%	Total
1979	6,508,493	50.6	4,253,207	33.0	1,690,599	13.1	421,553	3.2	12,873,852
1984	5,426,821	40.8	4,865,261	36.5	2,591,635	19.5	429,156	3.2	13,312,873
1989	5,331,098	34.7	6,153,661	40.1	944,861	6.2	2,931,647	19.1	15,361,267
1994	4,268,539	27.9	6,753,881	44.2	2,557,887	16.7	1,712,415	11.2	15,292,722
1999	3,578,203	35.8	2,803,820	28.0	1,266,549	12.7	2,353,681	23.5	10,002,253
2004	4,397,087	26.7	3,718,683	22.6	2,452,327	14.9	5,890,506	35.8	16,458,603

Table 12.03: Party Votes as Percentages of Electorate European Parliament Elections 1979-2004 (UK & GB)

	Conservative UK	Conservative GB	Labour UK	Labour GB	Liberal UK	Liberal GB	Others UK	Others GB	Non-Voters UK	Non-Voters GB
1979	15.8	16.2	10.4	10.6	4.1	4.2	2.4	1.1	67.3	67.9
1984	12.8	13.1	11.4	11.7	6.1	6.3	2.6	1.0	67.1	67.9
1989	12.3	12.7	14.3	14.6	2.2	2.2	8.1	7.0	63.2	63.5
1994	9.8	10.1	15.5	16.0	5.9	6.0	5.3	4.0	63.5	63.8
1999	8.0	8.3	6.3	6.5	2.8	2.9	7.0	5.4	76.0	76.9
2004	10.0	10.2	8.4	8.6	5.6	5.7	14.6	13.7	61.5	61.8

Table 12.04: Conservative and Labour Votes as Percentages of Two-Party Votes European Parliament Elections 1979-2004 (GB)

Party	1979	1884	1989	1994	1999	2004
Conservative	60.5	52.7	46.4	38.7	56.1	54.2
Labour	39.5	47.3	53.6	61.3	43.9	45.8

Table 12.05: Conservative, Labour and Liberal Votes as Percentages of Three-Party Votes European Parliament Elections 1979-2004 (GB)

Party	1979	1884	1989	1994	1999	2004
Conservative	52.3	42.1	42.9	31.4	46.8	41.6
Labour	34.1	37.8	49.5	49.7	36.7	35.2
Liberal	13.6	20.1	7.6	18.8	16.6	23.2

Table 12.06: Single Member Seats Won on a Minority Vote European Parliament Elections 1979-1994 (GB)

Election	C	Lab	L	Others	Total	% of seats
1979	16	10	0	1	27	34.6
1984	25	17	0	1	43	55.1
1989	31	21	0	0	52	66.7
1994	18	26	2	1	47	56.0

Table 12.07: Forfeited Deposits at European Parliament Elections 1979-2004

Election[1]	Con	Lab	L	PC	SNP	Others	Total	% of total opposed candidates
1979	0	1	37	3	0	24	65	23.0
1984	0	0	3	2	2	30	37	13.2
1989	0	0	33	0	0	48	81	21.5
1994	1	0	2	1	0	271	275	49.6
1999[2]	0	0	0	0	0	65 lists	65 lists	n/a
2004[2]	0	0	0	0	0	39 lists	39 lists	n/a

1. At the 1979 and 1984 elections a candidate forfeited the deposit of £600 if he failed to poll more than one-eighth of the total votes cast, exclusive of spoilt papers. In Northern Ireland the same sum of money was forfeited if the number of votes credited to a candidate at any stage of the count did not exceed one-quarter of the 'quota' figure. For the 1989 and 1994 elections the deposit was raised to £1,000 and the threshold in Great Britain lowered to one-twentieth of the total valid votes cast.

2. At the 1999 and 2004 elections a party list or independent candidate forfeited the deposit of £5,000 if it failed to poll more than 2.5% of the total valid votes cast in the region.

Table 12.08: Women Elected at European Parliament Elections 1979-2004

Election	C	Lab	L	Others	Total	% of total MEPs
1979	6	4	0	1	11	13.6
1984	6	5	0	1	12	14.8
1989	4	7	0	1	12	14.8
1994	2	13	0	1	16	18.4
1999	3	10	5	3	21	24.1
2004	2	7	5	4	19	23.1

Table 12.09: Women Candidates at European Parliament Elections 1979-2004

Election	C	Lab	L	Others	Total	% of total cands
1979	10	8	8	3	29	10.3
1984	13	11	12	15	51	18.2
1989	10	14	12	35	71	19.4
1994	13	24	22	49	108	19.5
1999	12	38	40	144	234	26.5
2004	16	37	32	129	214	31.3

Table 13.01: Electorate and Turnout at European Parliament Elections 1979-2004

	Total Electorate	Age of Register in months	Turnout %
1979			
ENGLAND	34,261,421	-	31.8
WALES	2,063,898	-	34.4
SCOTLAND	3,801,010	-	33.6
N. IRELAND	1,028,837	-	55.6
GREAT BRITAIN	40,126,329	-	32.1
UNITED KINGDOM	**41,155,166**	8	**32.7**
1984			
ENGLAND	35,392,982	-	31.6
WALES	2,124,967	-	39.7
SCOTLAND	3,911,128	-	33.1
N. IRELAND	1,064,045	-	64.4
GREAT BRITAIN	41,429,077	-	32.1
UNITED KINGDOM	**42,493,122**	8	**32.9**
1989			
ENGLAND	36,007,443	-	35.8
WALES	2,172,849	-	41.1
SCOTLAND	3,893,576	-	40.8
N. IRELAND	1,106,852	-	48.3
GREAT BRITAIN	42,073,868		36.5
UNITED KINGDOM	**43,180,720**	8	**36.8**
1994			
ENGLAND	36,170,925	-	35.5
WALES	2,204,465	-	43.1
SCOTLAND	3,916,080	-	38.2
N. IRELAND	1,150,304	-	48.7
GREAT BRITAIN	42,291,470		36.2
UNITED KINGDOM	**43,441,774**	8	**36.5**
1999			
ENGLAND	37,040,668	-	22.7
WALES	2,227,040	-	28.1
SCOTLAND	3,999,623	-	24.7
N. IRELAND	1,191,307	-	57.0
GREAT BRITAIN	43,267,331		23.1
UNITED KINGDOM	**44,458,638**	8	**24.0**
2004			
ENGLAND	37,025,997	-	38.8
WALES	2,218,649	-	41.4
SCOTLAND	3,839,952	-	30.6
N. IRELAND	1,072,669	-	51.2
GREAT BRITAIN	43,084,598		38.2
UNITED KINGDOM	**44,157,267**	-[1]	**38.5**

1. Rolling register introduced by the RPA 2000.

Table 13.02: Postal Ballot Papers – European Parliament Elections 1979-2004

	No. of ballot papers issued	No. of envelopes returned before close of poll	No. rejected[1]	Ballot papers included at the start of the count
1979				
ENGLAND	657,901	430,987	12,857	418,130
WALES	55,930	36,888	1,711	35,177
SCOTLAND	75,003	48,531	1,375	47,156
N. IRELAND	39,733	33,179	912	32,267
UNITED KINGDOM	**828,567**	**549,585**	**16,855**	**532,730**
1984				
ENGLAND	474,654	290,082	14,825	275,257
WALES	37,729	23,536	2,066	21,470
SCOTLAND	42,138	24,482	916	23,566
N. IRELAND	31,791	27,176	1,122	26,054
UNITED KINGDOM	**586,312**	**365,276**	**18,929**	**346,347**
1989				
ENGLAND	381,701	237,964	13,229	224,737
WALES	32,688	21,793	2,281	19,512
SCOTLAND	32,989	19,360	1,390	17,970
N. IRELAND	27,989	23,956	525	23,431
UNITED KINGDOM	**475,367**	**303,073**	**17,425**	**285,650**
1994				
ENGLAND	425,972	271,478	10,025	262,773
WALES	34,328	22,518	1,341	21,177
SCOTLAND	34,712	21,243	1,212	20,031
N. IRELAND	25,469	21,722	518	21,204
UNITED KINGDOM	**520,481**	**336,961**	**13,096**	**325,185**
1999				
ENGLAND	482,893	266,805	8,130	259,683
WALES	36,859	20,373	926	19,466
SCOTLAND	45,853	27,722	710	26,812
N. IRELAND	26,713	22,729	1,431	21,298
UNITED KINGDOM	**592,318**	**337,629**	**11,197**	**327,259**
2004				
ENGLAND[2]	16,077,378	7,458,914	156,164	7,307,057
WALES	223,393	131,440	5,617	125,823
SCOTLAND	182,380	120,979	2,536	118,443
N. IRELAND[3]	19,957	17,066	973	16,093
UNITED KINGDOM	**16,503,108**	**7,728,399**	**164,317**	**7,567,416**

1. Number of cases in which the covering envelope or its contents were marked "empty", "rejected", "declaration rejected" or "vote rejected".

2. The North East, North West, Yorkshire & The Humber and East Midlands regions were all postal voting pilot areas.

3. The rules for requesting a postal vote are different in Northern Ireland from elsewhere in the UK.

Table 13.03: Postal Ballot Papers (Summary) – European Parliament Elections 1979-2004

	Issued Postal Ballot Papers as % of total electorate	No. returned as % of No. issued	No. rejected as % of No. returned	No. of Postal Ballot Papers included at the start of the count as % of total poll
1979	2.0	66.3	3.1	4.0
1984	1.4	62.3	5.2	2.5
1989	1.1	63.8	5.7	1.8
1994	1.2	64.7	3.9	2.1
1999	1.3	57.0	3.3	1.7
2004[1]	37.4	46.8	2.1	44.1

1. The North East, North West, Yorkshire & The Humber and East Midlands regions were all postal voting pilot areas.

Table 13.04: Spoilt Ballot Papers – European Parliament Elections 1979-2004

	Want of official mark	Voting for more than one candidate	Writing or mark by which voter could be identified	Unmarked or void for uncertainty	Total	Average per constituency
1979						
ENGLAND	1,593	8,876	4,986	14,140	29,595	448
WALES	274	1,737	209	646	2,866	717
SCOTLAND	294	370	76	1,258	1,998	333
N. IRELAND	357	12,084	13	1,320	13,774	13,774
UNITED KINGDOM	**2,518**	**23,067**	**5,284**	**17,364**	**48,233**	**611**
1984						
ENGLAND	922	8,067	2,206	9,923	21,118	320
WALES	204	1,449	118	536	2,307	577
SCOTLAND	358	394	189	748	1,689	211
N. IRELAND	166	1,757	38	9,593	11,654	11,654
UNITED KINGDOM	**1,650**	**11,667**	**2,551**	**20,800**	**36,768**	**465**
1989						
ENGLAND	1,029	5,389	1,915	8,451	16,784	254
WALES	80	586	215	387	1,268	317
SCOTLAND	480	333	331	1,061	2,205	276
N. IRELAND	185	933	6	4,232	5,356	5,356
UNITED KINGDOM	**1,774**	**7,241**	**2,467**	**14,131**	**25,613**	**324**
1994						
ENGLAND	1,056	11,168	2,733	13,834	28,791	406
WALES	129	638	497	614	1,878	376
SCOTLAND	456	215	206	770	1,647	206
N. IRELAND	132	8,155	3	944	9,234	9,234
UNITED KINGDOM	**1,773**	**20,176**	**3,439**	**16,162**	**41,550**	**489**

Spoilt Ballot Papers – European Parliament Elections 1979-2004 (contd.)

	Want of official mark	Voting for more than one candidate	Writing or mark by which voter could be identified	Unmarked or void for uncertainty	Total	Average per constituency
1999						
ENGLAND	1,368	6,519	1,021	7,249	18,110[1]	-
WALES	132	1,120	84	1,348	2,684	-
SCOTLAND	654	916	130	663	2,363	-
N. IRELAND	129	838	1	857	1,825	-
UNITED KINGDOM	**2,283**	**9,393**	**1,236**	**10,117**	**24,982**[1]	-
2004						
ENGLAND	2,151	22,821	3,765	81,063	118,498[1]	-
WALES	144	4,066	66	6,813	11,089	-
SCOTLAND	843	1,237	1,094	575	3,806	-
N. IRELAND[2]	-	-	-	-	5,467	-
UNITED KINGDOM[2]	-	-	-	-	**138,860**[1]	-

1. The totals are correct but not all constituencies provided a breakdown by the individual categories.
2. A breakdown of the total number of rejected ballots at the count in Northern Ireland by reasons for rejection is not available.

Table 13.05: Polling Districts and Stations – European Parliament Elections 1979-2004

	Polling districts	Polling stations
1979	32,400	46,477
1984	33,579	43,916
1989	34,312	43,064
1994	35,638	41,476
1999[1]	21,440	25,944
2004[2]	n/a	28,949

1. A considerable number of constituencies failed to submit returns.
2. Regions with all-postal voting excluded.

Table 13.06: Candidates' Expenses – European Parliament Elections 1979-2004

Election	Agents¹	Clerks	Printing	Meetings	Rooms	Miscellaneous	Personal Expenses	Total	Average
	£	£	£	£	£	£	£	£	£
1979²	124,635	20,494	1,066,327	12,488	23,279	71,600	45,993	1,364,816	4,840
1984³	180,773	28,223	1,819,284	22,791	51,784	186,943	69,427	2,359,225	8,426
1989⁴	240,200	23,847	2,788,791	18,751	56,869	222,384	65,809	3,416,651	9,087
1994⁵	277,977	39,915	4,117,215	29,604	81,457	414,907	92,464	5,053,539	9,122
1999⁶	Expenditure breakdowns are no longer available.							5,606,976	-
2004⁶								9,642,800	-

1. Explanations of the headings can be found in Table 5.09.
2. The maximum a candidate could spend was limited to £5,000 plus 2p per elector. Personal expenses were excluded from this limit.
3. The maximum a candidate could spend was limited to £8,000 plus 3.5p per elector. Personal expenses were excluded from this limit.
4. The maximum a candidate could spend was limited to £10,000 plus 4.3p per elector. Personal expenses were excluded from this limit.
5. The maximum a candidate could spend was limited to £13,175 plus 5.7p per elector. Personal expenses were excluded from this limit.
6. The maximum a candidate or party could spend in a regional constituency was limited to £45,000 multiplied by the number of European parliamentary seats in the region. Personal expenses were excluded from this limit.

Table 14.01: European Parliament By-Elections 1945-1999

	Date	Result	%turn EP	%turn BE	Chng	Con EP	Con BE	Con% Chng	Lab EP	Lab BE	Lab% Chng	LD EP	LD BE	LD% Chng	Con/Lab swing¹	Con/LD swing¹	Lab/LD swing¹
1 London South West	20/09/1979	Con held	31.4	19.4	-12.0	52.0	41.2	-10.8	32.2	32.7	0.5	13.2	23.9	10.7	-5.7	-10.8	-5.1
2 Midlands West	05/03/1987	Lab held	27.4	28.6	1.2	37.2	36.5	-0.7	50.7	39.2	-11.5	12.1	24.3	12.2	5.4	-6.5	-11.9
3 Hampshire Central	15/12/1988	Con held	31.0	14.1	-16.9	51.7	49.0	-2.7	24.1	21.4	-2.7	24.2	17.3	-6.9	0.0	2.1	2.1
4 Merseyside West	12/12/1996	Lab held	26.2	11.3	-14.9	20.0	21.8	1.8	58.4	53.8	-4.6	14.1	15.1	1.0	3.2	0.4	-2.8
5 Yorkshire South	07/05/1998	Lab held	28.6	23.4	-5.2	13.8	17.7	3.9	72.7	52.2	-20.5	7.9	18.5	10.6	12.2	-3.4	-15.6
6 North East Scotland	26/11/1998	SNP held	37.7	20.5	-17.2	18.6	19.7	1.1	28.4	19.1	-9.3	8.3	9.7	1.4	5.2	-0.2	-5.4

1. Positive figure = swing to first named party; negative figure = swing to second named party. For a full explanation of swing see Introductory Notes.

Note: Since 1999 European Parliament By-elections have not been held. Vacancies are filled by the party originally allocated the seat.

Elections Within The United Kingdom

15. **General Election Results by Region and Nation, 1955-2005***

* The data for the English standard regions (plus Central London) from 1955 to 1987 inclusive are based on a data set compiled and kindly made available by Professor Danny Dorling. On occasion there are slight discrepancies between the vote totals in individual regions and the overall total for England as a whole which is taken from the tables in Chapter 1. Standard regions in England were replaced by Government Office regions in 1997.

16. **Elections in Major Urban Areas**

17. **Devolution Elections**

Table 15.01: General Election Results in East Anglia 1955-1997

		Con	Lab	Lib	Other	Total
1955	Votes	395,102	358,205	9,342	-	762,649
	% share	51.8	47.0	1.2	-	
	Candidates	18	18	2	-	
	Elected	13	5	-	-	
1959	Votes	401,072	338,992	44,134	-	784,198
	% share	51.1	43.2	5.6	-	
	Candidates	18	18	6	-	
	Elected	14	4	-	-	
1964	Votes	382,955	335,969	88,690	776	808,390
	% share	47.4	41.6	11.0	0.1	
	Candidates	18	18	12	-	
	Elected	13	5	0	-	
1966	Votes	386,663	377,287	58,161	1,208	823,319
	% share	47.0	45.8	7.1	0.1	
	Candidates	18	18	13	-	
	Elected	11	7	0	-	
1970	Votes	475,026	366,862	51,462	2,980	896,330
	% share	53.0	40.9	5.7	0.3	
	Candidates	18	18	14	-	
	Elected	17	1	0	-	
1974 (F)	Votes	436,569	325,913	254,110	3,406	1,019,998
	% share	42.8	32.0	24.9	0.3	
	Candidates	17	17	17	-	
	Elected	14	2	1	-	
1974 (O)	Votes	415,165	336,685	195,331	1,202	948,383
	% share	43.8	35.5	20.6	0.1	
	Candidates	17	17	17	-	
	Elected	12	4	1	-	
1979	Votes	532,287	341,671	167,161	5,897	1,047,016
	% share	50.8	32.6	16.0	0.6	
	Candidates	17	17	17	-	
	Elected	13	3	1	-	
1983	Votes	539,418	216,902	298,624	2,934	1,057,878
	% share	51.0	20.5	28.2	0.3	
	Candidates	20	20	20	-	
	Elected	18	1	1	-	
1987	Votes	601,421	249,894	297,041	5,217	1,153,573
	% share	52.1	21.7	25.7	0.5	
	Candidates	20	20	20	-	
	Elected	19	1	0	-	
1992	Votes	635,754	348,353	242,984	18,424	1,245,515
	% share	51.0	28.0	19.5	1.5	
	Candidates	20	20	20	-	
	Elected	17	3	0	-	
1997	Votes	460,612	456,417	213,474	60,735	1,191,238
	% share	38.7	38.3	17.9	5.1	
	Candidates	22	22	22	-	
	Elected	14	8	0	-	

Table 15.02: General Election Results in East Midlands 1955-1997

		Con	Lab	Lib	Other	Total
1955	Votes	807,101	893,688	23,849	916	1,725,554
	% share	46.8	51.8	1.4	0.1	
	Candidates	38	38	5	-	
	Elected	15	23	0	-	
1959	Votes	847,457	883,707	75,530	1,331	1,808,025
	% share	46.9	48.9	4.2	0.1	
	Candidates	38	38	12	-	
	Elected	18	20	0	-	
1964	Votes	769,289	877,678	173,477	1,579	1,822,023
	% share	42.2	48.2	9.5	0.1	
	Candidates	38	38	26	-	
	Elected	14	24	0	-	
1966	Votes	738,277	946,275	108,904	1,660	1,795,116
	% share	41.1	52.7	6.1	0.1	
	Candidates	38	38	28	-	
	Elected	11	27	0	-	
1970	Votes	900,510	900,201	85,521	8,606	1,894,838
	% share	47.5	47.5	4.5	0.5	
	Candidates	38	38	31	-	
	Elected	19	19	0	-	
1974 (F)	Votes	869,366	867,972	358,400	37,602	2,133,340
	% share	40.8	40.7	16.8	1.8	
	Candidates	39	39	29	-	
	Elected	19	19	0	1.0	
1974 (O)	Votes	764,400	837,830	356,795	27,699	1,986,724
	% share	38.5	42.2	18.0	1.4	
	Candidates	39	39	38	-	
	Elected	18	21	0	-	
1979	Votes	1,008,349	833,426	294,531	20,204	2,156,510
	% share	46.8	38.6	13.7	0.9	
	Candidates	39	39	39	-	
	Elected	23	16	0	-	
1983	Votes	1,013,406	600,624	517,098	17,266	2,148,394
	% share	47.2	28.0	24.1	0.8	
	Candidates	42	42	42	-	
	Elected	34	8	0	-	
1987	Votes	1,127,237	696,760	487,168	9,128	2,320,293
	% share	48.6	30.0	21.0	0.4	
	Candidates	42	42	42	-	
	Elected	31	11	0	-	
1992	Votes	1,149,514	922,399	376,610	18,037	2,466,560
	% share	46.6	37.4	15.3	0.7	
	Candidates	42	42	42	-	
	Elected	28	14	0	-	
1997	Votes	800,958	1,097,639	311,264	84,889	2,294,750
	% share	34.9	47.8	13.6	3.7	
	Candidates	44	44	44	-	
	Elected	14	30	0	-	

Table 15.03: General Election Results in Greater London 1955-1997

		Con	Lab	Lib	Other	Total
1955	Votes	2,179,652	2,086,657	119,930	13,270	4,399,509
	% share	49.5	47.4	2.7	0.3	
	Candidates	104	104	27	-	
	Elected	56	48	0	-	
1959	Votes	2,177,693	1,889,502	315,454	17,462	4,400,111
	% share	49.5	42.9	7.2	0.4	
	Candidates	104	104	55	-	
	Elected	62	42	0	-	
1964	Votes	1,720,904	1,783,235	516,935	28,640	4,049,714
	% share	42.5	44.0	12.8	0.7	
	Candidates	104	104	80	-	
	Elected	49	54	1	-	
1966	Votes	1,633,548	1,929,141	383,763	26,380	3,972,832
	% share	41.1	48.6	9.7	0.7	
	Candidates	104	104	85	-	
	Elected	37	66	1	-	
1970	Votes	1,736,208	1,676,739	257,809	23,733	3,694,489
	% share	47.0	45.4	7.0	0.6	
	Candidates	104	104	86	-	
	Elected	49	55	0	-	
1974 (F)	Votes	1,475,225	1,587,448	814,381	47,170	3,924,224
	% share	37.6	40.5	20.8	1.2	
	Candidates	92	92	89	-	
	Elected	40	52	0	-	
1974 (O)	Votes	1,310,546	1,540,551	594,757	61,706	3,507,560
	% share	37.4	43.9	17.0	1.8	
	Candidates	92	92	92	-	
	Elected	41	51	0	-	
1979	Votes	1,693,587	1,459,085	438,021	90,136	3,680,829
	% share	46.0	39.6	11.9	2.4	
	Candidates	92	92	92	-	
	Elected	50	42	0	-	
1983	Votes	1,517,154	1,031,435	853,332	55,862	3,457,783
	% share	43.9	29.8	24.7	1.6	
	Candidates	84	84	84	-	
	Elected	56	26	2	-	
1987	Votes	1,680,093	1,136,893	770,109	26,589	3,613,684
	% share	46.5	31.5	21.3	0.7	
	Candidates	84	84	84	-	
	Elected	58	23	3	-	
1992	Votes	1,630,569	1,332,456	572,432	60,747	3,596,204
	% share	45.3	37.1	15.9	1.7	
	Candidates	84	84	82	-	
	Elected	48	35	1	-	
1997	Votes	1,036,082	1,643,329	485,511	156,126	3,321,048
	% share	31.2	49.5	14.6	4.7	
	Candidates	74	74	74	-	
	Elected	11	57	6	-	

Table 15.04: General Election Results in Northern 1955-1997

		Con	Lab	Lib	Other	Total
1955	Votes	689,031	894,275	20,112	368	1,603,786
	% share	43.0	55.8	1.3	0.0	
	Candidates	37	37	3	-	
	Elected	10	27	0	-	
1959	Votes	721,152	923,342	37,687	0	1,682,181
	% share	42.9	54.9	2.2	0.0	
	Candidates	37	37	6	-	
	Elected	13	24	0	-	
1964	Votes	623,938	912,279	78,125	2,916	1,617,258
	% share	38.6	56.4	4.8	0.2	
	Candidates	37	37	12	-	
	Elected	6	31	0	-	
1966	Votes	551,864	939,475	42,061	4,960	1,538,360
	% share	35.9	61.1	2.7	0.3	
	Candidates	37	37	13	-	
	Elected	6	31	0	-	
1970	Votes	628,534	912,464	45,205	369	1,586,572
	% share	39.6	57.5	2.8	0.0	
	Candidates	37	37	15	-	
	Elected	7	30	0	-	
1974 (F)	Votes	606,300	882,700	215,200	27,620	1,731,820
	% share	35.0	51.0	12.4	1.6	
	Candidates	37	37	21	-	
	Elected	6	29	1	1	
1974 (O)	Votes	482,123	841,164	266,274	22,510	1,612,071
	% share	29.9	52.2	16.5	1.4	
	Candidates	37	37	37	-	
	Elected	6	30	1	-	
1979	Votes	627,993	876,276	216,159	26,671	1,747,099
	% share	35.9	50.2	12.4	1.5	
	Candidates	37	37	37	-	
	Elected	6	30	1	-	
1983	Votes	589,127	684,020	424,992	2,507	1,700,646
	% share	34.6	40.2	25.0	0.1	
	Candidates	36	36	36	-	
	Elected	8	26	2	-	
1987	Votes	578,970	830,785	376,675	4,635	1,791,065
	% share	32.3	46.4	21.0	0.3	
	Candidates	36	36	36	-	
	Elected	8	27	1	-	
1992	Votes	603,893	914,712	281,236	8,704	1,808,545
	% share	33.4	50.6	15.6	0.5	
	Candidates	36	36	36	-	
	Elected	6	29	1	-	
1997	Votes	360,973	991,745	215,900	60,322	1,628,940
	% share	22.2	60.9	13.3	3.7	
	Candidates	36	36	36	-	
	Elected	3	32	1	-	

Table 15.05: General Election Results in North West 1955-1997

		Con	*Lab*	*Lib*	*Other*	*Total*
1955	Votes	1,743,691	1,530,909	59,053	4,495	3,338,148
	% share	52.2	45.9	1.8	0.1	
	Candidates	76	77	7	-	
	Elected	43	33	1	-	
1959	Votes	1,751,291	1,562,309	156,191	2,834	3,472,625
	% share	50.4	45.0	4.5	0.1	
	Candidates	76	77	18	-	
	Elected	41	35	1	-	
1964	Votes	1,444,691	1,547,549	356,810	13,377	3,362,427
	% share	43.0	46.0	10.6	0.4	
	Candidates	77	77	41	-	
	Elected	29	48	0	-	
1966	Votes	1,334,402	1,628,870	247,440	14,214	3,224,926
	% share	41.4	50.5	7.7	0.4	
	Candidates	77	77	43	-	
	Elected	23	53	1	-	
1970	Votes	1,569,585	1,534,464	244,875	12,611	3,361,535
	% share	46.7	45.6	7.3	0.4	
	Candidates	77	77	50	-	
	Elected	37	40	0	-	
1974 (F)	Votes	1,391,210	1,515,414	722,778	25,724	3,655,126
	% share	38.1	41.5	19.8	0.7	
	Candidates	76	76	69	-	
	Elected	27	47	2	-	
1974 (O)	Votes	1,277,684	1,538,771	620,680	13,397	3,450,532
	% share	37.0	44.6	18.0	0.4	
	Candidates	76	76	76	-	
	Elected	24	51	1	-	
1979	Votes	1,581,328	1,537,618	469,236	23,429	3,611,611
	% share	43.8	42.6	13.0	0.6	
	Candidates	76	76	72	-	
	Elected	30	44	2	-	
1983	Votes	1,405,468	1,266,111	822,241	23,179	3,516,999
	% share	40.0	36.0	23.4	0.7	
	Candidates	73	73	73	-	
	Elected	36	35	2	-	
1987	Votes	1,400,993	1,518,698	758,141	8,969	3,686,801
	% share	38.0	41.2	20.6	0.2	
	Candidates	73	73	73	-	
	Elected	34	36	3	-	
1992	Votes	1,395,718	1,660,023	582,168	56,349	3,694,258
	% share	37.8	44.9	15.8	1.5	
	Candidates	73	73	73	-	
	Elected	27	44	2	-	
1997	Votes	905,877	1,812,401	477,547	147,330	3,343,155
	% share	27.1	54.2	14.3	4.4	
	Candidates	70	69	69	-	
	Elected	7	60	2	1	

Table 15.06: General Election Results in South East 1955-1997

		Con	Lab	Lib	Other	Total
1955	Votes	2,108,113	1,432,770	72,182	6,514	3,619,579
	% share	58.2	39.6	2.0	0.2	
	Candidates	82	82	15	-	
	Elected	75	7	0	-	
1959	Votes	2,259,627	1,397,773	321,274	3,744	3,982,418
	% share	56.7	35.1	8.1	0.1	
	Candidates	82	82	47	-	
	Elected	77	5	0	-	
1964	Votes	2,111,161	1,501,668	678,374	3,906	4,295,109
	% share	49.2	35.0	15.8	0.1	
	Candidates	82	82	75	-	
	Elected	70	12	-	-	
1966	Votes	2,110,611	1,683,074	578,261	38,767	4,410,713
	% share	47.9	38.2	13.1	0.9	
	Candidates	82	82	77	-	
	Elected	62	19	0	1	
1970	Votes	2,534,798	1,592,416	551,013	55,470	4,733,697
	% share	53.5	33.6	11.6	1.2	
	Candidates	82	82	79	-	
	Elected	76	5	0	1	
1974 (F)	Votes	2,508,889	1,550,610	1,513,104	17,359	5,589,962
	% share	44.9	27.7	27.1	0.3	
	Candidates	98	98	98	-	
	Elected	85	12	1	-	
1974 (O)	Votes	2,323,949	1,594,873	1,221,959	24,313	5,165,094
	% share	45.0	30.9	23.7	0.5	
	Candidates	98	98	98	-	
	Elected	80	17	1	-	
1979	Votes	3,090,165	1,514,709	988,495	54,533	5,647,902
	% share	54.7	26.8	17.5	1.0	
	Candidates	98	98	98	-	
	Elected	93	4	1	-	
1983	Votes	3,076,607	893,325	1,636,717	36,587	5,643,236
	% share	54.5	15.8	29.0	0.6	
	Candidates	108	108	108	-	
	Elected	106	1	1	-	
1987	Votes	3,382,849	1,023,521	1,653,544	27,603	6,087,517
	% share	55.6	16.8	27.2	0.5	
	Candidates	108	108	108	-	
	Elected	107	1	0	-	
1992	Votes	3,518,506	1,341,186	1,507,021	88,108	6,454,821
	% share	54.5	20.8	23.3	1.4	
	Candidates	109	109	109	-	
	Elected	106	3	0	-	
1997	Votes	2,521,508	1,945,998	1,303,360	326,671	6,097,537
	% share	41.4	31.9	21.4	5.4	
	Candidates	117	117	117	-	
	Elected	73	36	8	-	

Table 15.07: General Election Results in South West 1955-1997

		Con	*Lab*	*Lib*	*Other*	*Total*
1955	Votes	1,006,256	753,890	156,707	37,766	1,954,619
	% share	51.5	38.6	8.0	1.9	
	Candidates	45	45	22	-	
	Elected	35	10	1	-	
1959	Votes	1,036,707	709,935	299,616	2,707	2,048,965
	% share	50.6	34.6	14.6	0.1	
	Candidates	46	46	35	-	
	Elected	37	8	1	-	
1964	Votes	944,941	708,703	417,244	10,936	2,081,824
	% share	45.4	34.0	20.0	0.5	
	Candidates	46	46	42	-	
	Elected	36	8	2	-	
1966	Votes	965,995	814,905	337,353	2,755	2,121,008
	% share	45.5	38.4	15.9	0.1	
	Candidates	46	46	42	-	
	Elected	31	12	3	-	
1970	Votes	1,154,744	768,525	320,127	2,658	2,246,054
	% share	51.4	34.2	14.3	0.1	
	Candidates	46	46	43	-	
	Elected	37	7	2	-	
1974 (F)	Votes	1,090,256	656,747	734,983	8,811	2,490,797
	% share	43.8	26.4	29.5	0.4	
	Candidates	46	46	46	-	
	Elected	36	7	3	-	
1974 (O)	Votes	1,027,304	675,150	642,327	9,837	2,354,618
	% share	43.6	28.7	27.3	0.4	
	Candidates	46	46	46	-	
	Elected	35	8	3	-	
1979	Votes	1,317,449	620,132	568,398	33,248	2,539,227
	% share	51.9	24.4	22.4	1.3	
	Candidates	46	46	46	-	
	Elected	40	5	1	-	
1983	Votes	1,295,737	370,544	836,547	19,099	2,521,927
	% share	51.4	14.7	33.2	0.8	
	Candidates	48	48	48	-	
	Elected	44	1	3	-	
1987	Votes	1,386,857	436,358	906,288	13,049	2,742,552
	% share	50.6	15.9	33.0	0.5	
	Candidates	48	48	48	-	
	Elected	44	1	3	-	
1992	Votes	1,388,330	561,917	916,955	52,199	2,919,401
	% share	47.6	19.2	31.4	1.8	
	Candidates	48	48	48	-	
	Elected	38	4	6	-	
1997	Votes	1,020,635	734,361	869,486	153,564	2,778,046
	% share	36.7	26.4	31.3	5.5	
	Candidates	51	51	51	-	
	Elected	22	15	14	-	

Table 15.08: General Election Results in West Midlands 1955-1997

		Con	*Lab*	*Lib*	*Other*	*Total*
1955	Votes	1,120,424	1,116,920	28,356	4,350	2,270,050
	% share	49.4	49.2	1.2	0.2	
	Candidates	53	53	4	-	
	Elected	22	31	0	-	
1959	Votes	1,215,409	1,091,961	73,572	4,388	2,385,330
	% share	51.0	45.8	3.1	0.2	
	Candidates	53	53	11	-	
	Elected	29	24	0	-	
1964	Votes	1,122,599	1,079,784	190,642	6,331	2,399,356
	% share	46.8	45.0	7.9	0.3	
	Candidates	53	53	26	-	
	Elected	26	27	0	-	
1966	Votes	1,066,919	1,205,389	99,067	11,401	2,382,776
	% share	44.8	50.6	4.2	0.5	
	Candidates	53	53	30	-	
	Elected	22	31	0	-	
1970	Votes	1,239,793	1,097,245	103,675	9,047	2,449,760
	% share	50.6	44.8	4.2	0.4	
	Candidates	53	53	35	-	
	Elected	30	23	0	-	
1974 (F)	Votes	1,154,072	1,216,665	421,930	32,350	2,825,017
	% share	40.9	43.1	14.9	1.1	
	Candidates	56	56	38	-	
	Elected	23	33	0	-	
1974 (O)	Votes	992,685	1,159,987	470,977	20,427	2,644,076
	% share	37.5	43.9	17.8	0.8	
	Candidates	56	56	56	-	
	Elected	21	35	0	-	
1979	Votes	1,334,079	1,134,375	325,439	36,544	2,830,437
	% share		47.1	40.1	11.5	1.3
	Candidates	56	56	50	-	
	Elected	31	25	0	-	
1983	Votes	1,261,738	874,172	655,982	12,464	2,804,356
	% share	45.0	31.2	23.4	0.4	
	Candidates	58	58	58	-	
	Elected	36	22	0	-	
1987	Votes	1,346,505	984,023	615,699	10,401	2,956,628
	% share	45.5	33.3	20.8	0.4	
	Candidates	58	58	58	-	
	Elected	36	22	0	-	
1992	Votes	1,390,246	1,203,349	466,226	45,124	3,104,945
	% share	44.8	38.8	15.0	1.5	
	Candidates	58	58	58	-	
	Elected	29	29	0	-	
1997	Votes	953,465	1,326,822	388,807	156,731	2,825,825
	% share	33.7	47.0	13.8	5.5	
	Candidates	58	58	58	-	
	Elected	14	43	1	1	

Table 15.09: General Election Results in Yorkshire and Humberside 1955-1997

		Con	*Lab*	*Lib*	*Other*	*Total*
1955	Votes	1,091,054	1,288,578	81,503	1,461	2,462,596
	% share	44.3	52.3	3.3	0.1	
	Candidates	55	56	10	-	
	Elected	23	32	1	-	
1959	Votes	1,148,572	1,287,596	126,135	1,373	2,563,676
	% share	44.8	50.2	4.9	0.1	
	Candidates	55	56	16	-	
	Elected	24	31	1	-	
1964	Votes	985,550	1,234,865	275,455	4,650	2,500,520
	% share	39.4	49.4	11.0	0.2	
	Candidates	56	56	34	-	
	Elected	19	37	0	-	
1966	Votes	904,068	1,331,529	181,782	6,276	2,423,655
	% share	37.3	54.9	7.5	0.3	
	Candidates	56	56	34	-	
	Elected	16	39	1	-	
1970	Votes	1,043,264	1,253,241	194,732	7,138	2,498,375
	% share	41.8	50.2	7.8	0.3	
	Candidates	56	56	40	-	
	Elected	20	36	0	-	
1974 (F)	Votes	976,920	1,238,979	541,071	15,248	2,772,218
	% share	35.2	44.7	19.5	0.6	
	Candidates	55	55	45	-	
	Elected	16	38	1	-	
1974 (O)	Votes	822,386	1,170,140	509,752	19,899	2,522,177
	% share	32.6	46.4	20.2	0.8	
	Candidates	55	55	55	-	
	Elected	16	38	1	-	
1979	Votes	1,069,868	1,208,118	410,432	23,617	2,712,035
	% share	39.4	44.5	15.1	0.9	
	Candidates	55	55	55	-	
	Elected	20	34	1	-	
1983	Votes	1,013,315	925,483	669,377	13,512	2,621,687
	% share	38.7	35.3	25.5	0.5	
	Candidates	54	54	54	-	
	Elected	24	28	2	-	
1987	Votes	1,040,749	1,128,875	602,709	7,811	2,780,144
	% share	37.4	40.6	21.7	0.3	
	Candidates	54	54	54	-	
	Elected	21	33	0	-	
1992	Votes	1,084,242	1,267,515	481,260	25,240	2,858,257
	% share	37.9	44.3	16.8	0.9	
	Candidates	54	54	54	-	
	Elected	20	34	0	-	
1997	Votes	720,771	1,339,170	412,216	106,016	2,578,173
	% share	28.0	51.9	16.0	4.1	
	Candidates	56	56	56	-	
	Elected	7	47	2	-	

Table 15.10: General Election Results in England 1945-2005

		Con	Lab	Lib	Other	Total
1945	Votes	8,269,191	9,972,519	1,913,917	383,393	20,539,020
	% share	40.3	48.6	9.3	1.9	-
	Candidates	507	494	265	97	1,363
	Elected	167	331	5	7	510
1950	Votes	10,499,392	11,050,966	2,248,127	155,963	23,954,448
	% share	43.8	46.1	9.4	0.7	-
	Candidates	504	505	413	106	1,528
	Elected	253	251	2	0	506
1951	Votes	11,622,704	11,630,467	537,434	35,490	23,826,095
	% share	48.8	48.8	2.3	0.1	-
	Candidates	502	506	91	13	1,112
	Elected	271	233	2	0	506
1955	Votes	11,165,436	10,355,892	571,034	43,768	22,136,130
	% share	50.4	46.8	2.6	0.2	-
	Candidates	509	510	95	20	1,134
	Elected	293	216	2	0	511
1959	Votes	11,559,240	10,085,097	1,449,593	33,839	23,127,769
	% share	50.0	43.6	6.3	0.1	-
	Candidates	509	511	191	23	1,234
	Elected	315	193	3	0	511
1964	Votes	10,106,028	9,982,360	2,775,752	73,111	22,937,251
	% share	44.1	43.5	12.1	0.3	-
	Candidates	511	511	323	64	1,409
	Elected	262	246	3	0	511
1966	Votes	9,692,356	10,886,408	2,036,793	77,138	22,692,695
	% share	42.7	48.0	9.0	0.3	-
	Candidates	510	511	273	69	1,363
	Elected	219	286	6	0	511
1970	Votes	11,282,524	10,131,555	1,853,616	93,201	23,360,896
	% share	48.3	43.4	7.9	0.4	-
	Candidates	510	511	282	100	1,403
	Elected	292	217	2	0	511
1974 (F)	Votes	10,508,977	9,842,468	5,574,934	215,239	26,141,618
	% share	40.2	37.7	21.3	0.8	-
	Candidates	516	516	452	190	1,674
	Elected	268	237	9	2	516
1974 (O)	Votes	9,414,008	9,695,051	4,878,792	203,218	24,191,069
	% share	38.9	40.1	20.2	0.8	-
	Candidates	515	516	515	220	1,766
	Elected	253	255	8	0	516
1979	Votes	12,255,514	9,525,280	3,878,055	313,401	25,972,250
	% share	47.2	36.7	14.9	1.2	-
	Candidates	516	516	506	536	2,074
	Elected	306	203	7	0	516
1983	Votes	11,711,519	6,862,422	6,714,957	183,748	25,472,646
	% share	46.0	26.9	26.4	0.7	-
	Candidates	523	523	523	431	2,000
	Elected	362	148	13	0	523

General Election Results in England 1945-2005 (contd.)

		Con	Lab	Lib	Other	Total
1987	Votes	12,546,186	8,006,466	6,467,350	113,520	27,133,522
	% share	46.2	29.5	23.8	0.4	-
	Candidates	523	523	523	213	1,782
	Elected	358	155	10	0	523
1992	Votes	12,796,772	9,551,910	5,398,293	401,531	28,148,506
	% share	45.5	33.9	19.2	1.4	-
	Candidates	524	524	522	758	2,328
	Elected	319	195	10	0	524
1997	Votes	8,780,881	11,347,882	4,677,565	1,252,384	26,058,712
	% share	33.7	43.5	18.0	4.8	-
	Candidates	528	527	527	1,363	2,945
	Elected	165	328	34	2	529
2001	Votes	7,705,870	9,056,824	4,246,853	861,215	21,870,762
	% share	35.2	41.4	19.4	3.9	-
	Candidates	529	529	528	1,002	2,588
	Elected	165	323	40	1	529
2005	Votes	8,114,979	8,050,366	5,201,129	1,337,828	22,704,302
	% share	35.7	35.5	22.9	5.8	-
	Candidates	529	529	528	1,231	2,817
	Elected	194	286	47	2	529

Table 15.11: General Election Results in Scotland 1945-2005

		Con	Lab	Lib	Nat	Other	Total
1945	Votes	964,143	1,144,310	132,849	30,595	117,995	2,389,892
	% share	40.3	47.9	5.6	1.3	4.9	-
	Candidates	68	68	22	8	18	184
	Elected	27	37	0	3	4	71
1950	Votes	1,222,010	1,259,410	180,270	9,708	55,286	2,726,684
	% share	44.8	46.2	6.6	0.4	2.0	-
	Candidates	68	71	41	3	29	212
	Elected	31	37	2	0	1	71
1951	Votes	1,349,298	1,330,244	76,291	7,299	14,705	2,777,837
	% share	48.6	47.9	2.7	0.3	0.5	-
	Candidates	70	71	9	2	8	160
	Elected	35	35	1	0	0	71
1955	Votes	1,273,942	1,188,058	47,273	12,112	21,869	2,543,254
	% share	50.1	46.7	1.9	0.5	0.9	-
	Candidates	71	71	5	2	7	156
	Elected	36	34	1	0	0	71
1959	Votes	1,260,287	1,245,255	108,963	21,738	31,270	2,667,513
	% share	47.2	46.7	4.1	0.8	1.2	-
	Candidates	70	71	16	5	10	172
	Elected	31	38	1	0	1	71
1964	Votes	1,069,695	1,283,667	200,063	64,044	17,070	2,634,539
	% share	40.6	48.7	7.6	2.4	0.6	-
	Candidates	71	71	26	15	14	197
	Elected	24	43	4	0	0	71

General Election Results in Scotland 1945-2005 (contd.)

		Con	*Lab*	*Lib*	*Nat*	*Other*	*Total*
1966	Votes	960,675	1,273,916	172,447	128,474	16,868	2,552,380
	% share	37.6	49.9	6.8	5.0	0.7	-
	Candidates	71	71	24	23	17	206
	Elected	20	46	5	0	0	71
1970	Votes	1,020,674	1,197,068	147,667	306,802	16,024	2,688,235
	% share	38.0	44.5	5.5	11.4	0.6	-
	Candidates	70	71	27	65	23	256
	Elected	23	44	3	1	0	71
1974 (F)	Votes	950,668	1,057,601	229,162	633,180	16,464	2,887,075
	% share	32.9	36.6	7.9	21.9	0.6	-
	Candidates	71	71	34	70	19	265
	Elected	21	40	3	7	0	71
1974(O)	Votes	681,327	1,000,581	228,855	839,617	7,721	2,758,101
	% share	24.7	36.3	8.3	30.4	0.3	-
	Candidates	71	71	68	71	12	293
	Elected	16	41	3	11	0	71
1979	Votes	916,155	1,211,445	262,224	504,259	22,554	2,916,637
	% share	31.4	41.5	9.0	17.3	0.8	-
	Candidates	71	71	43	71	28	284
	Elected	22	44	3	2	0	71
1983	Votes	801,487	990,654	692,634	331,975	7,830	2,824,580
	% share	28.4	35.1	24.5	11.8	0.3	-
	Candidates	72	72	72	72	26	314
	Elected	21	41	8	2	0	72
1987	Votes	713,081	1,258,132	570,053	416,473	10,069	2,967,808
	% share	24.0	42.4	19.2	14.0	0.3	-
	Candidates	72	72	72	71	21	308
	Elected	10	50	9	3	0	72
1992	Votes	751,950	1,142,911	383,856	629,564	23,417	2,931,698
	% share	25.6	39.0	13.1	21.5	0.8	-
	Candidates	72	72	72	72	53	341
	Elected	11	49	9	3	0	72
1997	Votes	493,059	1,283,350	365,362	621,550	53,427	2,816,748
	% share	17.5	45.6	13.0	22.1	1.9	-
	Candidates	72	72	72	72	143	431
	Elected	0	56	10	6	0	72
2001	Votes	360,658	1,001,173	378,034	464,314	109,522	2,313,701
	% share	15.6	43.3	16.3	20.1	4.7	-
	Candidates	71	71	71	72	122	407
	Elected	1	55	10	5	1	72
2005	Votes	369,388	907,249	528,076	412,267	116,907	2,333,887
	% share	15.8	38.9	22.6	17.7	5.1	-
	Candidates	58	58	58	59	149	382
	Elected	1	40	11	6	1	59

Table 15.12: General Election Results in Wales 1945-2005

		Con	Lab	Lib	Nat	Other	Total
1945	Votes	316,729	779,184	198,553	14,321	21,884	1,330,671
	% share	23.8	58.6	14.9	1.1	1.6	-
	Candidates	27	34	17	6	3	87
	Elected	4	25	6	0	0	35
1950	Votes	418,668	887,984	193,090	17,580	11,232	1,528,554
	% share	27.4	58.1	12.6	1.2	0.7	-
	Candidates	35	36	21	7	6	105
	Elected	4	27	5	0	0	36
1951	Votes	471,269	925,848	116,821	10,920	4,591	1,529,449
	% share	30.8	60.5	7.6	0.7	0.3	-
	Candidates	33	36	9	4	2	84
	Elected	6	27	3	0	0	36
1955	Votes	428,866	825,690	104,095	45,119	29,954	1,433,724
	% share	29.9	57.6	7.3	3.1	2.1	-
	Candidates	32	36	10	11	2	91
	Elected	6	27	3	0	0	36
1959	Votes	486,335	841,450	78,951	77,571	6,950	1,491,257
	% share	32.6	56.4	5.3	5.2	0.5	-
	Candidates	34	36	8	20	3	101
	Elected	7	27	2	0	0	36
1964	Votes	425,022	837,022	106,114	69,507	9,377	1,447,042
	% share	29.4	57.8	7.3	4.8	0.6	-
	Candidates	36	36	12	23	5	112
	Elected	6	28	2	0	0	36
1966	Votes	396,795	863,692	89,108	61,071	12,769	1,423,435
	% share	27.9	60.7	6.3	4.3	0.9	-
	Candidates	36	36	11	20	8	111
	Elected	3	32	1	0	0	36
1970	Votes	419,884	781,941	103,747	175,016	35,966	1,516,554
	% share	27.7	51.6	6.8	11.5	2.4	-
	Candidates	36	36	19	36	11	138
	Elected	7	27	1	0	1	36
1974 (F)	Votes	412,535	745,547	255,423	171,374	8,964	1,593,843
	% share	25.9	46.8	16.0	10.8	0.6	-
	Candidates	36	36	31	36	9	148
	Elected	8	24	2	2	0	36
1974 (O)	Votes	367,230	761,447	239,057	166,321	3,785	1,537,840
	% share	23.9	49.5	15.5	10.8	0.2	-
	Candidates	36	36	36	36	6	150
	Elected	8	23	2	3	0	36
1979	Votes	526,254	795,493	173,525	132,544	8,772	1,636,588
	% share	32.2	48.6	10.6	8.1	0.5	-
	Candidates	35	36	28	36	19	154
	Elected	11	22	1	2	0	36
1983	Votes	499,310	603,858	373,358	125,309	7,151	1,608,986
	% share	31.0	37.5	23.2	7.8	0.4	-
	Candidates	38	38	38	38	17	169
	Elected	14	20	2	2	0	38

General Election Results in Wales 1945-2005 (contd.)

		Con	Lab	Lib	Nat	Other	Total
1987	Votes	501,316	765,209	304,230	123,599	3,742	1,698,096
	% share	29.5	45.1	17.9	7.3	0.2	-
	Candidates	38	38	38	38	6	158
	Elected	8	24	3	3	0	38
1992	Votes	499,677	865,663	217,457	154,947	11,033	1,748,777
	% share	28.6	49.5	12.4	8.9	0.6	-
	Candidates	38	38	38	35	31	180
	Elected	6	27	1	4	0	38
1997	Votes	317,145	886,935	200,020	161,030	54,932	1,620,062
	% share	19.6	54.7	12.3	9.9	3.4	-
	Candidates	40	40	40	40	63	223
	Elected	0	34	2	4	0	40
2001	Votes	288,665	666,956	189,434	195,893	31,598	1,372,546
	% share	21.0	48.6	13.8	14.3	2.3	-
	Candidates	40	40	40	40	64	224
	Elected	0	34	2	4	0	40
2005	Votes	297,830	594,821	256,249	174,838	68,981	1,392,719
	% share	21.4	42.7	18.4	12.6	5.0	-
	Candidates	40	40	40	40	90	250
	Elected	3	29	4	3	1	40

Table 15.13: General Election Results in Northern Ireland 1974-2005

		UU	UDUP	SDLP	SF	APNI	Other	Total
1974 (F)	Votes	326,404	58,656	160,437	-	22,660	149,469	717,626
	% share	45.5	8.2	22.4	-	3.2	20.8	
	Candidates	14	2	12	-	3	17	48
	Elected	7	1	1	-	0	3	12
1974 (O)	Votes	256,065	59,451	154,193	-	44,644	187,741	702,094
	% share	36.5	8.5	22.0	-	6.4	26.7	
	Candidates	7	2	9	-	5	20	43
	Elected	6	1	1	-	0	4	12
1979	Votes	254,578	70,975	126,325	-	82,892	161,117	695,887
	% share	36.6	10.2	18.2	-	11.9	23.2	
	Candidates	11	5	9		12	27	64
	Elected	5	3	1		0	3	12
1983	Votes	259,952	152,749	137,012	102,701	61,275	51,236	764,925
	% share	34.0	20.0	17.9	13.4	8.0	6.7	
	Candidates	16	14	17	14	12	22	95
	Elected	11	3	1	1	0	1	17
1987	Votes	276,230	85,642	154,087	83,389	72,671	58,133	730,152
	% share	37.8	11.7	21.1	11.4	10.0	8.0	
	Candidates	12	4	13	14	16	18	77
	Elected	9	3	3	1	0	1	17
1992	Votes	271,049	103,039	184,445	78,291	68,665	79,604	785,093
	% share	34.5	13.1	23.5	10.0	8.7	10.1	
	Candidates	13	7	13	14	16	37	100
	Elected	9	3	4	0	0	1	17

General Election Results in Northern Ireland 1974-2005 (contd.)

		UU	UDUP	SDLP	SF	APNI	Other	Total
1997	Votes	258,349	107,348	190,814	126,921	62,972	44,358	790,762
	% share	32.7	13.6	24.1	16.1	8.0	5.6	
	Candidates	16	9	18	17	17	48	125
	Elected	10	2	3	2	0	1	18
2001	Votes	216,839	181,999	169,865	175,933	28,999	36,739	810,374
	% share	26.8	22.5	21.0	21.7	3.6	4.5	
	Candidates	17	14	18	18	10	23	100
	Elected	6	5	3	4	0	0	18
2005	Votes	127,414	241,856	125,626	174,530	28,291	19,885	717,602
	% share	17.8	33.7	17.5	24.3	3.9	2.8	
	Candidates	18	18	18	18	12	21	105
	Elected	1	9	3	5	0	100	118

Table 15.14: General Election Results in Government Office Regions 1992-2005*

		Con	Lab	LD	Other	Total
EAST MIDLANDS						
1992	Votes	1,149,514	922,399	376,610	18,037	2,466,560
	% share	46.6	37.4	15.3	0.7	
	Candidates	44	44	44	-	
	Elected	29	15	0	-	44
1997	Votes	800,958	1,097,639	311,264	84,889	2,294,750
	% share	34.9	47.8	13.6	3.7	
	Candidates	44	44	44	-	
	Elected	14	30	0	-	44
2001	Votes	727,386	879,886	300,831	43,799	1,951,902
	% share	37.3	45.1	15.4	2.2	
	Candidates	44	44	44	-	
	Elected	15	28	1	0	44
2005	Votes	747,438	785,944	372,041	109,859	2,015,282
	% share	37.1	39.0	18.5	5.5	
	Candidates	44	44	44	-	
	Elected	18	28	1	0	44
EASTERN						
1992	Votes	1,636,990	823,743	618,106	38,503	3,117,342
	% share	52.5	26.4	19.8	1.2	
	Candidates	56	56	56	-	
	Elected	52	4	0	-	56
1997	Votes	1,164,777	1,137,637	504,416	140,337	2,947,167
	% share	39.5	38.6	17.1	4.8	
	Candidates	56	56	56	-	
	Elected	33	22	1	-	56
2001	Votes	1,053,197	926,3447	440,405	99,105	2,519,051
	% share	41.8	36.8	17.5	3.9	
	Candidates	56	56	56	-	
	Elected	34	20	2	0	56

General Election Results in Government Office Regions 1992-2005* (contd.)

		Con	Lab	LD	Other	Total
EASTERN (contd.)						
2005	Votes	1,147,180	790,372	578,741	133,520	2,649,813
	% share	43.3	29.8	21.8	5.0	
	Candidates	56	56	56	-	
	Elected	40	13	3	0	56
GREATER LONDON						
1992	Votes	1,630,569	1,332,456	572,432	60,747	3,596,204
	% share	45.3	37.1	15.9	1.7	
	Candidates	74	74	74	-	
	Elected	41	32	1	-	74
1997	Votes	1,036,082	1,643,329	485,511	156,126	3,321,048
	% share	31.2	49.5	14.6	4.7	
	Candidates	74	74	74	-	
	Elected	11	57	6	-	74
2001	Votes	841,751	1,307,229	482,888	128,855	2,760,723
	% share	30.5	47.4	17.5	4.7	
	Candidates	74	74	74	-	
	Elected	13	55	6	0	74
2005	Votes	931,966	1,136,587	638,373	212,204	2,919,130
	% share	31.9	38.9	31.9	7.3	
	Candidates	74	74	74	-	
	Elected	21	44	8	1	74
NORTH EAST						
1992	Votes	461,767	801,311	232,150	6,402	1,501,630
	% share	30.8	53.4	15.5	0.4	
	Candidates	30	30	30	-	
	Elected	4	25	1	-	30
1997	Votes	266,294	862,262	169,270	48,764	1,346,590
	% share	19.8	64.0	12.6	3.6	
	Candidates	30	30	30	-	
	Elected	1	28	1	-	30
2001	Votes	233,802	651,821	182,824	28,454	1,096,901
	% share	21.3	59.4	16.7	2.6	
	Candidates	30	30	30	-	
	Elected	1	28	1	0	30
2005	Votes	214,389	580,453	256,295	47,039	1,098,176
	% share	19.5	52.9	23.3	4.3	
	Candidates	30	30	30	-	
	Elected	1	28	1	0	30
NORTH WEST (incl. Merseyside)						
1992	Votes	1,537,844	1,773,424	631,254	58,651	4,001,173
	% share	38.4	44.3	15.8	1.5	
	Candidates	76	76	76	-	
	Elected	27	48	1	-	76

General Election Results in Government Office Regions 1992-2005* (contd.)

		Con	*Lab*	*LD*	*Other*	*Total*
NORTH WEST (incl. Merseyside)						
1997	Votes	1,000,556	1,941,884	524,177	158,888	3,625,505
	% share	27.6	53.6	14.5	4.4	
	Candidates	76	75	75	-	
	Elected	9	64	2	1	76
2001	Votes	848,899	1,469,700	485,262	95,987	2,899,848
	% share	29.3	50.7	16.7	3.3	
	Candidates	76	76	76	-	
	Elected	9	64	3	0	76
2005	Votes	845,196	1,327,669	629,250	142,875	2,944,990
	% share	28.7	45.1	21.4	4.9	
	Candidates	76	76	76	-	
	Elected	9	61	6	0	76
SOUTH EAST						
1992	Votes	2,517,270	865,796	1,131,899	68,029	4,582,994
	% share	54.9	18.9	24.7	1.5	
	Candidates	83	83	83	-	
	Elected	79	4	0	-	83
1997	Votes	1,817,343	1,264,778	1,012,418	247,069	4,341,608
	% share	41.9	29.1	23.3	5.7	
	Candidates	83	83	83	-	
	Elected	54	22	7	-	83
2001	Votes	1,590,628	1,090,367	879,228	151,383	3,711,606
	% share	42.9	29.4	23.7	4.1	
	Candidates	83	83	83	-	
	Elected	53	22	8	0	83
2005	Votes	1,754,247	951,323	990,480	205,098	3,901,148
	% share	45.0	24.4	25.4	5.3	
	Candidates	83	83	83	-	
	Elected	58	19	6	0	83
SOUTH WEST						
1992	Votes	1,388,330	561,917	916,955	52,199	2,919,401
	% share	47.6	19.2	31.4	1.8	
	Candidates	51	51	51	-	
	Elected	39	6	6	-	51
1997	Votes	1,020,635	734,361	869,486	153,564	2,778,046
	% share	36.7	26.4	31.3	5.5	
	Candidates	51	51	51	-	
	Elected	22	15	14	-	51
2001	Votes	946,629	645,121	765,824	98,766	2,456,340
	% share	38.5	26.3	31.2	4.0	
	Candidates	51	51	51	-	
	Elected	20	16	15	0	51
2005	Votes	985,346	582,522	831,134	154,313	2,553,315
	% share	38.6	22.8	32.6	6.0	
	Candidates	51	51	51	-	
	Elected	22	13	16	0	51

General Election Results in Government Office Regions 1992-2005* (contd.)

		Con	*Lab*	*LD*	*Other*	*Total*
WEST MIDLANDS						
1992	Votes	1,390,246	1,203,349	466,226	45,124	3,104,945
	% share	44.8	38.8	15.0	1.5	
	Candidates	59	59	59	-	
	Elected	31	28	0	-	59
1997	Votes	953,465	1,326,822	388,807	156,731	2,825,825
	% share	33.7	47.0	13.8	5.5	
	Candidates	58	58	58	-	
	Elected	14	43	1	1	59
2001	Votes	818,776	1,049,242	343,929	128,459	2,340,406
	% share	35.0	44.8	14.7	5.5	
	Candidates	59	59	58	-	
	Elected	13	43	2	1	59
2005	Votes	848,664	937,490	450,110	186,952	2,423,216
	% share	35.0	38.7	18.6	7.7	
	Candidates	59	59	58	-	
	Elected	16	39	3	1	59
YORKSHIRE AND THE HUMBER						
1992	Votes	1,084,242	1,267,515	481,260	25,240	2,858,257
	% share	37.9	44.3	16.8	0.9	
	Candidates	56	56	56	-	
	Elected	22	34	0	-	56
1997	Votes	720,771	1,339,170	412,216	106,016	2,578,173
	% share	28.0	51.9	16.0	4.1	
	Candidates	56	56	56	-	
	Elected	7	47	2	-	56
2001	Votes	644,802	1,037,114	365,662	86,407	2,133,985
	% share	30.2	48.6	17.1	4.0	
	Candidates	56	56	56	-	
	Elected	7	47	2	0	56
2005	Votes	640,553	958,006	454,705	145,968	2,199,232
	% share	29.1	43.6	20.7	6.6	
	Candidates	56	56	56	-	
	Elected	9	44	3	0	56

* 1992 results are based on 'notional' results. See Introductory Notes.

Table 16.01: Representation of the Major Towns 1950-2005

The following table shows the party representation in the major towns after each General Election since 1950. Substantial boundary changes took place at the General Elections of 1955, 1974(F), 1983 and 1997.

	1950	1951	1955	1959	1964	1966	1970	1974(F)	1974(O)	1979	1983	1987	1992	1997	2001	2005
BELFAST																
UDUP	-	-	-	-	-	-	-	0	0	2	1	1	1	1	2	2
UU	4	3	4	4	4	3	3	3	3	1	2	2	2	2	1	0
SDLP	-	-	-	-	-	-	-	1	1	1	0	0	1	0	0	1
Others	0	1	0	0	0	1	1	0	0	0	1	1	0	1	1	1
BIRMINGHAM																
C	4	4	4	7	5	4	6	3	2	5	5	5	3[4]	1[4]	1[4]	1[4]
Lab	9	9	9	6	8	9	7	9	10	7	6	6	9	10	10	9
L	0	0	0	0	0	0	0	0	0	0	0	0	0	0	0	1
BOLTON																
C	0	1	1	1	0	0	2	1	0	0	2	2	2	0	0	0
Lab	2	0	0	0	2	2	0	1	2	2	1	1	1	3	3	3
L	0	1	1	1	0	0	0	0	0	0	0	0	0	0	0	0
BRADFORD																
C	1	1	2	2	1	0	1	0	0	0	1	0	0	0	0	0
Lab	3	3	2	2	3	4	3	3	3	3	2	3	3	3	3	3
BRISTOL																
C	2	2	1	3	3	1	3	2	1	2	3	3	2	0	0	0
Lab	4	4	5	3	3	5	3	3	4	3	1	1	2	4	4	3
L	0	0	0	0	0	0	0	0	0	0	0	0	0	0	0	1
CARDIFF																
C	1	1	1	1	1	0	1	2	2	2	3	2	1	0	0	0
Lab	2	2	2	2	2	3	2	2	2	2	1	2	3	4	4	3
L	0	0	0	0	0	0	0	0	0	0	0	0	0	0	0	1
COVENTRY																
C	0	0	0	1	0	0	0	0	0	1	1	1	1	0	0	0
Lab	3	3	3	2	3	3	3	4	4	3	3	3	3	3	3	3
EDINBURGH																
C	4	4	4	4	4	4	4	4	4	4	4	2	2	0	0	0
Lab	3	3	3	3	3	3	3	3	3	3	2	4	4	5	5	4
L	0	0	0	0	0	0	0	0	0	0	0	0	0	1	1	1

Representation of the Major Towns 1950-2005 (contd.)

	1950	1951	1955	1959	1964	1966	1970	1974(F)	1974(O)	1979	1983	1987	1992	1997	2001	2005
GLASGOW																
C	7	7	7	5	2	2	2	2	2	1	0	0	0	0	0	0
Lab	8	8	8	10	13	13	13	11	11	12	10	11	11	10	9	6
L¹	0	0	0	0	0	0	0	0	0	0	1	0	0	0	0	0
Speaker	-	-	-	-	-	-	-	-	-	-	-	-	-	-	-	1
KINGSTON UPON HULL																
C	2	2	1	1	0	0	0	0	0	0	0	0	0	0	0	0
Lab	2	2	2	2	3	3	3	3	3	3	3	3	3	3	3	3
LEEDS																
C	2	2	2	2	2	2	2	2	2	2	2	2	2	0	0	0
Lab	5	5	4	4	4	4	4	4	4	4	3	4	4	6	6	5
L	0	0	0	0	0	0	0	0	0	0	0	0	0	0	0	1
LEICESTER																
C	1	1	1	1	1	1	2	1	0	0	2	0	0	0	0	0
Lab	3	3	3	3	3	3	2	2	3	3	1	3	3	3	3	3
LIVERPOOL																
C	5	5	6	6	2	2	2	1	1	2	0	0	0	0	0	0
Lab	4	4	3	3	7	7	7	7	7	5	5	5	5	5	5	5
L¹	0	0	0	0	0	0	0	0	0	1	1	1	1	0	0	0
LONDON²																
C	12	14	15	18	10	6	9	42	41	50	56	58	48	11	13	21
Lab	31	29	27	24	32	36	33	50	51	42	26	23	35	57	55	44
L¹	0	0	0	0	0	0	0	0	0	0	2	3	1	6	6	8
Respect	-	-	-	-	-	-	-	-	-	-	-	-	-	-	-	1
MANCHESTER																
C	3	4	4	4	2	2	2	1	1	1	1	0	0	0	0	0
Lab	6	5	5	5	7	7	7	7	7	7	4	5	5	5	5	4
L	0	0	0	0	0	0	0	0	0	0	0	0	0	0	0	1
NEWCASTLE UPON TYNE																
C	1	1	1	2	1	1	1	1	1	1	1	0	0	0	0	0
Lab	3	3	3	3	3	3	3	3	3	3	2	3	3	3	3	3

Representation of the Major Towns 1950-2005 (contd.)

	1950	1951	1955	1959	1964	1966	1970	1974(F)	1974(O)	1979	1983	1987	1992	1997	2001	2005
NOTTINGHAM																
C	0	0	2	3	1	0	1	0	0	0	3	2	0	0	0	0
Lab	4	4	2	1	3	4	3	3	3	3	0	1	3	3	3	3
PLYMOUTH																
C	0	1	2	2	2	1	1	2	2	2	2	2	2	1	1	1
Lab	2	1	0	0	0	1	1	1	1	1	0	0	1	2	2	2
L[1]	0	0	0	0	0	0	0	0	0	0	1	1	0	0	0	0
PORTSMOUTH																
C	3	3	3	3	3	2	2	1	1	2	2	2	2	0	0	0
Lab	0	0	0	0	0	1	1	1	0	0	0	0	0	1	1	1
L	0	0	0	0	0	0	0	0	0	0	0	0	0	1	1	1
SHEFFIELD																
C	2	2	2	2	2	1	2	1	1	1	1	1	1	0	0	0
Lab	5	5	4	4	4	5	4	5	5	5	5	5	5	5	5	5
L	0	0	0	0	0	0	0	0	0	0	0	0	0	1	1	1
STOKE-ON-TRENT																
Lab	3	3	3	3	3	3	3	3	3	3	3	3	3	3	3	3
TEESSIDE[3]																
C	-	-	-	-	-	-	-	0	0	0	0	1	1	0	0	0
Lab	-	-	-	-	-	-	-	4	4	4	3	3	3	5	5	5
L[1]	-	-	-	-	-	-	-	0	0	0	1	0	0	0	0	0
WOLVERHAMPTON																
C	1	1	1	1	1	1	1	1	1	1	1	2	1	0	0	0
Lab	1	1	1	1	1	1	1	2	2	2	2	1	2	3	3	3

1. SDP/Liberal Alliance 1983-87; Liberal Democrat 1992 onwards.
2. Constituencies within the area covered by the London County Council and subsequently the Greater London Council plus the city of London.
3. An amalgamation of Middlesbrough, Redcar, Stockton-on-Tees and Thornaby-on-Tees. The 'county' was disaggregated in 1996.
4. Including Sutton Coldfield.

Table 17.01: Northern Ireland Assembly Election 1998 (25 June)

% Turnout 70.0

Party	No. of candidates	First preference votes	% share	Number of seats	% seats
APNI	22	52,636	6.5	6	5.6
Ind UU	1	2,976	0.4	1	0.9
NIWC	8	13,019	1.6	2	1.9
SDLP	38	177,963	22.0	24	22.2
SF	37	142,858	17.6	18	16.7
UDP	9	8,651	1.1	0	0.0
UDUP	34	146,917	18.1	20	18.5
UKUP	13	36,541	4.5	5	4.6
Union	5	8,332	1.0	1	0.9
United	2	8,152	1.0	1	0.9
UPUP	12	20,634	2.5	2	1.9
UUP	48	172,225	21.3	28	25.9
Others	66	19,341	2.4	0	0.0
Total	**295**	**810,245**		**108**	

Table 17.02: Northern Ireland Assembly Election 2003 (26 November)

% Turnout 64.0

Party	No. of candidates	First preference votes	% share	Number of seats	% seats
APNI	21	25,372	3.6	6	5.6
UDUP	40	177,944	25.3	30	27.8
UPUP	11	8,032	1.1	1	0.9
SDLP	36	117,547	16.7	18	16.7
SF	38	162,758	23.2	24	22.2
UUP	43	156,931	22.4	27	25.0
UKUP	6	5,700	0.8	1	0.9
Others	61	47,965	6.8	1	0.9
Total	**256**	**702,249**		**108**	

Table 17.03: Scottish Parliament Election 1999 (6 May)

% Turnout 58.2

Party	Constituency votes	% share	candidates	elected
Con	364,425	15.6	73	0
Lab	908,346	38.8	73	53
LD	333,179	14.2	73	12
SNP	672,768	28.7	73	7
SSP	23,654	1.0	18	0
SLP	5,268	0.2	5	0
Others	34,848	1.5	24	1
Total	**2,342,488**		**339**	**73**

Scottish Parliament Election 1999 (6 May) (contd.)

Party	List votes	% share	with lists	elected
Con	359,109	15.4	8	18
Lab	786,818	33.6	8	3
LD	290,760	12.4	8	5
SNP	638,644	27.3	8	28
SSP	46,714	2.0	8	1
SLP	55,153	2.4	8	0
Green	84,023	3.6	8	1
P L	9,784	0.4	5	0
SUP	7,011	0.3	3	0
Liberal	5,534	0.2	2	0
H&IA	2,607	0.1	1	0
Others	52,757	2.3	31	0
Total	**2,338,914**		**98**	**56**

Party	Total elected	% of seats
Con	1 8	14.0
Lab	5 6	43.4
LD	1 7	13.2
SNP	3 5	27.1
SSP	1	0.8
Green	1	0.8
Others	1	0.8
Total	**129**	

Table 17.04: Scottish Parliament Election 2003 (1 May)

% Turnout 49.4

Party	Constituency votes	% share	candidates	elected
Con	318,279	16.6	73	3
Lab	663,585	34.6	73	46
LD	294,347	15.4	73	13
SNP	455,742	23.8	73	9
SSP	118,764	6.2	70	0
Others	65,877	3.4	45	2
Total	**1,916,594**		**407**	**73**

Party	List votes	% share	with lists	elected
Con	296,929	15.5	8	1 5
Lab	561,375	29.3	8	4
LD	225,774	11.8	8	4
SNP	399,659	20.9	8	18
SSP	128,026	6.7	8	6
Green	132,138	6.9	8	7
Others	171,950	9.0	59	2
Total	**1,915,851**		**107**	**56**

Party	Total elected	% of seats
Con	1 8	14.0
Lab	5 0	38.8
LD	1 7	13.2
SNP	2 7	20.9
SSP	6	4.7
Green	7	5.4
Others	4	3.1
Total	**129**	

Table 17.05: Welsh Assembly Election 1999 (6 May)

% Turnout 46.4

Party	Constituency votes	% share	candidates	elected
Con	162,133	15.8	40	1
Lab	384,671	37.6	40	27
LD	137,657	13.5	40	3
PC	290,565	28.4	40	9
Un Soc	3,967	0.4	9	0
Green	1,002	0.1	1	0
Others	43,023	4.2	29	0
Total	**1,023,018**		**199**	**40**

Party	List votes	% share	with lists	elected
Con	168,206	16.5	5	8
Lab	361,657	35.4	5	1
LD	128,008	12.5	5	3
PC	312,048	30.5	5	8
Green	25,858	2.5	5	0
NLP	3,861	0.4	5	0
SLP	10,720	1.0	3	0
Un Soc	3,590	0.4	4	0
Others	7,909	0.8	7	0
Total	**1,021,857**		**44**	**20**

Party	Total elected	% of seats
Con	9	15.0
Lab	28	46.7
LD	6	10.0
PC	17	28.3
Others	0	-
Total	**60**	

Table 17.06: Welsh Assembly Election 2003 (1 May)

% Turnout 38.2

Party	Constituency votes	% share	candidates	elected
Con	169,832	19.9	40	1
Lab	340,515	40.0	40	30
LD	120,250	14.1	40	3
PC	180,185	21.2	40	5
Others	40,061	4.7	40	1
Total	**850,843**		**200**	**40**

Party	List votes	% share	with lists	elected
Con	162,725	19.2	5	10
Lab	310,658	36.6	5	0
LD	108,013	12.7	5	3
PC	167,653	19.7	5	7
Green	30,028	3.5	5	0
UKIP	29,427	3.5	5	0
Others	41,048	4.8	21	0
Total	**849,552**		**51**	**20**

Welsh Assembly Elections 2003 (1 May) (contd.)

Party	Total elected	% of seats
Con	11	18.3
Lab	30	50.0
LD	6	10.0
PC	12	20.0
Others	1	1.7
Total	**60**	

Table 17.07: Greater London Authority Assembly Election 2000 (4 May)

% Turnout 34.0

	Constituency vote	%	Seats	List vote	%	Seats
Con	526,707	33.2	8	481,053	29.0	1
Lab	501,296	31.6	6	502,874	30.3	3
L	299,998	18.9	-	245,555	14.8	4
Green	162,457	10.2	-	183,910	11.1	3
Others	95,612	6.0	-	246,238	14.8	-
Total	**1,586,070**		**14**	**1,659,630**		**11**

Table 17.08: Greater London Authority Assembly Election 2004 (10 June)

% Turnout 36.0

	Constituency vote	%	Seats	List vote	%	Seats
Con	562,047	31.2	9	533,696	28.5	-
Lab	444,808	24.7	5	468,247	25.0	2
L	332,237	18.4	-	316,218	16.9	5
UK Ind	181,146	10.0	-	156,780	8.4	2
Green	138,242	7.7	-	160,445	8.6	2
Respect	82,301	4.6	-	87,533	4.7	-
CPA	43,322	2.4	-	54,914	2.9	-
Other	19,064	1.1	-	4,968	0.3	-
BNP	-	-	-	90,365	4.8	-
Total	**1,803,167**		**14**	**1,873,166**		**11**

Local Government Elections (GB)

Table 18.01: Turnout at Local Government Elections (Summary) 1945-2006

	England	Wales	Scotland		England	Wales	Scotland
1945	45.5[1]	57.7[1]	50.9	1976	42.3	52.9	-
1946	36.8[1]	52.1[1]	44.8	1977	41.9	51.0	48.2
1947	50.8[1]	53.9[1]	55.1	1978	39.9	-	45.0
1948	44.2	72.3	-	1979[2]	76.0	76.9	-
1949	46.4	56.1	52.1	1980	37.4	-	46.2
1950	46.6	51.3	44.2	1981	42.8	48.6	-
1951	45.0	50.0	42.2	1982	41.0	-	43.2
1952	47.5	59.5	50.5	1983	44.5	46.3	-
1954	44.1	50.6	41.9	1984	40.0	43.2	44.8
1953	46.0	51.4	41.6	1985	41.6	45.2	-
1955	41.0	56.0	43.7	1986	41.9	40.0	45.6
1956	38.5	45.4	37.9	1987	45.0	51.4	-
1957	42.0	49.9	36.8	1988	40.8	41.5	45.5
1958	38.0	54.4	42.0	1989	39.2	44.2	-
1959	41.4	48.2	41.4	1990	47.5	45.5	45.9
1960	37.8	44.6	39.8	1991	46.0	53.4	-
1961	38.9	53.5	45.2	1992	35.1	35.9	41.4
1962	41.6	45.4	42.4	1993	37.2	38.8	-
1963	43.7	48.8	41.3	1994	41.5	37.8	45.1
1964	41.1	50.9	45.4	1995	39.2	48.8	44.9
1965	38.7	44.5	40.2	1996	33.2	-	-
1966	38.4	44.3	39.6	1997[2]	72.5	-	-
1967	39.8	50.8	45.7	1998	28.8	-	-
1968	37.3	45.1	47.0	1999	32.2	49.7[3]	59.4[3]
1969	37.8	45.3	39.9	2000	29.6	-	-
1970	36.3	48.5	44.1	2001[2]	62.1	-	-
1971	40.1	44.8	42.6	2002	33.3	-	-
1972	38.3	43.4	42.2	2003[4]	35.6	-	50.1
1973	38.7	52.5	33.0	2004	40.5	43.2	-
1974	36.3	-	50.5	2005[2]	63.8	-	-
1975	32.7	-	-	2006	36.5	-	-

1. See footnote 4, Table 18.02.
2. A parliamentary general election was held on the same day as the local elections.
3. Inaugural elections for the Scottish Parliament and Welsh Assembly were held on the same day as the local elections.
4. Scottish Parliament elections were held on the same day as the local elections.

Average Turnout in each decade 1945-1999

	England	Wales	Scotland
1940s	44.7	58.4	50.7
1950s	43.0	51.7	42.2
1960s	39.5	47.3	42.7
1970s[1]	38.5	48.9	43.7
1980s	41.4	45.1	45.1
1990s[2]	37.9	44.3	47.3

1. Excluding England and Wales in 1979. See footnote 2 above.
2. Excluding England in 1997. See footnote 2 above.

Table 18.02: Turnout at Local Government Elections by Local Authority Type 1945-1972

ENGLAND

	Counties[1]	County Boroughs	Non-County Boroughs & Urban Districts[1]	Rural Districts	London County Council[2]	London Metro-polian Boroughs[3]
1945	-	45.4	47.4[4]	-	-	35.1
1946	29.5	42.4	40.4[4]	45.7	26.4	-
1947	-	52.6	49.6[4]	36.0	-	-
1948	-	-	-	44.2	-	-
1949	42.4	52.3	48.4	49.5	40.7	38.3
1950	-	45.3	47.6	46.2	-	-
1951	-	44.3	45.5	44.9	-	-
1952	42.7	49.8	50.4	49.5	43.4	-
1953	-	45.2	48.4	47.3	-	39.9
1954	-	42.6	45.4	47.0	-	-
1955	37.0	43.6	45.0	48.2	32.4	-
1956	-	37.5	41.3	41.3	-	30.9
1957	-	39.8	43.9	45.1	-	-
1958	33.2	40.1	42.4	43.3	31.5	-
1959	-	40.8	44.2	42.0	-	32.1
1960	-	35.2	40.1	37.3	-	-
1961	35.1	40.5	41.5	42.4	36.4	-
1962	-	40.1	45.1	41.5	-	32.3
1963	-	41.2	45.9	41.2	-	-
1964	38.3[5]	40.3	45.7	43.3	44.2	35.7
1965	27.9[6]	37.6	42.7	38.2	-	-
1966	-	35.3	41.9	36.0	-	-
1967	36.9	40.1	41.9	40.7	41.1	-
1968	-	35.6	40.2	35.7	-	35.9
1969	-	35.4	40.7	36.0	-	-
1970	32.5	37.3	39.7	40.3	35.2	-
1971	-	39.1	42.2	35.7	-	38.7
1972	-	36.6	40.3	38.0	-	-

WALES

	Counties[1]	County Boroughs	Non-County Boroughs & Urban Districts	Rural Districts
1945	-	50.4	61.5[4]	-
1946	51.8	45.2	49.2[4]	65.3
1947	-	54.5	53 3[4]	85.5
1948	-	-	-	72.3
1949	53.6	52.1	56.8	65.1
1950	-	48.6	53.9	80.4
1951	-	45.6	53.7	68.6
1952	55.8	53.2	61.6	68.9
1953	-	47.5	55.2	92.4
1954	-	46.4	54.8	62.5
1955	54.7	47.9	57.6	65.4

Turnout at Local Government Elections by Local Authority Type 1945-1972 (contd.)

WALES

	Counties[1]	County Boroughs	Non-County Boroughs & Urban Districts	Rural Districts
1956	-	41.1	49.3	92.3
1957	-	46.8	53.5	60.7
1958	54.4	46.9	54.2	64.7
1959	-	45.5	51.1	81.7
1960	-	40.8	48.2	59.3
1961	51.0	44.5	57.3	61.9
1962	-	41.7	49.1	-
1963	-	43.5	53.6	57.0
1964	48.9	43.6	53.7	60.0
1965	-	40.3	47.9	-
1966	-	40.4	47.6	62.9
1967	46.9	45.3	54.1	60.8
1968	-	40.0	49.4	81.9
1969	-	39.8	50.5	63.0
1970	45.6	44.1	50.7	55.5
1971	-	41.1	48.4	75.7
1972	-	39.1	47.6	81.3

SCOTLAND (to 1973)

	Counties	Counties of Cities	Large Burghs	Small Burghs	Districts
1945	54.6	43.1	54.5	58.6	55.3
1946	-	37.9	50.9	54.6	-
1947	-	52.3	58.9	58.5	-
1948	-	-	-	-	-
1949	60.6	48.6	53.1	51.6	62.8
1950	-	40.7	48.1	50.2	-
1951	-	37.6	47.0	49.1	-
1952	60.3	45.1	50.7	52.2	58.2
1953	-	37.4	45.3	50.3	-
1954	-	38.0	46.8	49.3	-
1955	58.5	46.4	36.0	50.2	57.4
1956	-	32.6	42.8	49.9	-
1957	-	31.1	42.2	50.2	-
1958	60.0	33.6	44.6	50.4	59.6
1959	-	37.1	45.2	51.6	-
1960	-	37.0	40.8	48.5	-
1961	57.8	40.9	43.8	50.1	54.6
1962	-	38.9	45.8	50.5	-
1963	-	38.6	40.9	50.2	-
1964	56.0	40.5	45.0	51.9	53.5
1965	-	36.1	42.0	49.7	-
1966	-	35.6	40.9	48.3	-
1967	54.9	41.2	44.6	48.9	54.9

Turnout at Local Government Elections by Local Authority Type 1945-1972 (contd.)

SCOTLAND (TO 1973)

	Counties	Counties of Cities	Large Burghs	Small Burghs	Districts
1968	-	44.4	48.7	51.6	-
1969	-	36.7	41.8	45.1	-
1970	53.6	39.4	43.8	46.9	53.3
1971	-	40.0	43.9	47.7	-
1972	-	39.7	44.0	46.5	-
1973	45.1	32.3	37.4	39.0	44.1

1. Excluding London
2. Greater London Council from 1964
3. Greater London Boroughs from 1964
4. Urban District Council elections were held in the spring of 1946, 1947 and 1948 but the figures of electorate and votes cast were not shown separately in the *Statistical Review* so the turnout percentages for 1945, 1946 and 1947 are not completely accurate as they include the Urban District elections which took place in the following years.
5. Excluding Essex, Kent and Surrey.
6. Essex, Kent and Surrey only.

Sources:

Registrar-General's Statistical Review of England and Wales, Part 2. Tables, Civil (until 1957), Population (from 1958).

Registrar-General for Scotland, Annual Report, Part 2. Population and Vital Statistics.

Table 18.03: Turnout at Local Government Elections by Local Authority Type 1973-2006

ENGLAND

	Metropolitan Counties	Non-Metro Counties	Metro-politan Districts	Non-Metro Districts	Greater London Council	Greater London Boroughs
1973	37.1	42.6	33.4	38.6	37.0	-
1974	-	-	-	-	-	36.3
1975	-	-	32.7	-	-	-
1976	-	-	38.1	44.3	-	-
1977	40.2	42.3	-	-	43.4	-
1978	-	-	37.2	42.4	-	42.9
1979[1]	-	-	74.7	76.6	-	-
1980	-	-	36.3	38.9	-	-
1981	39.5	43.7	-	-	44.4	-
1982	-	-	38.8	41.8	-	43.9
1983	-	-	42.0	45.6	-	-
1984	-	-	40.8	40.2	-	-
1985[2]	-	41.6	-	-	-	-
1986	Abolished	-	39.9	41.9	Abolished	45.5
1987		-	44.7	47.8		-
1988		-	40.1	41.5		-
1989		39.2	-	-		-

Turnout at Local Government Elections by Local Authority Type 1973-2006 (contd.)

ENGLAND

	Metropolitan Counties	Non-Metro Counties	Metro-politan Districts	Non-Metro Districts	Greater London Council	Greater London Boroughs
1990		-	46.2	48.6		48.1
1991		-	40.8	47.5		-
1992		-	32.5	37.8		-
	Unitaries[3]					
1993		37.2	-	-		-
1994		-	38.9	42.6		46.0
1995	39.7	-	33.8	41.0		-
1996	34.6	-	30.5	37.2		-
1997[1]	69.7	73.2	-	-		-
1998	27.8	-	24.8	30.8		34.6
1999	31.5	-	26.1	35.8		-
2000	28.5	-	26.0	32.2		-
2001[1]	57.6	62.5	-	-		-
2002	30.2	-	31.8	35.4		31.6
2003	36.8	-	33.1	35.8		-
2004	37.2	-	41.3	41.0		-
2005[1]	61.3	63.8	-	-		-
2006	33.7	-	34.7	37.0		39.9

WALES

	Counties	Districts		Counties	Districts
1973	55.0	50.0	1991	-	53.4
1974	-	-	1992	-	35.9
1975	-	-	1993	38.8	-
1976	-	52.9	1994	-	37.8
1977	51.0	-		*Unitaries*[3]	
1978	-	-	1995	48.8	
1979[1]	-	76.9	1996	-	
1980	-	-	1997	-	
1981	48.6	-	1998	-	
1982	-	-	1999 [4]	49.7	
1983	-	46.3	2000	-	
1984	-	43.2	2001	-	
1985	45.2	-	2002	-	
1986	-	40.0	2003	-	
1987	-	51.4	2004	43.2	
1988	-	41.5	2005	-	
1989	44.2	-	2006	-	
1990	-	45.5			

Turnout at Local Government Elections by Local Authority Type 1973-1999 (contd.)

SCOTLAND (from 1974)

Year	Regions & Islands	Districts	Year	Regions & Islands	Districts
1974	50.1	52.1	1991	-	-
1975	-	-	1992	-	41.4
1976	-	-	1993	-	-
1977	-	48.2	1994	45.1	-
1978	45.0	-	**Unitaries[3]**		
1979	-	-	1995	44.9	
1980	-	46.2	1996	-	
1981	-	-	1997	-	
1982	43.2	-	1998	-	
1983	-	-	1999[4]	59.4	
1984	-	44.8	2000	-	
1985	-	-	2001	-	
1986	45.6	-	2002	-	
1987	-	-	2003[5]	50.1	
1988	-	45.5	2004	-	
1989	-	-	2005	-	
1990	45.9	-	2006	-	

1. A parliamentary general election was held on the same day as the local elections.
2. The Greater London Council and the six metropolitan counties were abolished in 1986. No elections were held in 1985.
3. A number of all purpose unitary authorities were established and had elections from 1995 onwards. They replaced the previous county/region-district two tier structure in parts of (mainly) urban England and throughout Scotland and Wales.
4. The inaugural elections for the Scottish Parliament and Welsh Assembly were held on the same day as the local elections.
5. Scottish Parliamentary Elections were held on the same day as the local elections.

Sources:

Electoral Statistics (Office of Population, Censuses and Surveys) (to 1979). Registrar-General for Scotland, Annual Report, Part 2. Population and Vital Statistics. (to 1984).

C. Rallings and M. Thrasher (eds), Local Elections in Britain: A Statistical Digest, 1st edition (to 1992); C. Rallings and M. Thrasher (eds), Local Elections in Britain: A Statistical Digest, 2nd edition (to 2003). Files of the Local Government Chronicle Elections Centre, 1992 on.

Table 19.01: Number of Councillors Returned (Summary) 1973-2006[1]

a: Total returned   b: Returned unopposed   c: % of total unopposed

	England			Wales			Scotland		
	a	*b*	*c*	*a*	*b*	*c*	*a*	*b*	*c*
1973	19,875	2,149	10.8	2,098	390	18.6	-	-	-
1974	1,867	22	1.2	-	-	-	1,617	300	18.6
1975	806	21	2.6	-	-	-	-	-	-
1976	14,442	2,217	15.4	1,510	316	20.9	-	-	-
1977	3,816	379	9.9	577	122	21.1	1,114	247	22.2
1978	3,518	54	1.5	-	-	-	508	134	26.4
1979	13,147	2,278	17.3	1,516	396	26.1	-	-	-
1980	2,982	120	4.0	-	-	-	1,123	289	25.7
1981	3,693	123	3.3	578	122	21.1	-	-	-
1982	4,841	57	1.2	-	-	-	520	110	21.2
1983	11,190	1,383	12.4	1,268	304	24.0	-	-	-
1984	2,756	105	3.8	76	6	7.9	1,150	247	21.5
1985	3,002	61	2.0	559	145	25.9	-	-	-
1986	4,714	80	1.7	81	2	2.5	524	89	17.0
1987	10,894	791	7.3	1,232	282	22.9	-	-	-
1988	2,656	91	3.4	65	6	9.2	1,154	158	13.7
1989	3,005	64	2.1	504	145	28.8	-	-	-
1990	4,629	114	2.5	68	9	13.2	524	73	13.9
1991	10,961	835	7.6	1,367	331	24.2	-	-	-
1992	2,626	116	4.4	59	7	11.9	1,158	152	13.1
1993	2,998	60	2.0	502	111	22.1	-	-	-
1994	4,528	54	1.2	53	4	7.5	537	76	14.2
1995	10,855	552	5.1	1,272	208	16.4	1,161	54	4.7
1996	3,022	69	2.3	-	-	-	-	-	-
1997	3,247	37	1.1	-	-	-	-	-	-
1998	4,344	38	0.9	-	-	-	-	-	-
1999	10,809	544	5.0	1,270	200	15.7	1,222	56	4.6
2000	3,374	27	0.8	-	-	-	-	-	-
2001	2,484	2	0.1	-	-	-	-	-	-
2002	5,914	53	0.9	-	-	-	-	-	-
2003	10,430	630	6.0	-	-	-	1,222	61	5.0
2004	4,813	18	0.4	1,263	152	12.0	-	-	-
2005	2,396	8	0.3	-	-	-	-	-	-
2006	4,425	20	0.5	-	-	-	-	-	-

1. Data for elections from 1945-1972 (1973 Scotland) can be found in Tables 12.05-07 in the fifth edition of this book.

Table 19.02: Number of Councillors Returned by Local Authority Type 1973-2006[1]

ENGLAND

a: Total returned   b: Returned unopposed   c: % of total unopposed

Year	Metropolitan Counties / Unitaries a	b	c	Non-Metropolitan Counties a	b	c	Metropolitan Districts a	b	c	Non Metropolitan Districts a	b	c	Greater London Council a	b	c	Greater London Boroughs a	b	c
1973	601	22	3.7	3,127	396	12.7	2,511	66	2.6	13,544	1,665	12.3	92	0	0.0			
1974																1,867	22	1.2
1975																		
1976							806	21	2.6	13,591	2,204	16.2						
1977	598	6	1.0	3,126	373	11.9	851	13	1.5				92	0	0.0			
1978							938	7	0.7	675	47	7.0				1,905	0	0.0
1979							987	9	0.9	12,160	2,269	18.7						
1980							1,364	11	0.8	1,619	109	6.7						
1981	600	2	0.3	3,093	121	3.9							92	0	0.0			
1982							1,339	5	0.4	1,588	50	3.1				1,914	2	0.1
1983							845	7	0.8	10,345	1,376	13.3						
1984							850	14	1.6	1,906	91	4.8						
1985	Abolished			3,002	61	2.0							Abolished					
1986							861	25	2.9	1,939	52	2.7				1,914	3	0.2
1987							873	13	1.5	10,021	778	7.8						
1988							857	16	1.9	1,799	75	4.2						
1989				3,005	64	2.1												
1990							860	53	6.2	1,855	58	3.1				1,914	3	0.2
1991							840	37	4.4	10,121	798	7.9						
1992							843	12	1.4	1,783	104	5.8						
1993	*Unitaries*			2,998	60	2.0												
1994							850	29	3.4	1,761	25	1.4				1,917	0	0.0
1995	788	0	0.0				842	31	3.7	9,225	521	5.6						
1996	658	3	0.5				836	34	4.1	1,528	32	2.1						
1997	1,044	4	0.4	2,203	33	1.5												
1998	206	1	0.5				849	18	2.1	1,372	16	1.2				1,917	3	0.2
1999	1,274	11	0.9				836	11	1.3	8,699	522	6.0						
2000	882	12	1.4				884	6	0.7	1,608	9	0.6						
2001	269	0	0.0	2,215	2	0.1												

Number of Councillors Returned by Local Authority Type 1973-2006[1] (contd.)

ENGLAND

a: Total returned   b: Returned unopposed   c: % of total unopposed

	Unitaries			Non-Metropolitan Counties			Metropolitan Districts			Non Metropolitan Districts			Greater London Council			Greater London Boroughs		
	a	b	c	a	b	c	a	b	c	a	b	c	a	b	c	a	b	c
2002	527	1	0.2	-	-	-	838	1	0.1	2,688	48	1.8				1,861	3	0.2
2003	1,626	10	0.6	-	-	-	836	2	0.2	7,968	618	7.8				-	-	-
2004	644	0	0.0	-	-	-	2,445	9	0.4	1,723	9	0.5				-	-	-
2005	127	1	0.8	2,269	7	0.3	-	-	-	-	-	-				-	-	-
2006	361	3	0.8	-	-	-	827	3	0.4	1,376	17	1.2				1,861	0	0.0

WALES

a: Total returned   b: Returned unopposed   c: % of total unopposed

	Counties			Districts		
	a	b	c	a	b	c
1973	577	109	18.9	1,521	281	18.5
1974	-	-	-	-	-	-
1975	-	-	-	-	-	-
1976	-	-	-	-	-	-
1977	577	122	21.1	1,510	316	20.9
1978	-	-	-	-	-	-
1979	-	-	-	1,516	396	26.1
1980	-	-	-	-	-	-
1981	578	122	21.1	-	-	-
1982	-	-	-	-	-	-
1983	-	-	-	1,268	304	24.0
1984	-	-	-	76	6	7.9
1985	559	145	25.9	-	-	-
1986	-	-	-	81	2	2.5
1987	-	-	-	1,232	282	22.9
1988	-	-	-	65	6	9.2
1989	504	145	28.8	-	-	-
1990	-	-	-	68	9	13.2
1991	-	-	-	1,367	331	24.2
1992	-	-	-	59	7	11.9

SCOTLAND - from 1974

	Regions and Islands			Districts		
	a	b	c	a	b	c
1974	507	77	15.2	1,110	223	20.1
1975	-	-	-	-	-	-
1976	-	-	-	-	-	-
1977	508	134	26.4	1,114	247	22.2
1978	-	-	-	-	-	-
1979	-	-	-	1,123	289	25.7
1980	-	-	-	-	-	-
1981	-	-	-	-	-	-
1982	520	110	21.2	-	-	-
1983	-	-	-	-	-	-
1984	-	-	-	1,150	247	21.5
1985	-	-	-	-	-	-
1986	524	89	17.0	-	-	-
1987	-	-	-	-	-	-
1988	-	-	-	1,154	158	13.7
1989	-	-	-	-	-	-
1990	524	73	13.9	-	-	-
1991	-	-	-	-	-	-
1992	-	-	-	1,158	152	13.1
1993	-	-	-	-	-	-

Number of Councillors Returned by Local Authority Type 1973-2006[1] (contd.)

a: Total returned **b: Returned unopposed** **c: % of total unopposed**

WALES

	Counties			Districts		
	a	*b*	*c*	*a*	*b*	*c*
1993	502	111	22.1	-	-	-
1994	-	-	-	53	4	7.5

	Unitaries			Districts		
	a	*b*	*c*	*a*	*b*	*c*
1995	1,272	208	16.4			
1996	-	-	-			
1997	-	-	-			
1998	-	-	-			
1999	1,270	200	15.7			
2000	-	-	-			
2001	-	-	-			
2002	-	-	-			
2003	-	-	-			
2004	1,263	152	12.0			
2005	-	-	-			
2006	-	-	-			

SCOTLAND - from 1974

	Regions and Islands			Districts		
	a	*b*	*c*	*a*	*b*	*c*
1994	537	76	14.2	-	-	-

	Unitaries		
	a	*b*	*c*
1995[2]	1,161	54	4.7
1996	-	-	-
1997	-	-	-
1998	-	-	-
1999	1,222	56	4.6
2000	-	-	-
2001	-	-	-
2002	-	-	-
2003	1,222	61	5.0
2004	-	-	-
2005	-	-	-
2006	-	-	-

1. Data for elections from 1945-1972 (1973 Scotland) can be found in Tables 12.05-07 in the fifth edition of this book.
2. The boundaries of the 3 Islands authorities of Orkney, Shetland and the Western Isles were unchanged and they did not have elections in 1995.

Table 19.03: Party Political Control of Councils 1973-2006

Year	Con	Lab	L	Ind	SNP	PC	No overall control	Total[1]
1973	90	155	1	87	0	0	122	455
1974	99	170	1	109	1	0	137	517
1975	103	166	1	109	1	0	137	517
1976	216	107	0	98	1	1	94	517
1977	248	83	1	98	4	1	82	517
1978	257	78	1	97	4	1	79	517
1979	244	109	2	82	4	0	76	517
1980	223	144	3	82	0	0	65	517
1981	200	160	4	81	0	0	72	517
1982	198	153	4	81	0	0	81	517
1983	197	154	4	74	0	0	88	517
1984	188	155	5	73	1	0	95	517
1985	179	150	5	72	1	0	110	517
1986	151	160	9	70	1	0	119	510
1987	150	155	13	56	1	0	135	510
1988	155	157	13	52	1	0	132	510
1989	162	161	13	52	1	0	121	510
1990	151	168	11	53	1	0	126	510
1991	105	180	28	59	1	0	137	510
1992	110	164	27	57	1	0	151	510
1993	94	166	29	56	1	0	165	511
1994	74	173	37	53	1	0	173	511
1995	13	199	50	22	3	1	154	442
1996	14	207	55	24	3	1	137	441
1997	23	206	50	24	3	1	133	440
1998	24	203	42	23	3	1	144	440
1999	75	167	27	18	1	3	149	440
2000	93	150	27	18	2	3	147	440
2001	102	148	25	18	2	3	142	440
2002	109	136	27	21	2	3	142	440
2003	137	103	32	18	1	3	146	440
2004	151	94	31	16	1	1	146	440
2005	156	92	32	16	1	1	142	440
2006	169	75	33	14	1	1	147	440

1. Totals vary owing to local government structural changes and to on-going reviews of the boundaries of and number of councillors elected by each ward.

Table 19.04: Party Affiliation of Councillors 1973-2006

Year	Con	Lab	L	Nat	Other	Total[1]
1973	7,709	9,781	1,427	65	5,183	24,165
1974	8,102	10,325	1,474	145	5,664	25,710
1975	8,301	10,117	1,462	145	5,685	25,710
1976	11,077	8,213	1,113	223	5,132	25,758
1977	12,370	7,115	950	349	4,965	25,749
1978	12,645	6,644	923	349	4,920	25,481
1979	12,222	7,410	1,059	301	4,388	25,380
1980	11,738	8,011	1,149	186	4,325	25,409
1981	10,545	8,999	1,455	172	4,208	25,379
1982	10,447	8,774	1,850	177	4,099	25,347
1983	10,557	8,782	2,171	175	3,570	25,255
1984	10,393	8,870	2,331	179	3,515	25,288
1985	10,191	8,746	2,633	177	3,432	25,179
1986	9,216	8,759	2,971	191	3,364	24,501
1987	9,141	8,525	3,640	203	2,974	24,483
1988	9,150	8,601	3,518	254	2,968	24,491
1989	9,242	8,636	3,343	258	2,958	24,437
1990	9,020	8,920	3,265	264	2,968	24,437
1991	7,985	9,504	3,672	292	2,997	24,450
1992	8,288	9,102	3,728	334	2,977	24,429
1993	7,802	9,213	4,123	358	2,948	24,444
1994	7,286	9,257	4,551	392	2,941	24,427
1995	4,883	10,461	4,942	294	2,157	22,737
1996	4,276	10,929	5,078	298	2,157	22,738
1997	4,449	10,608	4,754	301	2,076	22,188
1998	4,772	10,411	4,629	304	2,083	22,199
1999	6,144	9,134	4,485	444	1,973	22,180
2000	6,785	8,529	4,457	447	2,071	22,289
2001	6,941	8,487	4,382	418	2,091	22,319
2002	7,178	8,117	4,379	415	2,094	22,183
2003	7,768	7,207	4,551	388	2,125	22,039
2004	8,038	6,669	4,714	355	2,213	21,989
2005	8,193	6,518	4,743	357	2,233	22,044
2006	8,495	6,176	4,723	364	2,273	22,031

1. Totals vary owing to local government structural changes and to on-going reviews of the boundaries of and number of councillors elected by each ward.

Table 20.01: Referendums on Elected Mayors

Authority	Date	Yes	%	No	%	T'out	% Electorate voting 'Yes'	All Postal
Berwick-upon -Tweed *	7.6.01	3,617	26.2	10,212	73.8	63.8#	16.7	N
Cheltenham	28.6.01	8,083	32.7	16,602	67.3	31.0	10.2	Y
Gloucester	28.6.01	7,731	32.1	16,317	67.9	30.8	9.9	Y
Watford	12.7.01	7,636	51.7	7,140	48.3	24.5	12.7	Y
Doncaster	20.9.01	35,453	64.6	19,398	35.4	25.4	16.4	Y
Kirklees	4.10.01	10,169	26.7	27,977	73.3	13.0	3.5	N
Sunderland	11.10.01	9,375	43.4	12,209	56.6	10.0	4.3	N
Brighton & Hove	18.10.01	22,724	37.9	37,214	62.1	31.6	12.0	Y
Hartlepool	18.10.01	10,667	50.9	10,294	49.1	33.9	17.3	Y
Lewisham	18.10.01	16,822	51.4	15,917	48.6	18.3	9.4	Y
Middlesbrough	18.10.01	29,067	84.3	5,422	15.7	33.9	28.6	Y
N. Tyneside	18.10.01	30,262	57.6	22,296	42.4	36.2	20.8	Y
Sedgefield	18.10.01	10,628	47.2	11,869	52.8	33.3	15.7	Y
Redditch	8.11.01	7,250	44.1	9,198	55.9	28.3	12.5	Y·
Durham	20.11.01	8,327	41.0	11,974	59.0	29.0	11.9	Y
Harrow	7.12.01	17,502	42.6	23,554	57.4	26.1	11.1	Y
Harlow	24.1.02	5,296	25.5	15,490	74.5	36.4	9.3	Y
Plymouth	24.1.02	29,559	40.8	42,811	59.2	39.8	16.3	Y
Newham	31.1.02	27,263	68.2	12,687	31.8	25.9	17.7	Y
Shepway	31.1.02	11,357	44.0	14,438	56.0	36.3	16.0	Y
Southwark † *	31.1.02	6,054	31.4	13,217	68.6	11.2	3.5	N
West Devon	31.1.02	3,555	22.6	12,190	77.4	41.8	9.4	Y
Bedford *	21.2.02	11,316	67.1	5,537	32.9	15.5	10.4	N
Hackney	2.5.02	24,697	70.1	10,547	29.9	26.8	18.8	Y
Mansfield *	2.5.02	8,973	55.0	7,350	45.0	21.0	11.5	N
Newcastle-u-Lyme *	2.5.02	12,912	43.9	16,468	56.1	31.5	13.8	N
Oxford	2.5.02	14,692	44.0	18,690	56.0	32.6	14.3	N
Stoke on Trent *	2.5.02	28,601	58.2	20,578	41.8	26.8	15.6	N
Corby	1.10.02	5,351	46.2	6,239	53.8	30.9	14.3	Y
Ealing *	12.12.02	9,454	44.8	11,655	55.2	9.8	4.4	N
Ceredigion † *	20.5.04	5,308	27.5	14,013	72.5	36.3	10.0	N
Isle of Wight *	5.5.05	28,786	43.7	37,097	56.3	62.4#	27.3	N
Torbay *	14.7.05	18,074	55.2	14,682	44.8	32.1	17.7	Y
Crewe & Nantwich *	4.5.06	11,808	38.2	18,768	60.8	35.3	13.6	N
Totals/averages		**498,369**	**45.9**	**550,050**	**54.1**	**30.0**	**13.4**	

\# Same day as General Election.

* Public petition triggered referendum.

† Referendum ordered by Secretary of State.

Table 20.02: Mayoral Elections

Authority	Date	No. of cands.	Elected	Party	First Vote	%	Valid 2nd vote	Combined vote	%	Runoff party	Turnout
London	May 4, 2000	11	Ken Livingstone	Ind	667,877	39.0	108,550	776,427	58.0	Con	33.6
	Jun 10, 2004	10	Ken Livingstone	Lab	685,541	36.8	142,839	828,380	55.4	Con	36.9
Doncaster	May 2, 2002	7	Martin Winter	Lab	21,494	36.8	4,213	25,707	67.9	Con	27.1
	May 5, 2005	7	Martin Winter	Lab	40,015	36.7	5,727	45,742	55.1	Ind	54.5 #
Hartlepool	May 2, 2002	5	Stuart Drummond	Ind	5,696	29.1	1,699	7,395	52.1	Lab	28.8
	May 5, 2005	7	Stuart Drummond	Ind	14,277	42.2	2,685	16,912	71.6	Lab	51.0 #
Lewisham	May 2, 2002	5	Steve Bullock	Lab	20,011	45.0	4,509	24,520	71.3	Con	24.8
	May 4, 2006	6	Steve Bullock	Lab	22,155	37.7	2974	25,129	57.1	LD	33.0
Middlesbrough	May 2, 2002	6	Raymond Mallon	Ind	26,362	62.8	-	-	-	-	41.6
Newham	May 2, 2002	6	Robin Wales	Lab	20,384	50.8	-	-	-	-	25.5
	May 4, 2006	5	Robin Wales	Lab	28,655	47.9	5,406	34,061	68.2	Respect	34.5
North Tyneside	May 2, 2002	5	Chris Morgan	Con	21,829	35.9	4,254	26,083	51.5	Lab	42.3
By-election	Jun 12, 2003	5	Linda Arkley	Con	18,478	43.1	2,821	21,299	56.5	Lab	30.8
	May 5, 2005	4	John Harrison	Lab	34,053	40.2	6,407	40,460	50.6	Con	61.4 #
Watford	May 2, 2002	6	Dorothy Thornhill	LD	10,954	49.4	2,519	13,473	71.9	Lab	36.1
	May 4, 2006	4	Dorothy Thornhill	LD	11,963	51.2	-	-	-	-	38.1
Bedford	Oct 17, 2002	8	Francis Branston	Ind	9,557	34.5	2,522	12,079	63.4	LD	25.3
Hackney	Oct 17, 2002	8	Jules Pipe	Lab	13,812	42.0	2,421	16,234	74.3	Con	25.2
	May 4, 2006	7	Jules Pipe	Lab	20,830	46.9	3403	24,233	73.4	Con	32.9
Mansfield	Oct 17, 2002	5	Tony Egginton	Ind	4,150	29.6	1,801	5,951	52.6	Lab	18.5
Stoke on Trent	Oct 17, 2002	12	Mike Wolfe	Ind	9,356	21.3	3,337	12,693	50.6	Lab	24.0
	May 5, 2005	7	Mark Meredith	Lab	27,253	32.9	9,708	36,961	61.5	Con	50.8 #
Torbay	Oct 20, 2005	14	Nicholas Bye	Con	5,283	21.9	1,813	7,096	57.7	LD	24.0

Same day as General Election

Table 21.01: The Local Electoral Timetable 2007-2017

Type of authority	2007	2008	2009	2010	2011	2012	2013	2014	2015	2016	2017
English counties	-	-	x	-	-	-	x	-	-	-	x
Districts (whole council elections)	x	-	-	-	x	-	-	-	x	-	-
Districts (part council elections)	x	x	-	x	x	x	-	x	x	x	-
London boroughs	-	-	-	x	-	-	-	x	-	-	-
Metropolitan boroughs	x	x	-	x	x	x	-	x	x	x	-
English unitary councils	x	x	-	x	x	x	-	x	x	x	-
Scottish unitary councils	x	-	-	-	x	-	-	-	x	-	x
Welsh unitary councils	-	x	-	-	-	x	-	-	-	x	-

Table 21.02: National Equivalent Vote at Local Government Elections 1979-2006

	Con	Lab	L	
1979	45	38	14	General Election result
1980	40	42	13	
1981	38	41	17	
1982	40	29	27	
1983	39	36	20	
1984	38	37	21	
1985	32	39	26	
1986	34	37	26	
1987	38	32	27	
1988	39	38	18	
1989	36	42	19	
1990	33	44	17	
1991	35	38	22	
1992	46	30	20	
1993	31	39	25	
1994	28	40	27	
1995	25	47	23	
1996	29	43	24	
1997	31	44	17	General Election result
1998	33	37	25	
1999	34	36	25	
2000	38	30	26	
2001	33	42	19	General Election result
2002	34	33	25	
2003	35	30	27	
2004	37	26	27	
2005	33	36	23	General Election result
2006	39	26	25	

Because local elections take place in different parts of the country each year and never encompass the whole of Great Britain, it is difficult to translate the results in terms of nationwide support for the political parties. Since 1979 a number of academics working for media clients have provided instant estimates of what the national vote shares might have been if local elections had been held throughout the country. This table reflects the work of Ivor Crewe and then John Curtice for the BBC and of Colin Rallings and Michael Thrasher for the Sunday Times. On occasion there have been slight differences between 'rival' estimates. This table has attempted to reconcile those differences following analysis of the full, rather than a sample of, local election results in each year.

Referendums

Table 22.01: Referendum on Membership of the European Economic Community 1975 (5 June)

Question:
Do you think that the United Kingdom should stay in the European Community (The Common Market)?

	Civilian Electorate	Civilian Turnout%[1]	Yes	%	No	%	Service Votes	Spoilt Ballot Papers
ENGLAND	**33,356,208**	**64.6**	**14,918,009**	**68.7**	**6,812,052**	**31.3**	**207,465**	**42,161**
Avon	665,484	68.7	310,145	67.8	147,024	32.2	499	635
Bedfordshire	326,566	67.9	154,338	69.4	67,969	30.6	829	385
Berkshire	443,472	66.4	215,184	72.6	81,221	27.4	2,666	571
Buckinghamshire	346,348	69.5	180,512	74.3	62,578	25.7	2,643	357
Cambridgeshire	375,753	62.9	177,789	74.1	62,143	25.9	3,840	354
Cheshire	633,614	65.5	290,714	70.1	123,839	29.9	128	663
Cleveland	392,672	60.2	158,982	67.3	77,079	32.7	47	308
Cornwall	298,706	66.8	137,828	68.5	63,478	31.5	2,321	572
Cumbria	349,596	64.8	162,545	71.9	63,564	28.1	83	415
Derbyshire	653,005	64.1	286,614	68.6	131,452	31.4	NIL	687
Devon	676,378	68.0	334,244	72.1	129,179	27.9	4,239	991
Dorset	429,752	68.3	217,432	73.5	78,239	26.5	3,200	976
Durham	444,783	61.5	175,284	64.2	97,724	35.8	24	453
East Sussex	511,437	65.8	249,780	74.3	86,198	25.7	104	775
Essex	1,010,317	67.7	463,505	67.6	222,085	32.4	2,648	1,119
Gloucestershire	347,218	68.4	170,931	71.7	67,465	28.3	1,304	504
Greater London	5,250,343	60.8	2,201,031	66.7	1,100,185	33.3	114,900	6,874
Greater Manchester	1,932,717	64.1	797,316	64.5	439,191	35.5	82	2,843
Hampshire	975,440	68.0	484,302	71.0	197,761	29.0	20,142	1,379
Hereford & Worcester	419,866	66.4	203,128	72.8	75,779	27.2	867	642
Hertfordshire	662,177	70.2	326,943	70.4	137,266	29.6	621	1,239
Humberside	607,890	62.4	257,826	67.8	122,199	32.2	1,207	765
Isles of Scilly	1,447	75.0	802	74.5	275	25.5	NIL	8
Isle of Wight	86,381	67.5	40,837	70.2	17,375	27.8	NIL	116
Kent	1,035,313	67.4	493,407	70.4	207,358	29.6	3,653	1,120
Lancashire	1,000,755	66.4	455,170	68.6	208,821	31.4	460	1,302
Leicestershire	590,780	67.2	291,500	73.3	106,004	26.7	1,557	835
Lincolnshire	370,518	63.7	180,603	74.7	61,011	25.3	6,149	445
Merseyside	1,147,920	62.7	465,625	64.8	252,712	35.2	138	1,602
Norfolk	485,229	63.8	218,883	70.1	93,198	29.9	3,016	605
Northamptonshire	351,653	66.7	162,803	69.5	71,322	30.5	166	507
Northumberland	212,846	65.0	95,980	69.2	42,645	30.8	401	231
North Yorkshire	468,998	64.3	234,040	76.3	72,805	23.7	5,853	738
Nottinghamshire	705,183	63.1	297,191	66.8	147,461	33.2	550	1,052
Oxfordshire	355,977	67.7	179,938	73.6	64,643	26.4	4,065	449
Salop	249,463	62.0	113,044	72.3	43,329	27.7	1,860	238
Somerset	293,191	67.7	138,830	69.6	60,631	30.4	1,251	300
South Yorkshire	954,539	62.4	377,916	63.4	217,792	36.6	941	1,060
Staffordshire	706,230	64.3	306,518	67.4	148,252	32.6	973	657
Suffolk	397,626	64.9	187,484	72.2	72,251	27.8	1,993	472
Surrey	720,440	70.1	386,369	76.2	120,576	23.8	2,518	770
Tyne and Wear	872,253	62.7	344,069	62.9	202,511	37.1	110	469
Warwickshire	327,967	68.0	156,303	69.9	67,221	30.1	879	391
West Midlands	1,972,987	62.5	801,913	65.1	429,207	34.9	NIL	2,153
West Sussex	464,396	68.6	242,890	76.2	75,928	23.8	750	719
West Yorkshire	1,485,749	63.6	616,730	65.4	326,993	34.6	65	1,860
Wiltshire	344,833	67.8	172,791	71.7	68,113	28.3	7,723	555

Referendum on Membership of the European Economic Community 1975 (5 June) (contd.)

	Civilian Electorate	Civilian Turnout%[1]	Yes	%	No	%	Service Votes	Spoilt Ballot Papers
WALES	**2,011,136**	**66.7**	**869,135**	**64.8**	**472,071**	**35.2**	**3,855**	**4,339**
Clwyd	272,798	65.8	123,980	69.1	55,424	30.9	554	515
Dyfed	241,415	67.5	109,184	67.6	52,264	32.4	980	491
Gwent	314,369	68.2	132,557	62.1	80,992	37.9	NIL	808
Gwynedd	167,706	64.3	76,421	70.6	31,807	29.4	694	240
Mid Glamorgan	390,175	66.6	147,348	56.9	111,672	43.1	NIL	900
Powys	76,531	67.9	38,724	74.3	13,372	25.7	272	170
South Glamorgan	275,324	66.7	127,932	69.5	56,224	30.5	1,355	705
West Glamorgan	272,818	67.4	112,989	61.6	70,316	38.4	NIL	510
SCOTLAND	**3,688,799**	**61.7**	**1,332,186**	**58.4**	**948,039**	**41.6**	**9,295**	**6,451**
Borders	74,834	63.2	34,092	72.3	13,053	27.7	NIL	160
Central	188,613	64.1	71,986	59.7	48,568	40.3	32	331
Dumfries & Galloway	101,703	61.5	42,608	68.2	19,856	31.8	60	179
Fife	235,166	63.3	84,239	56.3	65,260	43.7	1,255	589
Grampian	321,140	57.4	108,520	58.2	78,071	41.8	2,625	507
Highland	127,925	58.7	40,802	54.6	33,979	45.4	NIL	257
Lothian	548,369	63.6	208,133	59.5	141,456	40.5	2,002	960
Orkney	13,157	48.2	3,911	61.8	2,419	38.2	NIL	15
Shetland	13,411	47.1	2,815	43.7	3,631	56.3	163	29
Strathclyde	1,759,889	61.7	625,959	57.7	459,073	42.3	2,191	2,951
Tayside	282,160	63.8	105,728	58.6	74,567	41.4	666	422
Western Isles	22,432	50.1	3,393	29.5	8,106	70.5	301	51
NORTHERN IRELAND	**1,028,451**	**47.5**	**259,251**	**52.1**	**237,911**	**47.9**	**10,579**	**1,589**
UNITED KINGDOM	**40,084,594**	**64.0**	**17,378,581**	**67.2**	**8,470,073**	**32.8**	**231,194**	**54,540**

1. In calculating this figure the service votes have been deducted from and the spoilt ballot papers added to the total valid votes cast. Special arrangements were made to enable members of the forces and their spouses to vote irrespective of whether or not they were included in the electoral register as service voters. Service votes were counted in such a way as to prevent separate 'Yes' and 'No' totals for the forces alone becoming available. More detailed notes are provided following Table 13.02 of the fifth edition of this book.

Table 22.02: Referendum on Devolution for Scotland 1979 (1 March)

Question:
Do you want the provisions of the Scotland Act 1978 to be put into effect?

	Electorate	T'out %	Yes	%	No	%	Spoilt Ballot Papers
Borders	77,565	66.4	20,746	40.3	30,780	59.7	92
Central	197,772	65.9	71,296	54.7	59,105	45.3	198
Dumfries & Galloway	105,202	64.1	27,162	40.3	40,239	59.7	114
Fife	246,097	65.3	86,252	53.7	74,436	46.3	254
Grampian	343,527	57.2	94,944	48.3	101,485	51.7	415
Highland	136,445	64.7	44,973	51.0	43,274	49.0	90
Lothian	567,255	65.9	187,221	50.1	186,421	49.9	324
Orkney	13,937	54.1	2,104	27.9	5,439	72.1	17
Shetland	14,882	50.3	2,020	27.0	5,466	73.0	18
Strathclyde	1,769,077	62.5	596,519	54.0	508,599	46.0	1,302
Tayside	293,188	63.0	91,482	49.5	93,325	50.5	282
Western Isles	22,365	49.9	6,218	55.8	4,933	44.2	27
Total	**3,787,312**[1]	**63.0**	**1,230,937**	**51.6**	**1,153,502**	**48.4**	**3,133**

1. A provision of the Scotland Act was that not less than 40% of persons entitled to vote voted 'Yes' in the referendum. The Secretary of State for Scotland estimated that of the total electorate on March 1, 26,400 had died; 2,000 were convicted prisoners in prisons and 11,800 were students and nurses registered at more than one address. The official estimated number of the electorate was therefore reduced to 3,747,112 and of this the total 'Yes' vote was 32.8% and the 'No' vote was 30.8%. The turnout was increased to 63.6%.

Source: The Certificate of the Chief Counting Officer (Cmnd. 7530 of 1979-80).

Table 22.03: Referendum on Establishment of Scottish Parliament 1997 (11 September)

At the referendum 2,391,268 valid votes were cast, representing 60.2% of the Scottish electorate. Voters were asked two questions. First, 1,775,045 (74.3%) agreed that there should be a Scottish Parliament and 614,400 (25.7%) did not agree. A 'Yes' majority of almost 3 to 1. There were 11,986 spoilt ballot papers. Second, 1,512,889 (63.5%) agreed that the Scottish Parliament should have tax-varying powers and 870,263 (36.5%) did not agree. A 'Yes' majority of 642,626. On this question there were 19,013 spoilt ballot papers. The results of the referendum were counted and announced for each local authority area in Scotland.

i) Question on establishing a Scottish Parliament

Council	% Turnout	Yes	%	No	%
Aberdeen	53.4	65,035	71.8	25,580	28.2
Aberdeenshire	56.7	61,621	63.9	34,878	36.1
Angus	60.0	33,571	64.7	18,350	35.3
Argyll & Bute	64.6	30,452	67.3	14,796	32.7
Clackmannan	65.8	18,790	80.0	4,706	20.0
Dumfries & Galloway	63.1	44,619	60.7	28,863	39.3
Dundee	55.3	49,252	76.0	15,553	24.0
East Ayrshire	64.5	49,131	81.1	11,426	18.9
East Dunbartonshire	72.3	40,917	69.8	17,725	30.2
East Lothian	64.9	33,525	74.2	11,665	25.8
East Renfrewshire	68.0	28,253	61.7	17,573	38.3
Edinburgh	59.8	155,900	71.9	60,832	28.1
Falkirk	63.4	55,642	80.0	13,953	20.0
Fife	60.9	125,668	76.1	39,517	23.9
Glasgow	51.2	204,269	83.6	40,106	16.4
Highland	60.3	72,551	72.6	27,431	27.4
Inverclyde	60.0	31,680	78.0	8,945	22.0
Midlothian	64.9	31,681	79.9	7,979	20.1
Moray	57.5	24,822	67.2	12,122	32.8
North Ayrshire	63.1	51,304	76.3	15,931	23.7
North Lanarkshire	60.4	123,063	82.6	26,010	17.4
Orkney	53.2	4,749	57.3	3,541	42.7
Perthshire & Kinross	62.7	40,344	61.7	24,998	38.3
Renfrewshire	62.4	68,711	79.0	18,213	21.0
Scottish Borders	64.4	33,855	62.8	20,060	37.2
Shetland	51.3	5,430	62.4	3,275	37.6
South Ayrshire	66.4	40,161	66.9	19,909	33.1
South Lanarkshire	62.8	114,908	77.8	32,762	22.2
Stirling	65.5	29,190	68.5	13,440	31.5
West Dunbartonshire	63.4	39,051	84.7	7,058	15.3
West Lothian	62.3	56,923	79.6	14,614	20.4
Western Isles	55.3	9,977	79.4	2,589	20.6
Total	**60.2**	**1,775,045**	**74.3**	**614,400**	**25.7**

Referendum on Establishment of Scottish Parliament 1997 (contd.)

ii) Question on the Parliament having tax-varying powers

Council	Yes	%	No	%
Aberdeen	54,320	60.3	35,709	39.7
Aberdeenshire	50,295	52.3	45,929	47.7
Angus	27,641	53.4	24,089	46.6
Argyll & Bute	25,746	57.0	19,429	43.0
Clackmannan	16,112	68.7	7,355	31.3
Dumfries & Galloway	35,737	48.8	37,499	51.2
Dundee	42,304	65.5	22,280	34.5
East Ayrshire	42,559	70.5	17,824	29.5
East Dunbartonshire	34,576	59.1	23,914	40.9
East Lothian	28,152	62.7	16,765	37.3
East Renfrewshire	23,580	51.6	22,153	48.4
Edinburgh	133,843	62.0	82,188	38.0
Falkirk	48,064	69.2	21,403	30.8
Fife	108,021	64.7	58,987	35.3
Glasgow	182,589	75.0	60,842	25.0
Highland	61,359	62.1	37,525	37.9
Inverclyde	27,194	67.2	13,277	32.8
Midlothian	26,776	67.7	12,762	32.3
Moray	19,326	52.7	17,344	47.3
North Ayrshire	43,990	65.7	22,991	34.3
North Lanarkshire	107,288	72.2	41,372	27.8
Orkney	3,917	47.4	4,344	52.6
Perthshire & Kinross	33,398	51.3	31,709	48.7
Renfrewshire	55,075	63.6	31,537	36.4
Scottish Borders	27,284	50.7	26,497	49.3
Shetland	4,478	51.6	4,198	48.4
South Ayrshire	33,679	56.2	26,217	43.8
South Lanarkshire	99,587	67.6	47,708	32.4
Stirling	25,044	58.9	17,487	41.1
West Dunbartonshire	34,408	74.7	11,628	25.3
West Lothian	47,990	67.3	23,354	32.7
Western Isles	8,557	68.4	3,947	31.6
Total	**1,512,889**	**63.5**	**870,263**	**36.5**

Table 22.04: Referendum on Devolution for Wales 1979 (1 March)

Question:
Do you want the provisions of the Wales Act 1978 to be put into effect?

	Electorate	T'out %	Yes	%	No	%	Spoilt Ballot Papers
Clwyd	284,639	51.1	31,384	21.6	114,119	78.4	227
Dyfed	247,431	64.6	44,849	28.1	114,947	71.9	463
Gwent	319,387	55.3	21,369	12.1	155,389	87.9	189
Gwynedd	171,051	63.4	37,363	34.4	71,157	65.6	276
Mid Glamorgan	394,264	58.6	46,747	20.2	184,196	79.8	929
Powys	80,817	66.0	9,843	18.5	43,502	81.5	175
South Glamorgan	282,907	58.7	21,830	13.1	144,186	86.9	595
West Glamorgan	275,853	57.5	29,663	18.7	128,834	81.3	455
Total	**2,056,349** [1]	**58.3**	**243,048**	**20.3**	**956,330**	**79.7**	**3,309**

1. A provision of the Wales Act was that not less than 40% of persons entitled to vote voted 'Yes' in the referendum. The Secretary of State for Wales estimated that of the total electorate on March 1, 14,900 had died; 800 were convicted prisoners in prisons and 2,600 were students and nurses registered at more than one address. The official estimated number of the electorate was therefore reduced to 2,038,049 and of this the total 'Yes' vote was 11.9% and the 'No' vote was 46.9%. The turnout was increased to 58.6%.

Source: Welsh Office

Table 22.05: Referendum on Establishment of Welsh Assembly 1997 (18 September)

At the referendum 1,112,117 valid votes were cast, representing 50.1% of the Welsh electorate. There were 3,999 spoilt ballot papers. Of those voting, 559,419 (50.3%) agreed that there should be a Welsh Assembly and 552,698 (49.7%) did not agree. A 'Yes' majority of just 6,721.The results of the referendum were counted and announced for each local authority area in Wales.

Council	% Turnout	Yes	%	No	%
Anglesey, Isle of	56.9	15,649	50.9	15,095	49.1
Blaenau Gwent	49.3	15,237	56.1	11,928	43.9
Bridgend	50.6	27,632	54.4	23,172	45.6
Caerphilly	49.3	34,830	54.7	28,841	45.3
Cardiff	46.9	47,527	44.4	59,589	55.6
Carmarthenshire	56.4	49,115	65.3	26,119	34.7
Ceredigion	56.8	18,304	59.2	12,614	40.8
Conwy	51.5	18,369	40.9	26,521	59.1
Denbighshire	49.7	14,271	40.8	20,732	59.2
Flintshire	41.0	17,746	38.2	28,707	61.8
Gwynedd	59.8	35,425	64.1	19,859	35.9
Merthyr Tydfil	49.5	12,707	58.2	9,121	41.8
Monmouthshire	50.5	10,592	32.1	22,403	67.9
Neath Port Talbot	51.9	36,730	66.5	18,463	33.5
Newport	45.9	16,172	37.4	27,017	62.6
Pembrokeshire	52.6	19,979	42.8	26,712	57.2
Powys	56.2	23,038	42.7	30,966	57.3
Rhondda Cynon Taff	49.9	51,201	58.5	36,362	41.5
Swansea	47.1	42,789	52.0	39,561	48.0
Torfaen	45.5	15,756	49.8	15,854	50.2
Vale of Glamorgan	54.3	17,776	36.7	30,613	63.3
Wrexham	42.4	18,574	45.3	22,449	54.7
Total	**50.1**	**559,419**	**50.3**	**552,698**	**49.7**

Table 22.06: Referendum on Northern Ireland Remaining Part of the United Kingdom 1973 (8 March)

Question:
Do you want Northern Ireland to remain part of the United Kingdom?
OR
Do you want Northern Ireland to be joined with the Republic of Ireland outside the United Kingdom?

Electorate	T'out %	Remain part of UK	%	Joined with Republic	%	Spoilt Ballot Papers
1,018,712	58.7	591,820	98.9	6,463	1.1	5,973

Source: House of Commons Papers 1974-75 (Cmnd. 5875) xxviii, 1.

Table 22.07: Referendum on Northern Ireland Assembly and Associated Changes 1998 (22 May)

Electors in Northern Ireland were asked whether they supported 'the agreement reached at the multi-party talks on Northern Ireland and set out in Command Paper 3883?'.

T'out %	Yes	%	No	%	Spoilt Ballot Papers
81.1	676,966	71.1	274,879	28.9	1,738

Electors in the Republic of Ireland were asked whether they approved of 'the proposal to amend the Constitution contained in the 19th Amendment of the Constitution Act 1998?'.

T'out %	Yes	%	No	%	Spoilt Ballot Papers
55.6	1,442,583	94.4	85,748	5.6	17,064

Table 22.08: Referendum on Establishment of Greater London Authority 1998 (7 May)

At the referendum 1,709,172 valid votes were cast, representing 34.1% of the London electorate. There were 26,178 rejected ballot papers. Of those voting, 1,230,759 (72%) were in favour of the government's proposals for a Greater London Authority and 478,413 (28%) were not in favour. A 'Yes' majority of 752,346 or 44%. The results of the referendum were counted and announced for each London borough.

London Borough	% Turnout	Yes	%	No	%
City of London	30.6	977	63.0	574	37.0
Barking & Dagenham	24.9	20,534	73.5	7,406	26.5
Barnet	35.3	55,487	69.6	24,210	30.4
Bexley	34.7	36,527	63.3	21,195	36.7
Brent	35.6	47,309	78.4	13,050	21.6
Bromley	40.2	51,410	57.1	38,662	42.9
Camden	32.8	36,007	81.2	8,348	18.8
Croydon	37.2	53,863	64.7	29,368	35.3
Ealing	32.5	52,348	76.5	16,092	23.5
Enfield	32.8	44,297	67.2	21,639	32.8
Greenwich	32.3	36,756	74.8	12,356	25.2
Hackney	33.7	31,956	81.6	7,195	18.4
Hammersmith & Fulham	33.5	29,171	77.9	8,255	22.1
Haringey	29.9	36,296	83.8	7,038	16.2
Harrow	36.0	38,412	68.8	17,407	31.2
Havering	33.9	36,390	60.5	23,788	39.5
Hillingdon	34.4	38,518	63.1	22,523	36.9
Hounslow	31.8	36,957	74.6	12,554	25.4
Islington	34.1	32,826	81.5	7,428	18.5
Kensington & Chelsea	27.9	20,064	70.3	8,469	29.7
Kingston upon Thames	41.0	28,621	68.7	13,043	31.3
Lambeth	31.6	47,391	81.8	10,544	18.2
Lewisham	29.3	40,188	78.4	11,060	21.6
Merton	37.5	35,418	72.2	13,635	27.8
Newham	27.8	33,084	81.4	7,575	18.6
Redbridge	34.9	42,547	70.2	18,098	29.8
Richmond upon Thames	44.5	39,115	70.8	16,135	29.2
Southwark	32.3	42,196	80.7	10,089	19.3
Sutton	34.9	29,653	64.8	16,091	35.2
Tower Hamlets	34.1	32,674	77.5	9,467	22.5
Waltham Forest	33.6	38,344	73.1	14,090	26.9
Wandsworth	38.7	57,010	74.3	19,695	25.7
Westminster	31.5	28,413	71.5	11,334	28.5
Total	**34.1**	**1,230,759**	**72.0**	**478,413**	**28.0**

Table 22.09: Referendum on Establishment of a Regional Assembly for the North East Region 2004 (4 November)

At the referendum 893,829 valid votes were cast representing 47.2% of the North East region electorate. Of those voting, 197,310 (22.1%) agreed that there should be an elected assembly for the region and 696,519 (77.9%) did not agree.

Question:

Should there be an elected assembly for the North East region?

Local authority	Electorate	% Turnout*	Yes	% Yes	No	% No	Total valid	Total rejected
Alnwick	25,213	57.4	2,771	19.2	11,666	80.8	14,437	40
Berwick-upon-Tweed	21,468	52.3	2,250	20.7	8,597	79.3	10,847	378
Blyth Valley	63,884	45.5	7,523	26.2	21,178	73.8	28,701	348
Castle Morpeth	38,357	57.2	4,776	22.0	16,952	78.0	21,728	210
Chester-le-Street	43,032	49.5	5,487	26.0	15,610	74.0	21,097	209
Darlington	76,178	49.0	4,784	12.9	32,282	87.1	37,066	293
Derwentside	66,942	49.1	9,718	29.8	22,888	70.2	32,606	282
Durham	71,052	48.3	9,791	28.9	24,106	71.1	33,897	410
Easington	70,517	42.5	8,065	27.3	21,520	72.7	29,585	397
Gateshead	143,782	49.3	17,011	24.5	52,459	75.5	69,470	1,480
Hartlepool	68,636	42.9	4,887	16.8	24,240	83.2	29,127	340
Middlesbrough	100,706	42.1	7,977	19.2	33,543	80.8	41,520	871
Newcastle upon Tyne	178,531	46.4	19,984	24.5	61,477	75.5	81,461	1,405
North Tyneside	140,478	50.7	15,203	21.6	55,121	78.4	70,324	882
Redcar & Cleveland	103,769	50.6	8,493	16.4	43,250	83.6	51,743	791
Sedgefield	68,383	48.3	9,040	27.7	23,583	72.3	32,623	431
South Tyneside	114,377	46.3	11,329	21.6	41,029	78.4	52,358	547
Stockton-on-Tees	132,848	48.3	11,050	17.5	52,040	82.5	63,090	1,048
Sunderland	209,195	43.4	17,927	20.0	71,893	80.0	89,820	1,008
Teesdale	19,887	56.9	2,020	18.4	8,972	81.6	10,992	321
Tynedale	47,451	55.4	5,146	19.7	20,975	80.3	26,121	189
Wansbeck	46,636	46.6	5,947	27.7	15,503	72.3	21,450	267
Wear Valley	48,420	49.9	6,131	25.8	17,635	74.2	23,766	391
Total	**1,899,742**	**47.7**	**197,310**	**22.1**	**696,519**	**77.9**	**893,829**	**12,538**

* Total votes (both valid and rejected) divided by total eligible electorate.

Electoral Irregularities

Table 23.01: Election Petitions 1832-2006

	Void Elections[1]	Undue Elections[2]	Elections upheld[3]	Petitions withdrawn[4]	Total
GENERAL ELECTIONS					
1832	7	10	23	8	48
1835	5	7	9	13	34
1837	1	13	40	31	85
1841	10	15	11	36	72
1847	17	1	11	22	51
1852	30	3	29	60	122
1857	7	2	24	39	72
1859	10	1	23	26	60
1865	14	2	19	34	69
1868	21	1	43	37	102
1874	16	3	8	9	36
1880	19	0	15	19	53
1885	4	1	4	3	12
1886	0	2	2	0	4
1892	5	1	6	1	13
1895	2	0	6	2	10
1900	2	0	3	2	7
1906	2	0	3	1	6
1910(J)	3	0	1	1	5
1910(D)	5	1	4	3	13
1922	1	0	1	0	2
1923	1	0	0	0	1
1929	0	0	1	0	1
1955	0	1	0	0	1
1959	0	1	1	0	2
1964	0	0	1	0	1
1997	1	0	1*	0	2*
Total	**183**	**65**	**289**	**347**	**884**

* See below for details of the case in the Newark constituency.

	Void Elections[1]	Undue Elections[2]	Elections upheld[3]	Petitions withdrawn[4]	Total
BY-ELECTIONS					
1832-35	1	1	3	1	6
1835-37	0	4	4	2	10
1837-41	5	2	10	1	18
1841-47	4	2	6	8	20
1847-52	6	1	4	10	21
1852-57	4	1	7	15	27
1857-59	1	0	0	2	3
1859-65	2	1	6	11	20
1865-68	2	1	2	3	8
1868-74	5	2	8	4	19
1874-80	6	1	5	3	15
1880-85	4	1	3	0	8
1892-95	2	0	1	0	3
1895-1900	0	0	0	1	1
1955-59	0	1	0	0	1
1959-64	0	1	0	0	1
Total	**42**	**19**	**59**	**61**	**181**

Election Petitions 1832-2006 (contd.)

The details of the petition trials since 1918 are as follows:

Date	Constituency	Allegations	Result
April 1923	Derbyshire, North Eastern	Irregularities in the reception, rejection and counting of votes	Election upheld
May 1923	Northumberland, Berwick-upon-Tweed	Exceeding maximum permitted election expenses	Void election
May 1924	Oxford	Exceeding maximum permitted election expenses	Void election
October 1929	Plymouth, Drake	Bribery, etc.	Election upheld
September 1955	Fermanagh and South Tyrone	Elected member disqualified as a felon	Undue election
October 1955	Mid-Ulster	Elected member disqualified as a felon	Undue election
April 1960	Kensington, North	Irregularities by the Returning Officer	Election upheld
July 1961	Bristol South East	Elected member disqualified as a Peer	Undue election
December 1964	Kinross and West Perthshire	Corrupt and illegal practices (failure to include cost of party political broadcasts in return of election expenses)	Election upheld
October 1997	Winchester	Irregularities by the Returning Officer	Void election
March 1999	Newark	Corrupt and illegal practices (fraudulent return of election expenses)	Void election
		Conviction overturned	Election upheld on appeal

1. A 'void' election was one in which the result was quashed and a new writ issued.
2. An 'undue' election was one in which the Committee or Election Court found the successful candidate not duly elected and ruled that another candidate was entitled to be declared elected. This category includes double returns. See Appendix 14 of the fifth edition of this book.
3. An election 'upheld' was one in which the Committee of Election Court dismissed the petition and found the Member duly elected.
4. A 'withdrawn' petition includes a number of cases in which petitions lapsed due to a legal technicality or the Dissolution of Parliament. Also included in this category are some instances of petitioners failing to appear for the hearing. Petitions which were withdrawn after a hearing or trial commenced are not included in this category but are treated as elections upheld.

Sources:
Journals of the House of Commons.
O'Malley and Hardcastle's Reports on Election Petitions, Vols. 1-7.
The Table, Vol. 24, pp. 59-76 (Fermanagh and South Tyrone: Mid Ulster).
All England Law Reports, 1960, Vol 2, p. 150 and *Weekly Law Reports*, 1960, Vol 1, p. 762 (Kensington, North).
All England Law Reports, 1961, Vol 3, p. 354 and *Weekly Law Reports*, 1961, Vol 1, p. 577 (Bristol, South-East).
Scots Law Times, 1965, p.186 (Kinross and West Perthshire).
House of Lords Record Office.
Public Record Office.
Royal Courts of Justice.

Table 23.02: Undue Elections 1832-2006

An 'undue' election is an election at which a Committee of the House of Commons or Election Court found the successful candidate not duly elected and ruled that another candidate was entitled to be declared elected. Double and treble returns are excluded but a full list can be found at Appendix 14 in the fifth edition of this book.

GENERAL ELECTIONS

Election	Constituency	Won by	Awarded to	Date[1]
1832	Caernarvon Boroughs[2]	C	L	March 6, 1833
		L	C	May 22, 1833
	Coleraine	C	L	May 17, 1833
	Galway Borough	R	R	May 2, 1833
	Longford	R(2 cands)	C(2 cands)	April 2, 1833
	Mallow	R	L	April 24, 1833
	Petersfield	L	C	March 5, 1833
	Salisbury	C	L	May 6, 1833
	Southampton	C	L	April 2, 1833
1835	Canterbury	L	C	March 26, 1835
	Cork Borough	C(2 cands)	L(2 cands)	April 18, 1835
	*Cork County	L	C	June 5, 1835
	Dublin Borough	L(2 cands)	C(2 cands)	May 16, 1836
	Windsor	L	C	April 6, 1835
1837	Bedford	C	L	May 21, 1838
	Belfast	L(2 cands)	C(2 cands)	March 8, 1838
	Evesham	C	L	March 20, 1838
	Ipswich	L	C	February 26, 1838
	Kingston upon Hull	C	L	May 7, 1838
	Kinsale	L	C	April 11, 1838
	Norwich	C	L	May 14, 1838
	Petersfield	C	L	February 14, 1838
	Shaftesbury	L	C	April 3, 1838
	Stirlingshire	C	L	April 30, 1838
	Tralee	C	L	March 12, 1838
	Tynemouth & N Shields	L	L	February 3, 1838
1841	Athlone	C	L	June 10, 1842
	Clitheroe	L	C	March 21, 1842
	Flintshire	L	C	May 20, 1842
	Great Marlow	L	C	April 11, 1842
	Lewes	L	C	March 21, 1842
	Longford	R	C	April 18, 1842
	Lyme Regis	L	C	May 30, 1842
	**Wakefield	L	C	April 21, 1842
	Waterford Borough	C(2 cands)	L(2 cands)	June 10, 1842
	Weymouth & Melcombe Regis	C(2 cands)	L(2 cands)	April 4, 1842
	Wigan	C	L	April 11, 1842
1847	Dundalk	R	L	March 20, 1848
1852	Derby	C	L	March 9, 1853
	*Tavistock	L	L	February 21, 1853
1857	Sligo Borough	L	C	July 31, 1857
1865	Boston	L	L	March 21, 1866
	Bridgnorth	L	C	March 22, 1866

Undue Elections 1832-2006 (contd.)

GENERAL ELECTIONS

Election	Constituency	Won by	Awarded to	Date[1]
1868	Taunton	C	L	March 8, 1869
1874	Boston	L	C	June 23, 1874
	Wigtown Burghs	C	L	June 1, 1874
1886	Yorkshire, Buckrose	L	C	January 27, 1887
	Londonderry Borough	C	N	January 27, 1887
1892	Greenock	L	LU	August 9, 1892
1910(D)	Exeter	L	C	April 21, 1911
1955	**Fermanagh &South Tyrone	SF	C	October 25, 1955

BY-ELECTIONS

Election	Constituency	Won by	Awarded to	Date[1]
1832-35	Monaghan (1834)	L	C	July 30, 1834
1835-37	*Drogheda (1835)	L	C	June 29, 1835
	Carlow County (1835)	L(2 cands)	C(2 cands)	August 19, 1835
	Longford (1836)	L	C	May 4, 1837
1837-41	Devizes (1838)	L	C	May 25, 1838
	Carlow Borough (1839)	C	L	July 11, 1839
1841-47	**Newcastle-under- Lyme (1842)	L	C	July 22, 1842
	Bridport (1846)	C	L	April 27, 1846
1847-52	Horsham (1848)	C	L	September 4, 1848
1852-57	**Peterborough (1853)	L	L	August 15, 1853
1859-65	Barnstaple (1863)	L	C	April 15, 1864
1865-68	Helston (1866)	L	C	July 5, 1866
1868-74	Bewdley (1869)	C	L	April 30, 1869
	Galway County (1872)	HR	C	June 13, 1872
1874-80	**Tipperary (1875)	Ind N	C	May 27, 1875
1880-85	Evesham (1880)	L	C	January 6, 1881
1955-59	**Mid-Ulster (1955)	SF	C	October 25, 1955
1959-64	**Bristol, South-East (1961)	Lab	C	July 31, 1961

1. The dates given are those on which the House of Commons made an order for the Return of Members of Parliament to be amended. In a few cases the Clerk did not attend to amend the Return until a few days later. At Wigtown Boroughs (1874) and Londonderry Borough (1887) the Return did not require to be amended as in the case of Wigtown the member declared elected had been appointed a Judge and the seat was vacant, and at Londonderry the member had also been returned for another constituency but chose to represent Londonderry.

2. The only case where the result of a petition was reversed by a second petition.

* Lack of property qualification to be elected.

** Disqualified from being elected.

Table 23.03: Void Elections 1832-2006

The following is a list of constituencies in which on petition the election was declared void and a by-election would be held unless the House of Commons decided to suspend the issue of a new writ. The cause of the void election was bribery and/or corrupt practices unless otherwise stated. Double vacancies are indicated.

GENERAL ELECTIONS

Election	Constituency	Party
1832	• Carrickfergus	Conservative
	• Hertford	Conservative (2 vacs)
	Montgomery Boroughs	Conservative
	Oxford	Liberal
	*Tiverton	Liberal
	• Warwick	Conservative
1835	Carlow County	Conservative (2 vacs)
	*Drogheda	Liberal
	Ipswich	Conservative (2 vacs)
1837	*Marylebone	Liberal
1841	Athlone	Liberal
	Belfast	Conservative (2 vacs)
	Ipswich	Liberal (2 vacs)
	Newcastle-under-Lyme	Liberal
	Southampton	Conservative (2 vacs)
	• Sudbury[1]	Liberal (2 vacs)
1847	Aylesbury	Conservative
	Bewdley	Conservative
	Carlisle	Liberal (1 vac)
		Conservative (1 vac)
	Cheltenham	Conservative
	Derby	Liberal (2 vacs)
	Great Yarmouth	Conservative (2 vacs)
	Harwich	Conservative
	Horsham	Liberal
	Kinsale	Conservatlve
	Lancaster	Liberal
	Leicester	Liberal (2 vacs)
	Lincoln	Liberal
	*Sligo Borough	Repealer
1852	Barnstaple	Conservative (2 vacs)
	Berwick-upon-Tweed	Liberal (2 vacs)
	Blackburn	Liberal
	Bridgnorth	Conservative
	Cambridge	Conservative (2 vacs)
	Canterbury	Conservative (2 vacs)
	Chatham	Conservative
	Clare	Liberal (2 vacs)
	Clitheroe	Liberal
	^Frome	Liberal
	Harwich	Conservatlve
	Huddersfield	Liberal
	Kingston upon Hull	Liberal (2 vacs)
	Lancaster	Liberal

Void Elections 1832-2006 (contd.)

GENERAL ELECTIONS

Election	Constituency	Party
1852 (contd.)	Liverpool	Conservative (2 vacs)
	Maidstone	Conservative
	Maldon	Conservative (2 vacs)
	Plymouth	Conservative
	Rye	Liberal
	Sligo Borough	Liberal
	Taunton	Conservative
	Tynemouth and North Shields	Conservative
1857	* Beverley	Liberal
	Falkirk	Liberal
	Galway Borough	Liberal
	Great Yarmouth	Liberal (2 vacs)
	Mayo	Independent Opposition
	Oxford	Liberal
1859	Beverley	Conservative
	Clare	Liberal
	Dartmouth	Liberal
	Gloucester	Liberal (2 vacs)
	Kingston upon Hull	Conservative
	Norwich	Liberal (2 vacs)
	Roscommon	Conservative
	Wakefield	Liberal
1865	Bridgwater	Conservative
	^Cambridge	Conservative
	Devonport	Conservative (2 vacs)
	Helston	Liberal
	•Lancaster[1]	Liberal (2 vacs)
	Northallerton	Conservative
	Nottingham	Liberal (2 vacs)
	•Reigate[1]	Liberal
	•Totnes[1]	Liberal
	Windsor	Liberal (2 vacs)
1868	•Beverley[1]	Conservative (2 vacs)
	Bewdley	Conservative
	Blackburn	Conservative (2 vacs)
	Bradford	Liberal
	Brecon	Conservative
	•Bridgwater[1]	Liberal (2 vacs)
	•Cashel Borough[1]	Liberal
	Drogheda	Liberal
	Dublin Borough	Conservative
	Hereford	Liberal (2 vacs)
	Norwich	Conservative
	•Sligo Borough[1]	Conservative
	Stafford	Liberal (1 vac)
		Conservative (1 vac)
	Westbury	Conservative
	^^Wexford Borough	Liberal
	Youghal	Liberal

Void Elections 1832-2006 (contd.)

GENERAL ELECTIONS

Election	Constituency	Party
1874	Dudley	Liberal
	Durham	Liberal (2 vacs)
	Durham, Northern	Liberal (2 vacs)
	^^Hackney	Liberal (2 vacs)
	^^Haverfordwest Boroughs	Liberal
	Kidderminster	Conservative
	Launceston	Conservative
	^^Mayo	Home Ruler (2 vacs)
	Poole	Liberal
	Stroud	Liberal (2 vacs)
	Wakefield	Conservative
1880	Bewdley	Liberal
	• Boston	Conservative (1 vac)
		Liberal (1 vac)
	^Bute	Liberal
	• Canterbury	Conservative (2 vacs)
	• Chester	Liberal (2 vacs)
	Dungannon	Liberal
	Evesham	Liberal
	• Gloucester	Liberal
	Gravesend	Liberal
	Knaresborough	Liberal
	Lichfield	Conservative
	• Macclesfield[1]	Liberal (2 vacs)
	Plymouth	Conservative
	Tewkesburv	Liberal
	Wallingford	Liberal
1885	Barrow in Furness	Liberal
	Ipswich	Liberal (2 vacs)
	Norwich	Conservative
1892	Northumberland, Hexham	Conservative
	Meath, North	Nationalist
	Meath, South	Nationalist
	Rochester	Conservative
	Walsall	Conservative
1895	Staffordshire, Lichfield	Liberal
	Southampton	Conservative
1900	Maidstone	Liberal
	Monmouth Boroughs	Conservative
1906	Cornwall, Bodmin	Liberal
	Worcester	Conservative
1910(J)	Dorset, Eastern	Liberal
	Hartlepools, The	Liberal
	Kerry, East[2]	Independent Nationalist
1910(D)	Cheltenham	Liberal
	Cork, East	Nationalist
	Kingston upon Hull, Central	Conservative

Void Elections 1832-2006 (contd.)

GENERAL ELECTIONS

Election	*Constituency*	*Party*
1910(D) (contd.)	Louth, North	Nationalist
	West Ham, North	Liberal
1922	Berwick-upon-Tweed	National Liberal
1923	Oxford	Liberal
1997	^^Winchester	Liberal Democrat

BY-ELECTIONS

1832-35	Dungarvan (1834)	Liberal
1837-41	Maidstone (1838)	Conservative
	Cambridge (1839)	Conservative
	Ludlow (1839)	Liberal
	^^Totnes[3] (1839)	Conservative (1 vac)
		Liberal (1 vac)
1841-47	Ipswich (1842)	Conservative (2 vacs)
	Nottingham (1842)	Conservative
	Durham (1843)	Conservative
1847-52	^^Rye (1847)	Liberal
	Cheltenham (1848)	Liberal
	Sligo Borough (1848)	Liberal
	Aylesbury (1850)	Liberal
	Harwich (March 1851)	Conservative
	^^Harwich (May 1851)	Liberal
1852-57	Durham (1852)	Conservative
	Peterborough (1852)	Liberal
	Clitheroe (1853)	Liberal
	Barnstaple (1854)	Conservative
1857-59	Limerick Borough (1858)	Liberal
1859-65	^Norwich (1859)	Liberal
	Lisburn (1863)	Liberal
1865-68	Coventry (1867)	Liberal
	Bristol [2] (1868)	Conservative
1868-74	Longford County (1869)	Liberal
	Waterford Borough (1869)	Liberal
	Bristol (1870)	Liberal
	Mallow (1870)	Liberal
	Norwich (1870)	Conservative
1874-80	Galway Borough (1874)	Home Ruler
	St Ives (1874)	Conservative
	Stroud (May 1874)	Conservative
	Stroud (July 1874)	Liberal
	Horsham (1875)	Liberal
	•Norwich (1875)	Liberal
1880-85	•Oxford (1880)	Conservative
	•Sandwich[1] (1880)	Conservative
	Wigtown Burghs (1880)	Conservative
	Wigan (1881)	Conservative

Void Elections 1832-2006 (contd.)

BY-ELECTIONS

Election	*Constituency*	*Party*
1892-95	**Gloucestershire, Cirencester (1892)	Conservative
	Pontefract (1893)	Liberal

*   Lack of property qualification to be elected

** Tie after recount and scrutiny

^   Disqualified from being elected

^^ Irregularity by Returning Officer

•   Writ suspended. No by-election held

1. Subsequently disfranchised -see Appendix 11 in fifth edition of this book.
2. Parliament Dissolved before a by-election could be held.
3. Double return -see Appendix 14 in fifth edition of this book.

Table 23.04: Void Elections Caused by Returning Officer Irregularity 1832-2006

GENERAL ELECTIONS

Election	*Constituency*	*Remarks*
1868	Wexford	Failed to hold poll after a second candidate had been nominated on the hustings but who subsequently withdrew.
1874	Hackney	Failure to provide sufficient ballot boxes and consequently at two of the polling places no poll was taken and at several others the polling was delayed.
	Haverfordwest	Refused to accept a second nomination without the candidate providing £40 security for the Returning Officer's costs.
	Mayo	Failed to hold a poll after a second candidate had been nominated on the grounds that the candidate had not appointed an election agent.
1997	Winchester	Election result declared void by the High Court following an investigation into voting papers disqualified for want of the official mark.

BY-ELECTIONS

1839	Totnes	Failed to give proper notice of the poll.
1847	Rye	Failed to give proper notice of the poll.
1851	Harwich	Closed poll early.

Table 23.05: Successful Candidates Found to be Disqualified 1832-2006

GENERAL ELECTIONS

Election	Name	Party	Constituency	Reason
1841	J. Holdsworth	L	Wakefield	He was Returning Officer for the Constituency and although he delegated his duties at the election he was held to be disqualified.
1852	Hon. R.E. Boyle	L	Frome	Secretary of the Most Illustrious Order of St. Patrick.
1865	W. Forsyth	C	Cambridge	Standing Counsel to the Secretary of State for India.
1880	T. Russell	L	Bute	Partner in a firm which held a government contract.
1955	P.C. Clarke	SF	Fermanagh & South Tyrone	Felon

BY-ELECTIONS

1842	J.Q. Harris	L	Newcastle-under-Lyme	Bribery by his agent at a previous election.
1853	G.H. Whalley	L	Peterborough	Guilty of 'treating' at a previous election.
1859	Viscount Bury	L	Norwich	Bribery by his agents at a previous election.
1875	J. Mitchel	Ind N	Tipperary	Felon
1955	T.J. Mitchell	SF	Mid-Ulster	Felon
1961	A.N.W. Benn	Lab	Bristol South East	Peer (Viscount Stansgate)

Public Opinion Polls

Table 24.01: Predicting General Election Results 1945-2005 (GB)

This table shows the errors in the final predictions of the major public opinion polls forecasting the results of General Elections since 1945. An over-estimate of a party's share of the vote is recorded as a positive figure; an under-estimate as a negative one.

As surveys are not normally carried out in Northern Ireland (Marplan in 1970 did cover Northern Ireland but their forecast has been adjusted to provide only Great Britain figures for the sake of uniformity) the figures relate only to Great Britain.   Polls carried out by Business Decisions in 1974 (both elections), Research Services in 1951,1964, 1966 and 1979 and the Daily Express from 1950-64 have been omitted for reasons of space but details appeared in a previous (4th edition) of this book, pp. 117-119. Telephone polls carried out for the Sun in 1983 and 1987 by Audience Selection Limited have not been included. The final opinion poll findings for each company were published in the following sources:

Gallup: *News Chronicle* (1945-59); *Daily Telegraph* (1964-2001).

Harris: *Daily Express* (1970-74); *The Observer* (1983); TV-AM (1987); ITN (1992); *Independent* (1997).

Marplan: *The Times* (1970); *Birmingham Evening Mail* (February 1974); *The Sun* (October 1974 and 1979); *Guardian* (1983 and 1987).

MORI: *Evening Standard* (1979-83); *The Times* (1987-2001); *Evening Standard* (2005).

NOP: *Daily Mail* (1959-79); Northcliffe Newspapers Group, 1983; *The Independent* (1987 and 1992); Reuters (1997); *Sunday Times* (2001); *Independent* (2005).

ORC: *Evening Standard* (1970 - October 1974).

ICM: *The Guardian* (1992-2005).

Rasmussen: *Independent* (2001).

Populus: *The Times* (2005).

YouGov: *Daily Telegraph* (2005).

Election	% share (GB)	Gallup	Harris	MORI	Marplan	NOP	ORC
1945							
C	39.3	1.7					
Lab	48.8	-1.8	NO	NO	NO	NO	NO
L	9.2	1.3	POLL	POLL	POLL	POLL	POLL
Others	2.7	-1.2					
1950							
C	43.0	0.5					
Lab	46.8	-1.8	NO	NO	NO	NO	NO
L	9.3	1.2	POLL	POLL	POLL	POLL	POLL
Others	0.9	0.1					
1951							
C	47.8	1.7					
Lab	49.3	-2.3	NO	NO	NO	NO	NO
L	2.6	0.2	POLL	POLL	POLL	POLL	POLL
Others	0.3	-					
1955							
C	49.3	1.7					
Lab	47.3	0.2	NO	NO	NO	NO	NO
L	2.8	-1.3	POLL	POLL	POLL	POLL	POLL
Others	0.6	-					
1959							
C	48.8	-0.3				-0.8	
Lab	44.6	1.9	NO	NO	NO	-0.5	NO
L	6.0	-1.5	POLL	POLL	POLL	1.3[1]	POLL
Others	0.6	-0.1				-	

Predicting General Election Results 1945-2005 (GB) (contd.)

Election	% share (GB)	Gallup	Harris	MORI	Marplan	NOP	ORC
1964							
C	42.9	1.6				1.4	
Lab	44.8	1.7	NO	NO	NO	2.6	NO
L	11.4	-2.9	POLL	POLL	POLL	-3.5	POLL
Others	0.9	-0.4				-0.5	
1966							
C	41.5	-1.5				0.1	
Lab	48.8	2.2	NO	NO	NO	1.8	NO
L	8.6	-0.6	POLL	POLL	POLL	-1.2	POLL
Others	1.1	-0.1				-0.7	
1970							
C	46.2	-4.2	-0.2		-5.2	-2.1	0.3
Lab	43.9	5.1	4.1	NO	6.7	4.3	1.6
L	7.6	-0.1	-2.6	POLL	-0.5	-1.2	-1.1
Others	2.3	-0.8	-1.3		-1.0	-1.0	-0.8
1974(F)							
C	38.8	0.7	1.4		-2.3	0.7	0.9
Lab	38.0	-0.5	-2.8	NO	-3.5	-2.5	-1.3
L	19.8	0.7	2.2	POLL	5.2	2.2	1.4
Others	3.4	-0.9	-0.8		0.6	-0.4	-1.0
1974(O)							
C	36.7	-0.7	-2.1		-3.4	-5.7	-2.3
Lab	40.2	1.3	2.8	NO	2.8	5.3	1.6
L	18.8	0.2	0.5	POLL	0.7	0.7	0.6
Others	4.3	-0.8	-1.2		-0.1	-0.3	0.1
1979							
C	44.9	-1.9		0.1	0.1	1.1	
Lab	37.8	3.2	NO	-0.8	0.7	1.2	NOW
L	14.1	-0.6	POLL	0.9	-0.6	-1.6	HARRIS
Others	3.2	-0.7		-0.2	-0.2	-0.7	
1983							
C	43.5	2.0	3.5	0.5	2.5	3.5	
Lab	28.3	-1.8	-3.3	-0.3	-2.3	-3.3	NOW
L[2]	26.0	0.0	0.0	0.0	0.0	0.0	HARRIS
Others	2.2	0.2	-0.2	-0.2	-0.2	-0.2	
1987							
C	43.3	-2.3	-1.3	0.7	-1.3	-1.3	
Lab	31.5	2.5	3.5	0.5	3.5	3.5	NOW
L[2]	23.1	0.4	-2.1	-1.1	-2.1	-2.1	HARRIS
Others	2.1	-0.6	-0.1	-0.1	-0.1	-0.1	
1992					*ICM*		
C	42.8	-4.3	-4.8	-4.8	-4.8	-3.8	
Lab	35.2	2.8	4.8	3.8	2.8	6.8	NOW
L	18.3	1.7	-0.3	1.7	1.7	-1.3	HARRIS
Others	3.7	-0.2	0.3	-0.7	0.3	-1.7	

Predicting General Election Results 1945-2005 (GB) (contd.)

Election	% share (GB)	Gallup	Harris	MORI	ICM	NOP
1997						
C	31.5	1.5	-0.5	-3.5	1.5	-3.5
Lab	44.3	2.7	3.7	3.7	-1.3	5.7
L	17.2	-3.2	-2.2	-1.2	0.8	-3.2
Others	7.0	-1.0	-1.0	1.0	-1.0	1.0
2001			*Rasmussen*			
C	32.7	-2.7	0.3	-2.7	-0.7	-2.7
Lab	42.0	5.0	2.0	3.0	1.0	5.0
L	18.8	-0.8	-2.8	-0.8	0.2	-0.8
Others	6.5	-1.5	0.5	0.5	-0.5	-1.5
2005		*YouGov*	*Populus*			
C	33.2	-1.2	-1.2	-0.2	-1.2	-0.2
Lab	36.1	0.9	1.9	1.9	1.9	-0.1
L	22.6	1.4	-1.6	0.4	-0.6	0.4
Others	8.1	-1.1	0.9	-2.1	-0.1	-0.1

1. These polls published a combined forecast of the Liberal and Others vote. This figure is therefore the error in prediction of the Liberal and Others vote combined.

2. SDP/Liberal Alliance.

Table 24.02: Final Polls Compared with Winning Party and Lead at General Elections 1945-2005 (GB)

Election	Winning Party & % lead		Gallup	Harris	MORI	Marplan	NOP	ORC	ICM	Average error
1945	Lab	9.5	-3.5	-	-	-	-	-	-	3.5
1950	Lab	3.8	-2.3	-	-	-	-	-	-	2.3
1951	Lab	1.5[1]	-4.0	-	-	-	-	-	-	4.0
1955	C	2.0	1.5	-	-	-	-	-	-	1.5
1959	C	4.2	-2.2	-	-	-	-0.3	-	-	1.3
1964	Lab	1.9	-0.1	-	-	-	1.2	-	-	0.7
1966	Lab	7.3	3.7	-	-	-	1.7	-	-	2.7
1970	C	2.3	-9.3	-4.3	-	-11.9	-6.4	-1.3	-	6.6
1974(F)	C	0.8[2]	1.2	4.4	-	1.2	3.2	2.2	-	2.4
1974(O)	Lab	3.5	2.0	4.9	-	6.2	-11.0	3.9	-	5.6
1979	C	7.1	-5.1	-	0.9	-0.6	-0.1	-	-	1.7
1983	C	15.2	3.8	6.8	0.8	4.8	6.8	-	-	4.6
1987	C	11.8	-4.8	-4.8	0.2	-4.8	-4.8	-	-	3.9
1992	C	7.6	-7.1	-9.6	-8.6	-	-10.6	-	-7.6	8.7
1997	Lab	12.8	1.2	4.2	7.2	-	9.2	-	-2.8	4.9
			Rasmussen			*Populus*		*YouGov*		
2001	Lab	9.3	7.7	1.7	5.7	-	7.7	-	1.7	4.9
2005	Lab	2.9	-	-	2.1	3.1	0.1	2.1	3.1	2.1

1. Labour won 1.5% more votes in Great Britain than the Conservatives but the latter obtained a majority in the House of Commons.

2. Conservatives won 0.8% more votes in Great Britain than Labour but the latter formed a minority Government.

Table 24.03: Overall Record at General Elections 1945-2005 (GB)

Poll	No. of elections covered	Minimum % error[1]	Maximum % error[1]	Average % error[2]	Average error on lead
Gallup Poll	16	0.2	5.1	1.5	3.8
National Opinion Polls	13	0.1	6.8	1.9	4.9
Marplan	6	0.1	6.7	1.9	4.9
Harris Poll	7	0.2	4.8	1.9	5.6
MORI	7	0.1	4.8	1.3	3.6
Opinion Research Centre	3	0.3	2.3	1.1	2.5
ICM	4	0.7	4.8	1.3	3.8
Rasmussen	1	0.3	2.0	1.4	1.7
Populus	1	0.9	1.9	1.4	3.1
YouGov	1	0.9	1.4	1.2	2.1

1. These figures are based on the forecasts for Conservatives and Labour only.

2. These figures are based on the forecasts for Conservative, Labour, Liberal (SDP/Liberal Alliance 1983-87; Liberal Democrat 1992 onwards) and Others.

Table 25.01: Voting Intention (Gallup) 1945-1979

The voting intention figures in this table reflect the answers to the question: 'If there was a General Election tomorrow, which party would you support?', including the answers of the 'don't knows' to an additional question: 'Which would you be most inclined to vote for?'. Those respondents replying 'Don't Know' to this additional question as well are excluded from the analysis. The percentage of the total sample excluded in this way is shown in the column headed (DK %).

If there was more than one poll in any month the figures given are those of the poll published nearest to the 15th of the month.

Date	Con %	Lab %	Lib %	Others %	(DK %)	% Con Lead
1945						
February	27½	47½	12½	12½	(12)	-20
April	28	47	14	11	(15)	-19
June	32	45	15	8	(?)	-13
1946						
January	32	52½	11	4½	(7)	-20½
May	40	43½	13	3½	(8)	-3½
1947						
January	41	44½	12	2½	(8)	-3½
March	43½	43½	10½	2½	(13)	-
June	42½	42½	12½	2½	(11)	-
July	42½	42½	12½	2½	(11)	-
August	44½	41	11	3½	(17)	3½
September	44½	39½	11½	4½	(12)	5
November	50½	38	9	2½	(13)	12½
1948						
January	44½	43½	10½	1½	(15)	1
February	46	42	8½	3½	(17)	4
March	46	43	8½	2½	(17)	3
April	42½	41	10½	6	(15)	1½
May	45	41½	11	2½	(18)	3½
July	48	39½	9	3½	(12)	8½
August	48	41	8½	2½	(17)	7
September	47½	41	10	1½	(20)	6½
October	46½	41½	9½	2½	(18)	5
November	46	43	8½	2½	(17)	3
1949						
January	44	40½	13	2½	(14)	3½
February	44½	43½	9½	2½	(15)	1
March	41½	43	13	2½	(14)	-1½
April	42	43½	13	1½	(15)	-1½
May	46	40	11	3	(15)	6
June	46	41½	10	2½	(18)	4½
July	44½	40½	12½	2½	(13)	4
August	46½	40½	11½	1½	(14)	6
September	46	40	12	2	(15)	6
October	45½	39½	12½	2½	(19)	6
November	43½	40	14	2½	(13)	3½
December	45	41	12½	1½	(13)	4

Voting Intention (Gallup) 1945-1979 (contd.)

Date	Con %	Lab %	Lib %	Others %	(DK %)	% Con Lead
1950						
January	44	41½	12½	2	(7½)	2½
February	43	44½	12	½	(11½)	-1½
March	43½	45½	8½	2½	(8)	-2
April	45½	47	7	½	(9)	-1½
May	43½	46½	9½	½	(9)	-3
June	43½	46	9	1½	(9)	-2½
July	42	43½	11	3½	(10)	-1½
August	44½	46	8½	1	(9)	-1½
September	43	45½	10	1½	(12)	-2½
October	42½	45	10	2½	(11)	- 2½
December	43	44	11½	1½	(12)	-1
1951						
January	51	38	10	1	(13)	13
February	51½	37½	9½	1½	(13)	14
March	51	36½	10½	2	(14)	14½
April	50½	38½	9	2	(13)	12
May	49	40	9½	1½	(13½)	9
June	48	41	10	1	(12)	7
July	49	39	10½	1½	(13)	10
August	50½	38	10½	1	(11½)	12½
September	52	41	6½	½	(11)	11
October	50½	44	4½	1	(11½)	6½
December	47	45	6½	1½	(9)	2
1952						
January	44½	48	6	1½	(10½)	-3½
February	41	47	10½	1½	(14)	- 6
March	41½	48	9½	1	(9)	- 6½
May	43½	49	7	½	(9)	- 5½
June	40½	49	9½	1	(6½)	-8½
July	40	50	8½	1½	(9)	-10
September	41	48½	9	1½	(9½)	-7½
October	41½	48	9	1½	(11)	-6½
November	43½	46½	9	1	(12½)	-3
December	44	45½	9½	1	(11½)	-1½
1953						
January	42½	46	10	1½	(11)	-3½
February	42½	46	10	1½	(11)	-3½
March	46½	44½	8	1	(11½)	2
April	47	45	7½	½	(13)	2
May	47	45	7½	½	(12½)	2
June	46	46	7	1	(11½)	-
August	45	46	8	1	(13)	-1
September	44½	47½	7	1	(12)	-3
October	45	47½	7	½	(11½)	- 2½
December	45	47	7	1	(12½)	- 2

Voting Intention (Gallup) 1945-1979 (contd.)

Date	Con %	Lab %	Lib %	Others %	(DK %)	% Con Lead
1954						
January	45½	46½	7	1	(14)	-1
February	45½	47	7	½	(13)	-1½
March	46½	45½	7	1	(12)	1
April	46½	46	7	½	(13)	½
May	45½	47½	6½	½	(12)	-2
June	45	47½	7	½	(12½)	-2½
August	42½	48½	8	1	(11)	- 6
September	43	48	8	1	(11)	-5
October	45	45½	8	1½	(16)	-½
November	46	47	6	1	(15)	-1
December	48	49½	2½	-	(13)	-1½
1955						
January	46½	45½	7	1	(14)	1
February	46½	44½	8	1	(13)	2
March	46½	44½	8	1	(13)	2
April	48	44	7	1	(14)	4
May	51	47	2	-	(12½)	4
July	47	43	9	1	(11)	4
August	44½	47½	7	1	(14)	- 3
September	48	44	7	1	(10)	4
October	46½	44½	8	1	(13)	2
November	44½	45½	9	1	(12½)	-1
December	45½	46½	7½	½	(12)	-1
1956						
January	45½	46½	7½	½	(12)	-1
February	44	46	9	1	(12½)	-2
March	44½	47½	7	1	(19)	-3
April	43	48	8	1	(17½)	-5
May	43	47	9	1	(15)	-4
July	42	49	8	1	(14½)	-7
August	43½	49½	6	1	(16)	-6
September	43	46½	10	½	(15)	-3½
October	42½	47	9½	1	(15)	-4½
November	45	46	8½	½	(17)	-1
December	45	46	8	1	(15)	-1
1957						
January	43½	48½	7	1	(10½)	-5
February	42	48	8½	1½	(19)	-6
March	40	51½	7½	1	(21½)	-11½
April	41	51	7	1	(14½)	-10
May	41½	50	7½	1	(16½)	-8½
July	41½	49½	8	1	(16)	-8
August	40½	48½	10	1	(17)	-8
September	33½	52	14	½	(25)	-18½
October	37	49	13	1	(16½)	-12
November	38½	49	12	½	(19½)	-10½
December	41½	47½	9½	1½	(16)	-6

Voting Intention (Gallup) 1945-1979 (contd.)

Date	Con %	Lab %	Lib %	Others %	(DK %)	% Con Lead
1958						
January	40	47½	12	½	(17)	-7½
February	36	44½	18½	1	(19)	-8½
April	38	46½	15	½	(18½)	-8½
May	34	47	19	-	(18½)	-13
June	39½	43	17	½	(13)	-3½
August	42½	42	15	½	(14)	½
September	44	43	13	-	(17)	1
October	45½	41½	12	1	(15½)	4
November	46½	42½	10	1	(15)	4
December	47	42½	9½	1	(15)	4½
1959						
January	45½	45	8½	1	(19)	½
February	43	47	8½	1½	(22½)	-4
March	45½	47	6½	1	(22)	-1½
April	44½	44	10	1½	(14)	½
May	45	44	10	1	(14½)	1
June	45	43½	11	½	(14½)	2½
July	45½	41½	12½	½	(15½)	4
August	47½	41½	10	1	(13½)	6
September	50½	43½	5½	½	(17½)	7
October	48	46	5	1	(16)	2
November	48	44	7	1	(11)	4
December	47½	44	7½	1	(15)	3½
1960						
January	47	43½	8½	1	(16)	3½
February	47	43½	9	½	(16)	3½
March	47	42	10	1	(17)	5
April	45	42½	11½	1	(17)	2½
May	45½	42½	11	1	(15½)	3
June	45½	43	10½	1	(14½)	2½
July	47	43	9	1	(17)	4
August	47½	42	10	½	(16½)	5½
September	47½	40½	11	1	(16)	7
October	50	37	12½	½	(19)	13
November	46	40½	13½	-	(14)	5½
December	47½	37½	14	1	(15)	10
1961						
January	45	41½	12½	1	(19)	3½
February	44	42	13	1	(18½)	2
March	44	40	15	1	(12)	4
April	43½	40½	15	1	(18)	3
May	44½	40½	14	1	(18)	4
June	43½	40	15	1½	(16½)	3½
July	44	41½	14	½	(18)	2½
August	38	43	17	2	(17)	-5
September	40	45½	13½	1	(18)	-5½
October	43½	43½	12	1	(14½)	-
November	41½	43	14½	1	(17)	-1½
December	38½	43	17½	1	(20)	-4½

Voting Intention (Gallup) 1945-1979 (contd.)

Date	Con %	Lab %	Lib %	Others %	(DK %)	% Con Lead
1962						
January	42	42	15	1	(18½)	-
February	40	42½	17	½	(18)	-2½
March	39½	44	16	½	(18)	-4½
April	33	41	25	1	(12½)	-8
May	34½	39½	25½	½	(17)	-5
June	35½	39	25	½	(14)	-3½
July	35½	41½	22	1	(14½)	-6
August	34	43	22	1	(13½)	-9
September	34	45	20	1	(15)	-11
October	34½	43½	20	2	(17½)	-9
November	39	47	13	1	(16)	-8
December	37	46	16	1	(17½)	-9
1963						
January	35	48	16½	½	(8½)	-13
February	32½	48	18½	1	(8)	-15½
March	33½	50	15½	1	(9½)	-16½
April	34	49½	16	½	(10)	-15½
May	36	47	16	1	(10½)	-11
June	31	51½	16½	1	(8)	-20½
July	33½	51½	14	1	(12½)	-18
August	34	50	15	1	(11)	-16
September	33½	49	16½	1	(10½)	-15½
October	36½	48	14½	1	(11)	-11½
November	37½	49½	12	1	(10½)	-12
December	39	47½	13	½	(11½)	-8½
1964						
January	39	47½	13	½	(10½)	-8½
February	39	48	12	1	(9½)	-9
March	39	48½	12	½	(9)	-9½
April	38½	50½	10½	½	(8)	-12
May	39	50½	10	½	(7½)	-11½
June	41	50½	8	½	(7½)	-9½
July	40½	49½	9½	½	(6½)	-9
August	43	49½	7½	-	(8½)	-6½
September	44½	47	8	½	(7)	-2½
October	44½	46½	8½	½	(3½)	-2
November	38½	50	11	½	(7)	-11½
December	40	50½	9	-	(6½)	-10½
1965						
January	42½	46½	10½	½	(8)	-4
February	45½	45	9	½	(6)	½
March	43½	46	9½	1	(8)	-2½
April	39½	47½	12½	½	(9½)	-8
May	44	43	12½	½	(9½)	1
June	47	42½	9½	1	(9½)	4½
July	46½	45	8	½	(10½)	1½
August	49	41½	8½	1	(10)	7½
September	42	48½	8½	1	(6½)	-6½
October	41½	49	9	½	(7½)	-7½

Voting Intention (Gallup) 1945-1979 (contd.)

Date	Con %	Lab %	Lib %	Others %	(DK %)	% Con Lead
1965 (contd.)						
November	42	48½	8½	1	(8½)	-6½
December	40½	48½	10	1	(7½)	-8
1966						
January	42	47½	9½	1	(8)	-5½
February	42½	50	7	½	(10½)	-7½
March	40	51	8	1	(7)	-11
May	35½	53½	10	1	(6)	-18
June	39½	52	7½	1	(7)	-12½
July	41	48½	8½	2	(9)	-7½
August	44½	44	10½	1	(9½)	½
September	42½	45	11½	1	(8½)	-2½
October	43	44½	11½	1	(7)	-1½
November	44	42	12½	1½	(9)	2
December	42	46	10½	1½	(6½)	-4
1967						
January	42½	45½	10½	1½	(7½)	-3
February	37	48½	13	1½	(5½)	-11½
March	42½	42½	12½	2½	(9½)	-
April	45½	41½	11	2	(9)	4
May	46½	40	12	1½	(8½)	6½
June	48	41	9½	1½	(11)	7
July	43½	41	13	2½	(9½)	2½
August	43	42	13	2	(11½)	1
September	45	41½	10½	3	(9)	3½
October	45	38	14	3	(7)	7
November	46½	36	11½	6	(9)	10½
December	49½	32	12	6½	(9½)	17½
1968						
January	45	39½	11	4½	(10)	5½
February	52½	30	12½	5	(12)	22½
March	50	31	15	4	(13½)	19
April	54½	30	12½	3	(12½)	24½
May	56	28	11	5	(13)	28
June	51½	28	14	6½	(12)	23½
July	50	30	13	7	(10)	20
August	49½	34½	11½	4½	(11)	15
September	47	37	11½	4½	(8)	10
October	47	39	9½	4½	(9)	8
November	50½	32	14	3½	(9½)	18½
December	55	29½	11	4½	(11½)	25½
1969						
January	53	31	11½	4½	(11½)	22
February	54½	32	11	2½	(13½)	22½
March	52½	34	10	3½	(11½)	18½
April	51	30½	13	5½	(12½)	20½
May	52	30½	13½	4	(13)	21½
June	51	35	12	2	(12)	16
July	55	31½	11	2½	(12½)	23½
August	47	34½	15½	3	(12)	12½

Voting Intention (Gallup) 1945-1979 (contd.)

Date	Con %	Lab %	Lib %	Others %	(DK %)	% Con Lead
1969 (contd.)						
September	46½	37	13	3½	(9½)	9½
October	46½	44½	7	2	(10½)	2
November	45	41½	10	3½	(9½)	3½
December	50	39½	9	1½	(12)	10½
1970						
January	48½	41	7	3½	(10½)	7½
February	48	41	9	2	(10)	7
March	46½	41	9½	3	(10½)	5½
April	47	42½	7½	3	(9)	4½
May	42	49½	7	1½	(8)	-7½
June	42	49	7½	1½	(8)	-7
August	47	43½	7½	2	(9½)	3½
September	46½	44	8	1½	(10½)	2½
October	46½	46½	6½	½	(13½)	-
November	43½	48	6½	2	(12)	-4½
December	46	44½	6	3½	(12)	1½
1971						
January	42½	47	8½	2	(10½)	-4½
February	41½	49	8	1½	(10)	-7½
March	38½	50½	8	3	(11)	-12
April	44½	48	6	1½	(10)	-3½
May	38	50	9½	2½	(8)	-12
June	36	54	8	2	(11)	-18
July	33½	55	8½	3	(8)	-21½
August	42	48½	7	2½	(10½)	-6½
September	35	54	8½	2½	(10½)	-19
October	40	50	8	2	(8½)	-10
November	42½	48½	7	2	(12½)	-6
December	42	48	7½	2½	(13)	-6
1972						
January	40½	48	9	2½	(11)	-7½
February	40½	49	8½	2	(11)	-8½
March	39½	48½	9½	2½	(9½)	-9
April	43½	44½	10	2	(10)	-1
May	40½	46½	11	2	(8½)	-6
June	41	47	10	2	(9½)	-6
July	39	49	9½	2½	(8½)	-10
August	40	49	7½	3½	(11½)	-9
September	38½	49½	9½	2½	(9½)	-11
October	40	48	8½	3½	(10½)	-8
November	37½	45½	15	2	(10)	-8
December	38	46½	12½	3	(11½)	-8½
1973						
January	38½	44	15½	2	(11)	-5½
February	38	47	12½	2½	(10½)	-9
March	39	43	16	2	(9)	-4
April	38	41	17½	3½	(11)	-3
May	38	43½	14½	4	(7½)	-5½
June	41	42	14½	2½	(10)	-1

Voting Intention (Gallup) 1945-1979 (contd.)

Date	Con %	Lab %	Lib %	Others %	(DK %)	% Con Lead
1973 (contd.)						
July	35½	45	17½	2	(10)	-9½
August	31½	38	28	2½	(8½)	-6½
September	33½	43	22	1½	(9½)	-9½
October	33	39½	25½	2	(11)	-6½
November	36½	38½	22½	2½	(9)	-2
December	36	42½	18½	3	(10½)	-6½
1974						
January	40	38	19	3	(10½)	2
February	39½	37½	20½	2½	(3½)	2
March	35	43	19	3	(7½)	-8
April	33	49	15½	2½	(7)	-16
May	33	46½	17	3½	(7½)	-13½
June	35½	44	17	3½	(9)	-8½
July	35	38	21	6	(10½)	-3
August	35½	39½	21	4	(10)	-4
September	37½	40½	18	4	(10½)	-3
October	36	41½	19	3½	(5)	-5½
November	35	46½	14½	4	(9)	-11½
December	33	47	16½	3½	(10½)	-14
1975						
January	34	48½	13	4½	(11)	-14½
February	45	41	11	3	(11)	4
March	42	44	11	3	(7)	-2
April	43	45	10	2	(10)	-2
May	45½	39½	11	4	(11)	6
June	44	40½	13	2½	(11)	3½
July	43	40½	12½	4	(8)	2½
August	40½	42	14	3½	(8)	-1½
September	38½	41½	16½	3½	(10½)	-3
October	42½	40½	13½	3½	(6)	2
November	39	44½	12½	4	(11)	-5½
December	40½	41	14	4½	(10½)	-½
1976						
January	40½	42	14	3½	(11)	-1½
February	45½	40½	10½	3½	(11½)	5
March	44	41½	9½	5	(9)	2½
April	41	46½	9	3½	(8½)	-5½
May	44	41	10½	4½	(11½)	3
June	44	40½	11	4½	(11½)	3½
July	41	41	13	5	(11)	-
August	44	41	10	5	(12)	3
September	42½	42	11	4½	(10)	½
October	48	36½	11½	4	(13)	11½
November	55	30	11½	3½	(9)	25
December	49½	34	11½	5	(11½)	15½
1977						
January	47	34	14½	4½	(10½)	13
February	46	33½	14	6½	(13)	12½
March	49½	33	13	4½	(10)	16½

Voting Intention (Gallup) 1945-1979 (contd.)

Date	Con %	Lab %	Lib %	Others %	(DK %)	% Con Lead
1977 (contd.)						
April	49	33½	11½	6	(11½)	15½
May	53½	33	8½	5	(10)	19½
June	47½	37	10½	5	(10½)	10½
July	49	34½	10½	6	(11)	14½
August	48½	37½	9	5	(11½)	11
September	45½	41	8½	5	(8)	4½
October	45	45	8	2	(8½)	-
November	45½	42	8½	4	(10)	3½
December	44	44½	8	3½	(9½)	-½
1978						
January	43½	43½	8½	4½	(10)	-
February	48	39	9	4	(8)	9
March	48	41	8	3	(9)	7
April	45½	43½	7½	3½	(10)	2
May	43½	43½	8½	4½	(9)	-
June	45½	45½	6	3	(9)	-
July	45	43	8½	3½	(9½)	2
August	43½	47½	6	3	(11)	-4
September	49½	42½	6	2	(10½)	7
October	42	47½	7½	3	(8)	-5½
November	43	48	6½	2½	(11)	-5
December	48	42½	6	3½	(10½)	5½
1979						
January	49	41½	6	3½	(11)	7½
February	53	33	11	3	(11)	20
March	51½	37	8½	3	(11½)	14½
April	50	40	8	2	(5)	10
May	43	41	13½	2½	(5)	2
June	42	43½	12	2½	(6)	-1½
July	41	46	11½	1½	(8)	-5
August	41½	44	12½	2	(6½)	-2½
September	40½	45	12	2½	(9)	-4½
October	40½	45	12½	2	(9½)	-4½
November	39	43½	15½	2	(8½)	-4½
December	38	42	18	2	(7)	-4

Source: Social Surveys (Gallup Poll) Ltd.

Table 25.02: Voting Intention/Satisfaction Ratings/Economic Optimism (MORI) 1979-2006

The voting intention figures in this table reflect the answers to the question: 'How would you vote if there were a General Election tomorrow?', together with the answers of those undecided or who refused to say to a further question: 'Which party are you most inclined to support?'. From November 2002 onwards the voting intention figures given are for those 'absolutely certain to vote'.

The satisfaction rating of the government is the % 'satisfied' with the way it is running the country. The satisfaction ratings for the Prime Minister (named) and the leader of the Opposition (named) are the % 'satisfied' with the way they are doing their job minus the % 'dissatisfied'. Economic Optimism is measured as the % who think that 'the general economic condition of the country will improve' minus the % who think it will 'get worse'.

Note: From Feb 1981 to March 1988 'Lib' includes all those saying they would vote 'Liberal', 'SDP', or 'Alliance'. From March 1988 onwards the figure is for Liberal Democrat. SDP included with 'Other' from March 1988 to May 1990.

	Voting Intention					Satisfaction			Economic Optimism
	Con	*Lab*	*Lib*	*Other*	*Con lead*	*Govt.*	*P.M.*	*Opp.leader*	
	%	%	%	%	%	*Con*	*Thatcher*	*Callaghan*	
1979									
August	44	45	9	2	-1	34	2	18	-50
September	42	43	12	2	-1	33	-1	13	-53
October	41	46	11	2	-5	35	-3	13	-52
November	40	45	13	3	-5	30	-8	12	-58
1980									
January	40	43	14	3	-3	30	-11	-6	-64
February	38	46	14	2	-8	26	-18	-4	-58
March	38	46	13	3	-8	28	-19	10	-61
April	39	44	14	3	-5	33	-7	4	-55
June	41	43	13	3	-2	32	-10	-6	-49
July	37	47	13	2	-10	32	-19	1	-39
August	37	48	13	2	-11	30	-19	-7	-42
September	37	46	15	2	-9	27	-23	0	-42
October	34	50	15	2	-16	27	-24	*Foot*	-38
November	36	50	13	1	-14	25	-29	2	-41
1981									
January	35	45	17	4	-10	26	-28	-13	-34
February	33	41	25	2	-8	23	-31	-21	-37
March	28	38	32	2	-10	16	-36	-27	-41
April	30	38	29	3	-8	24	-27	-26	-22
June	31	39	28	3	-8	25	-27	-18	-31
July	30	36	31	2	-6	22	-31	-26	-35
August	30	39	29	2	-9	22	-35	-27	-18
September	27	38	33	2	-11	20	-37	-24	-35
October	27	31	40	2	-13	22	-35	-32	-30
November	27	27	43	2	-16	20	-36	-46	-24
December	27	29	43	1	-16	18	-41	-48	-27
1982									
Jan	29	30	40	1	-11	23	-29	-40	-13
Feb	30	33	34	3	-4	23	-33	-44	-27
March	34	34	30	2	0	29	-21	-37	-4
April	35	30	33	2	2	34	-12	-35	4
May	44	30	24	1	14	49	16	-49	6

Voting Intention/Satisfaction Ratings/Economic Optimism (MORI) 1979-2006 (contd.)

	Con %	Lab %	Lib %	Other %	Con lead %	Govt. Con	P.M. Thatcher	Opp.leader Foot	Economic Optimism
	Voting Intention					Satisfaction			
1982 (contd.)									
June	48	28	24	1	20	51	23	-51	8
July	45	31	22	1	14	42	10	-54	-17
August	44	30	23	2	14	40	6	-56	0
Sept	42	30	27	1	12	37	-2	-50	-22
Oct	43	32	24	2	11	38	0	-44	-3
Nov	43	35	21	2	8	41	3	-36	-4
Dec	42	35	22	2	7	38	2	-38	-21
1983									
Jan	44	36	19	-	8	42	4	-44	-21
Feb	46	32	21	-	14	41	4	-52	-10
March	43	28	27	1	15	42	2	-47	-1
April	46	33	21	1	13	41	5	-45	6
May	46	32	22	-	14	43	9	-39	14
June	43	27	29	1	16	-	20	-51	2
July	44	30	25	1	14	43	6	-	-10
August	46	30	22	2	16	46	13	-	-2
Sept	45	27	26	1	18	42	7	*Kinnock*	-15
Oct	42	37	19	2	5	39	1	20	-12
Nov	39	37	22	2	2	-	-	-	-
Dec	42	37	20	1	5	-	-	-	-
1984									
Jan	42	37	20	1	5	40	3	13	7
Feb	41	38	20	2	3	38	0	14	-4
March	41	40	17	1	1	38	-9	17	3
April	40	39	20	-	1	-	-	-	0
May	40	38	21	1	2	36	-9	2	-11
June	39	39	21	1	-	32	-15	0	-17
July	37	40	20	2	-3	-	-	-	-
August	39	39	21	1	-	32	-11	-7	-17
Sept	42	36	19	2	6	35	-10	-16	-21
Oct	44	35	20	2	9	37	2	-15	-26
Nov	43	35	19	3	8	36	-3	-15	-17
Dec	40	36	22	2	4	33	-10	-19	-22
1985									
Jan	42	34	21	3	8	33	-5	-16	-13
Feb	39	35	24	2	4	30	-12	-25	-24
March	36	40	23	1	-4	29	-19	-13	-22
April	38	37	24	1	1	31	-19	-16	-11
May	33	35	30	2	-2	26	-23	-20	-26
June	35	36	27	2	-1	29	-16	-18	-26
July	33	34	32	2	-1	28	-18	-20	-15
August	31	35	31	3	-4	26	-27	-20	-17
Sept	30	33	35	2	-3	28	-23	-19	-19
Oct	37	36	25	2	1	30	-16	4	-15
Nov	36	36	26	2	0	31	-16	0	-7
Dec	35	35	29	2	0	30	-14	9	-14

Voting Intention/Satisfaction Ratings/Economic Optimism (MORI) 1979-2006 (contd.)

	Con %	Lab %	Lib %	Other %	Con lead %	Govt. Con	P.M. Thatcher	Opp.leader Kinnock	Economic Optimism
1986									
Jan	33	38	28	2	-5	28	-24	0	-9
Feb	34	35	30	1	-1	23	-35	-9	-9
March	34	36	27	2	-2	27	-29	-11	-8
April	34	39	25	2	-5	26	-29	-7	-9
May	32	40	26	2	-8	23	-35	-3	-18
June	34	40	24	2	-6	25	-32	-5	-13
July	36	37	25	2	-1	26	-31	-11	-11
August	37	37	24	2	0	24	-38	-16	-22
Sept	35	37	26	2	-2	26	-27	-14	-15
Oct	39	41	17	2	-2	30	-20	0	-18
Nov	41	39	19	2	2	32	-17	-8	-10
Dec	39	38	22	2	1	34	-16	-14	-5
1987									
Jan	39	38	21	2	1	32	-19	-10	-2
Feb	39	36	23	2	3	33	-16	-23	-2
March	41	29	29	1	12	37	-6	-30	16
April	44	31	24	2	13	40	1	-30	14
June	49	31	18	3	18	48	10	-13	23
July	49	33	16	3	16	47	16	-10	19
August	48	36	14	2	12	44	3	-12	7
Sept	49	36	12	3	13	44	3	-11	5
Oct	47	37	14	2	10	45	6	-8	8
Nov	50	38	12	1	12	44	5	-10	7
Dec	48	36	15	1	12	43	2	-15	7
1988									
Jan	50	36	12	2	14	40	-1	-15	12
Feb	46	38	14	3	8	37	-3	-14	4
March	46	37	8	9	9	39	-2	-14	11
April	44	42	6	8	2	38	-9	-8	11
May	44	40	7	9	4	39	-8	-12	15
June	48	38	7	7	10	42	3	-23	5
July	46	41	8	5	5	41	-3	-27	-5
August	50	36	8	6	14	44	5	-31	-9
Sept	44	39	8	9	5	38	-1	-21	-18
Oct	44	39	8	9	5	40	-2	-15	-12
Nov	45	37	8	10	8	37	-1	-21	-28
Dec	46	36	6	12	10	41	0	-34	-24
1989									
Jan	47	36	8	9	11	38	-2	-27	-14
Feb	42	39	9	10	3	34	-7	-19	-18
March	44	40	6	10	4	36	-9	-22	-14
April	41	41	9	9	0	32	-13	-19	-28
May	41	43	7	9	-2	33	-14	-10	-21
June	37	47	4	12	-10	28	-26	-4	-30
July	36	45	4	15	-9	28	-27	-11	-19

Voting Intention/Satisfaction Ratings/Economic Optimism (MORI) 1979-2006 (contd.)

	Con %	Lab %	Lib %	Other %	Con lead %	Govt. Con	P.M. Thatcher	Opp.leader Kinnock	Economic Optimism
	Voting Intention					Satisfaction			
1989 (contd.)									
August	40	45	4	11	-5	31	-19	-8	-18
Sept	38	43	6	13	-5	30	-13	-8	-18
Oct	38	48	5	9	-10	27	-25	-1	-27
Nov	42	46	5	7	-4	28	-30	-2	-33
Dec	39	46	6	9	-7	28	-31	-5	-24
1990									
Jan	36	48	5	11	-12	25	-34	-1	-31
Feb	34	51	5	10	-17	19	-37	-3	-38
March	30	54	6	10	-24	16	-56	0	-43
April	31	54	6	9	-23	17	-54	-6	-37
May	35	48	8	9	-13	23	-44	-6	-31
June	38	49	8	5	-11	24	-32	-8	-24
July	38	46	10	6	-8	24	-35	-13	-19
August	35	50	10	5	-15	25	-30	-8	-43
Sept	38	45	12	5	-7	25	-23	-2	-46
Oct	33	49	14	4	-16	22	-37	3	-21
Nov	38	46	12	4	-8	22	-46	1	-24
Dec	41	45	9	5	-4	31	15 (*Major*)	-14	-20
1991									
Jan	46	41	9	4	5	41	46	0	-30
Feb	44	41	11	4	3	34	44	0	-27
March	40	40	16	4	0	30	31	-9	-1
April	42	40	15	3	2	32	33	-11	5
May	37	43	16	2	-6	27	13	-8	-1
June	39	41	15	5	-2	27	16	-8	-9
July	38	43	15	4	-5	26	20	-11	-7
August	42	40	14	4	2	32	27	-11	7
Sept	39	39	17	5	0	31	25	-20	13
Oct	39	45	12	4	-6	30	19	-8	5
Nov	40	42	15	3	-2	29	15	-13	3
Dec	38	44	14	4	-6	26	12	-22	-17
1992									
Jan	42	39	16	3	3	28	13	-19	-1
Feb	39	40	18	3	-1	25	4	-18	-2
March	38	41	17	4	-3	29	4	-7	4
April	43	38	16	2	5	40	20	-20	21
May	43	38	16	3	5	41	21	-28	18
June	42	39	16	3	3	34	12	-33	-3
July	39	43	15	3	-4	27	8	18 (*Smith*)	-18
August	41	44	13	2	-3	25	1	7	-32
Sept	37	43	16	4	-6	18	-27	12	-32
Oct	35	45	15	5	-10	10	-51	16	-46
Nov	34	47	15	2	-13	12	-44	12	-34
Dec	34	47	16	3	-13	14	-36	4	-16

Voting Intention/Satisfaction Ratings/Economic Optimism (MORI) 1979-2006 (contd.)

	Con %	Lab %	Lib %	Other %	Con lead %	Govt. Con	P.M. Major	Opp.leader Smith	Economic Optimism
1993									
Jan	37	45	14	4	-8	17	-30	-2	-16
Feb	34	46	16	4	-12	14	-36	-1	-21
March	32	47	17	4	-15	13	-41	2	-9
April	32	46	20	2	-14	17	-37	1	14
May	28	44	24	4	-16	12	-50	-8	3
June	28	46	23	3	-18	10	-54	-7	-7
July	27	44	25	4	-17	12	-54	-3	7
August	28	42	25	4	-14	12	-49	-4	5
Sept	29	43	25	3	-14	11	-50	-4	-8
Oct	29	45	23	3	-16	11	-46	7	-11
Nov	29	47	22	3	-18	13	-50	3	-5
Dec	29	47	20	4	-18	13	-44	4	-6
1994									
Jan	28	48	20	4	-20	13	-50	0	-3
Feb	28	47	21	4	-19	11	-46	0	-14
March	27	49	20	4	-22	12	-52	0	-14
April	26	47	23	4	-21	11	-55	-4	-7
May	27	46	23	4	-19	12	-49	-	0
June	24	52	20	4	-28	11	-54	-	-9
July	23	51	21	5	-28	10	-54	*Blair*	-9
August	23	56	18	3	-33	11	-59	18	1
Sept	25	54	17	4	-29	12	-44	14	-9
Oct	25	57	14	4	-32	14	-39	27	-5
Nov	24	55	17	4	-31	12	-47	21	-6
Dec	22	61	13	4	-39	8	-56	31	-16
1995									
Jan	27	56	14	3	-29	10	-53	22	-14
Feb	24	58	14	4	-34	9	-51	26	-27
March	25	57	13	5	-32	11	-48	30	-18
April	26	56	15	3	-30	9	-47	23	-16
May	22	58	16	4	-36	10	-49	28	-18
June	29	56	13	3	-27	14	-36	29	-11
July	26	59	12	3	-33	11	-41	27	-20
August	25	56	15	4	-31	13	-39	17	-17
Sept	28	51	16	5	-23	14	-34	16	-19
Oct	27	56	13	4	-29	15	-36	26	-16
Nov	26	56	14	4	-30	15	-41	27	-18
Dec	28	55	13	4	-27	14	-36	25	-16
1996									
Jan	29	55	13	2	-26	14	-39	22	-11
Feb	26	57	14	3	-31	13	-40	19	-18
March	28	57	13	2	-29	14	-39	27	-17
April	28	54	14	4	-26	15	-33	22	-6
May	27	54	15	4	-27	14	-40	19	-10
June	31	52	12	5	-21	18	-32	19	-3
July	29	53	12	6	-24	15	-35	11	-9

Voting Intention/Satisfaction Ratings/Economic Optimism (MORI) 1979-2006 (contd.)

	Con %	Lab %	Lib %	Other %	Con lead %	Govt. Con	P.M. Major	Opp.leader Blair	Economic Optimism
	Con	*Lab*	*Lib*	*Other*	*Con lead*	*Govt.*	*P.M.*	*Opp.leader*	
1996 (contd.)									
August	30	51	13	5	-21	16	-34	9	2
Sept	29	52	14	4	-23	17	-32	7	-1
Oct	28	56	12	3	-28	18	-30	24	-1
Nov	33	50	12	4	-17	22	-19	21	0
Dec	30	51	13	4	-21	18	-32	14	-9
1997									
Jan	30	55	11	4	-25	21	-30	18	0
Feb	31	52	11	3	-21	21	-24	16	2
March	29	50	14	5	-21	23	-27	22	1
April	-	-	-	-	-	26	-26	19	13
						Labour	*Blair*		
May	-	-	-	-	-	46	60	*Hague*	28
June	24	58	15	3	-34	53	65	-1	19
July	23	57	15	5	-34	53	59	-3	10
August	28	54	15	3	-26	48	46	-6	-2
Sept	25	59	13	3	-34	57	62	-28	17
Oct	24	60	12	3	-36	55	57	-18	7
Nov	24	56	16	4	-32	52	50	-34	6
Dec	26	55	15	5	-29	43	34	-30	-4
1998									
Jan	28	54	14	4	-26	46	31	-23	-1
Feb	28	52	15	5	-24	44	29	-19	2
March	28	53	14	5	-25	46	34	-16	4
April	27	55	14	4	-28	54	46	-15	1
May	26	55	14	5	-29	52	44	-25	1
June	27	56	13	5	-29	49	34	-23	-19
July	28	53	14	6	-25	50	34	-25	-21
August	28	52	14	6	-24	47	39	-23	-27
Sept	24	56	15	4	-32	45	31	-31	-37
Oct	26	53	16	5	-27	47	33	-25	-46
Nov	29	53	13	4	-24	49	32	-21	-31
Dec	27	54	12	6	-27	46	31	-27	-30
1999									
Jan	24	56	14	6	-32	45	28	-27	-23
Feb	30	51	14	2	-21	45	24	-30	-15
March	27	54	13	5	-27	47	32	-26	-6
April	25	56	13	6	-31	50	35	-31	-8
May	28	52	14	6	-24	46	24	-35	-1
June	28	51	13	8	-23	45	22	-27	-4
July	28	51	14	7	-23	43	22	-23	3
August	27	49	17	7	-22	39	10	-32	-12
Sept	25	52	17	6	-27	47	24	-27	5
Oct	28	56	11	5	-28	42	16	-28	-7
Nov	25	55	14	5	-30	44	18	-19	4
Dec	28	54	13	5	-26	45	22	-30	1

Voting Intention/Satisfaction Ratings/Economic Optimism (MORI) 1979-2006 (contd.)

	Voting Intention					Satisfaction			Economic Optimism
	Con	*Lab*	*Lib*	*Other*	*Con lead*	*Govt.*	*P.M.*	*Opp.leader*	
	%	%	%	%	%	Lab	Blair	Hague	
2000									
January	30	50	15	5	-20	37	53	19	+2
February	29	50	15	6	-21	35	49	22	-10
March	29	50	14	7	-21	37	47	26	-5
April	27	51	15	7	-24	38	52	24	-13
May	32	48	15	5	-16	36	47	27	-11
June	34	47	14	5	-13	28	39	29	-14
July	33	49	12	6	-16	29	42	29	-10
August	29	51	15	5	-22	33	45	26	-7
September	39	35	21	5	4	26	32	23	-17
October	32	45	17	6	-13	29	37	28	-13
November	33	48	13	6	-15	35	42	26	-6
December	32	47	16	5	-15	34	43	25	-6
2001									
January	31	50	14	5	-19	37	47	25	-9
February	30	50	14	6	-20	39	48	25	-2
March	31	50	14	5	-19	40	47	25	-29
April	30	50	13	7	-20	37	44	25	-22
May	30	55	11	4	-25	-	-	-	-
June	25	49	19	7	-24	45	55	23	-4
July	25	52	17	6	-27	42	51	n/a	-15
August	25	53	16	6	-28	40	49	n/a	-31
								Duncan Smith	
September	27	53	15	5	-28	54	67	15	-56
October	25	57	13	5	-32	50	65	22	-43
November	25	56	15	4	-31	52	64	24	-29
December					*No Poll in December*				
2002									
January	27	51	16	6	-24	43	51	25	-20
February	28	51	16	5	-23	37	46	27	-21
March	28	47	19	6	-19	33	42	23	-21
April	27	50	16	7	-23	41	46	26	-5
May	30	46	17	7	-16	33	39	26	-22
June	29	48	17	6	-19	36	46	24	-17
July	27	48	18	7	-21	34	42	22	-27
August	25	53	16	6	-28	-	-	-	-
September	27	53	15	5	-26	37	42	22	-23
October	25	57	13	5	-32	-	-	-	-23
November	30	42	21	7	-12	32	40	22	-32
December	33	37	24	6	-4	32	38	19	-40
2003									
January	31	40	22	7	-9	26	33	18	-46
February	29	41	22	8	-12	25	31	16	-50
March	29	43	21	8	-14	35	43	21	-39
April	29	43	21	6	-14	35	47	22	-18
May	31	39	22	7	-8	30	38	23	-24
June	32	41	19	8	0	25	31	21	-20

Voting Intention/Satisfaction Ratings/Economic Optimism (MORI) 1979-2006 (contd.)

	Con %	Lab %	Lib %	Other %	Con lead %	Govt. Lab	P.M. Blair	Opp.leader Duncan Smith	Economic Optimism
2003 (contd.)									
July	38	35	21	6	3	26	32	25	-22
August	34	36	24	6	-2	24	30	20	-26
September	31	40	21	8	-9	27	29	19	-23
October	35	38	21	7	-3	25	31	22	-25
								Howard	
November	35	36	22	7	-1	27	32	26	-27
December	31	40	22	7	-9	29	36	22	-20
2004									
January	35	37	21	7	-2	25	32	30	-21
February	35	36	21	8	-1	27	31	29	-18
March	35	35	23	7	0	25	32	31	-22
April	34	36	22	8	-2	26	31	28	-18
May	34	35	18	14	-1	26	29	30	-25
June	31	34	19	15	-3	27	30	26	-22
July	31	32	24	13	-1	27	30	26	-16
August	32	36	21	11	-4	28	29	26	-27
September	33	32	25	10	1	29	32	26	-22
October	29	39	22	10	-10	28	30	23	-26
November	31	35	23	11	-4	28	32	23	-23
December	30	35	26	9	-5	31	33	22	-22
2005									
January	32	38	22	8	-6	32	33	22	-19
February	37	39	18	7	-2	31	35	25	-11
March	37	37	20	6	0	31	34	31	-15
April	32	39	22	7	-7	-	-	-	-11
May	30	37	26	7	-7	38	39	28	-20
June	29	42	21	8	-13	34	39	23	-14
July	28	41	25	6	-13	37	44	25	-18
August	31	39	24	6	-8	36	39	25	-25
September	29	39	25	7	-10	29	31	-	-35
October	34	40	21	5	-6	35	36	-	-32
November	32	42	19	7	-10	33	37	-	-27
December	40	31	21	8	9	31	33	22	-22
2006									
January	40	38	17	6	2	32	36	31	-23
February	35	38	20	7	-3	28	31	31	-28
March	34	39	19	8	-5	27	31	32	-26
April	30	30	25	15	4	22	29	29	-30
May	41	31	18	10	10	22	26	33	-32
June	36	33	21	10	3	27	32	32	-25
July	36	32	24	8	4	23	23	29	-33
August/Sept.	35	36	19	10	-1	24	26	30	-31
October	35	37	18	10	-2	27	32	31	-23
November	35	33	20	12	2	22	27	25	-33
December	37	36	18	9	1	26	30	28	-27

Source: MORI (Market and Opinion Research International). From 2005 Ipsos MORI.

Table 25.03: Voting Intention in Scotland 1974-2005 (System 3 Polls)

The voting intention figures in this table reflect the answers to a question about how respondents would vote in a U.K. parliament election. System 3 do not poll in December, but conduct 2 surveys in January. Throughout, the January figures are the average of these 2 polls.

From February 1976 to November 1979 inclusive, support for the break-away 'Scottish Labour Party' was also recorded.

Note: From September 1981 to February 1988 inclusive 'Lib' is a combined figure for the 'SDP/Liberal Alliance'.

	Con	Lab	Lib	SNP	Lab lead
1974					
October	16	47	4	33	14
November	22	40	6	32	8
1975					
January	24	40	6	30	10
February	28	40	3	29	11
March	29	40	6	24	11
April	31	37	5	27	6
May	28	40	5	26	12
June	33	39	5	24	6
July	39	42	5	22	3
August	32	38	5	24	6
September	34	35	4	27	1
October	30	39	4	26	9
November	26	42	5	26	16
1976					
January	28	32	4	36	-4
February	28	24	6	33	-9
March	28	34	4	29	5
April	28	31	5	30	1
May	32	35	4	25	3
June	32	34	4	27	2
July	31	33	5	27	2
August	31	30	4	30	-1
September	30	30	9	28	0
October	31	31	3	31	0
November	35	24	7	32	-11
1977					
January	29	31	6	32	-1
February	32	29	5	31	-3
March	27	27	5	36	-9
April	31	28	6	31	-3
May	26	33	4	35	-2
June	31	28	6	32	-4
July	26	32	5	33	-1
August	32	29	5	30	-3
September	32	31	6	28	-1
October	30	36	6	26	6
November	27	35	5	30	5
1978					
January	28	36	6	29	7
February	30	35	5	27	5
March	29	38	4	27	9

Voting Intention in Scotland 1974-2005 (System 3 Polls) (contd.)

	Con	Lab	Lib	SNP	Lab lead
1978 (contd.)					
April	24	47	3	24	23
May	27	47	4	20	20
June	26	47	4	22	21
July	30	48	4	18	18
August	24	52	3	18	28
September	27	48	4	19	21
October	23	51	3	21	28
November	25	48	4	21	23
1979					
January	31	43	4	21	12
February	37	40	4	18	3
March	29	45	6	19	16
April	30	42	11	17	12
June	21	53	7	17	32
July	29	47	8	12	18
August	23	54	6	16	31
September	25	51	9	13	26
October	31	42	9	17	11
November	22	53	8	15	31
1980					
January	24	51	8	14	27
February	27	49	10	14	22
March	29	46	10	14	17
April	24	53	7	16	29
May	23	53	8	15	30
June	22	52	9	15	30
July	21	53	8	17	32
August	20	57	9	14	37
September	19	59	7	15	40
October	21	54	10	15	33
November	18	56	9	16	38
1981					
January	19	47	13	18	28
February	16	54	9	17	37
March	17	46	10	22	24
April	15	51	11	19	32
May	18	51	11	18	33
June	15	55	9	18	37
July	18	51	9	18	33
August	17	51	9	19	32
September	15	52	16	17	35
October	14	42	22	21	20
November	15	40	27	17	13
1982					
January	19	39	25	17	14
February	17	46	18	18	28
March	19	39	23	19	16
April	23	42	20	15	19
May	25	46	14	15	21

Voting Intention in Scotland 1974-2005 (System 3 Polls) (contd.)

	Con	*Lab*	*Lib*	*SNP*	*Lab lead*
1982 (contd.)					
June	27	43	16	14	16
July	22	44	17	16	22
August	24	42	16	18	18
September	20	48	18	14	28
October	26	46	16	12	20
November	28	45	14	11	17
1983					
January	30	46	11	13	16
February	22	47	18	13	25
March	25	49	14	13	24
April	25	48	15	10	23
May	32	42	14	12	10
June	25	40	24	11	15
July	27	40	18	13	13
August	27	40	22	11	13
September	25	42	23	10	17
October	27	47	15	11	20
November	25	48	14	11	23
1984					
January	24	48	17	11	24
February	23	51	13	12	28
March	19	58	12	10	39
April	22	53	14	12	31
May	22	52	14	12	30
June	21	49	17	12	28
July	19	54	13	14	35
August	23	50	14	12	27
September	22	44	18	15	22
October	26	47	15	11	21
November	26	46	15	13	20
1985					
January	25	45	16	14	20
February	19	47	20	14	27
March	20	45	21	14	24
April	17	50	18	14	32
May	17	50	22	12	28
June	15	52	19	13	33
July	17	47	24	12	23
August	15	47	24	15	23
September	18	41	28	13	13
October	22	45	21	12	23
November	19	42	22	15	20
1986					
January	15	46	22	16	24
February	16	44	24	16	20
March	14	47	23	16	24
April	20	45	20	15	25
May	17	49	20	14	29
June	19	44	19	17	25

Voting Intention in Scotland 1974-2005 (System 3 Polls) (contd.)

	Con	*Lab*	*Lib*	*SNP*	*Lab lead*
1986 (contd.)					
July	21	44	21	15	23
August	15	47	22	15	25
September	16	50	16	18	32
October	22	52	13	13	30
November	19	49	14	18	30
1987					
January	19	49	18	14	30
February	19	50	20	11	30
March	18	42	25	14	17
April	21	42	23	13	19
May	19	45	19	17	26
June	21	49	15	15	28
July	19	53	14	14	34
August	24	48	15	12	24
September	23	50	12	14	27
October	22	50	15	12	28
November	23	45	16	16	22
1988					
January	23	49	13	16	26
February	18	51	13	18	33
March	23	48	8	18	25
April	22	49	6	21	27
May	22	46	6	22	24
June	25	40	8	23	15
July	25	44	6	22	19
August	23	49	2	21	26
September	23	47	6	19	24
October	23	45	8	20	22
November	21	39	7	30	9
1989					
January	20	39	8	30	9
February	20	41	8	27	14
March	20	41	7	27	14
April	19	42	8	27	15
May	21	47	5	25	22
June	19	46	5	24	22
July	21	45	6	22	23
August	16	48	5	22	26
September	19	48	7	18	29
October	18	55	5	17	37
November	21	49	5	20	28
1990					
January	19	49	6	20	29
February	21	52	5	17	31
March	15	54	7	20	34
April	19	49	8	20	29
May	17	49	5	23	26
June	19	48	6	23	25
July	19	52	4	20	32

282

Voting Intention in Scotland 1974-2005 (System 3 Polls) (contd.)

	Con	*Lab*	*Lib*	*SNP*	*Lab lead*
1990 (contd.)					
August	22	49	5	20	27
September	19	42	10	24	18
October	16	48	9	24	24
November	24	43	7	23	19
1991					
January	26	45	8	21	19
February	23	46	6	22	23
March	23	42	10	22	19
April	27	42	11	18	15
May	23	44	11	20	21
June	25	46	9	16	21
July	24	46	8	20	22
August	25	45	8	19	20
September	24	43	9	23	19
October	23	41	10	24	17
November	18	44	13	23	21
1992					
January	22	43	11	24	19
February	22	38	10	28	10
March	22	44	7	26	18
May	26	39	10	23	13
June	24	44	8	22	20
July	25	44	8	22	19
August	23	46	10	20	23
September	20	42	10	27	15
October	20	47	9	23	24
November	18	48	10	22	26
1993					
January	21	44	10	23	21
February	18	43	11	26	17
March	17	49	11	22	27
April	21	47	9	21	26
May	16	45	16	23	22
June	16	46	12	25	21
July	17	45	13	24	21
August	15	45	16	24	21
September	17	43	15	24	19
October	14	48	12	25	23
November	15	47	14	23	24
1994					
January	16	47	14	23	24
February	13	47	14	25	22
March	13	46	14	26	20
April	14	44	14	27	17
May	10	53	12	24	29
June	12	46	11	30	16
July	12	51	9	27	24
August	12	55	8	24	31
September	11	51	9	29	22

Voting Intention in Scotland 1974-2005 (System 3 Polls) (contd.)

	Con	*Lab*	*Lib*	*SNP*	*Lab lead*
1994 (contd.)					
October	13	47	10	27	20
November	12	55	8	25	30
1995					
January	12	56	10	23	33
February	11	52	10	25	27
March	11	53	9	25	28
April	13	52	12	22	30
May	11	53	9	27	26
June	11	57	8	23	34
July	12	54	11	22	32
August	12	52	8	26	26
September	13	46	11	30	16
October	13	52	10	23	29
November	13	57	8	21	36
1996					
January	12	53	11	23	30
February	12	54	9	23	31
March	13	54	10	23	31
April	13	53	9	23	30
May	12	54	8	24	30
June	15	54	9	25	29
July	15	51	10	23	28
August	15	48	7	29	19
September	13	49	12	24	25
October	11	55	8	23	32
November	12	53	10	24	29
1997					
January	16	51	9	24	27
February	16	46	10	26	20
March	17	52	9	20	32
April	14	49	11	24	25
May	9	57	10	23	34
June	12	54	10	23	31
July	10	54	9	24	30
August	14	50	11	25	25
September	13	55	9	23	32
October	14	55	8	22	33
November	12	51	12	24	27
1998					
January	12	50	11	26	24
February	14	46	11	28	18
March	12	48	9	28	20
April	14	44	10	30	14
May	14	46	10	29	17
June	14	43	9	33	10
July	13	48	8	28	20
August	13	46	8	31	15
September	13	45	10	31	14
October	14	43	12	29	14

Voting Intention in Scotland 1974-2005 (System 3 Polls) (contd.)

	Con	*Lab*	*Lib*	*SNP*	*Lab lead*
1998 (contd.)					
November	13	42	13	31	11
1999					
January	11	45	10	32	13
February	14	44	11	29	15
March	13	50	13	22	28
May	13	47	14	22	25
June	13	49	10	24	25
July	13	49	11	24	25
August	16	46	12	24	22
September	14	42	13	29	13
October	12	45	13	27	18
November	12	50	11	24	26
2000					
January	14	49	11	24	25
February	15	45	11	27	18
March	16	40	11	29	11
April	17	44	9	26	18
May	14	48	10	24	24
June	17	39	11	31	8
July	15	46	9	26	20
August	15	45	9	28	17
September	15	33	17	33	0
October	13	48	10	27	21
November	16	48	9	24	24
2001					
Early January[1]	13	46	9	28	18
Late January	13	46	11	28	18
February	16	45	9	29	16
March	12	52	8	25	27
April	15	47	9	27	20
May	13	47	11	26	21
ELECTION	*16*	*44*	*16*	*20*	*24*
June	11	50	12	24	26
July	13	44	15	21	23
August	13	49	12	21	28
September	13	52	11	20	32
October	9	54	10	23	31
November	14	47	10	25	22
2002					
Early January[1]	15	46	12	23	23
Late January	12	47	13	24	23
February	13	46	12	24	22
March	14	41	15	26	15
April	14	47	14	21	26
May	13	49	13	21	28
June	15	46	11	23	23
July	13	49	10	21	28
August	14	46	13	23	23
September	11	47	15	21	26

Voting Intention in Scotland 1974-2005 (System 3 Polls) (contd.)

	Con	Lab	Lib	SNP	Lab lead
2002 (contd.)					
October	13	45	16	22	23
November	12	43	15	25	18
2003					
Early January[1]	12	45	14	24	21
Late January	14	42	15	25	17
February	12	42	15	25	17
March	13	38	17	25	13
April	13	45	13	22	23
May	13	41	15	22	19
June	14	40	17	20	20
July	15	40	14	24	16
August	13	41	14	24	17
September	12	39	18	24	15
October	13	43	18	22	21
November	17	42	12	24	18
2004[2]					
Early January[1]	11	43	12	27	16
2005					
February	15	42	16	22	20
April	14	45	14	23	22

1. Fieldwork was normally conducted in the fourth week of each month (with the exception of the December poll, which was put back to early January to avoid a clash with the Christmas/New Year holiday period).
2. The publishing of monthly polls ceased in January 2004.

Source: TNS – System 3 Polls.

Appendix:

Election Records and Trivia

A miscellany of interesting facts, figures and feats covering voting in general and by-elections; election results; candidates and turnout.

Appendix: Election Records and Trivia 1918-2005

The following records have been established since the introduction of universal suffrage in 1918. University seats and those in Ireland from 1918-22 have been ignored in compiling the records.

Largest Majorities—General Elections (Over 50,000)

Sir A.C. Rawson (Brighton, C), 1931[1]	62,253
G.C. Tryon (Brighton, C), 1931[1]	62,041
C.C. Craig (Antrim, C), 1924[1]	58,354
R.W.H. O'Neill (Antrim, C), 1924[1]	58,250
Sir P. Cunliffe-Lister (Middlesex, Hendon, C), 1931	51,000
G.B.H. Currie (Down North, C), 1959	50,734
S.K. Cunningham (Antrim South, C), 1959	50,041

1. Two member-seat.

Largest % Majority—General Elections

Down North, 1959	Conservative majority	96.0%

Largest % Majorities—G.B. General Elections since 1964 (excluding Speaker)

Labour:

Abertillery, 1966	Labour majority	76.2%
Bootle, 1997	Labour majority	74.4%

Conservative:

Sutton Coldfield, 1979	Conservative majority	52.7%
Kensington, South, 1970	Conservative majority	51.4%

Largest Majorities—By-Elections (Over 30,000)

United Kingdom—Rev. I.R.K. Paisley (Antrim North, UDUP), January 23, 1986	33,024
Great Britain—E.E. Gates (Lancashire, Middleton and Prestwich, C), May 22, 1940	31,618

Largest % Majority—By-Elections

Lancashire, Middleton and Prestwich, May 22, 1940	Conservative majority	97.4%

Largest % Majorities—G.B. By-Elections since 1945

Abertillery, November 30, 1950	Labour majority	73.0%
Bootle, November 8, 1990	Labour majority	69.2%
Barnsley East, December 12, 1996	Labour majority	68.0%

Smallest Majorities—General Elections (Under 10)

A.J. Flint (Derbyshire, llkeston, N. Lab), 1931	2
M. Oaten (Winchester, LD), 1997	2
F.D. Acland (Devon, Tiverton, L), 1923	3
T.W. Stamford (Leeds West, Lab), 1924	3
Sir H. Nicholls, Bt. (Northamptonshire, Peterborough, C), 1966	3
G.G. Jones (Carmarthen, Lab), 1974(F)	3
Lord Colum Crichton-Stuart (Cheshire, Northwich, C), 1929	4
Hon. G.R. Ward (Worcester, C), 1945	4

Appendix: Election Records and Trivia 1918-2005 (contd.)

Smallest Majorities—General Elections (Under 10) (contd.)

L. Ropner (Durham, Sedgefield, C), 1923	6
E.L. Gandar-Dower (Caithness and Sutherland, C), 1945	6
F.J. Privett (Portsmouth Central, C), 1922	7
D.H. Hobden (Brighton Kemptown, Lab), 1964	7
D.H. Spencer (Leicester South, C), 1983	7
P.A. Tyler (Cornwall, Bodmin, L), 1974(F)	9

Smallest Majorities—By-Elections (Under 50)

Sir H.C. Lowther (Cumberland, Penrith and Cockermouth, Co C), May 13, 1921	31
O.W. Nicholson (Westminster, Abbey, C), March 19, 1924	43

Record Swings in By-Elections since 1945

Conservative and Labour

Con to Lab	29.1	Dudley West	15.12.94
Lab to Con	22.6	Walsall North	4.11.76

Conservative and Liberal

Con to Lib	35.5	Paisley	20.4.61
Lib to Con	17.2	Sowerby	16.3.49

Labour and Liberal

Lab to Lib	44.2	Bermondsey	24.2.83
Lib to Lab	18.2	Mid Staffordshire	22.3.90

To Nationalists

Scotland	37.9	Hamilton (Lab to SNP)	2.11.67
Wales	29.2	Rhondda West(Lab to PC)	9.3.67

From Nationalists

Scotland	13.6	Kinross and Perthshire W (SNP to Lib)	7.11.63
Wales	10.6	Swansea East (PC to Lib)	28.3.63

Largest Number of Votes Cast for a Candidate—General Elections (Over 65,000)

Sir A.C. Rawson (Brighton), C), 1931[1]	75,205
G.C. Tryon (Brighton, C), 1931[1]	74,993
Sir R. Blair (Middlesex, Hendon, C), 1935	69,762
C.F. Entwistle (Bolton, C), 1931[1]	66,385
Sir P. Cunliffe-Lister (Middlesex, Hendon, C), 1931	66,305

1. Two member-seat.

Largest Number of Votes Cast for a Candidate—By-Elections (Over 50,000)

C.H. Mullan (Down, C), June 6,1946[1]	50,699

1. Two member-seat.

Smallest Number of Votes Cast for a Candidate—General Elections (Under 25)

Ms. C. Taylor-Dawson (Cardiff North, Vote[1]), 2005	1*
M. Kyslun (Derbyshire West, No label[2]), 2005	5
B.C. Wedmore (Finchley, Ind), 1983	13
J.F. Brennan (Sedgefield, No label), 2005	17
W.G. Boaks (Devon North, Ind), 1979	20

Appendix: Election Records and Trivia 1918-2005 (contd.)

Smallest Number of Votes Cast for a Candidate—General Elections (Under 25) (contd.)

Mrs K. Purie-Harwell (Battersea, Ind), 1983	22
Ms. S. Dunn (Folkestone & Hythe, PAP[3]), 2005	22
R.G. Weiss (Wimbledon, Vote[1]), 2005	22

* Although Taylor-Dawson is officially recorded as having received a single vote, there must be some doubt. She stood under the same label in the other 3 Cardiff constituencies and polled between 37 and 167 votes.

1. Vote for Yourself Rainbow Dream Ticket Party.
2. No label = candidate whose description on the ballot paper was left blank.
3. Peace and Progress Party.

Smallest Number of Votes Cast for a Candidate—By-Elections (Under 10)

W.G. Boaks (Glasgow Hillhead, Ind), March 25, 1982	5
K.S. Trivedi (Kensington, Ind), July 14, 1988	5
E.L. Bevan (Bermondsey, Ind Lab), February 24, 1983	8

Highest Turnout—General Elections

United Kingdom—Fermanagh and South Tyrone, 1951	93.4%
Great Britain—Lancashire, Darwen, 1924	92.7%

Lowest Turnout—General Elections

Lambeth, Kennington, 1918	29.7%

Highest Turnout—GB By-Elections

Ashton-under-Lyne, October 29, 1928	89.1%
Tiverton, June 21, 1923	88.1%
Darlington, February 17, 1926	87.6%
Carmarthen, February 28, 1957	87.4%
Stockport, September 17, 1925	85.7%
Brighouse and Spenborough, May 4, 1950	85.4%

Lowest Turnout—GB By-Elections

Poplar, South Poplar, August 12, 1942	9.3%

Excluding war-time by-elections:

Leeds Central, June 10, 1999	19.6%
Shoreditch and Finsbury, November 27, 1958	24.9%
Wigan, September 23, 1999	25.1%

Longest Periods without a Parliamentary By-Election

566 days -Beckenham/Winchester, November 20, 1997 to Leeds Central, June 10, 1999
545 days -Langbaurgh, November 7, 1991 to Newbury, May 6, 1993
1998 is the only recorded calendar year in which no parliamentary election took place in the U.K.

Candidates

There is only one instance of 15 candidates contesting a single seat at a General Election. This was at Sedgefield, the seat of the Prime Minister, in 2005. The previous record was the 11 candidates who contested Finchley (then too the seat of the sitting Prime Minister) in 1983.

Appendix: Election Records and Trivia 1918-2005 (contd.)

Candidates (contd.)

There is only one instance of nineteen candidates contesting a single seat at a by-election. This was at Newbury on May 6, 1993. The previous record was the 17 candidates who contested Chesterfield on March 1, 1984. 18 candidates contested Kensington and Chelsea on November 25, 1999.

At the General Election of October 1974, H. Smith and T.L. Keen of the Campaign for a More Prosperous Britain contested respectively twelve and eleven constituencies each. Smith polled a total of 2,192 votes and Keen 2,036. At the 2005 General Election R.G. Weiss of the Vote for Yourself Rainbow Dream Ticket Party contested 13 constituencies (all in London) polling a total of 1,289 votes.

One person, D.E. Sutch (Screaming Lord Sutch), was a candidate at 41 contests under various party labels. He first contested a seat at a by-election in Stratford in August 1963 and his last contest was at a by-election in Winchester in November 1997. At the 1992 general election he was a candidate in the constituencies of the Conservative, Labour, and Liberal Democrat party leaders. In all the contests he polled a total of 15,657 votes— his highest was 1,114 and his lowest 61. He forfeited his deposit each time. He died aged 58 in June 1999.

Two candidates, W.G. Boaks (Ind) and W.E. Gladstone (L formerly C) were candidates at twenty eight elections. Boaks first contested a seat at the General Election of 1951 and his last contest was at a by-election in October 1982. In all the contests he polled only a total of 1,772 votes— his highest was 240 and the lowest was 5. He forfeited his deposit each time. He died aged 81 in April 1986.

W.E. Gladstone fought eighteen contested elections and was returned unopposed ten times. He was only defeated on three occasions and the elections covered the period 1832-92 and fifteen General Elections and eight by-elections. He died in May 1898 aged 88. Tony Benn fought 17 contests with 1 defeat and 1 unseeking.

Jennie Lee (Lab) holds the record for the number of elections contested by a woman candidate (13).

Electorate

The constituency with the largest ever electorate was Essex, Romford. At the General Election of 1935 there were 167,939 electors on the Register. At the same election Middlesex, Hendon claimed 164,786 electors. When the last pre-war Electoral Register was published in 1939 the figures had risen to 208,609 at Hendon and 207,101 at Romford. Both constituencies were divided in the redistribution which took place in 1945.

The constituency with the smallest electorate was the City of London, a two-member seat. At the General Election of 1945 there were only 10,851 electors on the Register of whom 6,608 qualified for a vote on account of business premises in the constituency. Southwark North holds the record for the smallest electorate in a single member seat—14,108 electors at the General Election of 1945.

Expenses

James Maxton (Glasgow, Bridgeton, ILP) created a record when he retained his seat at the General Election of 1935 and only spent £54 in election expenses.

Forfeited Deposits

The Scottish Universities by-election (22-27/11/46) created an unusual record when out of five candidates, four forfeited their deposits.

From November 1947 until December 1954 no Liberal candidate was able to save his deposit at a by-election.

At the Newbury by-election (6/5/93) seventeen of the nineteen candidates lost their deposits. At the Kensington and Chelsea by-election (25/11/99) fifteen of the 18 candidates forfeited their deposits.

Appendix: Election Records and Trivia 1918-2005 (contd.)

Forfeited Deposits (contd.)

At both the Bermondsey (24/2/83) and Chesterfield (1/3/84) by-elections fourteen candidates lost their deposits. At Bermondsey there were sixteen candidates and at Chesterfield seventeen.

Minorities

At the General Election of 1992, the successful Liberal Democrat candidate at Inverness, Nairn and Lochaber polled only 26.0% of the total votes cast. Just 1,741 votes separated the winner from the candidate in fourth place.

At the General Election of 1922, the successful Conservative candidate at Portsmouth Central polled only 26.9% of the total votes cast.

Turnout

There was so much local interest in the result of the Ashton-under-Lyne by-election (29/10/28) that the Mayor arranged for coloured rockets indicating the party of the successful candidate to be fired from the roof of the Town Hall. The by-election resulted in a Labour victory and yellow rockets (the local Labour colour) were fired which could be seen throughout the town by many people awaiting the result. Despite a steady downpour of rain throughout polling day the by-election achieved a turnout of 89.1%. A record for a by-election which has never been exceeded in Great Britain.

At the five General Elections from 1922 to 1931, the turnout at Lancashire, Darwen always exceeded 90.0%.

Camberwell, North holds the record for the smallest number of votes cast in a parliamentary election. At a by-election on March 30, 1944, two candidates polled a total of oniy 3,329 votes. The turnout was 11.2%.

Gains and Losses

When the Liberals won Devon, Torrington (27/3/58) it was the first Liberal gain at a by-election for twenty-nine years. The previous occasion had been at Lincolnshire, Holland with Boston on March 21, 1929.

When Labour won Lewisham, North (14/2/57) from the Conservatives it was the first time that they had gained a seat from the Conservatives at a by-election for over seventeen years. The previous occasion had been at Lambeth, Kennington on May 24, 1939.

When the Conservatives won Sunderland, South (13/5/53) it was the first occasion since 1924 that a Government had won a seat from the Opposition at a by-election and only two such previous victories had been recorded since 1918. These were Liverpool, West Toxteth (22/5/24) when Labour won the seat from the Conservatives, and Woolwich, East (2/3/21) when the Conservatives won the seat from Labour. There have been only two occasions since 1953 that a Government has won a seat from the Opposition at a by-election. These were at Brighouse and Spenborough (17/3/60) when a National Liberal and Conservative candidate won the seat from Labour, and at Mitcham and Morden (3/6/82) when the sitting Labour MP resigned and contested the by-election as an SDP candidate. The Conservatives won the seat.

When the Conservatives held Uxbridge (31/7/97) it was the first occasion since 1989 that the party had retained a seat at a by-election. The previous occasion had been at Richmond (Yorks) on February 23, 1989. Subsequently the Conservatives suffered fifteen consecutive by-election losses.

Appendix: Election Records and Trivia 1918-2005 (contd.)

Counts

Brighton, Kemptown and Northamptonshire, Peterborough claim the joint record for recounts—seven.

At Brighton, Kemptown at the General Election of 1964, the Labour candidate D.H. Hobden was returned with a majority of seven votes after seven recounts. No official figures of the recounts were issued but from local press reports it appears that the first count resulted in a Labour majority of 302 but there was a discrepancy in the number of ballot papers counted of about 400. On the first recount the Labour majority was reduced to thirty eight. A second recount put the Conservative candidate ahead by one vote but the Labour lead was restored in the third, fourth and fifth recounts with majorities of twenty-nine, ten, and six. At 2.40 a.m. the count was adjourned until 9 a.m. when two further recounts both gave the Labour candidate a majority of seven votes. The result was finally declared just after 10 a.m. There were 60 spoilt ballot-papers.

At Northamptonshire, Peterborough at the General Election of 1966 the Conservative candidate, Sir Harmar Nicholls, Bt., was returned with a majority of three votes after seven recounts. The first count gave the Labour candidate a majority of 163 and the first recount produced the same result. Uncounted ballot-papers were then discovered in a ballot box and the second recount gave Labour a majority of two votes. Third and fourth recounts reversed the position and gave Sir Harmar majorities of two and then six votes. A fifth recount put Labour back in the lead by a single vote but a sixth recount showed Sir Harmar ahead once again this time with a majority of two votes. The seventh and final recount added another vote to Sir Harmar's majority. There were thirty-eight spoilt ballot-papers and counting started at 9.00 a.m. but the result was not declared until 5.30 p.m.

Probably the longest time taken to count ballot-papers and declare a result can be claimed by Derby-shire, North-Eastern. At the General Election of 1922 the count commenced at 10 a.m. on the day after polling and continued until shortly after 1 a.m. the following morning when it was adjourned until 10 a.m. The result was finally declared, after three recounts and four adjustments, at 1.15 p.m. The final outcome was a majority of five votes for the Labour candidate but after a recount and scrutiny by an Election Court the majority was increased to fifteen votes. The total time taken to count the votes and declare the result was approximately 18¼ hours.

In Harlow, Essex in 2005 the result was not announced until 11.40 a.m. on the Saturday following polling day. Although there were only three formal recounts, counting was adjourned between 6 a.m. on the day after polling until 10 a.m. on Saturday because of the exhaustion of the counting staff.

Although the majority at Winchester at the 1997 General Election was just two votes, it is reported that only two formal recounts took place.

Index

296